CONTENTS

PREFACE TO THE PAPERBACK EDITION

When I first came to study the press after the repeal of the taxes on knowledge the field had long been virtually fallow. Now some furrows have appeared, more ploughs are out and are being sharpened, stones are being turned, (see my 'The British Press and its Historians', *Journalism Studies Review* no. 3, 1978, pp. 40-2). Some of the new work relating to this period has been published in the Acton Society Press Group's *Newspaper History*, eds. G. Boyce, J. Curran and P. Wingate (1978), and another volume is planned.

There should, however, be no illusions that the crop will ripen and be harvested all at once. Many of the problems remain intractable, or at least susceptible only to a long process of research and analysis. This applies especially to the issues of content and readership. This book was an attempt to deal with the structure rather than the content of the mid- and late Victorian press, and it would seem neither appropriate nor possible at this stage to alter that focus. Some have cast a reproving look at my self-confessed 'Marxist' approach, as if this had, perhaps, some political significance, or in one case as if I imagined that Marx originated the concern for the ownership and control of communications. I see that I ought to have made it clear that I was making only a methodological distinction between what Michael Burrage usefully, as I imagined, labelled the 'Marxist' and the 'Tocquevillian' approaches. I still believe this distinction to be of value, but, of course, the labels are not essential and may be discarded if wished. My concern with production, structure and control in this period, however, remains unaltered. I do not think that I have unduly neglected such issues as readership and content, or the wider impact of the press on society and of society on the press, but the groundwork for a 'Tocquevillian' analysis seems yet to be laid.

I have then left the substance of the book unchanged. Typographical and other errors which have come to light have been corrected, and I thank all those who have drawn my attention to them, but I have refrained from adding any fresh material or comment, even to the notes which were already voluminous.

Alan Lee

ACKNOWLEDGEMENTS

I am most grateful to the following for permission to cite and to quote from the collections for which they are responsible: Mr Mark Bonham Carter; the British Library Board; the British Library of Political and Economic Science; the University of Liverpool; the House of Lords Record Office; the National Register of Archives (Scotland); the National Trust, Hughenden Manor; the National Union of Conservative and Unionist Associations; Sheffield City Libraries; Lord Wemyss.

I must also acknowledge the generous assistance given me by the Nuffield Foundation in my study of newspaper companies. The results of this research will be published in another form, but I have made use here of some of the material obtained in the process.

My thanks are also due to the always helpful staff of libraries and depositories too numerous to list individually. Without them no scholar could hope to prosper. Pat Underhill of the Centre for Computer Studies at the University of Hull helped with the figures, and Derek Waite of the Brynmore Jones Library in the University of Hull drew the maps. To them my sincerest thanks. Innumerable friends and colleagues have at one time or another, wittingly or otherwise, helped in the thinking and writing of this book, and although no passing reference to them can be an adequate expression of my gratitude I hope they will accept this mere token of my thanks. The members of the British Politics Seminar at the London School of Economics, and of the Research Seminar at the Centre for the Study of Social History at the University of Warwick deserve special mention for their patience and kindness in giving me an opportunity to expose some of my work to sharp but sympathetic criticism. Finally, I must express my deep gratitude to Tony Mason for his characteristically generous labours in combing and criticising the entire work. To him the improvements are due; to me the remaining deficiencies and errors.

ABBREVIATIONS

AYR	*All the Year Round*
BM	*Blackwoods Magazine*
Boase	F.B. Boase, *Modern English Biography* (1892-1921; 1965 ed.)
CJ	*Chambers Journal*
CM	*Cornhill Magazine*
CN	*Central News* (agency)
Colburn's	*Colburn's New Monthly Magazine*
CP	*Central Press* (agency)
CR	*Contemporary Review*
DNB	*Dictionary of National Biography*
EHR	*English Historical Review*
EcHR	*Economic History Review*
FM	*Frasers Magazine*
FR	*Fortnightly Review*
GM	*Gentleman's Magazine*
H.C.Deb.	*House of Commons Debates*
HJ	*Historical Journal*
HJW	H.J. Wilson Papers
Jm.	*Journalism*
Jt.	*Journalist*
LPCPN	*London, Provincial and Colonial Press News*
MM	*Macmillan's Magazine*
NC	*Nineteenth Century*
NPA	*National Press Agency*
NPD	*Newspaper Press Directory,* C. Mitchell, ed.
NPP	*Newspaper Press*
NQR	*New Quarterly Review*
NR	*National Review*
NV	*Newsvendor*
NW	*Newspaper World*
PP	*Parliamentary Papers*
P&P	*Past and Present*
PRO	*Public Record Office*
QR	*Quarterly Review*
RR	*Review of Reviews*
SCNS	Select Committee on the Newspaper Stamp, 1851

Sell's	*Sell's Dictionary of the World's Press*
SR	*Saturday Review*
Trans NAPSS	Transactions of the National Association for the Promotion of Social Science
VS	*Victorian Studies*
WR	*Westminster Review*

LIST OF TABLES

LIST OF MAPS

For my mother, and to the memory of my father

1 INTRODUCTION

> We believe in reason, in the power of rational processes to
> determine truth and to present real choices in human affairs.
> We do not have any illusion that reason always prevails. . .
> The Times is. . .a Liberal newspaper.
>
> *The Times,* 21 November 1970.

It is commonplace that the theory of the press which prevails in most
western democracies, including Britain, is a 'liberal' theory.[1] Its
protagonists have fought for it in the name of 'liberalism' and continue
to do so. Historically the struggle both for political and economic
freedom of the press in Britain was conducted in the rhetoric of
liberalism and by liberals. For the first half of the nineteenth century
at least, there seemed to be as triumphant and as sweet an accord
between liberal theory and liberal achievement in the press as in
education or in free trade. By the end of the century, however, the
triumph and the achievement were matters of history. Party and press
seemed locked in parallel decline.

W.J. Fisher, sometime editor of the *Daily Chronicle,* wrote in 1904,
'the provincial Liberal press has become feebler and feebler, and in the
smaller towns has almost ceased to exist'.[2] The young liberal historian
G.M. Trevelyan wrote in 1901, 'the Philistines have captured the Ark of
the Covenant (sc. the printing press), and have learnt to work their own
miracles through its power.'[3] L.T. Hobhouse, social philosopher and
leading 'new liberal' journalist, wrote in 1909, 'the Press, more and
more the monopoly of a few rich men, from being the organ of
democracy has become rather the sounding-board for whatever ideas
commend themselves to the great material interests.'[4] It was evident
that the tension had grown too great between an ideology which
claimed 'the Fourth Estate' for its own,[5] and forces of production
which by then had made the press into an industry, subject to the logic
of an expanding market. The conditions under which the old ideology
had been forged were disappearing, and were being replaced by others
which were inimical to it.[6] The very character of the politics which had
been cherished and nourished by that ideology, a close-knit, personal
and community politics, focused on oligarchies and small elites, was
also changing. Its characteristic, vertically integrated structure

continued only in the more rural areas, which were, moreover, the
least suitable for the expansion of the press. A workable political
morality had been created out of the apparently conflicting theory and
practice of the older society, so as to avoid the threat of a levelling
democracy, but the changing situation made it increasingly difficult to
cling to the old principles of 'liberalism'. Late nineteenth- and early
twentieth-century radicals like Hobhouse or H.W. Massingham could
still use these principles to make their critiques brilliantly sharp and
penetrating, but their caustic broadsides seemed all too ineffective in
combating or even in coming to terms with the new conditions. For
them what was new in the 'new journalism' was not journalism, and
what was journalism was not, after all, new.

How far were their criticisms justified? Had the press, once the jewel
in the liberal crown, ceded its esteemed and rightful position by the
beginning of the twentieth century? If so, was this the result, as was
and often still is claimed, of the spread of elementary education? Had
good intentions paved the way to mediocrity? Had there been as a
consequence, or was it perhaps a cause, a deterioration in the quality of
politics, and a diminution in the intelligence of 'the people'? Had the
educator turned debaucher, the teacher demagogue? It is not, of course,
simply a question of justification. While it is relevant and important to
verify or to falsify the picture painted by the pessimists, it must be
remembered that that picture was a part of the reality. 'The important
question about any statement contained in a source', wrote Collingwood,
'is not whether it is true or false, but what it means.'[7] What did the
obsequies passed on the Liberal press before 1914 mean for the mostly,
but not entirely, Liberal and radical critics who gave voice to them?

It is only to be expected that there would be a certain degree of
confusion in the responses to the changes in process before 1914 in the
press. Before and for a little while after the repeal of the 'taxes on
knowledge', and again after the First World War, issues and
developments were much clearer than they were during the period from
the 1870s to the 1910s. The actual process of the industrialisation of
the press was itself complicated, with large overlaps of the old and the
new, with all the stresses and strains familiar in other industries in the
early throes of industrialisation. The period was one in which a massive,
although very incomplete, shift in the extent of political participation
took place, with the extension of the suffrage, the development of
party organisations, and of pressure groups. In this period too fell the
crucial testing-time for the new commitment to education, after the
reforms of the 1860s and the Act of 1870. Increasing prosperity also

meant changing patterns of consumption which were in some cases vital
to the development of the press, increasing both its sales and advertising
revenue. Finally there was a shift, noted above, in people's attitudes
towards politics and political morality, a shift in crude terms from a
community- to a class-based politics. Such changes were neither smooth
nor total, and they often resulted in confused, ambiguous and
conflicting views of the role of the press, whether actually or ideally
conceived. This study examines both the objective changes in society at
large and in the industry itself in the half-century after the repeal of the
newspaper stamp, and the ways in which the older liberal vision of the
press was affected by those changes.

It is not, therefore, an attempt to write 'a social history of the press'
during this period. There is indeed a great need for a serious history of
the British press, even if at this stage it would have to be rather tentative,
like the excellent and monumental *Histoire Générale de la Presse
Française.*[8] The available works on the subject are largely anecdotal,
fragmentary, scissors-and-paste studies, usually written by journalists.
Some groundwork on the structure and development of the press has,
therefore, had to be included in what is otherwise more of an
interpretative essay. It must be stressed, however, that most of this
fundamental work remains to be done.

There are, broadly speaking, two main avenues of approach to such
a study, from the side of production, and from that of consumption,
or, in political terms, from the side of the controllers and from that of
the controlled. If one takes the classic model of communications
research set up by H.D. Lasswell:[9]

Question	*Type of analysis*
Who?	Control
Says what?	Content
In which channel?	Media
To whom?	Audience
With what effect?	Effect

then a production approach will concentrate upon 'who' and 'in which
channel', the consumption approach upon 'to whom' and 'with what
effect'. The content analysis naturally has a place in both approaches,
on both sides of the question. One sociologist has suggested that one
might see this as a distinction between a Marxist approach, focusing on
'ownership of the media', and explaining 'the quality or content of the
media by the *supply*'; and the Tocquevillian approach, emphasising 'the

literacy and education level of the audience. . .thus (seeking) to
understand the state of the media (by looking) to the *demand*'.[10] For
a number of reasons this study concentrates upon a broadly Marxist
approach, as thus defined, and emphasises the supply rather than the
demand side of the process. The difficulties of a demand approach are
dealt with more fully below, but briefly it may be suggested that there
are serious methodological, not to say epistemological problems
involved in getting to know how communicated ideas and information
affect their recipients, particularly if the problem is given an historical
dimension. Again, what study there has been in this field has tended to
support the view that at best people select their channel of communication, and the specific content they expose themselves to, mainly to
support views and opinions which they already hold. In the face of such
evidence modern studies of 'effects' are tending now to go back to such
problems as 'control in the newsroom', and are widening the focus of
their attention to include a much wider area of enquiry than the original
model had done.[11] Furthermore, in a study of nineteenth-century
Britain there can be little dispute that the context of the whole issue
of the press was that of a developing capitalist system, in which,
somehow, the press, both as an industry and as an institution had to
find accommodation. One's attention then naturally turns to questions
of supply and production.

The press in the nineteenth century was the most important single
medium of the communication of ideas, and it is with its organisation,
working, and development that this study is concerned. It is concerned
with the control of the press, not so much actually in the newsroom,
about which we know little in this period, but in the board room. This
emphasis may seem in some ways paradoxical, for it played little part
in the theory of the press commonly used at the time, discussed at
greater length in Chapter Two, except right at the end of the period, in
the time of crisis. To understand this it is perhaps helpful to remember
that the role of the press in politically developed societies tends to be
less spectacular than in traditional or modernising societies. The press,
and other media, can play a large and even decisive part in the process of
early political socialisation and economic development. In older
cultures, where political socialisation has already progressed quite far,
and in a period before the advent of newer rival media, the press played
more of a stabilising than a galvanising role, despite what its friends
hoped and its enemies feared. So it was in Victorian England, where
the press had a distinctively integrative role to play. As political
sea-changes brought nearer the nationalisation of politics, and the

replacement of earlier and more local forms of politics and political
discussion by ones based on broad bands of class stratification, the press
proved suitably adaptable. These changes, however, were to transform
it eventually into a true mass medium, and thus made it less suited as
an institution for a liberal society of the classical sort, the logic of mass
media being the extinction of differences, and not their perpetuation
in a pluralist society. Such a society was perhaps always far from reality,
but it was a vision which did illumine liberal views of the press before
1914. The press was regarded as an independent watchdog of every
interest against all abuse. Liberals were always invoking eternal vigilance
as the price of liberty, and for ever asking *quis custodiet ipsos custodes?*
They were less apt to ask who owned the guardians. They tended to
reduce the problem to one of education, and to ignore Marx's point
that education was also a matter of power. The logic of the press as an
industry favoured the process of centralisation, which in turn precluded
the classical, exchange model of the communication of ideas. Whilst
this process was going on within the established power structures, it was
the control and structure of the press as an industry which was crucial,
and which is, therefore, the subject of this study.

The 'demand' side has not been entirely neglected. There are some
areas where the interdependence of demand and supply have made it
essential to discuss, for example, the ways in which education,
prosperity and leisure have played their part in the development of the
press, and, conversely, the ways in which the press has played its part in
the development of education, prosperity and leisure. It is, however, an
area of much greater uncertainty than the 'supply' side. Indeed, it was
such uncertainty which made the proprietors' job so difficult. Content
analysis might provide better answers and more decisive conclusions
than it has been possible to give here, but very little of this highly
demanding work has as yet been done for this period.

It will be noted, by some with exasperation, that the study is limited
to England, although reference is occasionally made to the other
countries of the United Kingdom. Desirable as it would have been to
have included the rest of Britain there seemed cogent reasons for not
doing so. The peculiar political structure of Ireland made it *sui generis*
as far as the press was concerned, as witnessed by the continuation of
close government supervision there into the twentieth century. It was
also an overwhelmingly agricultural country, with a scattered population,
with a relatively low level of literacy and education. Only in Dublin and
Belfast did the Irish press match the major English provincial papers.
Here they shared common news agencies and telegraphs, developed their

own proprietors' associations, and ran their papers on much the same lines as English proprietors, although there were few proprietorial links across the Irish Channel.

If Ireland is too different to include in this study, then it is arguable that Scotland is too important. There the political and economic conditions were closer to those in England, and the social and economic links were stronger, the political obstacles fewer. The press was larger than in Ireland and played its part on the national political stage along with the best of the English papers. A country for long better educated and more democratic than England, it also supplied, together with Ireland, an altogether disproportionate part of the personnel of English journalism. All this is an argument for a separate study of this major segment of the British press.

Wales was economically poorly developed, and for the most part sparsely populated, and proved a far less fruitful source of journalistic talent than either Scotland or Ireland. Some papers of importance took root in the larger urban areas, but these were few. A Welsh-language press flourished, but by its very nature it remained limited and introverted. Things began to change towards the end of the nineteenth century, when the political value of Wales became more apparent to English politicians, and then more interest was taken in the development of its press. As with Ireland and Scotland, however, this phase particularly could do with a separate study.

Finally, a methodological note. It will be found that the text contains some quantitative material, but it should be stressed at the outset that this is not an exercise in quantification. Figures have been used as indicators and illustrators of tendencies; they have not been relied upon to produce conclusions unsupported by other 'literary' evidence. Nor have they been statistically processed, and should not, therefore, run the risk of giving an impression of false concreteness, or spurious precision. In most cases the trends have been clear enough to be accepted without much doubt, but such is the unreliability of most newspaper statistics, above all of circulation figures, but also of the simple number of extant publications at any one time, that any figures used in this study should be treated with the appropriate caution.

Most of the book, however, is concerned with what men thought about the role of the press and the journalist in their society, with what they meant when they spoke of it in certain ways, with what they expected of it, with how they used it, and with how far it met or failed to meet their expectations.

2 LIBERALISM AND THE NEWSPAPER

I The Vision

Perhaps only the steam railway rivalled the newspaper press in the Victorian estimation of the progress of civilisation. Journalists in particular never tired of extolling the wonders of their industry, both in their journals and in multi-volumed histories of their profession. Liberty, progress, knowledge and even salvation were virtues commonly attributed to the newspaper.[1] Alexander Andrews, for example, spoke of 'the Giant which now awes potentates. . .this mighty Mind-Engine. . . this tremendous moral power'.[2] The often used mechanical metaphor was significant less of utilitarian dogma than of genuine, if naive, wonder. The *Edinburgh Review* claimed in 1821 that

> we need not say how much we revere the genuine freedom of the press as the fountain of all intellectual light, and the source of all that is great among mankind. . .The press has wrought with a power which in reverence may be assimilated, if aught human may be so assimilated, to the working of Almighty wisdom,

and so on.[3] This was impressive tribute as a prelude to an attack upon the licentiousness of 'this chartered instrument of evil'. The radical *Westminster Review* was predictable upon the subject in 1824.[4]

> The newspapers. . .are the best and surest civilisers of a country. They contain within themselves not only the elements of knowledge but the inducements to learn. . . It is necessary to have seen a people among whom newspapers have not penetrated, to know the mass of mischievous prejudices which these productions instantly and necessarily dissipate.

Lord Lytton's was a more balanced view:[5]

> Large classes of men entertain certain views on matters of policy, trade or morals. A newspaper supports itself by addressing these classes; it brings to light all the knowledge requisite to enforce or illustrate the view of its supporters; it embodies also the prejudice, the passion and the sectarian bigotry that belong to one body of

men engaged in active opposition to another. It is, therefore, the
organ of opinion; expressing at once the truth, the errors, the good
and the bad of the prevalent opinion it represents.

It was the theme of public opinion which was most attractive to those
groups aspiring to improved social and political position. 'Public
opinion', wrote William McKinnon in 1828, 'is a sentiment that depends
on the degree of information and wealth which together may be styled
civilisation, and also with a proper religious feeling that exists in any
community.'[6] He understood it to be a direct function of the class
structure. The rise of the middle class consequent upon the increase of
capital and machinery had fostered the growth of public opinion by
improving the dissemination of information, religious feeling,
communication and wealth. 'The form of government becomes liberal
in the exact proportions as the power of public opinion increases.'[7]
This is what 'liberals' and radicals had fought for for a long time. In the
struggle against the 1819 press laws, in 'the war of the unstamped' in
the 1830s, and in 'the great agitation' for the repeal of the taxes on
knowledge in the 1850s, it was all the while the power of public opinion
that was being fostered. Emblazoned on every issue of the *Poor Man's
Guardian* was the motto 'knowledge is power', and for a considerable
time in the mid-nineteenth century the successful cultivation of the
newspaper was associated with the political power of emerging
Liberalism.

The concept of the freedom of the press had, of course, long had a
place in liberal thought. One has only to look at the classical liberal
model of society to understand how central to it press freedom is. It
was a model, in its essentials, of the free interplay of individuals in
society, like the objects in a Newtonian universe, differing only in that
it was a model of process, a gradual approximation to a state of
harmony or equilibrium, a process which the nineteenth century
commonly called 'improvement'. The model operated upon several
planes, the political, the ethical, the economic, the intellectual, each
having its respective equilibrium, peace, freedom, wealth and truth.
Temporary states of disequilibrium and conflict would be ended by
the advance of reason, and the accumulation, dissemination and
absorption of knowledge. In the liberal pursuit of certainty it was as
much the pursuit as the certainty which counted, reflecting not an
indifference to ends, but a psychological attachment to a faith in the
ultimate harmony of all ends. Liberals generally embraced freedom on
the understanding that it entailed truth, and with the assumption that

neither freedom nor truth could harm either the individual or his universe.

In this light, on the intellectual if not on the economic plane, liberalism was a child of the seventeenth century, part of a movement against authority and hierarchy, of the modern against the traditional. For a century or so a tight rein had been kept upon an important weapon of that movement, the printing press. The men of 'independent' mind in the seventeenth century who resented and resisted the imposition of ecclesiastical, theological or political authority upon their own God-given wills, were quick to grasp the potential of the printed word. Milton's friend Hartlibb wrote in 1641, 'the art of printing will so spread knowledge that the common people knowing their own rights and liberties will not be governed by way of oppression.'[8] The purpose of the Puritans in fighting for a free press was to be able to defend and propagate their religion, but in doing so they set out the general arguments for press freedom which have become an established part of liberal thought. The *locus classicus* was Milton's '*Areopagitica* (1644), an attack on the Long Parliament's Ordinance against the press. He argued, firstly, that mistaken censorship might result in the irremediable loss of an element of truth. Only the furnace of continued debate could safeguard against this danger. Secondly, with censorship men are more likely to make mistakes, because the Truth is one, the good indistinguishable except by comparison with the bad. Thirdly, a hidden truth is no truth at all. Truth always being stronger than falsehood, it is trial alone which can and will make truth clear. Fourthly, the fear of being condemned for error would effectively stifle investigation and study. Finally, reason and virtue are predicated upon the freedom to choose. Independent men needed no tutors, and if they were not allowed to make mistakes they could never become independent, and could never act rationally or virtuously. These arguments were reiterated, usually more prosaically, throughout the next century and beyond, by those of liberal and radical disposition in Britain, France and America. The context of the debate was inevitably a political one. Reply had to be made to those who continued to claim that press freedom was mere licence and a threat to the security and stability of the state. Perhaps the most favoured argument was that truths have to be tested. 'The liberty of the press has its inconveniences, but the evil which may result from it is not to be compared to the evil of censorship', said Bentham.[9] Madison agreed: 'some degree of abuse is inescapable from the proper use of everything; and in no instance is this more true than in that of the press.'[10] In the early nineteenth century the most uncompromising statements of the general arguments were in the essays of Samuel Bailey. He restated the fundamentals, that truth and falsehood were so interdependent that they could only be admitted together, that truth needed no protection from falsehood, that it was on the contrary enhanced by open challenge, and, utilitarian that he was, that truth was conducive to and productive of happiness. He paid homage to 'a silent march of thought, which no power can arrest'.[11]

There had, however, always been room in the liberal model for the problem of the less rational, and for the play of sinister interest. Even liberal democrats were little able to suffer fools gladly. James Mill, for example, thought the freedom of the press was to allow 'the sufficiently enlightened', and 'the greatest number of qualified persons' to engage in open discussion and competition.[12] Some saw the danger as more directly commercial. The Italian-Swiss liberal Sismonde de Sismondi, writing in 1823, noted that 'the daily press is a power and its object is not public good, but to get the largest number of subscribers.'[13] In 1829 John Stuart Mill claimed that 'more affectation and hypocrisy are necessary for the trade of literature, and especially the newspapers, than for a brothel-keeper'.[14] In 1836, after the publication of de Tocqueville's first volume of *Democracy in America*, Mill noted that public opinion 'exercises most salutary influence' in small rather than in large societies. In the latter, successful persuasion 'depends not upon what a person is, but upon what he seems: mere marketable qualities become the object instead of substantial ones.' For Mill this could be remedied only by co-operation to limit the waste involved in intellectual competition arising from economic forces, and in moves 'to invigorate the individual character'.[15] Interestingly, Mill's conclusions were more pessimistic at this time than those of de Tocqueville himself. Of a conservative disposition, de Tocqueville did not regard the freedom of the press as supremely good, but loved it more for the evil which it prevented than for the benefits it bestowed. He agreed with the liberal argument, however, that even to accomplish this some risks had to be run, and that they were worth running. One of them, he concurred with Mill, was the possibly deleterious effects it might have upon the quality of a journalism which had become a trade, in the American rather than in the French mould. Nevertheless, such freedom as could be obtained was, he thought, a politically stabilising factor, and a means of mitigating the disintegrative effects of equality, a means of achieving what he considered was the main task, 'to educate democracy'.[16]

Most 'democrats', perhaps, saw the issue in this light, in the context of the general 'improvement' of society, and associated a cheap press with universal education. Some went further, and in a period when parliamentary reform was progressing but slowly, claimed that the press was 'a reserved power of the people', a valid alternative to deficient parliamentary representation.[17] Disraeli had Sidonia tell Coningsby, 'God made man in his own image, but the Public is made by Newspapers, Members of Parliament, Excise Officers, Poor Law Guardians.' Later Coningsby himself told his young friend Millbank, a manufacturer's son who should have needed no telling, 'Opinion is now supreme and Opinion speaks in print. The representation of the Press is far more complete than the representation of Parliament.'[18]

The arguments for freedom of opinion and its expression were not, of course, necessarily associated with the belief in popular democracy. Indeed, some of the most brilliant defenders of the former were amongst the most hostile opponents of the latter. It is clear why this was so. The freedom of opinion would award laurels to those whose opinions were the truest, the best, and the most rational. Universal suffrage, a purely individualistic and arithmetical institution, would give the laurels to those who thought not the best, but the most like other people. Given that one could not reasonably oppose the extension of the franchise, if one were a liberal (after all, the premise was of a developing rationality in society), then education, both academic and political, was the only solution. Practically speaking, if this failed only the abyss remained, and it is not surprising to find many liberals of the older type at the end of the century drawing precisely this conclusion from the operation of the 1870 Education Act![19] Whatever the outcome of the process, however, there did seem to be general agreement on the political potential of the press, for good or for ill, and during the 1840s and 1850s, and the expansion of the press which followed this, it was the Liberals who made most of the effort, and were the most successful at capturing this valuable political weapon. In part this was the consequence of a natural identity of interest between enterprising publishers and Liberal political and economic policies, although it also owed something to the fact that the aristocracy remained unhappy with and suspicious of the newspaper, and were usually inept in their attempts to control it. By 1861, with the disappearance of the paper duty, the Liberal idea of the press as an economic institution was firmly entrenched in reality, and as literacy, education and reform progressed, there was the prospect of the Liberal press becoming even more central to the sure and sound running of the country than it then was. The prospect of a golden age, both for Liberalism and for the press, was not then an illusion. The illusion was that it could be perpetuated indefinitely.

II Education

The association of knowledge with power had in the first decades of the nineteenth century been in part a class argument. Working-class radicals of the unstamped and the Chartist press looked towards knowledge to engineer political and social revolution.[20] The repeal of the taxes on knowledge took on a significance similar to that which had attached to the Charter.[21] It is still a matter of debate whether the unstamped agitation of the 1830s exacerbated or mollified class differences, but it is clear that the purpose of the working-class radicals in the movement, Carlile, Hetherington, Carpenter, Cleave and the rest, differed from the middle-class radicals, Brougham, Roebuck and W.J. Fox, and from Francis Place, who worked with them. For the latter group the agitation was linked both in ideas and in personnel with utilitarianism and the 'Steam Intellect Society'. They envisaged the freedom of the press as a weapon against aristocratic interest, but a weapon which would work only through the agency of knowlege. Believing with Milton and Bailey that good would always oust the bad in the market place, all forms of publication were welcomed as part of the educating process. Some actually urged that the role of the newspaper should be to spread middle-class ideology downwards.[22] This was the explicit purpose of the SDUK, and the driving idea behind the work of Charles Knight. Knight, amongst others, also argued that if there was to be a large newspaper press then education would be necessary to prevent the otherwise baleful influence it might have on a barely literate public.[23]

Yet if education was called upon to keep a check upon the press, the newspaper itself was also seen as an educational tool. One of the major arguments against the stamp duty after 1836 was that it prevented the development of a good cheap press, which was needed particularly in the rural areas. The Rev. Thomas Spencer, editor of the *British Temperance Advocate,* and uncle of Herbert Spencer, also argued that by educating parents through the press, the benefits would be passed on to the children, and a cumulative effect be started.[24] The London journalist F. Knight Hunt shared the view that the cheap newspaper was an essential adjunct of the spread of education, and reiterated to the 1851 Select Committee on the Newspaper Stamp the point that John Stuart Mill had made in 1834, that 'police reports are better digests of the laws which relate to the affairs of the poor, than are the term reports of the lawyers.'[25] The educational argument could, of course, be turned to many uses, and one finds Samuel Smiles arguing, inevitably, that 'we would mainly employ that mighty educator, the Press, to teach working men that they must be their own elevators, educators, emancipators. . .'[26] That the newspaper was a source of information for the working class, usually the major or even the sole source, was a point made repeatedly up to and indeed after the repeal of the taxes. Cobden complained in 1854 that 'there was no use in putting into the hands of the peasant books about France, Austria or Germany. If, however, he could read about a neighbour being taken before petty sessions for poaching. . .'[27] It was common for newspapers to be read aloud to groups, especially when important issues were being discussed, as, for example, Sunday closing.[28] Some notice was taken of the argument in the Revised Code on education in 1860, in which Standard VI included a test of being able to read a paragraph from a newspaper, and to write a paragraph dictated from the same paper.[29] A decade after repeal it was being claimed, albeit with some caution, that the educational argument for the removal of the taxes had been proved. In 1867 Ludlow and Jones admitted that[30]

> the cheap newspaper and periodical cannot perhaps be defined strictly as educators. Yet for good or evil, and probably on the whole for good, they are very powerful ones. . . Notwithstanding the many sins and shortcomings of the newspaper press, the working man of today, with his broadsheet for a penny is by its aid a man of fuller information, better judgement and wider sympathies than the workman of thirty years back who had to content himself with gossip and rumour, and whose source of information as to public events was the well-thumbed weekly newspaper in the public house.

Because the newspaper was such an important channel of information it was also recognised as a means of social control. When blame was cast upon newspaper agitation for the rural violence of the 1830s, the champions of the press retorted, 'the more newspapers the fewer rioters,' and 'readers are not rioters; readers are not rick-burners.'[31] It was later even boasted that 'in fact "Swing" was to be put out by a cheap press'.[32] However idle such a claim may have been, it indicated just what sort of a role was expected of the newspaper. In 1861 the Registrar-General commented that 'the excessive ignorance of the colliers of Staffordshire and Wales is a cause of incalculable evils, amongst others of explosions and probably of strikes'. In 1867 he warned against laying up trouble ten or twelve years hence by neglecting to educate young adults.[33] In 1851 the Association for the Repeal of the Taxes on Knowledge seized upon the argument to further their cause, by claiming that recent Welsh disturbances would have been less likely to have happened if cheap and easy methods of communicating grievances, such as newspapers, had been available.[34] Other areas of social control were also linked to the role of the press. The Select Committee on Drunkenness of 1834 recommended the repeal of the taxes on newspapers on the grounds that the working man would cease to have to resort to the public house in order to read a newspaper.[35] The Temperance Society was said in 1851 to have considered the stamp 'a premium upon drunkenness'.[36] In 1849 the Public Libraries Committee was told that the stamp was the cause of the workers having nothing good to read.[37] The manager of *The Times,* three years after 1848, even claimed that 'in the crisis of a country. . .a good press might be the saving of it'.[38] A more sophisticated version of this conservative view was put by J.F. Stephen in 1862:[39]

> Experience has seldom proved anything more conclusively than the proposition that in a rich and intelligent country, a perfectly free press is one of the greatest safeguards of peace and order. Under such circumstances it is nearly certain that the ablest newspapers will be both read and written by and for the comfortable part of society, and will err rather on the side of making too much of their interests than on that of neglecting them.

The accent on order and control, however, was weakened after the 1860s, partly, perhaps, because it had become a less obvious issue, and was less discussed. The problems of the 1840s seemed for a while at least to have been resolved. It was instead the educational value of the newspaper which became the main item in the credo of the 'golden age' of journalism after repeal. Information, guidance and the erosion of parochialism, these were considered to be the first tasks of the newspaper press.

The ways in which increasing literacy and improved education affected the quality and character of the newspaper, however, were not those which had been predicted at the mid-century. Edward Baines junior had claimed that education and the reading of newspapers and periodicals were mutually reinforcing activities, but it had already been observed that the working classes read hardly anything but newspapers and periodicals — 'give the working man his pint of beer, and he will not ask for tea, but he must have his newspaper.'[40] What sort of newspapers would such demands provide in the future?

III Literacy

Education, even as a means of social control, was not necessarily confined to the problem of literacy, but it was literacy, or more specifically the ability to read, which was crucial to the debate about the cheap press. In the earlier part of the nineteenth century literacy was a primary concern for educationists. Later, as the problem seemed in the process of solution, as illiteracy progressively diminished, attention shifted to other aspects of education, a shift which also affected the debate about the role of the press towards the end of the century. The simple ability to read, which would in theory at least follow from educational reform and expansion, was no guarantee as to the quality, content, or effect of what was read. Nevertheless, the ability to read was inescapably a major premise of the expansion of the cheap press, and the extent of literacy, particularly in the decade or so after the repeal of the taxes, must occupy an important position in any analysis of the development of the press.

The 1870 Education Act provided much of the framework for the subsequent expansion of elementary education. Additional legislation, and changes in practices and attitudes were still needed to achieve anything like an effective universal system. and there had been much progress before 1870, but the Act was an undeniably significant contribution to the whole process. One consequence of it, however, was the creation of a myth about literacy in nineteenth-century Britain. The Act was supposedly to turn out hundreds of thousands of Board School literates. It was, therefore, easily assumed that the previous level and extent of literacy must have been very poor. The years before 1870 thus came to be seen as a dark age. Recent work has shown up the myth for what it is, but it is equally important to remember that for generations after 1870 it was a very widely accepted version of the past, and judgements and analyses of the relationship of education to the press were made in its light. By the 1890s at the latest it had become a cliché to link the large circulation of the popular press with the effects of Board School education. Staking a claim for more daily papers in 1892, W.T. Stead wrote, 'the Education Act has practically created a new reading public, for which the morning daily, as we have it, makes next to no provision"[41] There were many, like Stead, who noted the potential readership created by the Act, but there were also many who noted it only to deplore what they considered to have been the production of mere readers, unable to concentrate upon more than a few lines at a time, and lacking entirely any critical faculty.[42] Before discussing the grounds on which these opinions might have been founded, it will be helpful to set them in perspective. The disillusion of the 1890s and 1900s was at least in part due to the exaggerated optimism which the 1870 Act had created, and the apparent bleakness of the previous period.

As Professor Webb has demonstrated, there seems to have been no marked break in the continuity of improvement in educational achievements at 1870. 'Some degree of literacy must have been nearly universally diffused in the portion of the working-classes which made up the great political potential in English society' in the early Victorian period.[43] This had been recognised by some of the more perceptive observers at the time. William Hunt, editor of the *Eastern Morning News* at Hull, and ex-President of the Provincial Newspaper Society, thought 'the increased attention given to education — although still far less than it ought to have been — had *before 1863* (the *Eastern Morning News* was founded in 1864) helped greatly to multiply newspaper readership.'[44] The point was spelt out by Thomas Wright, 'the journeyman engineer', in 1881.[45]

> It should be borne in mind that the Education Acts have not created a new system of education. They have simply extended the operations of a previously existing system. That system, as it did previously exist, was so large, and had been at work so long we can fairly judge of it by its fruits; and its fruits were not and are not culture. . . The extension of elementary education, as it has hitherto been understood, if left to its single self, will give us a large number of the people able to read the police intelligence of the lower types of weekly newspapers, and willing to read little else.

There had, of course, been anxiety expressed about the allegedly low rates of literacy in the mid-century, but there is evidence of a somewhat brighter picture. Henry Fowler, a printer and publisher, told the Excise Commission in 1835 that in Bristol only one in twenty could not read. In 1860 the founder of the *Driffield Times,* G.R. Jackson, based his whole enterprise on the claim that there existed in the area 'almost universal reading and writing'. In 1867 Ludlow and Jones, experienced observers, noted with satisfaction 'the decreasing proportion of educational marksmen in the population'.[46]

All of these observers had some interest in stressing the brighter side of the picture, but while such evidence does not constitute irrefutable proof of widespread literacy, such are the difficulties of obtaining information as to literacy it none the less warrants considerable attention. These difficulties are notorious. It is usual to look for evidence of reading ability, as this is judged the easier of the two skills involved in literacy, and the most widely and frequently used. Moreover, schools taught reading before writing, if, indeed, they taught writing at all up to the mid-century. Unfortunately reading is an activity which leaves few traces. Literacy questions have never been included in British censuses.[47] A few surveys conducted by those thankfully zealous fact-gatherers, the early British social scientists, have been expertly used by Professor Webb to supplement our picture, but they are still too few to admit of broad conclusions.[48] Some literacy statistics are also available from reports on the prison population. The proportion of those completely unable to read or write decreased from 35.8 per cent to 30.61 per cent from 1837 to 1845.[49] Such statistics have not been systematically examined, however, and conclusions differ. Roberts, in his book on *fin de siècle* Salford, for example, claims that the proportion of illiterate prisoners rose from 10 per cent in 1835 to more than 80 per cent in 1905.[50] Clearly, however, such statistics reflect changes only in the prison population and not in the population as a whole, although they probably also indicate changes in the standards of literacy in use at each date. The figures which may be gleaned from the returns of illiterate voters are similarly unrepresentative.[51]

For anything like a global picture of the situation one has to turn from reading to writing. Both contemporaries and later historians have based their estimates on the incidence of marks in marriage registers, recorded from 1839.[52] Before looking at such figures, however, their limitations must be considered. The Registrar's reasoning in 1861, that 'the signing of one's name is roughly equivalent to being able to read fluently', seems highly speculative, although, as Professor Stone has suggested, the ability to sign one's name some twelve or fifteen years after leaving school may be an indication of abiding literacy.[53] Even more dubious is the procedure of examining the marks to see which were firmly made and which were not, and trying to deduce from this whether delicacy on the part of the bride or harassment by the presiding officials caused a literate person to mark.[54] Then, again, the statistics thus gleaned form an idiosyncratic sample. If it is assumed that literacy declined rapidly after the termination of formal education,[55] aggregate figures taken at marriage age must underestimate the literacy of the younger age groups, and, if education and literacy were improving over time, such figures must tend to overestimate the abilities of the older age groups. Nor can they tell us anything about the development of literacy after marriage, so that one must assume that, like riding a bicycle, reading and writing are habits which, once acquired, are never lost. There are dangers also in using the married as representative of the unmarried. The strains of marriage in a poor family, in bad housing, would probably have an adverse effect on the persistence of literacy, while there may have been men and women who refrained from marriage at least in part to continue their self-education. The Registrar himself admitted that the sample would include 'very few of the infirm, idiotic, or others incapable of learning', and even if these disabilities may have caused people to remain unmarried, it is unreasonable to assume that anything like a majority of the unmarried would have been thus handicapped.[56] Again, as Webb has repeatedly stressed, the figures are geographically specific, and vary widely from parish to parish, according to the state of educational provision, the age and sex structure of the population, the levels of work and wealth, and the influence, probably, of religion. The influence of occupation, for example, is not always clear. It has been claimed that the early effects of industrialisation were to reduce the literacy requirements of the labour force.[57] After the 1840s, particularly with the growth of the distributive and service industries, literacy probably became more significant. In areas of small-scale industry, where more were their own masters, it is also likely that literacy and numeracy would have been higher, as they would have been valuable assets from a business point of view.[58] The problem of the sexual distribution of literacy is also important. As the marriage age of women tended to be lower than that of men, one would have expected a slightly better performance from the brides than from the bridegrooms. It was usual, however, for the opposite pattern to occur, and this may have been due to the inferior education provided for girls, to the fact that less, or at least different was expected of them than of men and boys, to the unwillingness of brides to embarrass their husbands, and to the pressure from those officiating to conform to the convention of female deference in these matters. It is also possible that women went into occupations which led to a quicker deterioration of literacy than those which men took up, whilst there were few occupations in which women were allowed to rise even to quasi-managerial positions. The wage differential would also have left women with less time and leisure to exploit their literacy. These are all problems which make the interpretation of overall literacy statistics extremely difficult, for they affected not only the actual pattern of literacy in the country, but also the way in which this was recorded.

These reservations must be borne in mind when examining the figures provided by the Registrar in this period, but taken together with the views of contemporaries such as those already noted in this section, the figures do perhaps provide a not entirely misleading guide to the changes which occurred in the last half of the nineteenth century. In England, after an initial faltering in the 1840s, the trend was steadily upwards, from a mean of about 61 per cent 'literate' in 1850, to 76 per cent in 1868. There then seems to have occurred a small plateau about 1870, before the final surge up to 97 per cent, in 1888. The gap between male and female literacy narrowed from about 16 per cent in 1841 to about 6 per cent in 1868 and 1 per cent in 1898, in favour of men. Closer investigation, however, reveals that there were more counties in 1888 with 10 per cent illiterate men (17), than there were with 10 per cent illiterate women (11). Women had always tended to do better in the south-east, their average being brought down by the industrial counties of the north, Lancashire, Cheshire, the West, and to a lesser extent the East Riding of Yorkshire, Nottinghamshire, Derbyshire and Staffordshire. Counties with a persistently poor overall record were scattered – Monmouthshire, Staffordshire and Bedfordshire for men and women, plus Suffolk for men, and Lancashire, Cambridgeshire, Durham and Cornwall for women. Those with the best records were the rural sparsely populated counties of Cumberland, Northumberland, Westmorland and the North Riding of Yorkshire. All Yorkshire, Devon, Gloucestershire and the southern Home Counties came into the running later on. London was an area of high literacy for both sexes. By 1898 no county fell below 90 per cent for either sex. Comparison of the figures for Northampton and Northamptonshire, which show the town to have had consistently higher figures for men, and lower figures for women than in the county, suggests that urban life may have favoured the development of male literacy, even perhaps at the expense of female literacy.[59] A proper study of the differences between literacy in the town and the country, and between classes, however, remains to be done.

Taking a broad view, what evidence has been used here seems to point to a quick growth in literacy over the whole country in something like thirty years, or a generation, and this, of course, to a large extent confirmed the confidence of the early Victorians in the knowledge revolution. It is now necessary to make a closer inspection of the wider process of readership before coming to the central problem of the relationship between the expansion of education, the growth of literacy, and the development of the press. Two points may be made at this stage, however, about the relationship of the press to the development of literacy. The first is that the improvement in literacy was reasonably steady, and there is nothing to suggest that the growth of newspaper circulations, or of the numbers of individual newspapers was directly linked to the supply of readers. Indeed, the myth about 1870 may have been more important in this respect than the reality, the promise of a new and untapped source of readers more alluring than any actual evidence of a reading revolution. The second point relates to the question as to whether the supply of readers or of newspapers was the shorter in the period under consideration. As neither literacy nor circulation figures can be relied upon, answers, at this stage at least, must be speculative. There were, with the possible exception of *The Times,* no national newspapers in England, and readership was, therefore, highly localised. Detailed comparison of local literacy and circulation figures might be made where these were available, but multiple readership and the sale of the paper over quite a large area would be likely to make most such studies unproductive. The trends which do appear, increasing literacy, growing population, increasing numbers of newspapers with increasing circulations, seem all to fit together, but it is still difficult to see exactly what the fit was. In the early 1870s the number of literate married people was perhaps just over one-third of the whole population, giving a potential pool of say six million readers. The circulation of the provincial press, with a small number of large papers and a large number of small ones, was, at a guess, about two and a quarter million a week (assuming that the people who bought a daily paper on one day would be those who bought it on the other days of the week). There were, in addition, about three million copies of the London dailies and weeklies a week, making a total of five and a quarter million papers a week, not far short of the potential pool of readership among married people. The circulation would have to be reduced, however, for those who read more than one paper a week, and the pool increased for the unmarried, at the very least. Then there would be an unknown reduction in the pool to be made for those excluded for financial reasons. Modern analyses tend to stress 'household coverage' for the purpose of advertising, and it is possible that, with the greater average size of the Victorian family, newspapers did in fact reach more people per copy than newspapers of later generations. But again there may have been restrictions upon certain members of the family reading some papers, or some parts of papers. These are quite obviously speculative remarks, and they are designed to show the extreme complexity of the relationship between the ability and the opportunity to read on the one hand, and the development of the newspaper press on the other.

IV Readership

There is an obvious distinction to be made between literacy and readership, even if it be accepted that the former can be measured in terms of reading ability. A person may be taught how to read, but he may not choose to do so, or he may have no opportunity for doing so. Personal caprice aside, the opportunity for reading depends upon a variety of circumstances. In the countryside for example, there would be less reading matter on view than in the poster-laden towns, and there would be a smaller variety of occupation and recreation involving reading and writing in the country than in the town.[60] In urban areas, where living conditions perhaps encouraged a closer community, the older forms of communication would linger. As Dr. Schofield has pointed out, in pre-industrial society there was 'a large area in which there was effective participation in the literate culture by essentially illiterate people', and, for example, the practice of reading newspapers aloud to groups persisted into the twentieth century, not only in country areas, but in the slums of Salford.[61] Opportunity would also depend upon the time available for reading, and for many working people in the nineteenth century there would be little enough of this, hence the popularity of the Sunday papers which could be read first on the only rest-day of the week, and intermittently thereafter. Such a situation also militated against female readership, as the working-class wife would rarely enjoy even the free time given to the men of the family. Poverty would affect the means available to buy newspapers, although when the breadwinner was employed this would not constitute a serious drain on resources. There were ways in which opportunities could be increased by co-operation, such as the use of a club, pub, or institute, or later of a public library, or, strictly speaking illegally, by the hiring out of newspapers, or by reading them aloud to groups, the members of which were not necessarily illiterate.[62] Reading aloud in offices and workshops was quite common, and meant that each person involved would hear from more than one newspaper a day.[63]

The method of distribution of newspapers was also important in determining the degree of opportunity. The methods before and after repeal of the stamp differed considerably, and the technical details will be discussed later, but the effect of the system is relevant here. Each copy of a newspaper before repeal, and probably for a long while afterwards, was seen by perhaps half a dozen readers, either in pubs or coffee houses, or sent free through the post after the initial purchase, or hired at a penny an hour, or read around country subscription circles at a halfpenny a day.[64] In the towns news and reading rooms had existed since the eighteenth century, and had multiplied greatly in the nineteenth. Libraries and Exchanges commonly had reading rooms and newsrooms, and in the last quarter of the century, if not before, such rooms were the rule in any such institution. In Hull for example the new Mechanics Institute, founded in 1842, the Anglican Church Institute in 1845, the new Young People's Institute in 1864, and the James Reckitt Library in 1889, were all complete with their own newsroom. In addition there had been a subscription newsroom over the Exchange since 1805, and an Operative Conservative News Room since at least 1851.[65] The Public Libraries Act of 1850 had also called for the provision of free newsrooms in the new Free Libraries.[66] The coffee house, perhaps more even than the pub, was also a centre of newspaper reading. Peel's in Fleet Street was famous for its provision of all the provincial press. Even into the 1870s the association of the coffee house with the newspaper was axiomatic.[67]

Then, of course, there were the Mechanics Institutes, which for a while in the 1820s and 1830s fought unsuccessfully for the allegiance of the working class. They suited and were subscribed to for the most part by the middle classes, who tried to control the contents of and behaviour in the newsrooms to such an extent that the working classes were driven out.[68] There were clashes between patrons and members of the Institutes over the specific newspapers which were to be supplied, clashes which led in both Manchester and in Crewe to the secession of groups who formed their own rival institutions.[69] The question of providing newsrooms at all constituted a source of conflict. 'In almost every case', claimed Thomas Hogg, secretary to the Union of Mechanics Institutes in Lancashire and Cheshire, newsrooms had been objected to by patrons on political grounds, although in some cases those who had withdrawn their support for fear of encouraging radicalism were persuaded to restore it after they had witnessed the social benefits it had bestowed.[70] There was, on the part of the working classes, it seems, a general dislike of the condescending and 'classy' air of the establishments, but perhaps the commonest specific complaint was against the rule of silence. Working men preferred to be able to discuss what they read, and found that they could do so more freely in the pubs than in the Institutes.[71] This, and the fact that, as Hogg admitted, the Institutes attracted mostly 'young men in offices, and others engaged in retail establishments and the like', drove some to found separate working-class institutions.[72] A commentator on the Carlisle working men's reading room noted that, in contrast to that exercise in self-help, 'the worthy folks who patronise the lower orders, who dispense fountains of soup, mints of copper and small change — parcels of left-off clothes for flattery — condescend not to bless, but to demoralise the victims of their ignorant attention.' In 1851 this reading room took two daily papers, thirteen weeklies, and fifteen periodicals, and possessed a library of some 708 volumes. The committee consisted only of those who earned a weekly wage. Those who fell behind with their subscriptions were expelled, except in cases of unemployment.[73] In 1853 James Hole argued that these working-class reading rooms were inferior to those provided by the Institutes, because they did not provide both sides of the arguments. Reading newspapers, he admitted, inculcated 'the habit of reasoning which is of great value in the affairs of life', but he thought there might be too much newspaper reading, and would have prohibited persons of under twenty-five from using the Institute's rooms, and included the charge for the newsroom in the overall charge for membership of the Institute, in order to discourage those who came merely to read newspapers.[74]

The repeal of the taxes on knowledge, and the appearance of the cheap penny and halfpenny press did not do any detectable harm to the newsrooms. The clubs and other similar institutions played a very important role in nineteenth-century social life, for all classes, both for recreation and for politics. The men, at least, spent their leisure increasingly away from the hearth and home, and this meant that until the growth of street distribution and the spread of rail and tram commuting, the majority of newspapers would have been read in the clubs and pubs. Both provided a vast selection of newspapers and periodicals, all for a very modest fee. In fact, the newsroom as an institution was probably strengthened in the 1870s and 1880s by the growth of the press during those decades. In 1884, for example, it was estimated that 10,000 people a day used Birmingham's newsrooms.[75] Of course, the morning papers were also read at the breakfast table, particularly by the middle classes, where the head of the family would not have usually had to leave home before the morning delivery. When the evening papers came into their own towards the close of the century they were read at the tea-table, and as early as the 1870s suburban trains were left strewn with the litter of thousands of newspapers every morning.[76] Indeed, in 1866, commuter reading was credited with saving people half an hour at the office every morning, and with enabling them to avoid having to stare at advertisements or other people during the journey. In fairness one should note that it was possible that the noise of the vehicles may have made conversation impossible![77]

In the 1860s most newspapers were still written by and for the middle classes, or as Sala put it, 'the governing classes — aristocratic, official, parliamentary, financial and commercial — and were not read, to any very considerable extent, by the public outside the charmed sphere of those governing classes. . .and were to a great extent controlled and contributed to by members of the governing classes themselves.'[78] While there was still a smattering of radical papers, the unstamped and the Chartist press had almost disappeared by the 1860s. The London and provincial morning papers catered largely for the middle classes. In London the evening papers were taken by the clubs, until the appearance of the halfpenny *Echo* in 1868. The working classes read mostly on Sundays, and were provided for by the *News of the World*, the *Weekly Dispatch, Reynolds News* and *Lloyds Weekly News*. Local weekly papers tended to have more of a community readership, especially before the multiplication of newspapers gave rise to local competition. In the country areas especially the local weekly would be read by squire and labourer alike, although for different reasons.[79]

By the 1870s too, readership was being taken more into account by those who started and ran newspapers. Proprietors were beginning to realise their dependence on advertisement revenue, and realised that this revenue would in part depend upon an accurate determination of readership and circulation. As one commentator observed in 1853, 'before providing for the political ideals of the middle classes, the (London) Journal must provide for their interests'.[80] Newspapers were bought for their news, but often what determined the choice of paper was the sort of advertisement the reader could expect to find there. This applied particularly to those in search of employment. The *Morning Post,* it was said, was read by gentlemen and by gentlemen's gentlemen, by ladies, and by ladies' maids.[81] The *Daily News* became the labour exchange of the journalistic world. The *Daily Telegraph* catered for lower-middle-class employment, the *Daily Chronicle* and the *Echo* more for working-class employment.[82] In the provinces all these needs were catered for by the same paper, except perhaps in the larger cities where some social differentiation may have existed. In addition there was also an enormous growth after repeal in class and trade papers, providing specialist reading for the enthusiast and information for occupational groups. The rule of 'find your readers' interests' applied here more than anywhere.

Lacking readership surveys, or detailed historical content analyses of the Victorian and Edwardian newspapers, we are forced to use, as above, the mostly unsubstantiated opinions of contemporaries. Much of this evidence, however, derives from journalists, and it seems unlikely that they would have been wildly wrong about the nature and habits of their readers. Edward Dicey wrote in 1905 that the penny dailies

> still represent the small trading classes, the shop keepers, the clerks, as distinguished from the working men proper. But I cannot doubt that the elector who earns his day's work and lodging for himself and and his family by the labour of his own hands is represented by the halfpenny Press.[83]

H.W. Massingham had anticipated this view more than a decade earlier when there were fewer halfpenny dailies. The penny and especially the halfpenny newspaper, he wrote, 'is to be met with in the common lodging house, and the furnished room of the worst slums, just as it is in the rural labourer's cottage'.[84] There seems little reason to doubt that these observations were tolerably accurate. More dubious was the opinion of G.R. Humphrey in 1893, not about the destination of the newspapers, but about the tastes of the workers and clerks. He thought the working men read more seriously than the middle-class clerks, who wanted only entertainment and were more susceptible to the sensational, the ephemeral and the trivial.[85] Now, this was a widely held opinion, but while there may have been an element of truth in it, it is supported by no firm evidence, and smacks rather of argument by stereotype. Other accounts tend to be a mixture of opinion and observation. Take, for example, the survey conducted by J. Leigh in 1904, in a part of industrial Lancashire. He published his report in the *Economic Review,* the organ of the Oxford Christian Union, and it reflected this body's broad-church view of working-class mores.[86] He noted, first, that the Free Library was well-stocked, but was used mainly by a few clerks, schoolteachers and 'higher artisans'. They borrowed popular fiction and history mostly, and few read the reviews, except on special issues such as tariff reform. Where books were to be found in working-class homes they would be the Bible, (which Leigh thought served rather as a fetish), Bunyan, Pike's *Guide to Disciples,* some G.A. Henty and Anthony Hope, with perhaps *Uncle Tom's Cabin, Mary Barton* and a temperance novel by Mrs Henry Wood. Most readers, he found, confined themselves to periodical literature, and to the sporting press, with an emphasis upon horse racing and football. The women read weekly novelettes with happy endings, often forming 'reading agencies' to circulate them. All sorts of religious weeklies were popular, especially amongst non-Church-goers, and were often of a very heterodox nature. Interestingly he found that the weekly editions of the provincial dailies which carried serialised fiction were even more popular than the usual Sunday papers, with one of every two homes taking one and sometimes two of them. The only widely read dailies were the sporting ones. Leigh thought the picture so bleak that he almost wished 'that the masses could not read'. Two years later James Haslam made similar observations about four districts of Manchester. In the Ancoats slums newsagents told him that the worst-off working-class readers wanted romances, the better-off, 'articles dealing with some sociological aspect of working life'. Crime, violence and sport were the best-sellers, and the shops were besieged by women at midday for the early edition of the sporting papers. In Salford a similar picture emerged, except that the bias was almost wholly towards sport. One newsagent claimed that reading had used to matter in the district, over the previous forty years, but that it did so no longer. In relatively better-off Harpushy fewer betting papers were sold, and these to the men, with fashion, romance and self-education generally more popular. In east Manchester Haslam found complaints about the burden of selling Sunday newspapers, and these he noted were the most corrupting sort of paper.[87]

Allowing for the fundamental disapproval exhibited in these studies, they do give an idea of how few daily newspapers were read by the poorer working classes, or even by the lower middle classes. The market created by economic prosperity and elementary education was, it seems, even up to the 1900s, still severely limited. Such revelations were a great disappointment to those who had cherished the liberal vision in the 1860s and 1870s. It was not that the people were not buying liberal or radical papers, it was that they were not buying newspapers at all in a serious sense. It was the failure of the papers of the golden age that they could not match the power of attraction of the 'new journalism' as practised after the 1890s. While the quantity of actual reading had indeed risen, its quality, and even its motivation seemed to have worsened from the liberal point of view.

If one compares the views expressed about public reading in the 1860s and in the 1900s certain similarities are apparent: the criticisms that popular literature was too radical, or too trivial, or associated with betting, vice and crime. Yet the tone of the two periods is different.

Efforts were made in the 1860s to point out how popular reading matter, and its readers, had improved, whereas in the 1900s it was almost always a case of emphasising, if not its actual deterioration, then certainly its failure to improve, and to live up to expectations. The assumption that improvement and seriousness were the right roads persisted, although entertainment was allowed a certain respectability, and given the role of leavening the drear gravity of the mid-century press. This disillusion was not mere sour grapes. The developing popular culture, however much it lacked an earlier authenticity,[88] posed a threat to the Victorian middle-class ideology, whether it was in the form of the press, the music hall or the cinema, and it was so whether interest or reason was stressed in the articulation of that ideology. On both counts the golden age of the press was a part of the ideology, whereas the 'new journalism', in its most advanced and dynamic form, was not. Hence it is not surprising to find that 'new liberals' in caustic denunciation of the popular press of their time. In fact the threat proved insubstantial, but it is important to note that it was regarded as a threat, particularly to the Liberal idea of politics which had held the field during the third quarter of the nineteenth century. For the present, however, it is necessary to return to the golden age itself.

3 THE MAKING OF A CHEAP PRESS

I A Model Agitation

The most important phase in the struggle for the freedom of the press
was the period during which the government tried to suppress what
Lord Ellenborough called 'the pauper press', in order to stop short of
'having statesmen at the loom and politicians at the spinning jenny'.[1]
In 1836, after two long and fierce rounds in the battle, the government
compromised with working- and middle-class radicals by reducing the
stamp duty on newspapers by 3d, bringing it down to 1d. The
advertisement tax had already been reduced from 3s 6d to 1s 6d in
1833, and now the paper duty was also slightly reduced. These measures
provided for a cheaper, but not for a cheap press. Disappointment at the
failure to achieve more was aggravated by proprietors reducing prices by
2d instead of 3d. Technically this was justified by the loss of the
discount which they had received on payment of the tax, but the loss
to proprietors from this source was only about $\frac{1}{3}d$ on each stamp, and
they were thus benefiting to the extent of $\frac{2}{3}d$ on each paper sold. It
was claimed, however, with some fairness, that only the London papers
and the large provincials, of which there were very few, gained in this
way, because smaller papers had always to sustain a loss on unused
stamps.[2]

The reduction of the taxes was made even less satisfactory because
it was accompanied by stricter enforcement of other controls. The use
of the common informer was ended, but the securities demanded of
printer and publisher were increased, while newspapers of more than
two sheets in size, or costing 6d or more, were no longer exempted
from the tax. Advertisement sheets were also brought under the rule
of the newspaper stamp. The fine for selling or for possessing an
unstamped newspaper was raised to £20, and for publishing a newspaper
without having made a declaration the fine was raised to £50.[3] Apart
from making it economically less attractive to produce unstamped
newspapers, the effect of the 1836 Act was generally to protect the
established papers, both in London and in the provinces, as Collett put
it, 'against interlopers'. Weaker rivals inevitably came to see it as having
created what they considered to be the monopolist power of *The
Times*.[4] In so far as it served to maintain the price of newspapers, and
thus inhibited the growth of smaller journals this criticism was not

without foundation, and the fears expressed by the Provincial Newspaper Society about floods of cheap, worthless papers were not substantiated. In the first year of operation of the Act the following return was made to Parliament.

Newspapers established since repeal (1836)

	London	Country
Daily	1	—
Twice a week	1	—
Thrice a week	—	1
Weekly	23	35
Fortnightly	1	—
Occasionally	1	—
(of which total 10 London and 6 Country papers had been discontinued or incorporated with other papers)		

Source: PP 1837 (291), xxxix

This was a very modest expansion, but having no yardstick some contemporaries thought it alarming, finding some consolation in the fact that the increase was rather in what they regarded as the more moderate provinces, than in the combustible metropolis.[5]

However one viewed these events it could not be claimed that the radicals had secured their cheap, or even free press. There were many who had no intention of ushering into existence any such animal, and who defended the stamp in terms of quality, tone and security, and their views were strengthened by the growth of Chartism in the 1840s.[6] For a time even the radicals became quiescent about this issue, less cowed by authority than distracted by other movements, notably by Chartism itself and by the Anti-Corn Law agitation. There were, however, important connections between the latent movement for a cheap press and these other two movements. The campaign against the taxes on knowledge was resumed by those who were members of the People's Charter Union, and consciously modelled upon the example of Anti-Corn Law League.

In 1849 the PCU decided to ask Richard Cobden to insert the repeal of the newspaper stamp in his 'national budget', and the appeal was couched in terms well calculated to elicit a positive response. The PCU argued that if national education was not to be achieved quickly, then at least the working classes should be allowed to educate themselves to fit them for the franchise. Only thus, it was added, could they learn the 'natural laws' of political economy.[7] A favourable reply from Cobden led to the formation within the PCU of the Newspaper Stamp Abolition Committee. Its members included Henry Hetherington (for the few months before his death), James Watson, and C.D. Collett, secretary of the PCU.[8] Francis Place became treasurer. Its first address appealed to the middle classes:[9]

> If the middle classes wish to improve the condition of those less fortunate than themselves, they have now a golden opportunity. The reduction of the duty (a measure of which they have reaped the chief benefit) was carried almost entirely without their assistance. Let them in their turn carry out that total repeal, which will benefit all who have an interest in the spread of knowledge or the progress of truth. It is only by their assistance that this can be done in the perfectly legal manner which is the peculiar characteristic of the middle class reformers of Great Britain.

The campaign was thus couched in terms of the improvement of class relations. Julian Harney lent the support of his *Democratic Review,* the Committee was joined by the secretary of the printers' trade union, Edward Edwards, and in 1850 the Society of Fraternal Democrats endorsed the campaign. The Committee decided to adopt the federative tactics of the Anti-Corn Law League, but the new campaign was to prove rather quieter and less plebeian than its model. Collett, its secretary, was trained as a lawyer, and was a master of detail, and Cobden instilled into it the importance of organisation. Balking a little at the Chartist habit of 'blending music and logic', he stressed that 'if you don't *sell* sufficient tickets, you ought to fill the room from the *highways* and *hedges.*' He begged Collett:

> cast your eye over the subscription list of the "Association", and you will see how exclusively, almost, we comprise steady, sober middle-class reformers — free trade, temperance, education, peace advocates — who will stand by you from year to year, and gather about them an increasing moral power, provided you handle them judiciously, and do not place them in a position in which they think they are committed to a *tone* of agitation which does not represent their feelings.[10]

As Cobden hinted, the Chartist flavour and personnel of the movement did seem to ebb away after a year or so, although a Chartist, Richard Moore, remained chairman until the dissolution of the Committee, by then called the Association for the Promotion of the Repeal of the Taxes on Knowledge, in 1870.[11]

In the beginning the Committee was not the only body concerned with the taxes on knowledge. In 1849 John Francis, publisher of the *Athenaeum,* together with some other newspaper proprietors, set up the London Committee for Obtaining the Repeal of the Duty on Advertisements, converted in 1853 into an association for the repeal of the paper duty.[12] In 1850 a paper manufacturer founded an Association for the repeal of the paper duty, but the PCU succeeded in putting a stop to it, on the grounds that the commercial motive for repealing only the paper duty was unacceptable. There were higher things at stake. In 1851 the Association for the Promotion of the Repeal of the Taxes on Knowledge (APRTK) was formed, its president Milner Gibson, its treasurer Francis Place. On the committee were Cobden, Bright, Holyoake, William Ewart, G.H. Lewes, Joseph Hume, Thornton Hunt and William Hickson.[13]

Part of the agitation consisted of meetings and pamphlets, and Cobden's skills were invaluable here. In 1854, for example, he put once more the educational arguments for repeal, arguments which he considered to be the Association's best weapons.[14]

> There were 2,000,000 of adult males, if not 3,000,000, who now never read a newspaper. Now there was a great mine, which it was the interest of the press to open, thus cultivating a taste for reading in the lower strata of the social system. The cheap paper would gradually increase the customers for the higher priced paper. . .
> *The Times.* . .at 5*d* was as cheap as any paper in the world. But then it was no consolation to the poor peasant, whose earnings were 15*d* or 18*d* a day, to tell him that *The Times* was at his disposal. It was too good and too large for him; he had not a table on which he could spread it out, and his feeble rush light would not help him over its vast surfaces of print. He looked over pages of advertisements announcing estates for sale, or he read the state of the Stock-Exchange; but these things possessed no interest for him. . .

More important than this sort of activity, however, was the establishment of a House of Commons Select Committee on the Newspaper Stamp, a markedly successful propaganda exercise initiated by Cobden and Milner Gibson in 1851. Gibson was chairman, and Cobden led most of the questioning. On their side were William Ewart, of the APRTK, Shafto Adair and Sir Joshua Warmsley. Three of the witnesses were also members of the APRTK, although this was not disclosed in the evidence. There were four on the other side, led by Henry Rich. George Hamilton seemed committed to neither side. The Report, written very largely by Gibson, claimed first that the law had been shown to be unworkable. Secondly, it was noted that the reduction of the duty in 1836 had been followed by an 'improvement' in the press, and that most of the evidence they had taken had refuted the claim that cheapness meant deterioration. Finally, 'it may be said with truth, that the newspaper stamp prohibits the existence of such newspapers as from their price and character would be suitable to the means and wants of the labouring classes'.[15] The evidence had in fact been overwhelmingly in favour of repeal, and some of the witnesses opposing it, especially Mowbray Morris, the manager of *The Times,* and Joseph Timm, the Solicitor for the Inland Revenue, caused more damage to their own than to the other side.

It is difficult to assess the impact of the Report, but it certainly provided ample material for the APRTK to work with, which it did with skill and pertinacity.

The first success of the campaign was the repeal of the advertisement duty in 1853. That this should have come first was only to have been expected, for, although the APRTK had not put it first on their list, it was a measure which aroused little opposition. The Provincial Newspaper Society had opposed the repeal of any of the taxes, but by 1852 it too had come to support the repeal of the advertisement and paper duties. Gladstone, the Chancellor of the Exchequer, prevaricated, and toyed with the alternative idea of abolishing the newspaper stamp on advertising supplements. As *The Times* was the only paper which issued such supplements this would have further damaged the position of the provincial press, as Cobden was quick to point out.[16] After a tactical struggle in the Commons Gladstone dropped the idea, and agreed to abolish the advertisement tax. At the same time, however, he increased the size of sheet permissible for a 1*d* stamp, once again to the advantage of *The Times.*

The prominence of *The Times* in these manoeuvres is of more than passing significance. The paper had since 1836 built up a very strong position, which its rivals claimed was the direct result of the privileges conferred upon it by the provisions of the 1836 Act. This was at best a half-truth. Without the 1*d* postage, (1½*d* for *The Times* with supplement), the paper could not have built up its circulation as it did.

In 1841 it sold twice the number of copies as the *Morning Post, Morning Herald* and *Morning Chronicle* put together, and by 1850 four times as many. These papers, however, also enjoyed the privilege of the stamp, but found it impossible to compete with *The Times*. The main reason for this was, as Mowbray Morris pointed out, the free advertisement sheet, which did not often pay for itself, and the occasional double supplement which never paid for itself, but both of which did serve to increase circulation.[17] The effect of the repeal of the advertisement duty, and not of the reduction of the stamp, did improve the by then established position of *The Times* as an advertisement medium, although the paper retained a markedly conservative advertising policy.[18] It had not only been a question of the supplements, however. The quality of the paper's production and editing under Barnes and then Delane simply surpassed that of its rivals, and continued to do so into the 1850s. It is in the context of this strength that the repealers' hostility to *The Times* after 1853 must be seen. The APRTK never made *The Times* its sole target, but Cobden's relations with the paper during the 1850s deteriorated sharply, and he came increasingly to speak in terms of the provinces against the metropolis, the small against the great, especially against *The Times*.

Fresh impetus was given to the campaign for repeal by the outbreak of the Crimean War. This did two things for the movement. It emphasised the power of *The Times* to such an extent that it provoked a natural reaction. By the time the stamp was abolished the paper had alienated both Aberdeen and Palmerston. The war also precipitated another spate of unstamped newspapers, the 'war telegraphs', which contained only war news, and, therefore, claimed exemption from the stamp. The Board of Inland Revenue quickly succeeded in frightening them out of existence, but the APRTK pursued the Board relentlessly over the matter, and eventually in 1855 Cornewall Lewis introduced the Bill for the repeal of the stamp.

The Times claimed as early as July 1854 that 'Mr. Cobden and his school wish to destroy the influence of the metropolitan press because it interferes as they think with the provincial.'[19] This was, perhaps, a slight exaggeration, but it was a view which received support from the fact that Gibson and Gladstone succeeded in getting the maximum weight for 1*d* postage on newspapers reduced from 6 oz. to 4 oz., after the abolition of the stamp. This meant that it was now below the average weight of *The Times*, and even its opponents considered this a blow below the belt.[20] *The Times*, having identified its opponents, claimed defiantly, 'we shall never descend to the level of a Manchester machine, to report speeches at command, and spin theories to order.'[21] Fonblanque, still the doyen of English journalists, warned that 'to kill the giant is all very fine, but it is not always pleasant to live with dwarfs.'[22] *The Times* was not killed by the measure, but its growth was seriously impaired, and the lead which it had built up over the past twenty years was quickly whittled away. By the time the Post Office had been persuaded to raise the weight to 6 oz. again, in 1858, the damage had been done. Robbed of a carefully fostered advertising advantage it had now to meet a new cheaper press on its own terms. It had first to turn to the railways for transport, where the rates were only ½*d*, but although it should have benefited from this, as Rowland Hill gloomily predicted in 1851, rail distribution was still a thing of the future.[23] *The Times* also tried to find a lighter weight of paper, and its wholesale agents took to mutilating the supplements in order to reduce the weight, but to little avail. The repeal of the stamp had made cheaper papers possible, especially in the provinces, and this was the main thing, as Cobden had well understood.[24]

The campaign did not finish in 1855. There remained the paper duty. The APRTK proceeded upon a plan of little by little, starting from a minor success in obtaining a drawback of duty on the waste cuttings of envelopes. From then on the astounding complexities of the paper duties ensured the repealers excellent opportunities to exploit their anomalies and inconsistencies. The campaign in the Commons was led once more by Milner Gibson, while outside the APRTK was joined, not by the Provincial Newspaper Society in England, but by its counterparts in London, Scotland and Ireland.[25] In 1860 Milner Gibson became President of the Board of Trade, and Gladstone proceeded to the work of repeal, on the grounds, first, of the 'boundless scope' of the material in question, namely paper, and second, that repeal would 'promote a diffused demand for rural labour'. There was resistance from paper manufacturers, who were more interested in protection,[26] from the savers of candle-ends who were already alarmed at the rate of income tax resulting from the Crimean war, and from those, like Robert Cecil, who thought talk of the paper duties as a 'tax on knowledge', 'a prostitution of real education'.[27] Nevertheless, the duties were abolished in October 1861, after a stubborn rearguard action in the Lords, which drove Gladstone to the constitutional innovation of incorporating all financial measures into one Bill, thus, in theory at least, destroying the power of the Lords in all matters of finance.[28] The agitation, noted the publisher Robert Chambers, had lasted two years longer than the siege of Troy. Indeed, it did not in fact stop at this point, for there was still the security system in force, which it took another eight years to abolish.

This 'model agitation', as Holyoake termed it, was an admirable text book example of the way in which a mid-Victorian pressure group worked. The easy manner in which Collett later described the work, the references to 'the usual means', indicate the expertise with which the agitation was conducted. Holyoake was not being in the least disparaging when he said that Collett 'had all the qualities of the great secretary'.[29] It was more than just a piece of pressure group politics, however. It was an affirmation of provincial England against central authority and the metropolitan press, and it was an agitation which pulled down some of the last obstacles to the provincial domination of the 1870s and 1880s, a domination which lay at the root of the triumph of Liberalism during that period, and which was so closely associated with the press. Conservatives prophesied that 'the cheap press will lead to the lower classes demanding and getting their own way', but the reformers had in mind a different, less fearsome prospect, the vision of using the press to educate the lower classes as to what 'their own way' really was, and to show them how it was compatible with the way which every rational man was already following.[30]

II A Host of Nobodies

Rhetoric and ideology aside, the Victorian newspaper was not just, or even primarily, a vehicle of national education or of political democracy. It was for those who ran it first and foremost a business, and had long been recognised as such. It will be argued later that there persisted a significant ambivalence between the political and the economic conceptions of the newspaper in the late nineteenth century. That ambivalence was also detectable in the years of the struggle for a cheap press.

There can be little doubt that the proprietors of early Victorian newspapers ran them in the vast majority of cases in order to make a profit. In many cases that profit had not to be substantial, but usually the least that was required was that the business should break even. Where the newspaper was part of a bigger printing and publishing enterprise, then losses could be borne or disguised, but the general rule of profitability was not often broken for long. When it was, Nemesis was never far away. In the course of making out a case for a new Chartist weekly paper William Lovett pointed out that[31]

the Newspaper Press, daily and weekly, is the property of capitalists who have embarked on the enterprise upon purely commercial principles, and with the purpose of making it contribute to their own personal and pecuniary interests. It is the course which is *profitable,* therefore, and not the course which is *just,* which necessarily secures their preference.

At a time of political and economic restriction, however, almost any tolerably run paper could expect to command a viable circulation, because that would be quite small. That there were many casualties was a reflection of the ease with which it was possible to enter the industry, not of the difficulty of making a go of it. One observer put it as follows, in 1863:[32]

starting a newspaper appears to have for some minds a singular fascination. Just as there are men who *must* have race-horses, or play chicken-hazard, so there are others to whom newspaper enterprise is a necessity of life.

Some men were certainly unfortunate in their undertakings. Abel Hinchcliffe, for example, started the *Rotherham Journal* (1857-61), the *Sheffield Argus* (1859-61), the *Hull Pilot* (1860-5), and the *Brigg Observer* (1861-2). He also bought the *Hull Daily Express* in 1859, but sold it again in 1863. He was associated with the more successful *Rotherham and Masborough Advertiser,* started in the name of Annie Hinchcliffe in 1858, and eventually sold to John Garnett in 1872. His last transaction seems to have been to sell his *Doncaster and Pontefract News* to William H. Caldicott in the 1880s.[33]

Newspaper organisation developed from the older sole proprietorship and family firm, through the small and usually private joint-stock company of the mid-nineteenth century, and the chains and syndicates of the last third of the century, to the trusts of the twentieth century. It was an uneven development, and older forms persisted and still persist. The family business remained the most typical form of organisation even in the late nineteenth century, ownership passing from father to son, or severally amongst members of the family. Thus were built up the great businesses of the Tillotsons of Bolton, the Woodheads of Huddersfield, the Stephensons of Southport, the Jeanses of Liverpool, the Baines of Leeds, and so on. Apart from the Walters of the *Times,* and the Borthwicks of the *Morning Post,* London papers tended to remain outside the family pattern, being more of a speculative phenomenon, and more subject to changes in the market.[34]

Before the coming of the cheap press the provincial proprietors
found it more difficult to start successful ventures than those in
London. This was partly the result of the difficulty of raising capital,
with country banking firms showing little enthusiasm for such
enterprises. The partnership and libel laws were also held to be a
deterrent to investment, but this would have applied equally to the
London papers.[35] On the other hand the capital required was not
necessarily very large, and might be raised on a private loan, or by
subscription by 'local residents', who were often attracted by the
opportunity to promote a political cause, or to open up an advertising
medium. An additional difficulty in the provinces was the lack of
jobbing firms to which the printing of small papers could be contracted
out. The concentration of the jobbing trade in London was a legacy of
the earlier seventeenth-century restrictions upon the spread of printing
presses, and had been reinforced by the pattern of trading activity in
the country as a whole, which tended to confine eighteenth-century
printing to the ports. This meant that newspaper proprietors tended
overwhelmingly to be publishers and printers in their own right, and
quite frequently apothecaries, the sale and distribution of medicines
having been closely connected with the distribution of newspapers and
other literature in the eighteenth century.[36]

The most expensive type of paper to start was the London daily. It
was estimated that it might have cost from £2,000 to £5,000 to
establish one in 1818.[37] In 1856 it took £4,500 to start the *Morning
Star*.[38] Michael Whitty, a Liverpool proprietor, told the 1851 Select
Committee that £10,000 was needed to start a London daily, half for
the machinery to print 20,000 in four hours, and half to run it.[39] The
maintenance or purchase of an established London paper could be even
more expensive. In 1842 a £25,000 mortgage was raised to prevent the
Morning Post from falling into the hands of free-traders.[40]

It was less expensive in the provinces. In 1830 it was estimated that
'the expense of getting out a middle sized country paper, published
once a week, is little more than half that of a London weekly newspaper',
but it was admitted that the cost of distributing a country paper was
greater, before the railways and the telegraph.[41] Even so Edward
Baines and William Byles had used £2,500 each in 1801 and 1834
respectively to start the *Leeds Mercury* and the *Bradford Observer*.
John Taylor used only £400 of the £1,000 which he had borrowed in
1821 to set up the *Manchester Guardian*. The *Stockport Advertiser*
began with £1,000 in 1822, but the *Leicester Chronicle* had only £760
in 1810.[42] Varied though they were, by the 1830s costs do seem on

average to have risen. One estimate was for £4,000 to £5,000 to establish and carry on a country paper over its first few years. The *Leeds Intelligencer* was actually sold for £4,000 in 1831, and the *Newcastle Courant* for £8,000 in the following year.[43] In fact, although these figures give some impression of what was at stake, the variety of enterprise, the scale of the paper, the ability of the proprietor and other factors were crucial in determining the level of capital costs. Thus Michael Whitty borrowed some capital and a one-cylinder printing machine to start the *Liverpool Journal,* and was successful enough within a few years to buy what must have been a new two-cylinder Middleton for £1,000.[44] On the other hand the *Newcastle Daily Journal,* an altogether larger proposition, was sold in 1867 for only £2,357.[45] Smaller weeklies fetched much less. The *Peterborough Times* went in 1869 for £300, the *Surrey Comet* for £200 in 1856.[46] Ailing papers, of course, would have fetched prices even below the cost of starting them, whilst prosperous ones would, as with any business, be sold at prices inflated by healthy prospects for the future.

There was always recognised to be a more or less direct relationship between the size of capital and the status of the project. The proprietors of the unstamped press before 1836 ran their businesses for the most part on a shoestring, and there were always men willing to gamble a small capital on a newspaper. The more respectable proprietors, however, had no wish to associate themselves with these projects, or with failures. Some of the biggest proprietors even refused to associate themselves publicly with their own Provincial Newspaper Society.[47] They were, after all, both capitalists and public men, strategically placed to ensure the working of the essentially liberal idea of public service by the economically successful. They were the standard-bearers of their class in the struggle for domination, and they were conscious of the fact. The unending list of councillors, aldermen and mayors boasted of by the provincial press speaks for itself. Michael Whitty, one of the most successful of Liverpool proprietors, had been the city's chief constable in the 1830s. The founder of the *Sunday Times,* Daniel Whittle Harvey, had also risen to the office of Commissioner of Police in the City of London, from 1840 to 1863, after retiring from more than twenty years in Parliament.[48] William Hobson, founder of the *Derbyshire Advertiser* in 1846, became a councillor in 1860, an alderman in 1879, and was mayor in 1883 and 1885. In 1880 he was appointed to the local Bench. Joseph Glover of the *Leamington Spa Courier,* President of the Provincial Newspaper Society in 1870, chairman of the Press Association in 1874, was a JP from 1876, and actually refused nomination for mayor in 1891.[49] These stories were the rule rather than the exception for any proprietor whose business had flourished for a number of years.

For most of the century the major organisation of provincial proprietors was the Provincial Newspaper Society.[50] It had been founded in 1836 as a result of concern about certain advertising practices, and had in the first instance been organised by advertising agents. It consistently refused to identify itself with any political opinions, and followed an invariably restrictive line of policy on the development of the newspaper press. It refused to admit as members proprietors whose papers depended on partly-printed sheets, on the reasonable grounds that they could not be expected to be entirely independent agents. In 1836 they set themselves firmly against the possibility of the growth of newspaper joint-stock companies. The 1836 Act, they claimed, had opened the door to such enterprises, and 'would become the occasion of newspapers being started by persons of no property who, to use a common phrase, are men of straw, who would push forward their plans in the shape of public companies'.[51] In the 1850s they opposed, on the same grounds, the repeal of both the advertisement taxes and the paper duties, and they continued to fight the repeal of the Stamp Acts until it was an accomplished fact. It was said that the effect of the latter 'would be to lower the character of the newspaper press in this country, by the competition for cheapness, and by the increase in number of publications diminishing the means of incurring the large outlay made for every respectable journal'. They were, said an ex-president and the Society's historian, haunted by the spectre of a 'host of nobodies'.[52]

These were attitudes shared, significantly, by Charles Mitchell, an advertising agent, and proprietor of the *Newspaper Press Directory,* who wrote in 1846:[53]

> the press has now so great and so extensive an influence on public opinion — it is so mixed up with all the relations of life — that it is most essential its *[sic]* conductors should be GENTLEMEN in the true sense of the word. They should be equally above corruption and intimidation; incapable of being warped by personal considerations from the broad path of truth and honour, and superior to all attempts at misrepresenting or mystifying public events.

In 1854 he warned again of the dangerous consequences which would follow the abolition of the stamp. 'Our experience convinces us that

such a step would completely destroy the respectability of the
newspaper press, and reduce it from its present position, that of the
highest in the world – to that of the American press.'[54] It was, of
course, to be expected that a canny advertising agent would follow the
opinion of his most important clients, the PNS, but the fact remains
that the Society, which represented the majority of major provincial
proprietors, remained far from enthusiastic about the prospective new
era of the cheap press, and it will be seen later that their anxieties
continued until at least the closing years of the century.

An example of what was feared was the so-called railway press of
1845-6, associated with the railway 'mania' of those years. About thirty
papers concerned with railway business were founded during those two
years, and few survived. In an effort to withstand the crash they began
campaigns resembling those of the 'new journalism' half a century later,
giving away globes and pianos and such like to regular subscribers.[55]
Some thought that this might easily extend into the business of
ordinary newspapers. Mowbray Morris told the 1851 Select Committee
'that persons who have capital and some stake in society, something to
lose should have these papers in their hands. . .it is an advantage to
confine the newspaper press as much as possible in the hands of a few
persons with large capitals.' When pressed by Cobden on this point he
allowed that they need not be very large capitals. Collett had already
claimed that 'capitalists will not venture their capital so long as they
can be interfered with', which, whilst being a neat retort to Morris, also
served to support the view that a cheap press should not, and need not
be based on mere speculation. The *Christian Socialist* and the *Red
Republican,* Collett claimed, were 'the sincere convictions of the
proprietors. . .I do not suppose that either paper is got up as a mere
speculation.'[56]

The effects of the abolition of the stamp, new advances in
production and distribution, and an increasingly literate and prosperous
population would make these fears and reassurances seem very short-
sighted within the next decade or two.

III Those Extraordinary Machines

Whether commercial or ideological, a matter of profits or of national
education, the need was recognised for a multiplication of readers and
of newspapers. Yet the aims of those who were to provide the papers
were relatively modest. Already awed by the scale of the industry,
already referring to 'those extraordinary machines', the prospects for
future expansion were not considered to be unlimited, and expansion

was thought of rather in terms of growth in the number of newspapers, than in the circulation of each.[57] It was accepted that profits were related to advertisement revenue, and advertisement revenue to circulation, but few considered that profits would increase proportionately, let alone more than proportionately with circulation. The vision of cheap newspapers, each catering for vast numbers of readers, was not really put into focus before it had become reality.

Nevertheless, proprietors realised that they could sell more papers cheap than they could dear, and the large papers in particular, *The Times* and *Lloyds Weekly News* for example, found that it was not just the law, or the want of education which inhibited the expansion of their businesses, but also, and perhaps primarily, the technical problems of producing large circulations quickly enough to reach the readers, and the lack of a distributive system capable of handling them.

The first and perhaps major breakthrough had come with the Koenig steam press, first used by *The Times* for its issue of 29 November 1814.[58] Until the beginning of the nineteenth century the printing press had hardly changed since its invention some three hundred and fifty years previously. To the simple platen press had been added a metal screw (1550), a sliding bed and an anti-twist device (1620), and a cast-iron frame (1800). Worked at top speed by strong men these hand presses could produce 250-300 impressions an hour. The application of steam, first by Koenig, and then in an improved fashion by Cowper and Applegarth, made it possible to print double size sheets at the rate of 1,000-1,200 an hour, and later up to 2,500 an hour, ten times the speed of the hand presses.[59] Apart from *The Times,* not even the London dailies had much use for such feats of production, and although more modest steam presses became the rule in the metropolis quite quickly, the provincial papers stuck to their Stanhopes, Columbians and Albions. The *Staffordshire Advertiser* and the *Western Times* acquired steam presses in 1829 and 1835 respectively, but they were probably exceptions.[60] On such presses they could produce their circulations in under two hours, and these were weekly papers. The pull had to come from the other end of the scale.

The main problem with the flat-bed reciprocating steam press was the quantity of energy required to drive it, and the difficulty of controlling the quality of the output. A bed weighing more than half a ton had to be moved 76 inches over 2,500 times an hour, stopped dead and re-accelerated each time. The machinery needed a great deal of maintenance, and the quality of impression left much to be desired. The only way out was the use of rotary motion, but it was not known how to fix movable type on to a cylinder. An answer had, in fact, been provided with the invention of the *papier maché* stereotype, but this was not taken up seriously until a way of locking type on to a cylinder had been developed by the American Richard Hoe. In 1846 he made the first rotary press, and sold it to the Paris paper *La Patrie.* The latter's circulation increased from 3,140 a day in 1846 to 24,500 in 1858.[61] In 1852 Hoe sold a six-cylinder machine to the *New York Tribune,* and in 1856 a similar one to Edward Lloyd, the first rotary press of its type in Britain. *The Times* had been using a faceted vertical cylinder press, but now it also purchased two of the new ten-feeder Hoe machines. Meanwhile the stereotype process had been developed in both France and in Britain, and first Girardin's *La Presse* (1852), and then *The Times* (1858) switched to the use of stereotypes on cylinders.[62] An additional advantage of stereotyping was the ability to cast as many plates as necessary of the same page, enabling production to be multiplied accordingly. This was the key to the development of the giant presses which appeared at the end of the century, and which were really sets of single presses linked together.

Before this sort of press could be used to the best advantage, however, the problem of feeding paper into them had to be solved. The multiplication of feeders at the mid-century was partly the result of having to use separate sheets of paper, in Britain because the Excise Office, before 1855, demanded that sheets be stamped separately and counted for duty. Although this restriction did not exist in America, it was not until 1865 that the first press to use a continuous web of paper was constructed in Philadelphia. In 1868 John Walter III started to use a web machine on *The Times,* thus doubling capacity. Hoe followed in 1874.[63] By the 1870s labour-saving web-fed rotaries had widely replaced sheet-fed machines. Even the provinces followed the fashion, with their small Marinonis, Prestonians and Whitefriarses. By this time a large number of smaller papers had progressed at least to steam-driven flat-bed presses, the Napiers and Middletons in the 1850s, the Wharfedales and Victories later in the 1870s.[64]

The production rate of a Walter web-rotary was 10,000 perfected (i.e. printed on both sides), eight-page papers an hour, compared to a maximum of 14,000 an hour for a Hoe machine. Modifications continued until in 1904 *Lloyds Weekly* was using seven Hoe double-octuplets (i.e. each equivalent to eight double-width web-rotaries), each producing 55,000 thirty-two page papers an hour. Circulations had by this time increased to justify these rates, at least for the mass circulation Sunday papers, but such vast capital expenditure and running costs could only be met by increasing advertising revenue. It was, as will be seen, this growing dependence on advertising that most concerned hostile critics at the turn of the century.

Another publishing problem was the supply of paper. Until the 1850s most paper was made from rags, which explains why newspapers produced before then tend to be more durable than their successors. The perfection of paper-making machines by the French, the improved quality of imported rags, mainly from Germany, and the improved processing of these rags, had resulted in a tremendous growth in paper production in the first half of the century. Economies of scale, competition and the temporary raising of the paper duties led to a concentration of the industry into a few firms, based mainly in the Thames and Medway valleys in the south, and in a few industrial districts in the north. Apart from a period from 1853 to 1860 when rags were in short supply, and much paper was being exported to the United States, there was sufficient competition in the industry to keep prices down. Considering the vigour of the resistance to the repeal of the paper duties, this seems to have had little effect in reducing prices still further, partly because rag duties remained, and partly due to a continued shortage of rags, itself in part a consequence of the cotton famine. These difficulties led to somewhat desperate attempts to find rag-substitutes. At first esparto grass was used, and Edward Lloyd was one of the first newspaper proprietors successfully to expand vertically into paper production, with a factory at Sittingbourne, based on the lease of over 100,000 acres of esparto in Algeria. Another major source of supply was Spain, but it was made unreliable by the political disturbances of the late 1860s.[65] In the 1880s came the use of wood-pulp, which reduced the price of newsprint so considerably that it became an important factor in the profitable management of the large popular papers towards the end of the century.[66]

Composition was another bottle-neck. Methods here had continued unchanged for even longer than the printing presses themselves. John Walter I had tried to speed up matters by a logographic system, whereby words instead of letters were set up, but seeking to impose rigidity upon an essentially flexible system it inevitably failed. A primitive mechanical composing machine had been made by Bessemer in 1842, but it was the Hattersley machine of the 1860s which really achieved the breakthrough, with its system of keyboard operation, and an additional distributing machine for returning the letters to their reservoirs.[67] The introduction of the Hattersleys, however, was determined by the strength of the typographical unions. The compositor was the aristocrat of the printing trades, highly skilled, necessarily literate, and well-paid,[68] but the unions were not uniformly strong, and their weakness in the provinces undoubtedly worked to the advantage of the provincial press. Thus it was in Hull in 1866, on the *Eastern Morning News* that Hattersleys were first used. The non-union shop of *The Times* then adopted them, but they were not accepted elsewhere in London until 1891, at the *Daily News*.[69]

The Hattersleys, however, were not the perfect answer. They suffered from repair and maintenance problems, and although they saved from one- to two-thirds on labour costs, cheap, often female and child labour had to be used for the redistribution of the type. The Cheshire newspaper magnate Alexander Mackie actually set up an all-female composing room at Crewe in 1880, and paid from one- half to one-quarter of the provincial established rates. The American Thorne machines were an improvement, as they had an automatic distributor. They became popular in the 1880s, but were soon overtaken by the American 'Linotype', which did away with the need to redistribute type altogether, by casting fresh type for every composition, and having only, automatically, to distribute keyed matrices. After only a brief struggle the unions accepted the innovation, and this eventually disposed of the problem of cheap labour, at any rate in the larger shops.[70] Once again the provinces were the first to take advantage of the process, at the *Newcastle Chronicle* in 1889, with the *Globe* in 1892 being the first London paper to adopt it.[71]

Generally speaking, newspaper proprietors seemed to have had remarkably few labour problems, although on one or two occasions they had to resort to the importation of Irish and Scottish labour to break strikes. The unions did campaign against the widespread transfer of stereos from 'fair' to 'unfair' shops in the 1880s, which had been used as a way of weakening provincial labour organisation, but this does not seem to have caused serious problems for the proprietors.[72] Working conditions seem if anything to have deteriorated in the large establishments with the introduction of bigger and faster machinery, which resulted in an increase in accident rates towards the end of the century.[73] Printers' early fears that the effect of a mass cheap press would be to cheapen their labour had been met with assurances that rates would be maintained, and that cheapness would create more work.[74] This forecast proved more or less accurate. In 1921 Robert Donald, by then one of most senior figures in the industry, complained that newspaper production was 'under the control of dictatorship of the proletariat with the help of the black-coats (viz. the *NUJ*)'.[75] Even

before 1914 the proprietors had been driven into organising themselves
as employers, rather than, as earlier, as professional men.

The part which technical developments played in the growth of the
press was not confined to the printing and composing rooms, or to the
paper mills. The communications revolution which so deeply affected
nineteenth-century society enabled news to be gathered, processed and
distributed at a pace and on a scale which became almost an obsession
of the Victorians. The question of speed was crucial, for it was the
speed of communication, together with the speed of production, which
made a mass press possible, albeit that before 1914 it had hardly
become a reality. Other aspects of the popular press were important —
style, capital, readership and so forth, but Victorians were quite rightly
most impressed by the sheer pace of it all.

The two crucial factors here were the railway and the telegraph.
They affected different parts of the whole process, but equally
profoundly. The railway did not improve much upon the actual
collection of news. The stage-coach, the dispatch-rider, the pigeon and
semaphore were all quite efficient in their way.[76] Regular trains from
the main centres, however, enabled collection to be cheapened and
regularised. By the 1840s provincial papers were able to have the
London and foreign news, and in a few years they could get in
stereotype anything and everything that would make up a newspaper,
all sent up to them in the same, or even in an earlier train, than that
which brought them the London papers. They were thus able to keep
not too far behind their bigger rivals. The railway, however, did benefit
the larger London dailies which could dispatch quantities of copies over
a large area very quickly. They took advantage of it slowly. The first
special train was run by agreement between *The Times* and George
Hudson on 14 August 1845, when the news of Hudson's election in
Sunderland was sent to *The Times,* processed and returned as
newspapers in nineteen hours.[77] Speeds were improved in subsequent
years. Bristol, Norwich, Birmingham and Southampton were still out
of reach of the London mornings by the start of business hours in
1868, but were arriving well beforehand by 1875.[78] The idea of running
special regular trains for newspapers originated with James Law of the
Scotsman, who used them between Edinburgh and Glasgow in the
1870s. The idea was exploited by W.H. Smith, or rather by his manager
Lethbridge, and in 1875 *The Times* was running specially equipped
trains, with their own sorters and labellers provided by Smith. Smith
had in fact provided ordinary trains at special times since 1847, but
fortunately for the provincial press the London papers made little use

of them whilst they were still served by the free postage guaranteed under the stamp duty. Papers thus distributed usually arrived in the afternoon, after the provincial dailies had been out all morning. Smith's scheme also had the disadvantage that neither he nor the country agents met the costs, which were passed on to the customers.[79]

The net effect, however, of the railways was to favour the metropolitan papers as against the provincials, and this continued to be the case until the electric telegraph became cheap enough to give the provincials the edge in 1870. The inimitable Charles Babbage had suggested in the 1830s that every church steeple be used as a telegraph pole, but the first message to be transmitted by telegraph for a newspaper was in May 1845 for the *Morning Chronicle* along the London and South Western Railway Company's line from Portsmouth to London.[80] Soon the telegraphs were taken over by the telegraph companies, the Electric TC (1846), the British Electric TC (1850), the English and Irish Magnetic TC (1851) and the International TC (1852), an offshoot of the Electric. The Electric and the International merged in 1855, and the British Electric and the English and Irish Magnetic in 1857. In 1859 the London District TC was founded, and in the following year the United Kingdom TC.[81] The first systematic news service dealt mainly with sports and exchange or business news, and was subscribed to by some 163 members, mainly newsrooms, clubs and public houses.[82] The inland service was used chiefly by the provincial papers, while the London dailies successfully exploited the continental and inter-continental links, although at great cost. The effect was perhaps greatest in Scotland, where it was noted in 1868 that the papers were becoming 'more cosmopolitan and imperial in their tone'.[83] By the 1860s, however, the three major companies had combined together to form one Intelligence Unit for the press, a virtual monopoly. This had made the service very expensive, and the provincial papers also found it unreliable. A paper could send its own news over the wires, but it then had to compete with normal commercial business and its delays, or hire private wires at prohibitive expense. Only nine private wires were rented by newspapers, five of them in Scotland. The Irish charges prevented any lines being taken at all.[84] At last, realising that they could not do without telegraphic facilities, the provincial proprietors in conjunction with some local chambers of commerce, who relied on the wires for market reports, were stung into action. In 1865 under the leadership of John Taylor of the *Manchester Guardian,* a group of provincial daily newspaper proprietors met in Manchester to create an agency of their own. They met resistance from the existing companies, however, and nothing effective was achieved. The idea of transferring the whole telegraphic system to government control had been in the air for some time. A Select Committee had warned that this might be necessary as far back as 1840. It was suggested in 1854 to Rowland Hill by the founder of one of the major companies, and again by Edward Baines junior in 1856, by Lord Stanley in 1860, by the chairman of a major company, and by the Edinburgh Chambers of Commerce in 1861. Only in 1868, however, were attempts made to intervene. Neither the newspapers nor the Post Office were thinking in terms of nationalisation at this stage. The campaign was rather for a government company to be formed in competition with the existing companies.[85]

In 1868 a Select Committee was set up, but just before it began its hearings, the provincial proprietors met again, this time in London, and established the Press Association, which was constituted in September 1868 with a capital of £18,000, and a rigorous procedure for ensuring that no proprietor or group of proprietors could get control of it for their own purposes.[86] The fight was a fierce one, with the companies threatening at least two major papers with the withdrawal of services if they continued to support reform.[87] After some deliberation, a change of government, and another Select Committee, it was decided to accept the modified view of the Post Office that a government monopoly was the answer. The press's anxiety over the possible political consequences of this was assuaged by the Post Office's decision to reduce transmission rates considerably. Unfortunately the Post Office had made no provision for dealing with the inevitable increase of traffic consequent upon this decision, and for several months after the take-over in February 1870 chaos reigned on the wires.[88] Soon, however, the change was recognised as an inestimable boon to the provincial, and especially to the cheap provincial, press. The cheap rates were in effect a Post Office subsidy to the newspapers. The large halfpenny evening press, the press of the working man, had only been made possible at all by these rates, it was claimed in 1893, and in 1876 MPs and proprietors protested vigorously when the Post Office discontinued the cheap rates for sports news. 'The press was an important educational machine and engine for the diffusion of knowledge,' claimed D.C. Cameron MP, and proprietor of the *North British Mail* of Glasgow. The burden on the Post Office, however, was considerable, and was made even worse by the proliferation of news agencies after nationalisation. There were some 20 in London alone in 1900, all benefiting from the cheap rates and free copy arrangements.

Even so nothing was done until 1920, and there was still strong opposition from proprietors and MPs worried about the effect on the reporting of their speeches which raising the rates might have.[89] In the 1870s the question of cheap rates had also exposed the deep conflict of interest which existed between the metropolitan and the provincial press, particularly perhaps between *The Times* and the smaller provincial papers. A *Times* staff man told the 1876 Select Committee that the telegraphs had made news 'a slop article'. From *The Times'* point of view the cheap telegraph, and especially the cheap second and further copy arrangements, made it, *The Times,* a prey to the parasitic provincial press, especially in the matter of expensive foreign news. On the other hand, George Harper, editor of the *Huddersfield Daily Chronicle,* urged that the state had a duty to subvene a commercial press as a public service,[90] a duty which, in fact, it continued to perform.

Several points arise from this aspect of the development of the machinery of the press which relate directly to the major themes of this essay. Firstly, the struggle against the telegraph companies was, as the struggle against the taxes on knowledge had been, a struggle in the name of free trade against monopoly, and was doctrinally, therefore, a liberal struggle. Secondly, it was waged in the main by the provincial press, because London was not keen to make easier the exploitation of a medium which would advantage its country rivals.[91] Thirdly, it was undertaken mainly by the more advanced and progressive provincial proprietors, the owners of dailies for which the telegraph was a necessity of life. Fourthly, these leading papers were, as the Provincial Newspaper Society rather bitterly pointed out, predominantly Liberal papers. The domination of the press in the provinces by the Liberals was thus in some sense at least admitted to be a reflection of their greater enterprise. Finally, although this enterprise was pursued in a commercial spirit, the main arguments put forward were necessarily political. There were few who considered it prudent to admit, even to themselves perhaps, that the government should establish a monopoly merely in order to make newspapers more profitable. The intervention of the state in the Victorian economy was invariably justified on grounds of public utility, not of economic opportunity. News was a public service and ought, therefore, to be safeguarded from the predacity of would-be monopolists. Such a situation had not arisen in the case of the railways, largely because they behaved more or less satisfactorily as common carriers, and had not sought to carve out a monopoly for themselves on the supply side of the industry.[92] There were, of course, some doubts about the advisability of thus delivering the press into the hands of the Post Office, but the Post Office had already become an acceptable government monopoly. It had at least overcome what Rowland Hill had referred to in 1851 as the 'great difficulty in controlling the public'.[93] When the possibility of government interference had been mentioned to advocates of the transfer they had dismissed it as an improbable event, and in any case a tolerable one if national security were at stake.[94] As to the danger of political bias, William Saunders, who later set up his own Liberal news agency, claimed before the event that the transfer would probably eliminate bias.[95] He was perhaps not being as disingenuous as this might sound, thinking either that the bias would necessarily be on the right side, and therefore be no real bias at all, or that it would be eliminated by the political competition of numerous agencies.

Looking back from 1887, Victoria's golden jubilee year, a liberal journalist and historian of the press made the following assessment.[96]

> Newspapers were, perhaps, at their highest level of real value, though not of influence or circulation, in 1870 and the few years ensuing. Nearly everything so far as we know, that could be done in the way of mechanical conveniences and freedom from fiscal and legislative restraints had by that time been done. It had come to be possible for a large and well-printed sheet, supplying intelligence from all parts of the world, put together at great cost, and edited with great care, to be sold for a penny, and the number of people able and anxious to read good newspapers had grown with the trade that catered for them. The competition between rival producers was keen enough to force them to use all their wits in seeking and winning public favour, but not yet so keen as to drive them to often unworthy ways of attracting and amusing readers.

In 1870 it had, indeed, been thought that 'improvement' would continue, agitations and nobodies in the past, the machines going on for ever. By 1887 doubts had begun to emerge, and in 1899 the author of the above assessment was writing that the cheap press was 'to some extent nasty by reason of its cheapness'.[97] This is, however, to anticipate. It is first necessary to examine what sort of cheap press the repeal of the taxes on knowledge had brought about.

IV Newsvending

If technical obstacles in the way of rapid and efficient distribution of newspapers were being overcome by the 1870s, the distributive system continued to raise questions concerning the operation of the market, and and the social costs involved. Large wholesalers were not only more efficient, but they could exercise a power which narrowed the choice of their customers. This was most obviously the case with the large circulating libraries, but it was also a problem for the newspaper. The relationship of the wholesaler to the retailer could also threaten this choice, the choice, it must be remembered, which was central to the liberal vision of the press. This was demonstrated when the new halfpenny papers met resistance from newsagents frightened for their profit margins, and had in consequence to set up their own distribution systems. The social costs of a system which worked through street selling, house-to-house deliveries, and large packing and dispatch stations, and which, therefore, relied to a large extent on cheap, casual and child labour, were very considerable. In addition, the relationship of reader to paper was changed by the more centralised, concentrated system of distribution.

The repeal of the stamp and the cessation of the privilege of free postage in 1870 changed the pattern of distribution, and of readership No longer would *The Times* be sent eight or ten times free through the post. With the cheapening of newspapers, the habits of collective purchase, collective reading and hiring out began to fade. An Act of 1789 had made hiring out newspapers illegal, but the practice had continued to be widespread. Newsvendors used to hire London morning papers out at 1*d* an hour, retrieving them in time for dispatch to their country subscribers by the evening mail or train.[98] Public houses, apart from charging to read newspapers inside, also used to hire them out at 1*d* an hour. Occasionally the barmaid would lend them free of charge to dissenting washerwomen and radical tailors, and use them on return to wrap tobacco plugs.[99] A blind man in Drury Lane in the 1840s ran a shop which hired out at 1*d* an hour, or a shilling a week, and used the shop itself as a newsroom.[100] Such practices began to die with the appearance of the cheap newspaper which could be bought outright for 1*d*, although, as we have seen, newsrooms, coffee-houses and pubs continued to be used as social venues.

As circulation increased the wholesale agents prospered, at their head W.H. Smith. Victorian journalists were, it seems, for ever showing their readers the inside of Smith's, 'our modern mercury', a hive of poorly paid industry.[101] Damp, reeking, and until the 1870s unfolded, sheets were bundled, labelled, tied and wrapped, for dispatch in sprung carts for the London railway termini, for suburban agents and the Post Office.

The railways had played a major part in determining the spread of
the newspaper, for the older messengers, newsboys and pedlars had
become few and far between. By the 1870s most rural areas were within
reach of a train, or at least of a milk-cart.[102] Once the paper had arrived
in the town it was often delivered by railway messengers to the houses
of the subscribers, but with the cheap papers it became more usual to
deliver them to certain shops, tobacconists, greengrocers, stationers,
booksellers and barbers, often run by radical self-educated artisans,
thrown out of employment and helped to start up a business by their
friends.[103] Outside London the system was usually on a cash basis, but
in the metropolis it had been traditional for news-sellers, usually the
very young, to build up a prosperous, if insecure, business by dealing on
credit with the wholesaler. The absence of any sale or return
arrangements, which seem to have been accepted partially only after
the Ripper murders, had early led to an open exchange market, in
Catherine Street, off the Strand, and in front of the General Post Office
in St. Martin's-le-Grand.[104] The object of this market was to provide
the newsboys with correctly constituted parcels of papers, which they
bundled up and rushed to catch the 6.00 p.m. post to the country.[105]

Street news-selling was an old tradition. Every public place had its
newsboy, even before 1855, but it expanded enormously after the
appearance of the cheap daily, and especially of the cheap evening
paper. The *Daily Telegraph* was, perhaps, the first to use uniformed
boys, while the *Echo* employed 500 boys wearing 'Echo' caps in 1869.
By 1874 similarly clad sellers were to be found everywhere, even in
Wales.[106] Later Newnes used the Boys Brigade to sell his *Tit-Bits* in
Manchester.[107] An indispensable adjunct to street selling was the
contents bill. In the early part of the century they had relied on very
detailed bills, printed on waste papers, which made them difficult to
read. Such a form of advertisement was found to be very effective
during the Crimean War, and by the third quarter of the century large
papers would have special printing machines for turning out such
posters. Crying newspapers was also extensively used, but in some areas,
like the City of London, this was prohibited. Some control, too, was
exercised over the use of contents bills, one newsboy being gaoled in
1873 for selling *The Globe* with the help of a placard proclaiming
Gladstone's death.[108] Edward Lloyd's gimmick of stamping coins of
the realm with 'Lloyds Weekly News' had been stopped by
Parliament.[109] Lloyd had other ways of advertising his paper, from
conventional wall-posters to the distribution of free copies of the
paper to tollgate keepers who displayed posters for him on their

premises.[110] The 'new journalism' outstripped all this with the use of insurance schemes, competitions and such like, advertised by every device in the advertisers' armoury. Papers still had to be sold, however, papers and money had to change hands, and advances here were less impressive.

Street selling inevitably attracted child labour, and eventually complaints were made about the condition and prospects of this child army of news-sellers, at first by newsagents who considered them unfair competition.[111] There was also some, perhaps more genuine, concern from other quarters. The *Manchester Guardian* arranged some sort of scheme for them which would enable them to earn a living when they grew up, and it was proposed in 1874 that a Newsboys Brigade be set up, with similar intentions.[112] The use of newsboys, on a semi-contractual system, however, went on with little or no change.[113] The editor of the *Yorkshire Post* and then President of the Provincial Newspaper Society, told the Departmental Committee on the Employment of Children in 1901, that street selling was 'necessary both in the interests of the trade and for the convenience of the public'. He claimed that it offered a means of subsistence to the poor, and did not contravene the Cruelty to Children Act.[114] There is no evidence that the industry regarded the use of such a system as at all inappropriate for an institution claiming to be a 'fourth estate'. There was, however, some conflict of status between the street arabs on the one hand and the more respectable news-sellers on the other. The former discredited the trade, it was claimed. Smith's stall managers and other agents were often well-educated and of good 'position'.[115] The wholesalers more or less appropriated the term 'newsvendor', and lent it an air of respectability which it has now lost. The old Newsvendors Benevolent Society and the Friendly Society of Dealers in Newspapers, formed in 1870, served to emphasise this respectability, while politically everything was crowned, of course, by the position of W.H. Smith himself.[116] Beneath them the old structure persisted, and the development of large-circulation 'new journalism' brought problems also to the middlemen, who had first reluctantly accepted the 1*d* paper, and then had held out against the halfpenny, forcing the publishers of the *Echo*, and in the 1880s and 1890s the *Star* and the *Morning Leader*, to establish their own distributing departments. On occasion their obstinacy had political foundations, as when George Cadbury had to arrange at his own expense the distribution of the radical anti-war *Morning Leader* in the north of England during the Boer War. The newsagents, however, had eventually to accept the cheaper papers, as

the most popular of them began to improve their terms, or, as with
Riddell of the *News of the World,* to establish a nation-wide network of
his own newsagencies.[117] This put great pressure upon the smaller
papers who were forced to offer similar terms, or adopt similar tactics,
and thus to endanger the viability of their businesses. There was, of
course, nothing before 1914 like the great circulation wars of the 1930s,
but the growing size of circulations and the development of the
distribution system were already leading in this direction.

V The Birth of the Cheap Press

What were the effects of the repeal of the taxes on knowledge on the
structure of the English press?[118] Without adequate checklists of the
newspapers published, including details of changes of title and price, it
is not possible to say precisely what happened.[119] As it is, there are a
few local studies which provide such details, where early runs of the
paper survive, and there are advertising lists and directories. Of the
latter perhaps the most useful is Mitchell's, but it must be handled
with caution. Alexander Andrews, author of a standard history of the
British press in 1859, and editor of the *Newspaper Press* (1867-72),
pointed out its failure to record ephemeral sheets, and the omission of
others due to oversight or to the ignorance of proprietors of such an
admirable publication as the *Directory*.[120] Mitchell relied on newspapers
informing him of their existence, as he was an advertising agent, not a
public information bureau. He consequently accepted much information
which was almost certainly inaccurate, particularly about the age of the
papers advertised. Nevertheless, he certainly provides us with a very
useful rough guide.

There had been provincial dailies before 1855. The oldest surviving
one in that year seems to have been the *Liverpool Telegraph and
Shipping Gazette,* a 3d information sheet first published in 1826.
Liverpool had also provided the next oldest provincial daily, the
Northern Daily Times (24 Sep. 1853-1862), which had taken advantage
of the repeal of the advertisement duty in August 1853. In October
1854 the Crimean War and the campaign against the stamp combined to
to produce the famous War Telegraphs, most of them weeklies, all
unstamped. Two of these in Manchester, and one in Edinburgh,
however, were dailies, the first penny dailies in Britain. In December
priprietors of the *Manchester Examiner* started the *Manchester Daily
Times,* stamped, and selling at 3d. In 1855 the *Examiner* itself became
a daily paper. Both the Manchester and the Liverpool *Daily Times* had
been Liberal papers, the Manchester one even radical. Two other less

well-authenticated productions appear in Mitchell's to go back to 1854, Stevenson's *Daily Express,* in Nottingham, which seems rather to have begun in July 1855, and the *Sunderland Daily News* published by a John Barnes, which is not recorded by other sources.

Interesting as these productions were, their numbers were few. It was only in anticipation of the repeal of the stamp duty in 1855 that the pace quickened. In April John Watson published a penny Liberal paper, the *Northern Daily Express,* at Darlington. In May C.S. Butcher issued the Liberal *Birmingham Daily Press* at 1½d, and in the same month a ½d daily called *Events* was published in Liverpool, becoming a regular publication in June. In that month many papers decided to anticipate repeal, banking on the probability that at that late stage they were unlikely to be prosecuted.[121] (See Table 1, p.274, for a timetable of this exceptionally busy phase.)

After this spate of publications no more dailies were started in 1855. Of the fourteen listed, six were avowedly Liberal, the others 'neutral'. Seven were completely new, the others new ventures on the part of established papers. Seven of them were sold for 1d, five for ½d. Only five of them failed to survive for five years, and four are still being published. The first crop of cheap dailies was, therefore, a sturdy one. (Table 2, p.275-6, shows the development up to 1870.)

In the first fifteen years of the cheap press in the provinces 78 new dailies were founded, 17 of these evening papers. In 1870, 59 of them survived, thirteen of them evenings, which were already increasing their share of the total dailies published. In so far as papers were being founded and were dying all the time, it is slightly to distort the picture to stop in any one year, but the rate of growth exhibited in this first period went on unchecked into the 1870s, and there is no reason to suppose that that year was in any radical way untypical of the whole period from repeal to the 1880s.

The dailies were, of course, founded for the most part in areas of large population. In 1870 only 8 of the survivors were published in towns of less than 50,000, 11 in towns of between 80,000 and 100,000, and 36 in towns of more than 100,000. Only Portsmouth and Salford of towns of more than 100,000 had no daily paper. (See Table 3 p.277). With the exception of those at Norwich and Brighton all were published to the north and west of a line drawn from Exeter to Hull. Thirteen were in Lancashire, 15 in Yorkshire, and 10 in Northumberland and Durham. The 11 distributed in Exeter, Plymouth, Bristol and Norwich reflected the older eighteenth-century pattern of newspaper distribution, but in general the new cheap press was a phenomenon of new urban industrial England. (See Maps).

The urban bias at this time inevitably tended to strengthen the grip of the Liberals on the provincial press. Their political strength was precisely in these urban and industrial areas, and the Conservatives would have to wait until the 1880s to make a significant mark either politically or journalistically here. Of the 59 survivors in 1870 some 26 were Liberal, and only 9 Conservative. (See Table 4, p.278.) It was, however, at this time the smaller towns which tended to obtain the highest proportion of dailies to inhabitants. Exeter had one daily for every 11,000 people, Plymouth and Darlington one for every 22,000 and 27,000 respectively. Birmingham, however, could provide only one for every 110,000, Liverpool one for every 100,000, and Manchester one for every 90,000. The papers of the smaller towns may have circulated in a large area around the town proper, which may have given an exaggeratedly low paper to population ratio, and the dailies of the larger towns naturally had much larger circulations than those of the smaller.

In London the effect of repeal was less dramatic. Excluding purely commercial sheets, there were before repeal six morning and four evening metropolitan dailies. (See Table 5 p.279.)

The immediate effect of repeal was to reduce the price of all of them by 1*d*. In June, however, a new 2*d* morning paper, the *Daily Telegraph,* was founded. It was rescued from disaster in September and its price reduced to 1*d*, and it became the first successful metropolitan penny daily.[122] In March the *Morning Chronicle* issued an edition called the *Morning News,* which continued until 1860. Then the Peace Society helped launch the famous radical *Morning Star,* in March 1856, at 1*d*. In June 1857 the *Morning Herald* began an evening edition at 2*d*, and the *Standard* became a morning paper, again at 2*d*. In 1860 the *Morning Chronicle* tried to replace its *Morning News* by making its other paper, the *Evening Journal,* into a 2*d* evening paper, but the venture quickly failed, and not for another five years were fresh attempts made to found a new metropolitan daily paper.

In 1865 there appeared the 2*d* Liberal *Pall Mall Gazette* and a form of 'society' paper called the *Glowworm,* also at 2*d*, and claiming to be Liberal. In the May of the following year a local London weekly paper, the *Clerkenwell News,* became the ½*d Daily Chronicle.* In December 1868 the *Echo* was launched, the first metropolitan halfpenny evening paper. By this time prices had been reduced all round, so that the picture in 1870 was substantially different from what it had been in 1855. (See Table 6, p.279.)

Thus, by 1870 the names familiarly associated with the golden age of journalism in the metropolis, as in the provinces, were established, and they remained dominant until the next wave of 'new journalism' came to challenge them in the 1880s and 1890s. These papers, with the exception of *The Times,* were not 'national' newspapers as the term is understood today, although some certainly had quite a large circulation in the major provincial centres, and through private country subscriptions. They circulated for the most part, however, within the confines of London and the Home Counties, and amongst quite a select stratum of London society. The more popular of them had circulations running into the hundreds of thousands, but within the London area they were supplemented by a host of metropolitan weekly parochial newspapers, which are of some interest. The earliest of them had been old suburban or country papers whose constituencies had been swallowed by the spreading metropolis. There were, for example, the *Surrey Standard* (1835-60), and the *Kent Mail* (1839-), the last moving its place of publication in 1860 out to Maidstone, away from the clutches of London. By 1870 there were some 43 of these papers, excluding the numerous local editions which some of them issued. (See Table 7, p.280.) The growth seems to have been almost exclusively a direct result of the repeal of the Stamp Acts. Not one of those surviving in 1870 had been founded before 1855, while almost a third were founded before or during 1860, and the figures take no account of those which had come and gone between 1855 and 1869. As Alexander Andrews had been quick to note in 1859, this new development was very significant, a response to 'the immense and rapid growth of the metropolis', the growth of an important vehicle of opinion in an area of government which was still notorious for its oligarchy and corruption.[123]   It was also, of course, from the ambitious proprietor's point of view, the growth of an expanding and prosperous market.

It was this, the market aspect of London, which made it inevitably the centre of periodical publishing for sectional and special interest groups. The administrative, financial and commercial hub of England was also, thanks to the continuing effects of seventeenth-century legislation, the centre of the printing industry. Here, therefore, were produced hundreds of 'class and trade' papers. There were literary, religious and academic papers, papers for gardeners, for soldiers and sailors, for lawyers, doctors and chemists, for bakers, tailors and pawnbrokers, for speculators and promoters, for women, for musicians and music lovers, for the Volunteers, for architects, for foreigners, for everybody. Papers also of all kinds, from the serious to the comic, from the drab to the illustrated. Together their circulation must have been considerable, and so diverse was their appeal there may have been few multiple readers.

Most of them were weeklies, some were monthlies. By far the most popular newspaper, however, was the weekly which catered for a wide public, and which was sold on Sundays, and perused and pored over for the rest of the week, by tens if not hundreds of thousands of households. Some were expensive, especially the sporting papers like *Bell's Life in London,* which dealt mainly with field sports and athletics, and cost 5*d* a copy. The *Observer* was 3*d*, the *Sunday Times* and the *News of the World,* less radical than they had once been, were still 2*d*, but the biggest sellers were those which sold at 1*d*, *Lloyds Weekly News, Reynolds News,* the *Weekly Dispatch,* and the *Weekly Times,* all radical, or at least Liberal, all catering for sensation, all containing stories and illustrations. They were in terms of readership the most popular papers in the country. It had been, after all, Edward Lloyd, not John Walter, who had first installed the new Hoe printing machine.

The greatest region of growth in terms of the numbers of individual papers, however, was that of the provincial weeklies. A number of them were little more than advertising sheets, some of them actually being given away free, like the *Penryn Commercial Shipping and General Advertiser* (1867), or the *Midland Counties Herald* 1846). Some were mere holiday resort 'visitors lists', issued only 'during the season', like the *Filey Advertiser* (1857), or the *Malvern Advertiser* (1856). Already there had appeared by 1870 local editions of papers which, but for their titles, were virtually identical. Nevertheless, the increase was remarkable, and far outstripped the growth of the metropolitan press, including the parochial weeklies. According to one directory, there were in 1874 410 London papers, 322 of which were 'neutral' or 'independent', indicating that they were mostly the 'class and trade' papers described above. In the English provinces there were 916 papers, of which 67 fell into the latter category. By 1880 the figures for London were 426 'neutral etc.' out of 514, and for the provinces 433 out of 1,055.[124] A growing proportion of non-party-political papers in the provinces is reflected in these figures, but still the most significant aspect of them is the absolute growth in the number of provincial newspapers.

1870 was probably, as contemporaries saw it, the threshold of post-repeal journalism, in terms both of quality and of quantity. The reformers' claims for the abolition of the taxes on knowledge had been fulfilled at least in one direction, namely in the numerical expansion of

the press. In addition there was in the metropolitan dailies especially a
new confidence and liveliness. Education, enfranchisement and
enterprise seemed at this point ready to join together to further the
claims which had been made about the political and social role of the
cheap press, and to justify the boast that it was indeed a 'fourth estate',
and an enlightened and wise one at that. *free from Political Pressure*

4 THE OLD JOURNALISM AND THE NEW

I Provincial and Metropolitan

'There are many persons in the country who are utterly unable to understand a London paper,' Collett had claimed in 1851.[1] If this was true then it was in part the consequence of deficiencies in the education of the country reader, but also, as Collett was suggesting, the London dailies were produced not for the country reader at all, but for the London reading middle classes, and more especially for those with some interest in fields such as politics, the theatre and London 'society'.[2] At the mid-century, *The Times* notwithstanding, the dailies published in London were not national papers. In so far as the 'ruling' or 'governing' classes, Parliament and other institutions of central government were located in the metropolis, national 'interest' was certainly involved, but it was to be long before this 'interest' was developed to an extent which made a national press a normal and accepted British institution. Until the 1870s, as we have seen, this development was held up partly by the inability of the railways to deliver the London papers in time for early morning distribution, but even with the advent of special newspaper trains, and earlier first edition deadlines, a 'national' press had still not fully developed by the turn of the century. By then, however, the trend towards centralisation had become unmistakable, just as had the decline of the provinces.[3]

The domination of *The Times* at the mid-century, however, did produce something of a feeling of provincial inferiority, and precipitated a response designed to restore provincial self-respect. For some of those who promoted the campaign for a cheap press the avowed intention had been to strengthen the provincial press, so as to reflect what was rightly felt to be the real strength of provincial opinion. Not everyone concurred in this objective. A tension had developed between the older provincial proprietors and journalists, who wanted to preserve the position they had built up under the Stamp Acts, and who were most faithfully represented by the Provincial Newspaper Society, and the more adventurous proprietors who, being of a more business-like turn of mind, and generally more sanguine about the prospects which a really cheap press opened up, wanted to develop newer and cheaper papers. The decisive moves were made with the formation of the Press Association, and the government take-over of the telegraphs, making it possible at last for provincial dailies, which were increasingly evening papers, to be masters in their own houses. They could now buy news from the agencies as quickly and as cheaply, indeed often more cheaply, than could the London papers. They could also add the local news which was so essential to their accustomed readers. If the 1870s and the 1880s were a 'golden age', it was so by and large with reference to the status and even influence of the provincial press.

It was in the provinces too that the press was most dominated by the Liberals, so that the success of the Liberal and of the provincial press, at least into the 1880s, were synonymous. But it was not the Liberals alone who lauded the quality of the provincial newspapers. Leading Liberals like Gladstone, Hartington and Morley often extolled the virtues of the provincial press, but Conservative politicians and journalists did so too, with a distinct note of envy in their voices. Joseph Hatton, editor of *The People*, remarked in 1882 that 'it is provincial England, not journalistic London, that makes and unmakes Parliaments.'[4] This had been recognised long back at the outset of one of the most successful ventures in Conservative journalism. The first leader of the *Yorkshire Post*, on 2 July 1866, put the point as follows.[5]

> When we consider that the population of two such counties as Lancashire and Yorkshire, to say nothing of the north of England in general, now draws its political opinions quite as much from the Press of Manchester, Liverpool and Leeds, as from the Press of London, we shall understand at once the whole extent of the power which, for good or evil, may be wielded by provincial journalists. .

A later editor of the paper, Charles Pebody, linked this view to a diagnosis of the sickness of Conservative journalism. The dearth of Conservative journalists, he suggested, both in the provinces and in London, was a result of their having been neglected by their Party, and to the Party's general failure to recognise the importance of the provinces. 'It is because the Provincial Press of this country is *not* a provincial press that it calls for notice at all.'[6] This was only to repeat the obvious at a time when the development of the news agencies, of London offices of provincial papers, and of 'London correspondents', together with the successful struggle for fairer representation in the Press Gallery and the formation of the Lobby, made the news and opinion of the provinces as important as those of London. This was reinforced by the fact that even national politics were still markedly regionalised, and it is significant from the journalistic point of view that the establishment of Manchester and Glasgow offices of London papers did not commence until the 1900s.[7]

In contrast the traditional country weekly paper underwent a partial eclipse after the 1850s. In 1865 James Macdonnell remarked bitterly on the intrigue and corruption which he detected in the local weeklies after the appearance of the provincial dailies.[8] The effect was perhaps less deleterious on the real country papers, which did not have the direct competition of the dailies to contend with. A Conservative journalist writing in 1880 observed that 'the old-fashioned high-priced and somewhat ponderous organ, which is published on market day in the county town, and which serves its subscribers for a week, still lingers on.'[9] He gave the *Hereford Times* as an example, but was of the opinion that this sort of paper 'had lost its power and influence'. Relative to the increasing prestige of the urban dailies this may well have been so, but as the agricultural journalist Richard Jefferies noted of the 1870s, 'the old weekly paper. . .is one of the institutions of agriculture', which during the agricultural distress of this time retained a considerable significance. It represented property, but was still read by tenants and labourers. In fact rural England now had more papers than ever before, even if they could not, and did not try to, compete with expanding daily press of the towns.[10]

The provincial newspaper's prestige was due in part to the quality of its journalism, but there were other factors. The total circulation of the morning and evening provincial press, even though it cannot be precisely measured, was certainly far in excess of that of the metropolitan press, and where they were direct competitors it was the local paper which usually did best. It had the advantage of containing local news, and had often built up a hard core of readership over many years. Larger circulations, which the London dailies were after, depended to some extent on recruiting working-class readers, who were apt to stick to their weeklies, or the cheaper local evening paper. The provincial papers also used much London press copy, sometimes unpaid for and unacknowledged. If it is a matter of assessing the 'influence' of the London press some account of this multiplier has to be taken, but it was the physical presence of the provincial sheet which mattered in terms of economic power and prestige, and which gave the edge to the local paper.[11] There were also some cases, it seems, in which local papers had a thinly spread national circulation.[12]

Thus to put the provinces at the centre of the stage does not mean that the London press was completely overshadowed. The daily and evening London press was the press of a minority, but it was an important minority, including a large proportion of the decision-makers. Individually the major metropolitan dailies had larger circulations by far than any provincial rival, and their more adventurous policies, their more lavish expenditure in the obtaining and making of news, gave them the pride of place in the advance of journalism. Without them the provincial papers would have been greatly impoverished.

II The Business of Newspapers

There was, as we have noted, an underlying ambivalence in the Victorian attitude towards the newspaper press, an ambivalence which increasing commercialisation and the emergence of a new sort of politics towards the end of the century, made more difficult either to conceal or to resolve. It is often dismissed with the comment that there are two sides to the newspaper industry, that the newspaper is 'simultaneously a commercial enterprise and a vehicle of opinion'.[13] Yet there might obviously be a conflict between these roles, and it was this possibility which was central to the problem of the place, function and meaning of the press in Victorian society. The political and social involvement of the newspaper, its owners and creators, was a highly complex phenomenon. Ambivalence existed not only between the business and political roles of the newspaper, but between business and politics in general. Yet in the commercial ambience of Victorian England, imbued with what has been termed 'the entrepreneurial ideal', there was little overt conflict between the conduct of a business and what has been referred to in the case of popular liberalism as 'sound government. . .improved by the new rhetoric of benevolence'.[14] In the case of the newspaper, on the other hand, such conflict was nearer the surface, for there was an often explicit presumption that its political and social role, the fulfilling of the liberal vision, should take precedence over other considerations, come what may.

This ambivalence was clearly demonstrated during the hearings of the Select Committee on the Law of Libel in 1879. John Hutchinson, MP for Halifax, a leading member of the Provincial Newspaper Society, and promoter of a Bill to amend the law of libel in favour of the press, expressed the opinion that 'by virtue of his general education, and the position that he occupies amongst those with whom he lives and the conscious sense of responsibility of the damage that may be done to his property, (the newspaper proprietor) is likely to guard against any unwarrantable interference with the reputation of other people.'[15] He put this point to A.K. Rollit, a Hull solicitor with local newspaper interests, who dealt with a great deal of press work in his business, and was representing the Provincial Newspaper Society before the Committee. Rollit, naturally, did not dissent from Hutchinson's proposition, but it is significant that he chose to support it rather by reference to economic interest than to status. [16]

> I should say that the capital invested in a first-class newspaper is a very ample protection on these points. No doubt (newspaper enterprise) has its commercial element, but on the other hand the advantages to the public of the existence of the press and of its presence at these (public) meetings are so unquestionable that we may say, I think, that the newspapers are a public convenience, and that the public derive benefit from them.

Pressed as to whether he was saying that proprietors invested their money for the public good, he admitted that that was not his meaning. 'I am afraid one does not invest one's energies, or one's capital in any line of life, simply for the public good.'[17] This was taken as Rollit intended, not as an expression of outrageous self-interest, but as a statement of the obvious. It was in the old Smithian tradition of the heterogeneity of ends, whereby men were held to accomplish the ends of society as a whole by each pursuing their own individual ends. It is perhaps not too much to say that without this underlying faith the symbiosis of business and philanthropy, in the nineteenth century, including public works and public service, cannot properly be understood. There was no simple distinction made between business and other interests. What there was, however, was an economic logic which required the less fortunate to choose between business and other interests, even if they had rather not done so. No money, no paper; no paper, no public, political or social service. There was no corresponding logic of public service which forced men to lose money without end to fulfil it. Even for the Quaker businessmen, who might seem exceptions to the rule, there came a point at which economic pressures prevailed. As the old Devonshire proprietor-journalist Isaac Latimer told the Select Committee, many proprietors such as himself ran their papers for 'political education', and would support them even at a loss. In fact most of them would not, could not support them regardless of the extent of the losses involved, and as the industry grew these became potentially much greater.

The structure of newspaper enterprise was dictated by the economic, political and legal framework within which it worked. With the repeal of the taxes on knowledge, the increasing prosperity of the 1850s and 1860s, the slackening of political control, and the pressure for political reform which found in the press a valuable weapon, the newspaper became an increasingly attractive field for investment. Technical advances, improved communications, the process of urbanisation, with its concomitant market opportunities, went even further to make the newspaper a profitable venture. All this, however, meant that the scale of the industry grew rapidly, and with increased scale came greater specialisation of employment, with distinctions more frequently made between proprietor, manager, and editor, although old labels were often retained. Joint-stock companies emerged which accelerated this process, and with all this went an improvement in status of those engaged in the press, not, it is true, equally across the board, but large proprietors and leading professional journalists were gradually accorded a social recognition previously denied them. Improvement in status, however, tended to heighten the ambivalence between business and political motivation. There were many directly commercial papers at the mid-century, from the sensational popular weeklies to the small advertising sheets and visitors' lists, and for these the claim of the Conservative MP Henry Drummond in 1855, that 'the press was a mercantile speculation, nothing else', was accurate.[18] At the other extreme, though, were the politically motivated papers like the *Morning Star,* financed by the Peace Society and Manchester School men, which made huge losses, and the *Beehive,* George Potter's trade unionist organ which, with some subsidisation, managed to keep its head above water even in the difficult 1860s.[19] By the 1870s and 1880s the commercial motives seemed to have become more important and widespread. The *Sheffield Daily Telegraph* had been started in 1855 by a group of 'capitalists in London and Manchester', who had soon lost interest in it and had left the printer to carry on as best he could. One of its staff later remarked, in 1876, that in contrast, 'capitalists nowadays are ever on the alert for new speculations, and in most cases anxious to be identified with them.'[20] In 1887 Fox Bourne was writing that 'it may be thought indeed, that in some newspaper enterprise of the present day there is too much, rather than too little of the prosaic commercial spirit. The community suffers, though the individuals connected with it may gain, when a paper is 'worked' for money-making purposes alone, like a shop or a factory or a patent medicine.' He was still optimistic enough to add, however, that 'this need not and does not very often happen.'[21]

Yet it is significant that from the owner's point of view it was complained in 1891 that 'the newspaper proprietor. . .may at any moment find his business marred by wealthy amateurs, who will start and maintain a paper from no business motive whatever, but simply and solely to advertise themselves or support their party.'[22] The worry was that ordinary enterprises, dependent on the market, could not compete with such political ventures, but as will be seen later, there was a great deal of opposition from inside the parties concerned to discourage such projects, and a growing realisation that what was needed was rather a viable business proposition which could then be made amenable to political interests, without destroying its commercial value. Before this issue can be discussed, however, it will be necessary to to examine first the organisation of the industry, second the proprietors themselves and their place in Victorian society, and third, their attitudes towards newspaper politics.

Organisation

It has already been noted that the nineteenth-century newspaper industry was built upon the basis of the family business, and family firms long continued to be a favoured form of organisation, although towards the end of the century it became usual to adopt at least the form of a joint-stock company. These companies had begun to emerge in the 1840s. By the 1850s 'chains' of newspapers were to be found, and by the 1880s 'syndicates' and corporations. At the turn of the century the foundations of 'the amalgamated press' had been laid.

After the family firm, the partnership was perhaps the commonest and earliest form of newspaper business. The French form of limited partnership was rare, however, in the newspaper industry as in other areas of British enterprise.[23] The ordinary partnership provided a means of raising capital, and was often dissolved within a short time in favour of one of the partners. Sometimes, as with the *Manchester Guardian* or the *Leeds Mercury*, the initial support was on less formal lines, merely the arrangement of a loan, but profitability and longevity could result in the establishment of a formal partnership, sometimes, as in the best self-help stories, cemented by marriage ties. Capital was also raised by informal groups of local men, like the 'company of Liberal Gentlemen' who started the *Kent Herald*, or the 'country gentlemen' who founded the *Chester Courant*. Between 1846 and 1873 there were 67 cases of 'Residents', 'a Residential Proprietary', or a 'Company of Residents' responsible for publishing papers recorded in Mitchell's *Directory*, including almost all the Birmingham newspapers in the 1850s. The

majority of these passed quickly into the hands of their printers or
publishers, and the motives for their enterprises remain obscure. Almost
certainly many of them were attempts to influence local politics at
municipal level. This was certainly the case with local papers which
have been studied in Leicester, Nottingham, Bradford and Rochdale,
although these were not termed 'residents' papers.[24]

Such groups became rarer with the growing respectability and
security of the joint-stock company. Some eighteenth-century papers
had been organised as joint-stock companies, the *Public Ledger,* for
example, in which Woodfull had published the Letters of Junius, and
in the early nineteenth century, before the 1845 Companies Act, there
were newspaper companies registered, two in London, two in Yorkshire,
and one in Coventry. Two more were proposed in 1846, but were never
fully registered. The real expansion came only after the 1856 and 1862
Companies Acts.[25] As it became accepted as normal business practice,
and as businessmen became more adept in its use, even the attractions
of complete family control were outweighed by the increased potential
for expansion and the greater security offered by limited liability.[26]
The much bruited danger of 'straw men', the bogey of the 1830s and
1840s, proved relatively slight. The real danger to the older type of
paper lay in the ability of companies to increase the scale of their
operations.

The extent and scale of joint-stock enterprise in the press may be
appreciated by examining the thirty years following the 1856
Companies Act, during which the effect of the repeal of the taxes on
knowledge was most immediately felt, and the Liberal predominance in
the press was first consolidated and then undermined.

A total of some 420 newspaper companies was formed between
1856 and 1885, 75 in the first decade, 125 in the second, and 225 in
the third, about an 80 per cent increase from decade to decade.[27]
Between 1856 and 1863 the average annual rate of formation was
between 5 and 6. The pace then quickened with 50 in the next four
years. Then the depression of the late 1860s meant that only 10 new
companies were founded from 1868 to 1869. From 1870 to 1880,
however, the average annual rate was almost 16, including in this
period the lean years of 1871 and 1878. Between 1881 and 1885 the
average rose to nearly 29 a year. The formation of a company, of
course, was no guarantee of its success. The 'infant mortality' of new
enterprises diminished considerably from 20 per cent in the first decade,
to 7 per cent and 6 per cent respectively in the following two decades.[28]
Of the 74 companies formed in the first decade after 1856 29 were

abortive or lasted for less than a year, a slightly lower proportion than for all companies.[29] The weeding out, as with other companies, came early, but once established, a newspaper property was a sound investment; more than a quarter of those founded between 1856 and 1865, which lasted longer than one year, survived for more than eleven years. (See Table 13.)

The size of most of these companies, according to their nominal capitals, was only moderate, most of them falling into the bracket between £1,000 and £10,000, but with a significant proportion falling into a higher, £10,000 to £100,000 bracket in the 1870s and 1880s, and a growing number of over £100,000, including five companies of £200,000 and over. (See Table 8.) The early rash of companies with very large nominal capitals was a reflection of the unhealthy tendency of companies to register with such inflated nominal capitals that their liability was virtually unlimited.[30] Such was the case of the National Newspaper League Company of 1856, which had a registered nominal capital of £250,000 . It was dissolved in 1868 having called on not more than £40,000 of this.[31] Once again the information on called capital in the returns is inadequate, but it does serve at this stage to give an indication of the general trend. (See Table 9.) It was most usual to call from £1,000 to £10,000, but the second most common category was that of companies calling less than £500. The discrepancy between the nominal and called capitals was partly a reflection of the youth of the companies. It was customary, and certainly prudent, to establish a nominal capital which would carry through the business for at least a year or two, in the hope that it would not all be needed. It was also partly the result of excessive caution, and partly of a misunderstanding of the principles of limited liability. In fact, no company before 1885 called upon more than £62,000, and that was in 1883. The Evening Post Company of 1887 was the first newspaper company to have called more than £100,000 from its shareholders in the first year of its existence.[32]

The returns also demonstrate a gradual loosening of the structure of ownership, shown by the rise in the average number of shareholders in each company. One or two companies boasted several hundred shareholders, including the Labour Trades Newspaper Company of 1861, and the News Newspaper Company of 1859. (See Table 10.) Most companies with more than ten shareholders had less than fifty, and in the middle of the 'golden age' there were three times as many companies with less than ten as with more. As the size of companies increased this disparity was reduced, but there is reason to believe that inside large communities of shareholders the distribution of shares was very unequal.[33] The size of share, an important variable of the number of shareholders, and of their voting power, conformed quite closely to the normal pattern of joint-stock enterprise of the time, with the vast majority between £1 and £10. In the 1880s, when *The Economist* remarked that 'one pound shares. . .have recently become very popular', about half of the newspaper companies had shares of £1 or less.[34]

Smaller shares were more attractive, but this was not a prime consideration of most newspaper companies. Their shares were not usually put on the open market. To have done so would greatly have increased the anxiety of proprietors, and probably also the ambivalence between the commercial and social-political roles of the newspaper. A rare example of public quotation occurred in the case of the National Newspaper League Company, originally founded in a religious interest as an unlimited company. It was launched in 1856 with a nominal capital of £250,000, and was probably responsible for the publication of the *Dial* newspaper. In 1867 its £10 shares, on which £2 had been called, were being offered for sale at 3s 0d each. The company was wound up in the following year.[35] It was only really with Harmsworth's Answers Ltd in 1893, and his Associated Newspapers Ltd in 1905 that the public at large was effectively given an opportunity to invest in the newspaper business, and very profitably too.[36]

A related fact was that most of the companies registered before 1882, after which the relevant details ceased to be provided in the returns, were reorganisations of existing businesses. It seems, therefore, that most of these companies were in effect private rather than public companies, although no such legal distinction was made until 1907. The speculation which they represented was almost entirely the affair of those already committed to newspaper enterprise. Until the rapid expansion of the 1890s the newspaper company continued to represent a form of compromise with fully-fledged commercialism, despite the fact that its structure conformed quite closely to the average middle and late Victorian light industry.

The companies, of course, were only a small proportion of the total newspaper firms in the country, even at the end of the century. They tended to be more geographically centralised than newspaper businesses as a whole, however, with about a third of them in London. (See Table 11.) This was due mainly to the fact that London was the economic, financial, administrative and political centre of the country, as well as the largest conurbation. As these companies came more and more to dominate the industry in the twentieth century, this meant that the process of centralisation, and the desertion of the provinces as regional centres, was hastened.

It is obviously difficult, if not impossible, to calculate the value of all newspaper enterprise at any one time. Even if the company returns were full and accurate there would still be a large sector of the industry unaccounted for, and there is some reason to believe that much of this was seriously undervalued. Thomas Shields' *Bradford Daily Telegraph,* for example, started in 1868, was incorporated thirty years later with a capital of £37,000, including an estimate of £30,000 goodwill. Even if this latter figure represented some window-dressing it was by any standards a valuable company at that time, a fact which until its incorporation may have been less than obvious, even to its proprietors.[37] Some idea of the growing scale of the industry, however, can be obtained from the parliamentary returns. (See Table 12.) The drop in nominal capital during the first decade indicates a hesitant start, dramatically rectified in following years. Even if part of the growth in called capital represents rather an improvement in the collection of returns, these figures, taken with the fact of an increasing survival rate, point to a considerable accumulation of capital in the industry even by the mid-1880s. By 1907 the First Census of Production estimated that newspapers represented something like £2,000,000 a year in capital and running costs.[38]

How expensive was it, after repeal, to establish and to operate a newspaper? We have seen that by the mid-century £10,000 to £20,000 was thought necessary for a London daily. By the 1870s estimates had risen to £100,000.[39] This may have contained an allowance for continuing the paper sufficiently long to build up a clientele and an advertising connection. When Edward Lloyd bought the *Clerkenwell News* in 1876 for £30,000, he spent £150,000 more on establishing it.[40] No company, however, was subscribed to this amount in the 1870s, and only two in the 1880s. In 1887 the London *Star* was registered with £100,000 nominal capital, just over £6,000 of which was called immediately, but another source puts the actually subscribed capital at £40,000, and it is certain that it ran only with the substantial financial assistance of Sir John Brunner.[41] When the Harmsworths bought the *Evening News* in 1893 they got it for the bargain price of £25,000. It had cost Coleridge Kennard, its Conservative banking proprietor, more than £100,000 by this time.[42] It was, of course, always more expensive to finance a continuing loss, than to set up a profitable enterprise, while prices and expenditure were also determined more by the proprietor's willingness to lose than on the inherent potential of the newspaper. Albert 'Baron' Grant lost a fortune on the

Echo in 1875-6, but the paper struggled on under the much more careful philanthropy of Passmore Edwards and others until 1905.[43]

There are few figures available for the post-1855 provincial press. By 1881 Robert Spence Watson, the Liberal political manager of Newcastle, reckoned £30,000 necessary to establish a new north-eastern daily.[44] Again for the 1880s there is a useful estimate by Arnot Reid for the costs of a provincial daily. He allowed £1,000 for the rent of two telegraph wires, another £1,000 for parliamentary telegraphic news, £4,000 on local news coverage, and £1,000 on a London Letter, making a total of £5,000 a year on editorial running costs alone, excluding the editor's salary, other wages, and other paper, printing and management costs. All in all, he thought a provincial daily ought to reckon on £20,000 more a year to run than a similar-sized London daily, but this seems a dubious deduction, and is not supported by other sources.[45]

Any estimate of the size and extent of newspaper enterprise must also take into account the often intimate relationship which existed between such businesses and printing and publishing firms. At least some of the printing and management costs would have been reduced where such connections existed. Attempts were also made to integrate distribution into the newspaper industry. In the cases of the *Echo,* the *Star* and the *Morning Leader,* and later of the *Tribune,* this was a consequence of the usual distributors considering the profit margins on the handling of cheap papers too slight to be worth their while. Such integration, however, probably increased rather than reduced both capital and running costs.

The actual management of a newspaper was a complex and risky process. Newspaper proprietors had customarily been recruited from the ranks of printers and publishers, and the tradition of proprietor-editor was deeply rooted and   long-lived. It was surely a major factor in the success of the family business, where experience both of the regular work of journalism and of the business management of a firm were found in the one man. Practice has always tended to vary with the size and frequency of publication of the paper, and with its location. There was the expected concentration of expertise in London, but there had early been established the two-way flow of professional journalists between the provinces and London and back again, so that practice was communicated fairly freely over the whole country. Inevitably the smaller and more remote country papers, often run by inexperienced amateurs, remained wedded to more primitive techniques, even hand-presses in some cases up to the turn of the century. Yet the

large provincial daily or weekly was as well, if not better managed than
its London counterpart. This is, however, not to say much, for standards
of management were universally poor. The few pictures that we have of
the day-to-day running of these businesses indicate that even in the case
of the largest concerns management was, if it existed at all, very basic.
Northcliffe was amazed and concerned at the state of *The Times'* books
when he took it over in 1908, and although the paper had seen better
days, it was probably typical of most newspapers in this respect in the
nineteenth century. This failure was in part a reflection of poor
management in industry as a whole, particularly at the mid-century
when business practice and ethics were still very unsettled. Even the
Press Association had the embarrassing and disquieting experience of
having its first manager embezzle most of its funds in 1870.[46] The
Manchester City News suffered more than once from the improbity
both of its managing editors and of its office boys. One writer on
newspaper management in 1891 was appalled at the slipshod way in
which the books, if there were any, were kept by most firms. He
endeavoured to persuade them to adopt double-entry accounting,
instead of what seemed to be the general practice of recording orders
and payments for advertisements only on the office copy of the
paper![47] Henry Wilson had received very sound advice in 1874 when
he commissioned a survey to discover the prospects for a new radical
paper in Sheffield. He was told that it was essential to have a first-class
book-keeping system, with double entry, and a comparatively
continuous audit by a first-class accountant.[48] Part of the trouble was
the habitual secrecy surrounding newspaper enterprise, borne of a fear
that disclosure would harm the property journalistically and
commercially.[49] Even the obligation to provide the Registrar of
Companies and the Inland Revenue with annual returns did not have
much effect in improving this state of affairs.

A newspaper's income consists of sales and advertising revenue, and
even before the repeal of the advertisement tax the latter had played a
very large part in the financing of any paper. Some newspapers, as we
have seen, were distributed free, relying wholly on advertisements as a
source of income. It was often a good way of getting a paper started, as
William Mitchell discovered in 1853 when he began the *West Sussex
Gazette* as a free paper, and built up a circulation of 3,000 to 4,000 a
week.[50] Co-operation between advertisers and proprietors had been
very close since at least the 1820s. Most advertisements were placed by
individuals, but increasingly agents came to play a vital part in the
process. From the papers' point of view it was a way of securing their

income. Advertisers commonly remained long in default, even bodies
like railway companies and local corporations.[51] For larger papers such
delays were normally tolerable. Their orders were usually placed for
long periods, and diminished seriously only in times of trade depression,
or a long-term decline in the position of the paper, or more rarely
because of a change in the politics of the paper. For the smaller
journals, however, short-term fluctuations could be fatal, and much
effort was spent on the use of canvassers and collectors in an attempt
to keep heads above water. This was where the agencies proved their
worth, by absorbing many of these temporary shocks. From the point
of view of the advertiser they also provided access to papers, especially
in the provinces, which their clients would never have known about,
hence the importance of the self-descriptions of the papers to be found
in the advertising agencies' lists and directories. It was an easy matter
to advertise, say in all the Conservative county papers in north-west
Lancashire, without having to know what these papers were. And, for
the papers, this was a way of advertising their presence to potential
clients and readers. It is hardly surprising, therefore, that the original
instigators of the Provincial Newspaper Society were advertising
agents.[52]

   Advertising, however, was a difficult aspect of newspaper
management, particularly for the new penny dailies at the outset of
their careers. 'In the provinces. . .the habit of daily advertising has not
yet been acquired,' lamented the *Birmingham Daily Post* in 1855. By
1859, however, it was managing to fill its front page with advertisements
every day.[53] Another complaint was that advertisers persisted in looking
at the cost of advertisements rather than at the circulation which they
were buying, a habit which, it was claimed, lured proprietors into
accepting very low rates, and into submitting to blackmail by those who
who, as a means of ensuring publicity, threatened to exclude reporters
from their meetings if free coverage were not afforded them.[54] It is
doubtful, however, whether such problems were encountered by larger
papers, and even the smaller ones could be obstinate. At the beginning
of the twentieth century the *Huddersfield Weekly News* was still
refusing to report meetings which had not previously been advertised,
at the normal rates, in its columns.[55]

   The prosperity of a paper could increasingly be gauged by the
quantity of advertising in its pages, and *The Times* supplement, of
course, had played a large part in making it such a prosperous paper in
the first half of the century. A count made on 21 March 1866 showed
2,140 advertisements in the *Clerkenwell News* (soon to be the *Daily*

Chronicle), 1,865 in *The Times,* 560 in the *Standard,* and 416 in the *Morning Star.* Much of the advertising of the first two was 'classified', but the discrepancy between the prosperous and the not so prosperous was nonetheless very clear.[56] A similar result was obtained twenty years later, when it was shown that 60.6 per cent of the columnage of the *Daily Telegraph,* 51 per cent of that of the *Standard,* 49 per cent of that that of *The Times,* 40.5 per cent of that of the *Scotsman,* and 26.5 per cent of that of the *Scottish News* was devoted to advertising.[57] It is difficult to make generalisations, but on the smaller provincial paper of the 1860s and 1870s the proportion of total revenue made up by advertising was between one-half and three-fifths. On the *South Wiltshire Express,* for example, in 1873, £1,040 of the annual income of £2,730 came from this source.[58] When the proportion fell below half it is probable that most papers would have been in trouble.

Despite this fact, English newspapers were not quick to exploit advertising after the 1850s. Before the repeal of the tax, advertisers had tended to resort to other types of display, and between 1830 and 1850 there was a plague of sandwich-board men, handbills, stencilled pavements, painted and postered walls, and placarded carriages. This gave rise to a vigorous campaign against the defacement of the environment, and the business came to be concentrated more in the hands of respectable and known agents. The newspapers benefited from all this, partly through the acquisition by the public of the habit of advertising, and of reading advertisements, and partly by the incentive the restrictions gave to newspaper advertising. Their response, however, was poor. The conservative, and cheap, column by column advertisement gave way only slowly, in the 1860s, to the use of blocks of type, woodcuts, reiteration, and patterning. The *Courier* had used display advertisements in the 1840s, and others had appeared sporadically, but English newspapers lagged considerably behind the Americans until at least the 1880s.[59] The most important innovation was the 'classified' advertisement, and the 'box number', the latter invented by J.M. Levy, proprietor of the *Daily Telegraph*, and the former used first and most fully by the same paper. Later the *Daily Chronicle* picked up the device, aiming at slightly lower social strata, so successfully, it was claimed, that it had diminished the number of agencies specialising in finding places for domestic servants.[60] *The Times* had always catered for the market for 'personal' advertisements, but these, especially those concerning matrimony and other sexual relations, spilled over into the other dailies, and as with employment, they began to take the place of the specialist agencies which had been founded in the early Victorian period.[61] It was not entirely due to a lack of initiative, however, that advertising policies remained relatively conservative. There were certain restrictions imposed by the limitation of printing machinery, and this helped produce a situation where demand was greater than supply, and there was, therefore, no great pressure upon papers to obtain more advertising. Advertising rates also bore no very clear relation to circulation.[62] The *Glasgow Herald* priced advertisements 'according to whether and how far they represented realised wealth, or were published with the object of making a living.'[63] By the beginning of the century the process had become, under the influence of Harmsworth, more rational, which made the position of the less popular papers more precarious than ever before.

On the costs side, printing and paper were the major items, accounting from 40 per cent to as much as 60 per cent of total costs. The weekly cost of producing the *Daily News* in the 1840s, for example, had averaged some £520, £200 for editorial and reporters' wages, £100 for correspondents, and £200 for printing and publishing, including, it must be supposed, paper costs.[64] On top of this there were the advertisement, paper and newspaper taxes. When these were removed the position became much healthier. The larger papers could exploit the economies of scale by obtaining discounts on purchases of paper, for example, but the smaller ones tended to rely on wage restraint as a control, a policy which in the end led to the formation of the National Union of Journalists in 1907. Only on the larger papers, where wages formed a much smaller proportion of outlay, were journalists' rewards substantially increased, and then only in the 1890s below the editorial level.

Generalisations, as has been stressed, are difficult to arrive at. Some of the problems involved, however, in calculating the cost to a proprietor of setting up and running a paper can be seen in the attempts of the Sheffield Radical MP, H.J. Wilson, to start a radical rival to the *Sheffield Independent*. His first enquiry in July 1872 had elicited the information that it would cost £1,530 to buy machinery, partly second-hand, capable of printing a four-page paper the size of the *Sheffield Independent*, including eight-page papers on two days of the week.[65] Two years later he was told by another informant that with the ending of the virtual monopoly of type-founding, and with the prices of paper and composing materials falling, the cost of establishing a ½d daily over four years would be £1,000 for machinery, £250 for materials and paper, and £250 to £300 for publicity.[66] Taking the new *Northern Echo* as a model (although this was a ½d morning paper), it was claimed that the weekly cost of production would be about £84 17s 0d, half of which was for paper and printing. With advertisement revenue of £48 and a net sales revenue of £17 7s 2d, a loss of £19 9s 10d a week would result in the first year. Losses would continue for the next three years, to a total of some £4,000, by which time the paper would begin making a profit each year. It is perhaps not surprising that Wilson decided not to proceed with the project on these somewhat speculative terms, especially as he was himself rather a cautious businessman. The next year, 1875, he solicited an estimate for a four-page evening paper at ½d, and received an optimistic reply from a local printer, suggesting £26 16s 0d a week for a circulation of 2,000, and a total weekly revenue of £30, which would have required an advertisement income of something like £26.[67] These figures are not conclusive, of course, but they do indicate the range of costs and revenue which a new provincial daily proprietor might have to cope with. If he were successful, however, he would find himself involved in a much larger enterprise altogether. Alfred Stephenson, for example, proprietor of the *Southport Visiter,* spent £44,000 on new machinery in the 1870s.[68]

For the successful, indeed, there were rich rewards. It had been estimated in 1836 that a country paper with a circulation of between 1,000 and 2,000, with 80 to 100 advertisements each week, should make between £800 and £1,200 profit a year.[69] This does not seem an exaggerated estimate when one considers that the much larger *Manchester Guardian* made an average annual profit between 1839 and 1844 of £6,777. In 1855 it made £12,000 profit, and between 1862 and 1865 £20,000 a year, a level which with temporary lapses it maintained until the end of the century.[70] Over some thirty to forty years the *North Eastern Daily Gazette* was said to have made Hugh Gilzean-Reid £250,000.[71] Before it took over the *Liverpool Daily Mercury* in 1905, the *Liverpool Daily Post* was making annual profits in excess of £43,000.[72]

The London papers were even more lucrative. T.H.S. Escott, an informed observer, reckoned that in the 1870s a London daily should expect to make a profit of £55,000 to £60,000 a year, on an expenditure of between £260,000 and £270,000.[73] Hatton reckoned that in 1882 the *Daily News* was making £30,000 a year, the *Standard* £60,000, and the *Daily Telegraph* £120,000.[74] The *Daily News,* before the lean times following the Home Rule split, was giving dividends of 133 per cent.[75] The proprietors of the *Daily Telegraph* and *Lloyds Weekly News* each left an estate in excess of half a million pounds.[76]

There were, however, no licences to print money, no guarantees of profit-rich seams. It was calculated, one does not know how accurately, that between 1860 and 1863 £250,000 was lost in newspaper bankruptcies.[77] As trade worsened in the late 1860s, and confidence waned after 1867, the amount must have increased. The *Newspaper Press* recorded 20 bankruptcies associated with newspapers in 1867, 28 in 1868, 24 in 1869, and 15 in 1870. Things improved after this, with only one case in each of the next two years. The majority of these bankruptcies were small-scale affairs, journalists, reporters and newsagents, but 15 proprietors went down in the five years from 1867 to 1871, and in addition 22 partnerships were dissolved.[78] Individual papers could lose fortunes. The *Morning Star* had run through at least £80,000 in its fifteen years, and the short-lived *Day* £12,000 in 1867.[79] In the early 1880s the London *Evening News* was losing £40,000 a year year.[80] Party papers, as their critics were always asserting, seemed especially bad risks. The Conservative papers the *North Times* and *Latest News* lost £16,000 between them in six months in 1882. The *Southport Daily News* was said to have lost £75,000 over the years, the *Yorkshire Gazette* £26,500 in ten months in 1884, and the *Blackburn Daily Star* £30,000 in 1904 to 1905, and all were Conservative papers, backed for political reasons.[81] On the other side the Radical MP Peter Taylor sank £10,000 into the London *Examiner* without success in the 1870s, and the radical *Birmingham Morning News* lost its proprietor some £30,000 at about the same period.[82]

Such risks as these losses point to, however, did not seriously deter new capital investment, with the possible exception of the late 1860s. The political, economic and social attractions were too great, while the risks themselves were not substantially greater, in the long term, than in other Victorian growth industries.

One of the marks of such an industry was the ability of individual concerns to expand, to absorb competitors. Newspaper entrepreneurs began surprisingly early to exploit the idea of diversification under centralised control. This took two major forms, the partly printed sheet, and the local edition. The former was a technique developed to overcome difficulties of communication in the provinces before the coming of the telegraph. Instead of awaiting the mail-coach, or even meeting it half-way, or later relying on the train for raw news, papers could contract with some London firms to be supplied with from two to four sheets already set up in type. A barrister named Douglas Straight seems to have originated the idea in 1850, and it was then taken further by William Eglington, but Charles Knight was the first to use it on a large scale with his *Town and Country Newspaper,* which local

proprietors could simply attach to their own papers.[83] It was begun
with the repeal of the stamp duty, and although it lasted only a couple
of years or so, it was widely imitated by others, including Cassells the
publishers, and once stereotyping had properly been developed, the
partly printed sheet played a major part in provincial journalism. By
1870 leaders, London Letters, reviews and general news could all be
purchased on what the *Globe* disapprovingly termed the 'communistic
principle'.[84] In the 1880s a political version was developed by the
Conservative agency, the Central Press, entitled the *Editor's Handysheet*,
a practice which continued on into the twentieth century.[85]

The larger provincial dailies disdained the use of such a device, but
they had created in the Press Association a bigger and a more respectable
respectable form of it. News agencies had begun in the 1860s with the
purpose of exploiting the telegraphs. The first large agency was the
Central Press, founded in 1863 by William Saunders and Edward
Spender, but the most famous was the Press Association, a response of
the provincial daily proprietors to the discovery that the telegraph
companies were exploiting the press. It went from strength to strength
after its formation in 1868, and played a major part in the campaign
for the government take-over of the telegraphs.[86] Competitors were
quickly on the ground, however. In 1870 Saunders formed another
agency, the Central News, while his Central Press passed to the
Conservatives. Later there came a Liberal offshoot of the latter, the
National Press Agency, and soon other more specialised ones were
started. The agencies used mainly to send telegraphic information, but
they also supplied the partly printed sheet in stereo form.

The other major type of proliferation and expansion was the local
edition, which seems to have been a device popular amongst proprietors
of the unstamped press in the early 1830s. There was, of course,
nothing untoward in the practice of publishing specific local editions of
a paper under local titles, but the practice was open to abuse, as a *cause
célèbre* of the 1860s demonstrated. In January 1865 a company was
floated with £3,000 nominal capital, £325 of which was actually
subscribed. Its purpose was to buy out the business of a Mr Manfield,
the owner of the *Dorset County Express* and fifteen other local Liberal
papers in the west of England. A Dorset magistrate, Mr Yeatman, 'a
gentleman of conservative opinions', acted as trustee, and with other
gentlemen and clergymen, accepted bills for Manfield's debts
amounting to about £2,000. The bills were not honoured and Manfield
sued Yeatman for liability. There was no real defence to offer, and
Yeatman won his suit, and the company was wound up in January

1868 with more than £4,000 liabilities.[87] It is the structure of the company, however, which is the interesting point here. The leading proprietor was an ex-editor of the *Dorset County Chronicle,* and founder of the Newspaper Press College in Dorchester, William Wallace Fyfe. What he and the company had bought were really fifteen editions of the *Express,* with different titles, such as the *Weymouth, Portland and Dorchester Telegram.* The company then bought out the old *Western Flying Post* and the *Yeovil and Somerset Times,* and proceeded to publish some nine further editions of these. The practice was not unknown, but the scale of operation seems to have been unusually large. In some cases, although not apparently in this, it was a way of getting advertisers to pay considerably more for their advertisements by having to buy space in a handful of papers instead of just one.[88] Alexander Andrews drew from this unfortunate story the moral 'that Newspaper Companies, limited or unlimited, will seldom succeed even when projected by honourable men and elaborately organised (as for instance the *Dial* was some years ago). We will back private capital and enterprise against them any day.'[89] He was to be proved very wrong, but the opinion is indicative of the caution that surrounded such enterprise in the 1860s.

Not all newspaper chains were merely strings of titles. In 1873 Mitchell's *Directory* listed five proprietors who owned five or more newspapers outside London. Robert Ackrill owned five in the West and North Ridings of Yorkshire; George Bacon, son of the more famous Richard Bacon of Norwich, and president of the Provincial Newspaper Society from 1848 to 1849, had six Liberal papers in Surrey, Sussex and Kent; Edwin Barrow Smith owned five, four of which were avowedly Conservative, in Kent, Essex and Surrey. The largest chain men were Alexander Mackie of Cheshire and W.E. Baxter of Sussex. Mackie had bought the *Warrington Guardian* from John Thompson in 1856, and on this he built up a network of *Guardians,* at Northwich in 1861, at Altrincham and Bowdon in 1862, at Runcorn, Nantwich and Crewe in 1863, and at Chester in 1867. All were supposed to be politically neutral, but Mackie was to become an important Conservative journalist in the 1870s. Baxter's enterprise was larger and older than Mackie's. He had been president of the Provincial Newspaper Society in 1854 to 1855, and only its second secretary from 1864 to 1869. He had begun in 1835 at the age of twenty-seven with the *Surrey Standard* in Guildford, to which he added the *Kent Mail* in 1839. In 1849 he took over his father's *Sussex Agricultural Express* (Lewes). In 1853 he brought out a Hastings edition of the *Express,* and in 1855 the *South London Journal.* In 1862 he began papers, probably local editions of his other papers, in Worthing, Tunbridge Wells and Dorking, and in 1863 more at Chichester, Eastbourne and Sutton, as well as buying one at Greenwich. In 1866 he added more at Brighton and Windsor, and as his most ambitious project took over the Home Counties paper the *Counties Herald,* which issued special editions in all the Home Counties and in Hampshire. On his death these editions were reduced to four, but the rest of the network continued to prosper under the eye of his son. All his papers were professedly Conservative or Independent, as one would expect from the area of his operations. Clearly both Mackie and Baxter were first and foremost, if not solely, entrepreneurs, whose main object was profit, an object which they accomplished with remarkable success.

The Proprietors

These were but two of the newspaper proprietors. It is now time to look at them as a group. They were, perhaps, somewhat less numerous than the total number of newspapers, as multi-ownership increased during the second half of the century. The deficiency may have been more than redressed, however, by those who were 'proprietors' by virtue of being shareholders or directors of newspaper companies. Counting is difficult. Many proprietors remained anonymous, especially before the Register was begun in 1881, while occupational censuses would often miss newspaper activity, it being subsumed under some other title, such as printing or publishing, or treated as entirely subsidiary by the proprietor himself. The category of 'newspaper proprietor' was not separately enumerated in the censuses, and was included at all only in those of 1861 and 1911. In 1861 it was bracketed with editors and publishers, and a gross underestimate of 114 was made for England and Wales, 8 of them female, 70 per cent between 35 and 40 years of age. In 1911 there were 2,880 newspaper proprietors and publishers, 99 of them female, 80 per cent of them between 20 and 45 years of age. Only 449 (16 per cent) of the males, and 25 (25 per cent) of the females, however, were self-employed. In both years they were found in the more thickly populated areas of Lancashire, the West Riding of Yorkshire, Staffordshire, Durham and Warwickshire, and in London and the Home Counties. In 1861 the older centres of journalism in the south-west were also prominent, with a few in the extreme north, in the Welsh Borders and the East Midlands. By 1911 they were found to be much more evenly scattered over the country.

Most proprietors seem to have been in the printing and publishing industry, whilst those that were not tended to form companies and put more qualified men in charge. In a sample of southern and eastern papers, in an area bounded roughly by a line from the Solent to the Wash, and mostly in the last half of the nineteenth century, 20 of 35 identifiable proprietors and directors were printers, publishers, booksellers or stationers. Of the rest two were journalists, two estate agents, two auctioneers, two drapers, a tailor (in the East End of London), a hairdresser, a coal merchant, a solicitor and a schoolmaster.[90]

The term 'journalist' was commonly used to include the newspaper proprietor until the close of the nineteenth century, but proprietors proper, whether they were really 'journalists' or not, succeeded in improving their status more rapidly than did the working journalists. As we have already seen, provincial proprietors had broken into public life by the 1860s, but it was a slow process. 'The chances of a seat in the legislature for the journalist (sc. proprietor) are indeed remote. He may get a county judgeship, he may become a county treasurer, he may be appointed a consul or vice-consul, a lunatic or sanitary secretary, a poor law, educational or factory inspector, but he must leave journalism if his ambition be beyond these rewards.'[91] Indeed, the several MPs who had been proprietors, such as D.W. Harvey and Sir Edward Watkins, founders respectively of the *Sunday Times* and the *Manchester Examiner,* had left journalism before their election. Even as late as 1874 it was complained, by a possibly aggrieved author, that 'if a vice-consulship, a school inspectorship, or a county court treasurership should by a fluke fall into the hands of any of the class (of newspaper proprietors) it falls into his hands surreptitiously, is challenged by the opposition at once as a bribe or as the acknowledgement of a secret and perhaps dishonourable service.'[92] The way was becoming easier, however. In 1868 W. Newton of the *East London Observer,* C.W. Dilke of the *Athenaeum* and Sebastian Evans of the *Birmingham Daily Gazette* were all candidates in the general election.[93] By the end of the century at least thirty proprietors were sitting in the Commons.[94] Besides these there were numerous MPs who had acquired newspaper interests for a political advantage, such as S.W. Cowes, Conservative MP for Leicester North from 1868 to 1880, who was a proprietor of the *Leicester Express,* and Robert Yerburgh, Conservative MP for Chester from 1886 to 1906, who was a proprietor of the *Chester Courant.* Both these MPs, moreover, kept the company of Dukes in their newspaper interests, the Dukes of Rutland and Westminster being respectively shareholders in the *Leicester Express* and the *Chester Courant.*[95] This sort of proprietorship, of course, did not receive very much publicity, but the involvement of such men in the newspaper business was a significant step in the improvement of the standing of those who owned and ran it.

The issue of proprietorial status raised the problem of the ambivalent attitude towards the press previously noted. Proprietorship was seen in part as contributing to the ideal of public duty, but it was combined with an imperative of commercial success, producing in the end a kind of *capitaliste oblige.* The Provincial Newspaper Society had steadfastly tried to defend and promote the gentlemanly status of the profession, and it remained wedded to that concept throughout the century. In 1890, for example, it refused to act as an orthodox employers' organisation in the matter of labour relations, so the Linotype Users Association was formed, which in 1896 made the first national agreement in the printing industry. There followed other regional organisations, the Lancashire Newspaper Society, and the Northern Federation of Newspaper Owners, both in 1904, the London Newspaper Proprietors Association in 1906, and the Federation of Southern Newspaper Owners in 1909.[96] This was a new type of activity, indicative not only of the way in which the structure of the industry was being modernised, but of a changing attitude to the role of the proprietor in society. Ruskin had castigated them as 'ill-educated and mostly dishonest, commercial men', a typically exaggerated judgement.[97] They were probably no less well-educated than the class to which they belonged, a class, of course, which Ruskin considered to be ill-educated anyway, and whilst they were undoubtedly commercial men there is no reason to suppose that they were any less honest than other commercial men. The difficulty was that they claimed also to be a profession, even, occasionally, to be following a calling, and they expected to be treated as considerably more than just tradesmen.

There is no doubt that the increasing scale of newspaper enterprise, the removal of state regulation and fiscal burdens, and an increasing political pressure which tended to enhance the utility of the newspaper as a link between parties and voters, all served to improve the status of the proprietor. There remained, however, residual elements of the older system which understandably irritated those seeking power and respectability.

There was, first, the matter of the security system. Created by one of the notorious 'Six Acts' of 1819, it had not been abolished in 1855. Since 1830 the security demanded had been £400, but what had

originally been a matter of safeguarding government authority had
gradually come to be defended on the grounds that it gave individuals
security against being libelled, by excluding the worst elements of the
tribe. Some prosecutions were successfully carried out by the Inland
Revenue after the repeal of the stamp under this law, and in response
Acton Ayrton pressed two Bills forward to remedy the situation, but
without success. However, until 1869 no further prosecutions were
attempted. In that year the *Camden and Kentish Town Gazette* and
Bradlaugh's *National Reformer* were prosecuted. The former's case
never came to trial, and the latter's was abandoned on the introduction
by Ayrton, now Secretary to the Treasury in Gladstone's new
government, of a Bill to repeal the security system. Thus security was
abolished more than a decade after the stamp, and registration became
optional, few proprietors availing themselves of the opportunity.[98]

With the security system removed the conflict between the press
and the government was more or less confined to the law of libel. Its
critics had long accused the press of harbouring in its bosom hosts of
straw men, against whom actions could not be brought to recoup
damages for injuries caused to character and position through a libel.
In England[99] the use of the law of libel by the government as a method
of political censorship had by the 1870s much diminished. Although
they often felt affronted by what was published, the governing classes
no longer had good reason to fear it. When they acted now it was
usually in the interests not of political stability, but of public morality.
In 1870, for example, the Oswestry magistrates instructed the police
to warn, even to summons without hope of conviction, persons who
sold publications the like of the *Illustrated Police News.* In the same
year a London paper called the *Ferret* was suppressed, which seems to
have been in the same style as the notorious *Town.*[100] The law of libel,
however, was much more frequently used by private individuals to
defend their character, or speculatively to obtain monetary recompense.
Yet even in this sort of case the remedy of a criminal prosecution was
still open to the plaintiff, and was often used, it appears, to frighten
the defendants into settling out of court. Newspapers were inevitably
the chief objects of these prosecutions. On the one hand, therefore,
there was a body of opinion dissatisfied because of the difficulty of
getting at a responsible and substantial publisher or proprietor, and on
the other there were the proprietors who objected to the ease with
which it was possible for them to be prosecuted, to the penalties
imposed, and especially to the fact that the paper was invariably
required to pay the costs of the case, whether it won or lost.

One answer was some form of official registration. The registration associated with the duties and the securities had become defective after 1855, and more or less defunct after 1870. In the debates on the repeal of the stamp Disraeli had favoured a universal registration system, so that there should be available 'the name of a person whose station was such that redress might be obtained from him by those whom the journal might have injured'. George Butt, Conservative MP for Weymouth, urged that it should be along the same lines as company registration, so as to avoid the insidious 'straw men'.[101] Nothing, however, was done, so that the complaint was still heard in 1877 that 'it was well known that there was a class of newspaper established to write up bubble companies.'[102] This was still the issue. How was the bona fides of a newspaper proprietor to be established, how was the public to be safeguarded from charlatans and sharks, whilst also securing the freedom and security of the better part of the press from the depredations of professional litigants? This was not a problem peculiar to the press, except in so far as the libel laws applied mainly to newspapers, and there was much in the proprietors' claim to be treated like other businessmen. The freedom which they demanded, however, was in the nature of a privilege in many eyes, and there was much opposition to its being granted. Disraeli's simple solution, that a good indicator of the respectability of a newspaper was the amount of capital invested in it, might have impressed Victorian businessmen, and as we have seen it was a position with which the Provincial Newspaper Society had some sympathy, but it was also a formula which tended to guarantee the success of scurrilous litigants, and the bankruptcy of wealthy men.[103]

The first move toward reform came from outside the press. Two Liberals introduced a Bill in 1876 which would have required the registration of newspapers and proprietors, while making, in return, some slight alterations in the law of libel.[104] It was unsuccessful, but substantially the same Bill was introduced in 1877, and this time provoked some strong objections on the part of the proprietors. Joseph Cowen, Liberal MP for Newcastle and owner of the *Newcastle Daily Chronicle,* moved an amendment which would repeal what he termed 'the exceptional law which renders newspaper proprietors criminally as well as civilly responsible for the acts of the employees'. This must, he argued, be a *quid pro quo* for any registration legislation. He protested that 'there was no body of tradesmen who conducted their business in this country under more stringent restrictions than the newspaper proprietors.' They were subject to 'judge-made' law, unfairly administered.

> What he objected to was the *animus* that underlay the measure. The
> imputation was that newspapermen were not to be trusted, that
> they ought to be called upon to give guarantees as to their
> commercial stability. . . They were surely as much worthy of credit
> as an ordinary tradesman.[105]

Cowen's amendment was seconded by Dr Charles Cameron, Liberal MP
for Glasgow, and proprietor of the Glasgow *Mail.* The Bill's sponsor,
Samuel Waddy, Liberal MP for Barnstaple, retorted that the known
respectability of most proprietors was a reason why they should have
no fear of having to register their names. 'There was no disgrace in being
proprietor of a newspaper.'[106] Neither the amendment nor the Bill
went any further, but in 1879 a Select Committee was appointed to
investigate the problem, on the basis of yet another Bill drafted by
John Hutchinson, Liberal MP for Halifax and proprietor of the *Halifax
Courier.* After a career interrupted by the dissolution of 1880, the
reconstituted Committee delivered a Report in that year, the
recommendations of which were largely embodied in the Newspaper
Libel and Registration Act of 1881. The Act was a compromise,
requiring on the one hand that no proprietor, or any other responsible
person, should be liable to criminal prosecution for libel without the
fiat of the Director of Public Prosecutions, and on the other the
registration of newspapers and their proprietors, except in the case of
joint-stock companies which had already to be registered.

Argument for the measure in the Committee had been along classical
liberal lines, that the liberty of the press fully and freely to report
events was more important than the prevention of an occasional injury
to an individual unable to obtain redress. It was demanded that the
press be accorded, in the reporting of all public meetings, the privilege
it enjoyed in the reporting of the courts of law and of Parliament.[107]
It was thus claimed not only that newspaper proprietors should be
treated as other tradesmen, as Cowen had asked, but that they should
be given legal recognition as guardians of the nation's rights and
liberties. It was this point which raised most opposition, both in the
Committee and during the debates on the Bill. Other issues were not
so contentious. Most witnesses opposed the re-introduction of the
security system, although typically enough the solicitor for *The Times*
favoured both security and registration. Unfavourable comparison was
made with the position in Scotland, where it was not open to the

individual to seek a criminal prosecution. The main area of dispute, however, remained the question of privilege in the reporting of public meetings. The outcome of discussion in the Committee and of the debates on the Bill was the cumbersome second section of the 1881 Act. This accorded privilege to the reporting of public meetings 'lawfully convened for a lawful purpose, and if such a report was fair and accurate, and published without malice, and if the publication of the matter complained of was for the public benefit'. This effectively left the courts to decide not only what was libellous, but what was a public meeting. Both political parties had complained of the intrusion of the press at party meetings, the Liberals in 1875, and the Conservatives in 1880.[108] It remained unclear as to whether these meetings, or MPs' meetings with their constituents, or shareholders' meetings, or, most importantly, local government meetings, were privileged within the meaning of the Act. It had not been until 1868 that the reports of Parliament had been accepted as privileged, and progress along these lines was to continue only very slowly.[109] It is not clear what the general practice of local councils, boards of guardians, and Petty and Quarter Sessions was concerning the admission of the press. A series of Acts since 1848 had stressed the importance of magistrates' hearings being public, but the justices retained their right to sit when and where they chose, and there is some evidence that they did try to exclude the press on occasion.[110] Coroners and Poor Law Guardians were also suspicious, and reporters were expelled from inquests and guardians' meetings.[111] There were also many cases in which newspapers were successfully prosecuted for their reports, indicating that where entry was granted, privilege did not follow. The matter of admission was left to the bodies themselves, and the 1881 Municipal Corporations Act did not specify that either the public or the press be admitted to council meetings, while the County Councils Act of 1888 led to a rash of press exclusions.[112] The 1894 Local Government Act did stipulate that parish meetings be open to the press, but the LCC had decided in 1889 to exclude the press from committees. The matter came to a head in 1907 when Tenby Corporation sought to have the proprietor of the *Tenby Osbserver* stopped from attending its meetings, although they would have accepted one of his reporters. The judgement hinged on the 1882 Act, which had not specified the admission of the press, and the corporation won its case. This led Arthur Henderson to introduce a Bill giving the press the right of admission to meetings of local authorities, education committees, guardians, and rating and other bodies. There would be no right of admission to committees, except where these constituted the actual authority or where they chose to allow the press to attend. These provisions became law in 1908, and the fact that any council or other body could delegate most of its business to committees, or render itself a committee for special purposes, and thus avoid the public gaze, did not alter the fact that the press now had a legal if precarious position in local government.[113]

As serious a shortcoming of the 1881 Act as the inadequate definition of public meetings and rights of admission thereto, was the failure of section 2 to provide any substantial protection for the press in the reporting of libellous matter. It was quickly ruled in the courts that the Act did not apply to the most common form of criminal prosecution for libel, the criminal information. Only after the Lord Chief Justice had ruled in 1884 that the old rule held, whereby criminal information should be allowed only where the libelled person held high office, and the libel was an imputation of that office, were these proceedings virtually stopped. Even then private prosecutions began to increase rapidly, and proprietors found themselves vulnerable. It was ruled that for privilege to apply, what had to be in the public interest was not the report as a whole, but the particular words complained of, which as one Irish judge had it, meant that if a statement were found to be libellous, it could not possibly be in the public interest! The *Manchester Courier* fell victim to this trap in 1885.[114]

Finally, the Act had not dealt with the question of whether ignorance of the fact of publication might constitute a justification. A celebrated case, Reg. v. Holbrook (1877), had left the law unsettled, after two retrials and the death of the plaintiff. The Lord Chief Justice had given one opinion, but the majority of judges involved in the case had come to the opposite conclusion.[115]

Dissatisfied with the Act the proprietors succeeded in pushing through the Libel Law Amendment Act in 1888. This sought to remove proprietors from the danger of criminal prosecution, except by order of a judge in chambers, an application to whom could be defended. This was aimed at the indiscriminate issue of *fiats* under the 1881 Act. In practice the Act did not result, as the proprietors may have hoped, in the disappearance of such prosecutions, but it may have helped in their reduction.[116] The Act also provided for the consolidation of actions for libel, so as to make it impossible for a plaintiff to obtain exorbitant damages merely by pursuing separate actions on different papers for the same libel. Section 4 of the Amendment Act did something to extend privilege to reports of all public meetings, provided that they did not involve malice, blasphemy or indecency, and provided that the paper had not refused to publish an apology, explanation or contradiction. As with the second section of the earlier Act, however, this was so clumsily and obscurely drafted that much of its force was lost.[117] Also like its predecessor this Act failed to resolve the Reg. v. Holbrook question, and in 1910 in Jones v. Hulton & Co. it was no help against the judgement that want of intention was no justification of libel.[118]

Despite their shortcomings there is little doubt that these Acts had enhanced the legal status of the newspaper proprietor. Part at least of the claims to be allowed to act as a proper 'fourth estate' had been accepted in the 1888 Act, and in legislation establishing certain public bodies. These were significant advances on the position as it stood in 1855.

The press had a commercial as well as a social interest in the law. Crime and its punishment were news, and the newspaper and its staff had to live within close proximity, if not of the criminals, then of the police and the agents of justice. Having discussed the ways in which the newspapers themselves could become victims of the law it is convenient here to turn to two areas in which further friction arose, and which also throw some light on the nature of proprietorship.

Relations with the police varied, but there seems to have been a good deal of suspicion of the press in that quarter. In the 1880s particularly there were many complaints by the press of the failure of the police to co-operate with them, and of a lack of mutual trust.[119] In London, relations had been strained by the unemployed demonstrations of 1887, during which reporters claimed to have been among the first victims of police batons. This gave rise to a suggestion that press badges be worn and prominently displayed on such occasions. Relations were further exacerbated by the failure of the police over the Ripper murders, but hope was expressed that the new Metropolitan Police Commissioner might be more sympathetic. At other times and outside London, relations between the press and the police remain obscure, but it may perhaps be surmised that many proprietors who were also well-known local public figures would have been on very good terms with the local Chief Constable.[120]

The other area of interest concerns the reporting of executions. In 1868 that greatest of circulation boosters, the public execution, had been abolished. Henceforth, executions would be carried out within prisons. No provision was made for the press to be admitted to these occasions, but the Sheriffs were empowered to admit anyone they chose, and this, it seems, usually included reporters. By the 1890s, however, there seem to have been fewer Sheriffs willing to admit the press, and this led the Institute of Journalists to debate a resolution in December 1894 that, in the interests of the public, the press should be admitted to executions, and that every paper should receive equal treatment. Some speakers argued that the latter part of the resolution was the most important part, that it mattered less whether they were admitted or not, than that they should all be treated alike. This was a line which clearly put the commercial in front of the social or political role of the press. J.H. Dalziel, proprietor of *Reynolds News,* pointed out, however, that admission had to be secured if any credence were to be given to reports at all. Garbled and varying reports of the same execution had already appeared as a result of exclusions, and the use of Governors' descriptions, apart from their being in all probability less sensational than the papers required, would, it was argued, only add to the confusion. Herbert Asquith, the Home Secretary, was unsympathetic to the Institute's case, and the Home Office consistently took the line that the presence of reporters did not, by the press's own admission, guarantee accurate reports, and that in any case the decision was by law entirely in the hands of the Sheriffs. The matter blew up again in 1903 when the governor of Chelmsford prison complained that there had been so many reporters (eight) at the execution of 'Dougal' that they had hampered the proceedings. Enquiry, however, showed that the only delay had been caused by the chaplain trying to extract a confession. In the following year Sir William Leng again raised the matter with the Home Office in relation to the various reports of the executions of the Wombwell murderers and of 'Billington', but without success. In May 1909 an enquiry was held into the practice in Western Australia, which seems to have been the last that was heard of the issue. The practice in Britain had been moving towards the exclusion of the press, with 26 of the 45 prisons where executions were carried out admitting the press in 1895, and only 18 out of 52 in 1909.[121] Gradually, too, the press lost interest, and the morbid tradition of publishing detailed descriptions of executions, and of the executed, withered away, although eye-witness reports were still appearing in the 1920s.[122] Thus the proprietors had failed to prevail upon either the Sheriffs or the Home Office to help them further to pander to the more barbaric of the nation's tastes.

　　Finally, successful newspaper proprietors expected, just as other professionals and businessmen did, to rise to some form of local public office at the very least. The struggle for status in this respect had been a long and hard one. After years of pressure the Provincial Newspaper Society had succeeded in 1851 in having proprietors made eligible to sit on local councils, only to see the right spirited away again in 1875 when the Public Health Act omitted to mention it. As a result many proprietors had to resign their seats on local bodies, and the matter was only remedied, after several unsuccessful Bills, in 1885.[123] The local bench had been an even tougher nut to crack. In 1869 the proprietors of the *Darlington Times* and of the *South Eastern Gazette* were refused admission on the grounds that since at least 1851 the rule had been that clergymen, practising attorneys and solicitors, those connected with the wine, spirit and beer trade, and those connected with the local press should be excluded.[124] If this was so, however, it was a rule with exceptions. Thomas Latimer since 1851, John Jaffray since 1865 in Birmingham and since 1868 in Worcester, Thomas Wall since 1866, and John Watton since 1867, had all been appointed to the bench, and were recorded, by 1875 at least, as newspaper proprietors. Other proprietors sat on the bench in other capacities, such as J.J. Colman, since 1869, but as a merchant, not as a newspaper proprietor. Later F.B. Grotrian, appointed in 1877, continued to be referred to as a merchant even after he had founded the *Hull Daily Mail* in 1889. Alfred Hargrove was not listed as a newspaper proprietor until the 1893-4 returns, although this had been his major activity since before his appointment in 1877. Four of the original *Yorkshire Post* directors were JPs when it was founded in 1866.[125] Most of those listed as proprietors, however, were amongst the most respected and long-standing of provincial proprietors. The 'rule' seemed to prevail in most cases into the 1880s. In 1883 Selborne, the Lord Chancellor, refused to appoint two men to the bench on the specific grounds that they were newspaper proprietors. He explained that whilst there was no general rule of exclusion he had refused 'on account of general considerations applying to their positions, and the influence they might exercise within the local areas'. T. Wemyss Reid, editor of the *Leeds Mercury,* thought of raising the question again in the Commons, pointing out to Herbert Gladstone that 'as a matter of fact he (Selborne) only excludes the most important and responsible members of the class. At least half of the chief proprietors, and I believe *all* the managing proprietors of the *Yorkshire Post,* for example, are magistrates.'[126] Wemyss Reid had perhaps a partial view of who were the most important proprietors, but he was correct about the *Yorkshire Post.* Of nine directors in 1888, seven were JPs, three in Leeds, three in the West Riding, and one in both. Of the 23 directors appointed since the foundation of the paper in 1866, but not holding office in 1888, seven were JPs.[127] The Provincial Newspaper Society added its voice to the protest in 1883, but it was all to no avail.[128] It should be remembered, however, that this was a time when the political manipulation of the bench was notorious, and it was always useful to have grounds for refusal, even though they need never be disclosed. In 1910 the permanent secretary to the Lord Chancellor told the Royal Commission on Justices of the Peace that the exclusion of newspapermen

> is practically obsolete now, but it used to be the rule at one time, and on this ground, especially in the smaller places, that the local newspaper commented upon the cases in the local court, and it was not thought desirable that the proprietor of the local newspaper should also be a justice. I remember that, and it used to be a pretty rigid exclusion before, I should think, the year 1885.[129]

It was true that their exclusion had virtually ceased by 1910, the process of establishing this particular mark of social and political status had taken more than half a century after the repeal of the newspaper stamp. It was, however, an important process, and did add considerably to the status of the proprietor, and served further to wipe out the earlier stigma of being a 'nobody'.

III The Profession of Journalism

'Men of great ability and high character (who) gave their best to what they conceived to be a public service without seeking recognition or reward beyond a very moderate emolument for their labour,' was how J.A. Spender described the mid-Victorian journalist.[130] A change was evident in the profession by the end of the century, although there still were men of the type that Spender described, himself amongst them. The change was put succinctly by Harmsworth's associate in the *Evening News,* Kennedy Jones, who claimed to have remarked to that model of the old journalism, John Morley, 'you left journalism a profession, we have made it a branch of commerce.'[131] Both observations referred back to what has come to be seen as the 'golden age' of the 1860s and 1870s.[132] If the changing social and political role of the press in the last half of the century is to be understood, it is necessary first to examine the development of the economic position and status of the journalist.

It has been argued by L. O'Boyle that for the first half of the century journalists were rescued from the political patronage of the aristocracy and Old Corruption largely by the demands of commerce, and journalism became less corrupt as it grew to be more businesslike. After a brief, and perhaps illusory period of independence, it is argued, it succumbed to the equally demanding patronage of those commercial men who had liberated it from the old patronage, the men who now ran it, more or less, as a business.[133] Thus the swords of one generation became the fetters of the next. This is, moreover, a thesis which fits not only Britain, but France, Germany, and, it might be added, the United States. The process varied in detail and in pace from country to country, roughly according to the extent of industrialisation, but it seems to have been a process common to most sooner or later. Thus, what its critics regarded as a disastrous betrayal of the cause of the press in the 1880s and 1890s in England, may be seen, in larger perspective, as part of a quite 'normal' development in the history of the newspaper in the industrial revolution, and not as an unfortunate aberration. This is not to deny that 'normal' development might be totally undesirable to the critics, but it is to emphasise that there were deeper and stronger forces determining the path of development than the critics often allowed for. For them the 'golden age' tended to perform the function of a myth to enable them to ignore the unpleasant realities which followed.

Professionalisation was slow to start in journalism. The struggles of the early radical journalists had not improved their status, because their new-won freedom was widely considered to have spilt over into venality, licentiousness and sedition. In 1807 they were prevented from being called at Lincoln's Inn, and even such champions of a free press as Henry Brougham and John Roebuck shared the view that the men of the press were not gentlemen. This meant that[134]

the Newspaper Press is thus degraded from the rank of a liberal profession: the employment and the class engaged in it sink: and the conduct of our journals falls too much into the hands of men of obscure birth, imperfect education, blunt feelings and coarse manners, who are accustomed to a low position in society, and are contented to be excluded from a circle in which they have never been used to move.

Even in the 1840s social place was reserved for only a few of the most eminent journalists with aristocratic connections, hence Disraeli's much-quoted reference to the 'gilded saloons' to which they were admitted, and a future editor of the *Daily News,* W. Weir's complaint that 'the cry about the degraded status of journalists has been brought up by a knot of kid-gloved democrats, who wish to be pets of the saloons, as some French journalists are'.[135] The quest for equality of status with French journalists was a reflection of the latter's political influence, and it continued without ever having great success.[136] In 1860 a *Times* reporter was disqualified from the local bench on the grounds that he was a reporter, and a man was barred from a local book club because he was an editor.[137] There lingered the old feeling that in some sense journalists were really spies against whom 'Society' should be secured. Thomas Barnes had, when editor of *The Times*, been refused membership of the Athenaeum, Douglas Jerrold had only narrowly escaped being blackballed at the Reform Club, and Brooks' had excluded a Liberal politician because he was suspected of having written for the newspapers.[138] Lord Derby wrote to Disraeli in 1867 that 'Grosvenor has established a newspaper – the *Day* – and has engaged Kebbel, an Oxford man, well acquainted with the Press, *but* a fine writer, and scholar, and editor.'[139] In 1868 John Jaffray, editor of the *Birmingham Daily Post,* was vilified at an election contest in East Staffordshire on the grounds that he was a newspaperman.[140] At a national level there was also 'a fear of the newspaper', and of 'Typocrats', based largely on an antipathy to *The Times* borne of its policies and activities during the Crimean War.[141] The situation improved, but patchily and slowly. A Leeds councillor, J.S. Curtiss, remarked in 1875, 'fill the Council Chamber. . .with journalists and – the idea makes me laugh until my pen's broken.'[142] Five years later G.A. Sala complained that 'the English journalist has no definitely ascertained social position.'[143] The problem was, therefore, clear, but the reasons for journalists having failed to secure a higher status are complex.

There was, as has been noted, a certain distrust of men whose job it was to disclose unpalatable and often embarrassing facts. The journalist 'is associated with the general fear of espionage and feeling of insecurity which the custom of anonymous writing necessarily produces', wrote Lord Lytton in 1833.[144] Taking stock in 1851 William Johnston wrote[145]

> The profession of a journalist gives no social distinction, and the occupation is not even avowed, except to intimate friends. . .the feeling of society towards journalists is more that of fear or curiosity than that of respect or esteem.

Johnston, however, seems to have had in mind in this passage those who 'contributed' to the press, rather than those who made their living from it. As to that, H.B. Thompson, as he set about guiding the aspiring sons of the middle classes towards the professions in 1857, warned them that journalism is not a profession 'a man would willingly enter when a competence is open to him'.[146] By his criteria journalism, if a profession at all,[147] was certainly a lowly one, for it was completely open to anyone who cared to enter, and provided little if any security. Thompson put it on a level with the architect, the sculptor, the civil engineer, the educator, the parliamentary agent and the actuary, and he was almost certainly speaking here of only the higher echelons of the profession. This was demonstrated by the case of E.C.G. Murray, who in 1857 had been disciplined by the Foreign Office for having written for the press. Murray wrote a long, anonymous tract attacking this attitude, and one of his reasons for anger was that 'after the age of thirty all the liberal professions, all honorable means of obtaining a respectable livelihood, are virtually closed to a man.'[148] The option of going into full-time journalism obviously held little appeal for him.

It was true that journalism, even into the 1880s, could claim few of the generally accepted qualifications of a profession. It could provide little stability, no great remuneration, was hardly recognised by the state, and had no position of monopoly privilege. It sought instead to emphasise the only asset which it was accredited with, influence.[149]

The question of influence is one that must be returned to later in this study, but there are certain aspects of it which are convenient to discuss here. It was often argued that influence was a result, in part, of the English tradition of anonymous journalism. While this may have been true for the profession as a whole, or for particular papers, however, anonymity laid the individual journalist open to unlimited competition, and made it impossible for him to improve his worth by selling his name. The arguments over anonymity went on into the twentieth century. Most of the literature on the subject was predictably critical, and related mostly to the difficulty of controlling the abuses to which it was open, such as the difficulty of bringing a newspaper rather than a person to book for libel, or the power without responsibility which was consistently attributed to *The Times*. As John Morley put it, the worst aspect of the practice was the entrusting of 'the most important social influences at this moment to what is, as far as the public is concerned, a secret society'.[150] Cobden noted, predictably, but rather inaccurately, that the provincial press was free of the plague of anonymity, and in so far as this may have been so it was because the editors and journalists of provincial papers were likely to be well-known to their readers.[151] As Morley pointed out, however, if that were the case, it was difficult to see why formal anonymity was retained.[152] It was also claimed that people read leading articles, the most common form of anonymous matter, quite uncritically, which they would be less inclined to do if such pieces were signed.[153] In an age of fierce political partisanship and change Morley thought the practice politically dangerous and professionally unwise, respectable journalists being unable to avoid being tarred with the same unflattering brush as their less estimable colleagues. Want of discrimination between the ranks of journalists had been raised as an issue before.

> It is by (the penny-a-liner) we judge all writers for the press, and it is not surprising that to many minds the name of Journalist recalls a *mélange* of self-sufficiency, ridiculous pretension, and vulgar manners, which some French novelists have attributed to the class of travelling clerks.[154]

The other side of that penny, however, was to argue that it was precisely the traditional stigma of journalism which encouraged writers to remain anonymous.[155] Those who defended the practice, particularly for leaders, argued that these might in any case be the work of a number of hands, and constituted the identity of the paper.[156] It was also claimed that anonymous writing provided an entry for young journalists into the profession, but this was a thin case. Usually it meant merely depressing the price they could get for their work, and it was this that eventually drove increasing numbers of journalists towards the end of the century to refuse to write anonymously, except for leaders.[157]

If influence, and the acquisition of an identity, were positive aspects in the struggle for professionalisation, remuneration and life-style were the major debit items.

At the top journalists could earn a comfortable living. In the 1830s an editor of a London daily could expect between £600 and £1,000 a year, with *The Times,* the *Courier,* the *Globe* and *Lloyds Weekly News* all paying the £1,000. Until the 1870s, however, he was unlikely to have have got more. Charles Dickens managed to extract £2,000 from the *Daily News* in 1846, but he lasted only a few weeks. The editor of the *Morning Star,* on the other hand, received only 10 guineas a week in the 1860s.[158] By the 1870s £1,000 was probably the average London morning rate, with Chenery of *The Times* at £5,000, and the new editor of the *Morning Advertiser* in 1876 at £500.[159] Arthur Arnold, editor of the *Echo* from 1868 to 1874, and his counterpart on the *Pall Mall Gazette,* Frederick Greenwood, each received £1,000, while the editor

of the *Globe* managed only £600.[160] Papers which relied less on
editorial than on sub-editorial skills had no need to match these rates.
The *Weekly Dispatch,* for example, paid only £4 a week in the early
1870s.[161] Rates improved in the 1870s, so that John Morley was getting
£2,000 at the *Pall Mall Gazette* at the end of the decade, and the editor
of the *Morning Advertiser* £1,500. Harmsworth seems to have paid the
top rate of £5,000 to the editor of the *Daily Mail,* perhaps by the end
of the century, and in the next decade there were substantial increases
on the more successful papers, so that with bonuses, dividends, and
other additions the most successful editors may have obtained more
than £10,000 before the First World War.[162]

In the provinces the profession was less lucrative, but it could still
afford comfort. The successful provincial editor of the 1830s could
have got from £400 to £600, but more usually from £100 to £250.
Rarely could country editors, often still their own masters and,
therefore, paying themselves no salary, expect to earn more than £150
before the 1870s, and some £300 to £500 after this.[163] When
W.T. Stead took over the *Northern Echo* in 1872, for example, his
salary was £200, which seems to have been about average.[164] By then
only in Edinburgh, Glasgow, Birmingham, Manchester and Leeds were
the provincial rates on leading dailies up to London levels, at about
£1,000. Generally speaking, of course, the smaller the paper the smaller
the salary, so that in the 1890s an editor of a small weekly or bi-weekly
might get no more than £70 or £80, although this would have been
supplemented by other work.[165]

These salaries were low compared to those received at the upper
reaches of other professions.

> A barrister getting into practice may come to £5,000 a year, and the
> rank of a judge. A physician who is becoming popular may come to
> £6,000 a year, and a knighthood or a baronetcy. The man who only
> writes what concerns the public interests of his country and
> influences the minds of hundreds of thousands upon questions
> which, next to those of religion, are the most important of all
> questions is by no means likely to arrive at more than a decent
> competence. . . The lot of those who have written most and most
> effectively for the public press, is to live in obscurity and to die in
> neglect.[166]

An ordinary editor, it was claimed in 1858, could earn less than a
banker's or merchant's clerk, which by the 1870s would have been

between £80 and £400, with an average of £150.[167] Nevertheless, the elite of editors by the 1870s were perhaps amongst the top two per cent of those who earned their income, and were at the level at which it has been estimated that professional men could meet together, that is at £1,000 a year.[168] If there were no fortunes to be made, there were at least a sufficient number of well-paid editors to add lustre to the profession by the 1870s.

Beneath the editor there came the sub-editor, 'generally between forty and fifty years of age. . .not ordinarily one of your press Bohemians, but quiet, severe and respectable'.[169] On a London daily in the 1860s he would have got about a quarter to a third of the editor's salary, say about £250, but this varied greatly with the paper. By the end of the century the leading London dailies were paying £400 to £500, the rest £250 to £300.[170] Provincial rates were about two-thirds of those in London, from £150 to £300 in the 1870s and 1880s, up to £400 in the 1890s.[171] Again there were variations. The chief sub-editor of a popular London daily could get up to £2,000 a year at the turn of the century, while in the provinces even some of the large dailies paid only £75 in the 1900s.[172] The average rates, however, in the 1870s put the sub-editor on a level with the experienced bank or insurance clerk, and at the top of the scale with the coroner or an average medical man.[173] The majority, employed on small papers, had to combine their duties with many others, often unpaid. They had probably been first introduced to control the penny-a-liners, but it was the telegraph which made them indispensable, with their scissors and paste-pots.[174]

Between the editor and the sub-editor in terms of pay and status came the leader writer, and probably also the parliamentary reporters on large, and the foreign correspondents on the largest papers. Leader writers, when not occasional or free-lance, as they often were, could by the 1870s get about £1,000 a year in London. The Rev. Mozeley of *The Times* received £1,800 in the 1850s and 1860s, and C.E. Montague actually extracted the coveted £1,000 from the exiguous *Manchester Guardian* in 1899, but most had to be content with less.[175] It was reckoned that a good provincial daily in 1885 paid up to £400.[176] They usually enjoyed a very high status. Many were recruited directly from Oxbridge, and were duly isolated from the rest of the staff. In the 1860s they constituted a small group of about a hundred educated, comfortably off men, barristers waiting for briefs, unattached clergymen and government officials.[177] This class distinction caused some tension in the offices, so that by the 1880s Harold Spender recalled, 'Fleet Street hated the Universities. They despised our degrees;

scorned our knowledge; mocked at our modest river prides,' an attitude which T.E. Kebbel thought had begun in the 1850s.[178] No less of an elite were the parliamentary reporters. Arrangements in the House of Commons were such that there could only physically be a small number of them, and they too were usually recruited from the lower ranks of the bar, the Church and the services.[179] Their privileged position and habitual association with each other made 'the Gallery' a tight self-conscious clique, expanded only a little, and grudgingly, by the emergence in the 1870s of 'the Lobby'. In 1830 it was said they could get £200 to £300 a year. By the end of the century this had only risen to £250 to £400, but there were then ample opportunities of working for more than one paper. The latter rate, which had obtained from about 1894, persisted until 1906, but by then journalistic and political changes had made the job much more precarious, with four London morning papers having discharged their parliamentary men in 1904-5, preferring for financial reasons to use agency reports instead.[180]

Of the reporters the foreign and war correspondents were probably superior to the others in status, the latter having appeared since the Crimean and Franco-Prussian wars. They were both paid as a rule on a piecework basis, or on short-term contracts, and little is known about their average earnings. Even at the turn of the century they seem to have been rather poorly rewarded, a war correspondent getting some £80 a month during a war, and £25 a month in peace, plus a £300 a year pension for the widows of those killed in action.[181] The ordinary reporter in London appears to have got about £200 a year in the late 1860s, up to £500 or £600 in the 1890s, and between £500 and £1,000 in 1912.[182] In the provinces the larger papers paid between thirty shillings and £2 a week in the 1830s, and the *Leeds Mercury* offered F.R. Spark £80 a year in 1855.[183] The smaller journals, however, paid only £1 a week in the 1890s, and lower rates prevailed for so-called apprentices and junior reporters, less than ten shillings in the middle of the century.[184] In 1901 it was said that a junior reporter in London and a senior man in the provinces could get £150 to £200 a year on the best papers, but there were probably not many such jobs.[185] For the posts of reporter and sub-editor on the *Southampton Southern Echo* in 1889 the paper received 'eager petitioning. . .from honours men at the Universities, as well as from middle-aged men with families, and asking for salaries ranging from as little as seventeen shillings a week'.[186] At the upper level a reporter's wage was comparable with a top-grade clerk or better, but the average man in terms of income could match only the low grade, or young clerk, or schoolmaster.[187] In the 1870s Thomas

Frost had complained that the country journalist could earn only three-quarters of the wage of a bricklayer.[188] It was long accepted that reporters, and even the editors of some country weeklies, would be much more poorly paid than the printers who produced their papers. In 1913, 2,100 of the National Union of Journalists' 3,600 members were insured under the National Insurance Act, and were earning less than £160 a year, whilst the majority of the worst paid were not even members of the union. One of the leading journalists in the country, the editor of the *Daily Chronicle,* Robert Donald, told his colleagues in 1913 that this situation was discreditable to the profession. A proprietor had noted in 1910 that he had had applications for jobs at twenty-five shillings a week from competent reporters of forty and fifty years of age with families.[189] At this level things were slow to change, and the 'golden age' had always been an inappropriate epithet. The only improvement, perhaps, had been the virtual extinction of the old 'penny-a-liner', 'a very inferior race of reporters', who had been superseded by the combination of the telegraph and the sub-editor. Earning upwards of three-halfpence a line, they had constituted the casual labour force of journalism before the appearance of the penny dailies. They had had no contracts, were frequently driven to dishonesty and corruption, and were even more frequently the worse for drink, the source of 'copy furnished by the most ignorant of scavengers'.[190] By working many papers it was claimed that they could earn £30 or £40 a week, but this seems implausible and certainly exceptional. They were correctly seen as having got the profession a bad name, and their disappearance was much to the advantage of the other journalists.[191]

The poor remuneration of the rank and file was compensated in part by a 'middle-class' status. In late nineteenth-century Lancashire 'young men sometimes of good education though generally self-taught, who had dreaded the atmosphere of mill or factory. . .had sought to become what came to be called 'black-coated workers', mostly respectable but inevitably poor'.[192] As F.H. Rose, one of the prime movers of union organisation amongst journalists, remarked in 1906, they had the status of receiving a 'salary' instead of 'wages', and of accepting an 'engagement' rather than a 'job'.[193] Yet in terms of respectability and security the journalist held a low position amongst the professional men of whom he claimed to be one. Most lived on the fringe of the intelligentsia, but were not a part of it, a fact which had led Lord Lytton to explain the radicalism of newspapermen in terms of their further separation from the aristocracy than was usual in the rest of the middle classes.[194] This was an image repeated in the mid-century picture of the journalist as Bohemian, chiefly metropolitan, but also of the pubs and clubs of the provinces. Edward Dicey recalled of his contemporaries of the 1860s, men like Henry Mayhew, George Sala and Thornton Hunt, that while they had had little formal education, they could write lucidly and rapidly, that they belonged not to the 'swell' West End Clubs, but instead haunted the City taverns, the Cheshire Cheese, the Cock, the Edinburgh Castle, which used to remain especially open for them far into the night, and, finally, that they were men of little social ambition.[195] Some such pattern of life was dictated by the necessarily nocturnal habits of the daily journalist, but it was undoubtedly a pattern which attracted the rootless product of an expanding society, and men seeking the upward social mobility of the burgeoning professions in far greater numbers than the professions could provide places for them.[196] It was a profession which also provided an important niche for the many Irish and Scottish exiles who came to lend England the benefit of their wit and intellect. With an expansiveness perhaps indicating pride rather than prejudice it was claimed by a Scottish magazine in 1849 that three-quarters of London reporters were Irish or Scottish.[197] Certainly no fictional newspaper story of the Victorian period was complete without its Irishman.[198]

In such a competitive field, unorganised, as we shall see, on the supply side, job security was never high. It was also tied up with the security or otherwise of the papers themselves. As proprietors could ill afford to continue their journals merely to give journalists their due notice, and were usually unable or unwilling to pay wages in lieu of notice, journalists often found themselves cast out suddenly and without compensation. The custom of the trade was never firmly established. Some senior members of the bankrupt *Day* had in 1867 successfully sued for a month's salary in lieu of notice, but by the 1880s the courts were upholding the practice of instant dismissals.[199] On large papers the effect could be catastrophic for those involved, as with the *Tribune* in 1908.[200] Not until the National Union of Journalists became strong did matters really improve.

The insecure and erratic nature of the employment was a contributory cause of the traditional and widespread addiction of journalists to alcohol. This received a great deal of attention at a time when temperance was a militant movement. H.B. Thompson noted defensively in 1857 that 'at present the reporters are as quiet and as punctual as any other class of professional men, even though their late hours oblige them to seek refreshment and employment in places of public entertainment'.[201] By 1904, however, Edward Robbins, President of the Press Association, assured aspiring journalists that there was not one-twentieth of the drinking that there used to be.[202] The life of the journalist was not, indeed, confined to the billiard hall and the tap room. Towards the end of the century even London journalists were becoming suburbanised, and had taken to living in Clapham and Brixton. In 1891 most authors and journalists in London were to be found in the north and south-west of the city.[203]

More important, however, than life-style in securing a higher status for the journalist was the need to obtain some form of state recognition, as the major professions had done. The proprietors had organised, and successfully put pressure upon the state, but the journalists lagged far behind. At first the only provision made for 'decayed or distressed' journalists was the Newspaper Benevolent Fund, set up by the proprietors in 1864.[204] Next came the National Association of Journalists in 1886, again a proprietors' organisation. There had been Press Clubs in the provinces since the 1860s, but they were in no sense professional organisations.This was what the National Association, started in Birmingham, was intended to supply. It began with a membership of 221, which rose to 830 in 1888. Its avowed aim was respectability, and in only four years it had been achieved, with the granting of a charter in 1890, making it the Institute of Journalists. By 1894 there were 3,556 members.[205] From the start there was tension between the proprietors and the working journalists, initially over the control of the Newspaper Press Fund, and then over wages. It was complained in December 1887 that the trade union aims of the Association had already been forgotten. In 1889 a 'Non-member' asked what 'were the Institute going to do about wages?' A member replied it was

> absurd to suppose that the Institute can help working journalists to higher wages whilst newspaper proprietors are members. It is high time editors and reporters combined on the basis of a trades union, and not content themselves with the empty farce of subscribing to an institution which up to the present has not given the slightest return for the half guinea invested.

The low level of wages it was said only detracted from the quality and status of journalism as a whole.[206] This conflict of interest within the Institute was to continue until the working journalists broke away in 1907.[207]

The Institute did contribute slightly towards the raising of the status of the profession, and took up such issues as the admission of reporters to public meetings, and the relationship of the press with the police. It was true, however, that it was hardly effective as a trade union. Sometimes it intervened with some success in strikes at local offices, as at the *Preston Herald* in 1897, but it was careful not to get directly involved in such disputes, and, therefore, failed to allay the suspicions of the rank and file.[208] The first organisation of working journalists, independent of proprietors, was J.R.B. Cassello's Northern Society of Journalists, founded in 1900, which continued until the Union was founded in 1907, and which actually paid unemployment benefits.[209] In 1905 and 1906 many local branches of the Institute resolved to exclude the proprietors, and in the latter year F.H. Rose began a campaign in the *Clarion* to get journalists to accept the status of an ordinary working man, and to come closer to the printers. Eventually in 1907, on the groundwork of the Manchester journalist W.N. Watts, the National Union of Journalists was founded as the profession's first effective labour organisation.[210]

The Institute had also been of little use in another and as important a field of organisation, the control of entry into the profession. Other professions and trades attempted to do this by requiring qualifications and providing training. In journalism this was done in a very informal way by the 'apprenticing' of young journalists to small local papers, from which, if they were exceptionally fortunate and persistent, they might move to Fleet Street, or to one of the major provincial dailies. The system, however, provided little if any control on entry. The job had always been populated with amateurs, free lances and casuals, a truly rootless semi-intelligentsia. It had always been a popular system of out-relief for the unemployed of every other profession, including the notoriously insecure and unremunerative one of politics. It is doubtful whether either the Irish Nationalists or the Labour Party could have provided any MPs had it not been for the opportunity which journalism provided for them to support themselves. Understandably this caused some resentment amongst ordinary journalists against Labour MPs who took advantage of the situation, without joining an appropriate organisation.[211] There had been isolated attempts to provide training. In 1869 John Wisker had made a specific plea for the proper training of journalists, in order to prevent the profession becoming a trade, but the first School of Journalism seems to have been established in 1879 at Crewe, a short-lived private venture.[212] The difficulty was, what training should be provided? The only specialist skill, and this was not widespread until the end of the century, was shorthand.[213] Pressure for training built up in the 1880s, and in 1889 the Birmingham and Midland

Counties District of the Institute demanded an examination system for
young journalists. Why, it was asked, could not 'the gates that limit
entrance to other professions. . .be adapted to limit entrance to
journalism'?[214] The Institute, in response, tried to establish certain
standards of competence at the lower levels, but on a very informal
basis.[215] The difficulty was twofold. There were few skills that could
not be picked up in a short spell in a newspaper office, and to demand
more than these, such as academic qualifications, or language skills,
would have meant raising wage rates to a level unacceptable to the
proprietors. Inside the Institute there was no way in which to bring
pressure to bear upon the proprietors to raise wages.

Journalism had traditionally, except at the higher literary levels,
been a male preserve. By the 1880s, however, there were quite a
number of women in the profession and the Association reluctantly
admitted them as members.[216] In 1895 they formed the Society of
Women Journalists, which sought to improve the status of the woman
journalist, rather than challenge the men on their own terms. In 1897
it was reported that the Society 'have contended against poverty,
against considerable discouragement', but that it had, none the less,
grown slowly. They demanded to be taken seriously. 'We do not
welcome the crowd, or endeavour to encourage the amateur,' and they
were indignant when some mistook them for 'a sort of Ladies
Employment Society'.[217] In other words, they were shrewdly aware of
the dangers of overpopulation which constantly beset the men. For
some time they seem to have functioned more as a women's press club
than as a professional society, but with the support of radical
journalists like William Archer, H.W. Massingham and Bernard Shaw,
they managed to maintain a small benevolent fund, and by 1901
boasted about 200 members in London.[218]

We may now return to Kennedy Jones' remark quoted at the
beginning of this section. Had the 'profession' become a 'trade'? In so
far as journalism had ever become a profession, it had been a long and
incomplete process, the trappings of professionalisation which it did
manage to obtain proving much less effective in protecting its members
than was the case with other professions. When told that journalism
was a profession, Sir Marmaduke Rowley protested, 'but a barrister's
profession is recognised as a profession among gentlemen,
Mr. Stanbury,' in Trollope's *He Knew He Was Right.*[219] Yet what came
to be thought of as the norm of the 'golden age' in journalism, and
persisted amongst the elite even when the 'new journalism' had
overtaken them, was very like the norm of what have been called the

'new professions', which 'brought one scale of values — the gentleman's — to bear upon the other — the tradesman's — and produced a specialised variety of business morality which came to be known as "professional ethics" or "etiquette" ' [220] This, of course, was closely related to the proprietorial ethic, or *capitaliste oblige,* noted above. The same forces pushed both towards a resolution of their delicately balanced positions in favour of business and trade respectively. These changes were at the heart of the debate on the 'new journalism'. When critics of the latter referred to the commercialisation of journalism, the turning of it into a trade, they were not referring as Jones seems to have been, to the replacement of the amateur by the professional, the unskilled by the skilled, the casual labourer by the craftsman, but to the increasing subjection of the journalist to the uncontrollable laws of the market. The changing status of the journalist reflected the growing absorption of the press by the economy as a whole, and its dedication to the pursuit of profit, which was necessarily inimical to the old style of principled journalism. It had become more difficult, without private means, to perform the functions of the 'clerk', in the old sense, or of the 'intellectual', unimpeded by the demands of business. By the turn of the century, if not before, the profession had, indeed, all but succumbed to its new capitalist patrons.

Before looking at the 'new journalism', the tribute paid by Mercury to Mammon, it will be useful to recall what the classical liberal ideology required from the profession. It demanded first, a market situation in which adequate remuneration was accompanied by a wide choice of employment within the profession; second, a work situation which secured independence from either managerial or proprietorial control; and third, a status situation in which the journalist was expected to provide 'facts' and informed opinion as a matter of course, a status as high as the politician's, and higher than the mere 'educator'. When it transpired that none of these had been obtained, the rational foundation of liberal politics was felt increasingly to be in danger. This was the significance from a liberal point of view of the 'new journalism' in its widest sense.

IV The New Journalism

'The new journalism' quickly became the conventional term for developments in the press in the 1880s and after. It was rarely used precisely, or to describe exactly the same developments on each occasion, however, and while some 'new journalists' relished the title, others did not. Detractors delighted in the epithet, using it to sum up most of those facets of their society which they disliked, and which they claimed were reflected in and encouraged by it. The classic, if rather obscure origin of the term was in 1887 in a short regular commentary on the month's news in *Nineteenth Century* by Matthew Arnold. 'No plain reasonable man outside of politics', he thought, would be fooled by the insincerities of politicians.

> But we have to consider the new voters, the *democracy,* as people are fond of calling them. They have many merits, but among them is not that of being, in general, reasonable persons who think fairly and seriously. We have had opportunities of observing a new journalism which a clever and energetic man has lately invented. It has much to recommend it; it is full of ability, novelty, variety, sensation, sympathy, generous instincts; its one great fault is that it is *feather-brained.* It throws out assertions at a venture because it wishes them true; does not correct either them or itself, if they are false; and to get at the state of things as they truly are seems to feel no concern whatever. Well, the democracy, with abundance of life, movement, sympathy, good instincts, is disposed to be, like this journalism, *feather-brained;* just as the upper class is disposed to be selfish in its politics, and the middle class narrow.

The disposition was most marked, he added, in the industrial centres where the classes had least contact with each other, which is where, of course, the newspapers most flourished.[221]

The man Arnold referred to was almost certainly W.T. Stead, who had in the previous year published two articles setting out his journalistic credo. He had anticipated Arnold's strictures, and had repudiated them in advance, disowning the very term 'new journalism', which he had himself used in passing. What he had had in mind when he spoke of 'Government by Journalism' was more a personal notion than anything which came close to the popular conception of the 'new journalism'. He wanted the press to act as an extra-parliamentary pressure group of enlightened journalists interpreting the will of the people.[222] Yet this was no more than to restate, more arrogantly it is true, Delane's attitude in the 1850s. How else can one interpret that remarkable statement of *The Times* that 'the duty of the Press is to speak; of the statesman to be silent'?[223] Stead's work in Darlington during the Bulgarian agitation of the 1870s had conformed to this ideal, but when Frederick Greenwood suggested that this was the real beginning of the 'new journalism' he did not refer mainly, if at all, to the ideal, but to the style of the thing. The creed which Stead set himself at that time in his private journal was significantly not so much about the actual politics of the 'new journalism', but the politics which Stead wanted to use his paper to convey. Neither of the main aspects of the 'new journalism' singled out by Stead, 'political education' and 'the prophetic character of the journalist's vocation', were in fact characteristic of the genre, and neither was new. Nor could it be said that other practitioners of the 'new journalism' echoed Stead's claim that the aim was *'to reproduce in a paper the ideal of God'.*[225] What was new was 'the moral thrust, social conviction, directness of language and political ambition' of Stead's work, but even this was not what the 'new journalism' was in most people's conception. To claim, as Professor Baylen does, that the end of the Maiden Tribute agitation in 1885 marked the beginning of the decline of the 'new journalism' unduly narrows the focus of attention.[226] That Stead repudiated later developments made by the great weekly magazine magnates who entered the daily newspaper business seems rather to indicate that he failed to appreciate the 'new journalism' in all its complexity. It was a style of journalism, which when free of the political mill-stones with which Stead had sought to encumber it, was a commercial success. The political pressures and structures proved much weaker than the commercial dynamic which has been discussed earlier in this chapter. Stead had wanted to solve the conflict between politics and business by a frontal political attack, but if God was on his side, the strength of the Devil was with business, as most proprietors were well aware. Some compromise or compact with the Devil was inevitable. Even Stead, whose virtue tended towards the pharisaical, was vulnerable. His zeal for journalism led him to ignore the side-effects of his actions in the Eliza Armstrong affair, while he showed a remarkable willingness to change an article on the Prince of Wales, in 1891, according to advice from above.[227]

Later in the field, but less idiosyncratic than Stead, was T.P. O'Connor. He emphasised that the 'new journalism' was indeed a matter of style, and he instanced passages in Macaulay, J.R. Green, and, of course, Carlyle, to show that liveliness was neither new nor reprehensible.[228] He argued that one should present life as it was, rather than as it ought to be, and not as entirely serious, nor as unrelentingly political. When the press did turn to politics, he went on, it should be to an identifiable politics. An 'independence' which entailed depreciating one's friends and eulogising one's enemies would be bad politics and bad journalism.[229] O'Connor, Stead, and Arnold were

agreed, however, that the 'new journalism' was more than an approach
to politics, and it is the purpose of this section to examine what more
it was, leaving the political implications to a later chapter.

Arnold's strictures about the style of the 'new journalism' were no
newer than some aspects of the style itself. It was compalined in 1851,
before even the emergence of the cheap press, that there was a
morbidness, a forced humour, a maudlin sentimentality, and a penchant
for creating its own news in the press of the day.[230] Much of the
criticism of the American press at that time was motivated by a distaste
for similar characteristics, and Ruskin had long scorned the 'thousand
leagues square of dirtily printed falsehood every morning at
breakfast'.[231] In the 1860s and 1870s the journalism of the *Daily
Telegraph* and the *Pall Mall Gazette* created a furore because they had
broken with the staid traditions supposedly set by *The Times,* although
neither was trivial or frivolous in its treatment of the news.[232] These
strains were to be the common accompaniment of the 'new journalism'
in the 1880s, which can best be described as a mixture of journalistic
and typographical devices, which taken together constituted a new style
of journalism, a style which reflected a changing relationship between
the newspaper and its readers.[233]

The most conspicuous feature of this mixture was typographical
innovation aimed at making the paper more readable. Cross-heads,
shorter paragraphs, larger and more informative headlines, and the
increasing use of illustration all helped break the drear monotony of
the mid-Victorian daily. There was no sharp break with tradition, and
compared to post-1914 developments it all seemed very staid, but
compared to the newspaper of the 1850s, that of the 1890s looked
very different.[234] Some of the changes had been for the worse. While
the design of the paper had in some ways become more attractive, the
quality of much of the production had deteriorated, with the use of
dingy, frail paper, and indefinite inks, and even in cases of large
circulation journals poor, broken and minuscule type. Lighting in the
more prosperous middle-class houses and in the better reading rooms
had improved during the century, but it was still far from adequate in
most homes. The decision to print the *Westminster Gazette* on green
paper was, therefore, not just a gimmick, but a thoughtful policy to
meet a real problem.[235] A major change which helped enliven the
newspaper was undoubtedly the increasing use of the front page for
news. This practice had been encouraged by the development of the
evening press in the 1870s. As long as the paper was delivered to the
door by newsboy or by post, it was treated much as a magazine or book,

with the outer pages serving as wrappers. The price and publication
time of the evening papers, however, meant that they had to a large
extent to rely on street sales, and the front page, therefore, became an
important sales weapon, the latest news the chief selling-point. The
railway news-stands had probably had some effect in this direction
previously, and some of the earlier dailies used to give over half the
front page to news, but it was street-selling and the exploitation of
impulse buying which mattered most. It was thus that the
respectability of the *Daily Mail* was enhanced when it appeared in
1896, without front page news.

Of the journalistic innovations the most notable were the descriptive
parliamentary sketch, introduced in the 1850s by the Liverpool
journalist E.M. Whitty; the London Letter, introduced by Edward
Spender in the 1860s and perfected by H.W. Lucy in the 1870s; the
interview, an American import used extensively by Stead; and the
'stop press', introduced in 1889.[236] Only the last two were properly
credited to the 'new journalism', but by the 1880s the combined effect
had produced an obvious transformation. More generally, there was by
then an increasing emphasis upon news as against opinion and
commentary. This had been encouraged by the freeing of the telegraphs
in 1870, and was in the eyes of its critics the 'new journalism's' most
damaging feature, for the news, especially foreign and telegraphed news,
tended to be shorter per item, 'snippety', and often trivial, and lacked
the guidance necessary to help its readers understand, or even to follow
it. The new journal concentrated on what the Americans had called long
since 'the human interest story'. What a journalist of the new school
needed, said one of its most successful pupils, was 'a quick
understanding of the smaller emotions and an ability to tell of them'.[237]
The relationship between paper and reader was thus being changed
from the ideal one of a tutorial and intellectual nature, to one of a
market character. Both qualities had always been there, of course, but
there does seem to have been, as the critics said, a change in the balance
of the two. As J.A. Spender put it, 'the new newspapers have changed
the old not only by taking readers from them, but by unsettling their
minds, and confusing their ideas about their own publics.'[238]

Part of the reputation of the old journalism for dullness and severity
rested upon what had been its pride and joy, the leading, or as some
wits had it leaden, articles. It was claimed that 'really good leading
articles. . .form the great part of the reading even of the most educated
part of the adult members of the busy classes.'[239] It was the custom in
the 1850s for each leader in the serious press to be three paragraphs

long, stretching for one and a quarter to one and a half columns. In its palmy period in the 1860s and 1870s the leader became slightly shorter, and harder-hitting under the influence of Sala, Hunt and Greenwood, but in 1899 it was still the rule for most London dailies to carry three leaders each of more than a column in length.[240] Even in the mid-century, however, there had been complaints that leaders tended to be disconnected, and that they were rarely followed up with any consistency. Spender himself was noted for trying to provide a more coherent diet when he took over the *Westminster Gazette* in the 1890s.[241] By then there was much less space to accommodate leisurely analyses of the news, and in any case journalists as politicians were tempted to fall back on the effects of the 1870 Education Act as an excuse for providing less demanding fare.[242]

In the old days one turned from the leaders to the speeches. There were few perhaps as extreme as John Bright in their faith in the effect of Parliamentary debates. 'I should fill every paper with debates in the House of Commons', he said, 'and omit all editorial comment.'[243] Yet the speech, inside or outside of Parliament, played an important role in mid-Victorian politics and journalism. *The Times* would often carry large eight column pages filled entirely with reports of speeches in small black print, broken only by the white around the name of the speaker, unparagraphed, and with the simple heading 'Mr Cobden said'. While at one time it may have been true that such reports would have helped disseminate political argument, it had certainly become less so by the 1890s. The fact that a verbatim report of Gladstone's Home Rule speech of 8 August 1886 was on the Edinburgh streets within four hours of its completion did not mean that its every word was eagerly devoured by every reader.[244] At a time, however, when politicians were still tied fairly closely to their localities, and when central organisations were trying to bring the localities under the closer control of the centre, speeches, especially those made in the provinces, continued to be important indications of policies, and of reactions to policies. Parliament was also very much of a part-time institution, and its short sittings left plenty of time for extra-parliamentary activity. The platform, particularly the provincial platform, however, was nothing without the newspaper. At election times in particular newspaper reports of speeches were invaluable to the parties. Gladstone's speeches, it was claimed, 'constituted text-books for his own followers'.[245] Even the adoption of the party political 'programme' in the 1890s, which reduced the significance of individual politicians' speeches, was for some a weapon of dissent, so that Chamberlain, for example, still relied very much on the press for his impact.

All this was very well understood, but from the newspapers' point of view, as sales were more important than the educational effects of their contents, the provision of such reports was an expensive and, in terms of circulation, an unrewarding affair. They began, therefore, to rely increasingly on the services of the agencies. The agencies relied on being able to sell their reports profitably to the papers. At first they offered a choice of 'verbatim', 'full' and 'summary' reports, the first two being in the first person, the third in the third person.[246] By the 1890s the 'verbatim' was becoming rare, while only the Prime Minister, Balfour, Rosebery and Chamberlain could be assured of 'full' reports. If the speeches were long, then by the 1890s they were edited, sometimes severely. 'Verbatim' and 'full' reports, in fact, came to be confined to local papers reporting local politicians or local speeches by national politicians. The big attractions disappeared. It was unlikely that anyone would have caused in the 1900s the £400 a year loss in revenue which the Press Association claimed that Gladstone had done when he died. Even Chamberlain was severely cut in his tariff campaign of 1903. By 1899 the agencies were offering half-column reports of Asquith, John Morley, and Campbell-Bannerman.[247]

Most of the outside speeches at this time were made by Parliamentarians. Inside Parliament the reporting of speeches also suffered a decline. There were alarming implications for Parliament in this tendency, not least because its own record consisted of reports made by the press in the Gallery, collated and often amended by the MPs themselves. Only in 1909 was an official, independent record started.[248] In the 1870s things had become so bad that a Select Committee was appointed, primarily to investigate the complaints of the provincial and the new metropolitan press that they were being unfairly treated as to admission to the Gallery. The enquiry revealed, however, a disquieting failure of the machinery to provide either the press or Parliament with an adequate service, partly it must be noted due to the absurd hours which the legislature then kept, and still keeps. There was some conflict of interest involved between the papers and Parliament, the former wanting reports to cater for readers, the latter demanding a full and reliable record.[249] *The Times* had tried to combine both roles, and had since 1861 paid Charles Ross £400 a year to provide his own report.[250] Pressures on space grew, however. The proprietor of the *Birmingham Daily Post* told the Committee of

the monopoly of space by meetings of local bodies which have been created over a short time, by expansion of advertising, and by lengthened Stock Exchange reports, and by that flow of foreign news which is now supplied and the existence of which is the creation of a very short time; so that we are almost compelled to condense what may be called the ordinary proceedings of Parliament.[251]

Ross thought 'few persons read the debates in *The Times* they are so long'.[252] The point was, however, that *The Times* and some other papers persisted in such reports out of a sense of public service. The editor of the *Leeds Mercury* admitted that 'the giving of good reports does not affect (the papers' circulation); but it maintains the character of the newspaper, to pay attention to what we consider and what everybody considers a very important matter'.[253] William Saunders, the Liberal proprietor of the Central News Agency, also agreed that interest in Parliament was waning, although there was still a great demand for local MPs in local newspapers.[254] In 1890 a Conservative MP claimed that the press had actually enhanced the position of the platform at the expense of the Commons by its reporting of extra-parliamentary speeches, but it is an opinion that should be treated with caution as the author was one of that new brand of businessmen MP who were apt to complain that politics took up too much of their time.[255] If the Commons had suffered, it was probably more as a result of the increasingly managed nature of parliamentary business after the pressures and obstruction of the 1870s and 1880s, which had led to increased government discipline in the House of Commons. This made it more likely than before that 'news' would be made outside of the House. Whilst these pressures had ensured that Parliament actually sat longer, the newspapers were always in session, and speech-making rarely out of season. Besides, if the Commons had lost ground to the platform, it is probably true to say that all political speeches had lost a great deal of ground to other news with the advent of the 'new journalism'. Rosebery, whilst still an active politician, thought this development a response 'to the mute inarticulate demands of the public'. He later recalled that 'when I was young. . .practically the whole family sat down after breakfast and read the whole debate through', unlike the modern public whose minds were dulled by the flood of 'news'.[256] Rosebery's family, of course, had been a professional political one, but the 'governing classes' probably conformed more or less to this picture of the old days, and nurtured on a diet of interminable sermons they may have tolerated newspapers written in the same manner quite easily.

The 'new journalism' no longer put them to the test, but the change should not be exaggerated. Politicians still put great store in having their speeches reported, and it is arguable that the pressures to which the press was subject after the 1880s were salutary in encouraging concision, in sharpening style, and in improving the effectiveness of communication.

If the 'new journalism' meant less politics, it also meant more 'sensation' and more 'sport', the staples of the popular nineteenth-century Sunday press. Both categories inevitably encountered resistance from some of the strongest pressure groups in Victorian society. Under Stead in the 1880s, of course, the 'new journalism' itself took up the banner of Nonconformist morality, but it did so in an indisputably sensational and often prurient manner. It is not, however, the intention here to analyse the content and style of the 'new journalism' in any detail. Instead reactions to two sorts of paper, the Sunday and the evening paper, and to the issue of sport and gambling in the press, will be examined for the light they shed on the reception of the 'new journalism'.

The whole affair of Sunday newspapers had been a long and contentious one. Strictly speaking the selling and 'crying' of newspapers on Sundays was illegal, but by the second half of the century it was usually tolerated.[257] It was accepted that there should be Sunday papers, delivered and enjoyed on the Sabbath, just as there was a Sunday post, and that there should be Monday papers, which had to be prepared and produced on Sundays. There seem to have been few objections. The newsvendors in 1820 who petitioned Parliament against their sale did so because it was claimed they kept people from Church, but one suspects that it was equally a means of securing their own day of rest.[258] W.H. Smith refused to distribute Sunday papers, and there was no Sunday work in his establishments, but this was recognised as exceptional.[259] They had traditionally been radical journals, but by the 1850s they were beginning to be accepted as having become less subversive than in their youth, and in 1856 the *Saturday Review* was even praising their quality and decorum.[260] There were by then also a host of popular weeklies which were undoubtedly sold and read on Sundays, many of them of a religious, temperance or 'family' character.

It was a little surprising then when popular outcry stopped the production of Sunday editions of the ordinary daily papers. The *Daily Telegraph,* closely followed by the *Daily Mail,* began these in April 1899.[261] First there came pressure from the newsagents, who claimed that they and their agents were having to work longer and harder for little extra recompense. The other newspapers, notably the radical *Morning Leader,* began a crusade against the practice in the name of religion and humanity. Public protest meetings were held up and down the country; formal protests were registered by town councils; the Archbishop of Canterbury, John Burns and Frederick Maddison associated themselves with the campaign. In a few weeks the patron of the Newsvendors Benevolent Institution, Lord Rosebery, made a public appeal to Levy and Harmsworth to desist, for the sake of the newsboys. A weightier consideration was that the campaign seems to have succeeded in effecting a collective withdrawal of advertising, but Harmsworth seized on Rosebery's appeal to make the first move, backed by a suitably respectful note of protest against Sunday work by the *Daily Mail* printers. A week later the *Daily Telegraph* followed suit.[262] Sunday papers continued to be sold and read, and Monday papers to be produced on Sundays, but at least the 'new journalism' had not been allowed to run roughshod over the hypocrisy which sanctioned such activity.

There was less resistance to the new evening papers, most of them started in the 1870s and 1880s, and sold at a halfpenny. The first recorded halfpenny papers were the London *Daily General Advertiser* of 1860, and the *London Halfpenny Newspaper* of 1861, both of them Sunday papers.[263] There followed the *Greenock Telegraph* (1863), the *Shields Gazette* (1864) and the *Bolton Evening News* (1867), all evening sheets, relying heavily on the telegraphs. In 1870 the first successful halfpenny morning paper was started by J.H. Bell in Darlington, the *Northern Echo* edited by the young W.T. Stead, and within a few years a number of halfpenny mornings were to be found in the provinces. In 1874 Bell himself supported an abortive plan for one of them in Sheffield; in 1875 the *Northern Daily Express* in Newcastle and the *Birmingham Morning News* both became halfpenny papers, while in London the *Echo* became for a short time a morning paper at its old halfpenny price. The halfpenny morning paper, however, did not really expand in London or the provinces until the 1890s and after. The 1870s were the decade of the evening paper. Its advantage to proprietors was obvious. If run in tandem with a morning paper capital and running costs were much reduced for both of them. It was excellent advertisement medium. Many people bought more than one edition, primarily for the sports results, but also for the 'latest' telegraphed news signalled on the contents bills. They were distinct from the slightly older London evening papers, the like of the *Pall Mall Gazette* and the *Echo,* which had a fairly restricted sale in terms of social class. The new

genre was meant to be popular and profitable. They were, as
H.J. Wilson was told in 1874, a way to 'reach further down into the
life of the people'.[264] Their most serious handicap as far as the
politically minded were concerned was their association with sport and
gambling. Indeed, it was probably true that they formed an important
part of the structure of both in the late nineteenth century. How
reprehensible this was was another matter.

The British taste for sport had long been catered for in the press by
special journals like *Bell's Life in London.* In 1863 there appeared
Sporting Life, and in 1871 the *Sporting Chronicle* in Manchester. The
sports covered changed over time, with field sports giving way first to
athletics and later to football, but from the public schools and the
universities to the public houses and the slag heaps the appetite seemed
insatiable. In 1880 Birmingham was supporting two sporting papers,
and by the 1890s some of the most expensive telegrams used in the
London papers were for the scores of Australian cricket matches.[265] It
was the evening press, however, that provided most suitably for these
tastes, quite early introducing the 'special' football edition.[266] The
telegraphs which in the 1850s had run results services straight to the
pubs and clubs now turned to the evening newspapers.

Unfortunately, it seemed to many Victorians, not only was this
interest in sport essentially trivial and distracting, but it also
constituted a standing temptation to gamble. The *Saturday Review*
might praise the sporting press in 1856, but it was only to be expected
that the *Congregationalist* would regard all forms of sports news as a
species of 'immorality'.[267] That 'proper' morning newspapers could be
involved in this was the cause of much criticism. In 1870 the three
Manchester morning papers agreed between them not to publish betting
news, but only the *Guardian* abided by the agreement for any length of
time, and at some financial loss. Provincial morning papers were on the
whole more reluctant to establish the practice than the metropolitan
ones, but with the exception of the fortunately placed *Bradford
Observer* they all succumbed in the end, so that Stead could look back
nostalgically in 1894 to the time when the *Northern Echo* published a
single line report of the Derby. The *Leeds Mercury* had held out against
it to the 1890s only with difficulty.[268] The temptations were indeed
very great. Frank Harris claimed that the circulation of the *Evening
News* was increased fivefold to 20,000 by the introduction of starting-
prices, and in 1906 O'Connor reckoned that the London evenings lost
between one-quarter and one-third of their circulations at the end of
the racing season.[269] The *Echo* had not published any betting news

since 1876, but it was never a financial success. The *Daily News* stopped using betting news when the Cadburys took it over in 1899, and this too needed financing. Furthermore, in 1910, when the Cadbury Trust took over the *Morning Leader* and the *Star,* which had become famous for their tipster 'Captain Coe', Cadbury's fellow-Quaker chocolate manufacturer Sir Edward Fry protested, while the *Spectator* ridiculed Cadbury's 'cant and hypocrisy'.[270] In Sheffield another stalwart guardian of the Nonconformist conscience, H.J. Wilson, stumbled for more than thirty years over the issue in his efforts to found a radical paper in the city. John Wilson once asked an adviser sardonically whether he *really* thought that a combination of the *Morning Advertiser* and *Sporting Life* could become a rival to their project.[271] However, they too were forced to concede the point in 1910, consoling themselves that a radical paper with betting news was better than no radical paper.[272]

The association of the press with gambling had often occasioned hostility. Public libraries used to block out racing news in their copies. In 1874 an Act had prohibited the advertisement of gambling facilities, particularly tipsters. In 1902 the House of Lords Select Committee on Betting was told that newspapers encouraged illegal street and shop betting, with newsagents frequently acting as bases for the business. In the previous year the National Anti-Gambling League had succeeded in having two coupon competitions, one to do with football, declared illegal.[273] Yet, in the face of all the opposition, the betting, gambling and sporting news continued to grow, as did the competitions, albeit in a more controlled way.[274] They were by the turn of the century inextricable parts of the 'new journalism', and the failure to stop the one necessarily meant a failure to stop the other.

With sport and gambling went sensation. It had always been the staple diet of the Sunday papers, and had spawned many local papers with the title of *Police News.* Some would have included in the category the scandal-mongering papers like the *World*, but generally it was confined to those which traded heavily on the news of crime and criminals. The success of the *Star* during the Ripper murders, and of the *Pall Mall Gazette* during the Maiden Tribute affair indicate how far the 'new journalism' came to benefit from sensation. Again, however, there was perhaps less novelty in this than was claimed. *The Times* had always benefited from its lengthy law reports, and in the 1880s its reporting of divorce cases was only slightly less 'sensational' than Frank Harris's in the *Evening News.*[275]

News, sensational or otherwise, was not the only ingredient of the

'new journalism'. The newspaper was coming to resemble more closely
the magazine, in response to the demand for papers to be entertaining
as well as informative. One aspect of this was the emergence of the
serialised novel in the ordinary press. It began in 1871 in the Tillotsons'
weekly *Bolton Journal and Guardian,* extending afterwards to their
chain of Lancashire papers.[276] In 1873 a new novel by Miss Braddon
appeared in serial form simultaneously in eight provincial papers, from
Plymouth to Cardiff, from Dundee to Dublin. The Press Association,
and the merchants of partly printed sheets were mainly responsible for
this. Later in 1889 Hawmon Quezal opened a 'novel bureau', and the
Tillotsons soon established their own 'Fiction Bureau' under Philip
Gibbs.[277]

The lighter touch was also evident in the increasing use of illustration,
which had hitherto collected a somewhat dubious reputation with the
woodcuts appearing in the weeklies. The first paper to be based upon
the art of illustration had been the *Illustrated London News* in 1842,
followed in 1855 by the *Illustrated Times.* In 1861 came the *Penny
Illustrated Paper,* in 1869 the *Graphic,* and in 1874 the *Pictorial World.*
The first pictorial daily was the *Evening Illustrated Paper* of 1881, and
the first daily morning paper the *Daily Mirror.* It was one of the few
developments that escaped harsh criticism from those who were
opposed to the 'new journalism', for there was little question that it
served to broaden the horizons of its audience and to reduce
parochialism, and not least to familiarise voters with politicians, which,
as the great Liberal cartoonist F.C. Gould noted, put a great
responsibility on the cartoonist.[278]

Finally, there were what might be called the linguistic aspects of the
'new journalism'. Journalism has probably always been saddled with
the blame for what some consider deteriorations in the use of language,
as J.F. Stephen in 1856 for example:

> our intelligent middle classes are not known for extensive reading,
> and it is easy to observe in their dialect, whenever it becomes at all
> pronounced, traces of the fact that they form their style upon the
> newspapers, and more especially on their penny-a-lining
> department.[279]

The language he complained of, however, tended to be flowery and
artificial. Compared to this, Frederick Greenwood, at the end of the
century, found the language of the 'new journalism' refreshing, with
its 'unpedantic, nervous, flexible good English of common life. . .which

men of education used in their talk and in their letters'.[280]   He
admitted that familiarity could be carried too far, and there was general
agreement that the simple direct language of the *Westminster Gazette*
was hardly to be compared to the simplistic disjunctive prose of the
Daily Mail. Criticism was directed mainly to the literalisation of spoken
slang, and to diverse effects which the press had upon grammar, syntax
and style, and upon the very mode of thought. It was complained that
the reiteration of error lent to it a spurious authority, that a limited
vocabulary led to sheer tedium, and that developments since 1855, or
at least since 1870, had led to a general acceptance of an inferior
standard of language use. This sort of criticism, however, easily shaded
off into a patronising analysis of the 'public' who deserved what they
got, because they demanded no more. It would take an extended essay
in literary criticism to explore this issue adequately, but it is one which
should not be forgotten in an assessment of the development of the
press during this period. Such an analysis would have to explore the
ways in which such usages made communication more, or less difficult,
precise, incisive, colourful, and in a real sense meaningful, and how
this affected the social and political role of the press.

In default of such an extended analysis the contrast between the
new and the old journalism may be succinctly illustrated in the form of
two mottoes, the one of James Henderson's *Weekly Budget* of 1861,
'To inform, to instruct, to amuse'; the other of C.A. Pearson's *Pearson's
Weekly* thirty years later, 'To Interest, to Elevate, to Amuse'.[281] They
applied to weekly papers, but could not less appropriately have applied
to the spirit of journalism in its entirety. The difference in tone is clear.
No longer was the paper 'to inform', but merely 'to Interest'; no longer
was it 'to instruct', but 'to Elevate'; no longer was it 'to amuse' but 'to
Amuse'. By the 1890s the reader was expected to be intellectually more
passive, morally less confident, attracted less by the prospect of greater
wisdom than by that of 'Elevated' status, and he was now appealed to
in a shrill capitalised format. This was not true of all journals or
journalists, of course, but it was a change characteristic of the general
spirit and informing values of journalism in general by the turn of the
century.

A Note on Numbers: It is difficult in such an open profession to estimate the
numbers engaged in it, but it seems probable that they grew somewhat faster than
did the numbers in the professional classes as a whole from 1851 to 1911. The
aggregate of 'authors, editors and writers', and 'other literary' persons in 1851 was
2,645 men and 106 women; for 'journalists, authors, editors and reporters' in
1911 it was 12,030 men and 1,756 women. This would have been about one and
a quarter to one and a third times the growth of the professions as a whole
according to Reader, op.cit., pp.152ff and 184.

5 THE PRESS AND PARTY POLITICS

I Quantities of Newspapers

The most striking consequence of the changes of the 1850s and 1860s was the multiplication in the number of newspapers. From the political point of view it was generally reckoned that the daily press was the crucial area of growth. In the counties the weeklies may have held their own, but the political balance was in any case tilting towards the towns, especially towards the large towns and the emerging conurbations. Here the daily press was supreme.

Tables 14-24 show the political distribution of provincial dailies in England in election years from 1868 to 1910. The first and most obvious point is that the total number, morning and evening, rose rapidly from 43 in 1868 to 139 in 1886. A fall in the number of 'independent' papers was responsible for reducing the total to 126 in 1892, but the ground was recovered by 1895, and a peak reached in 1900 with 171 dailies. Thereafter the process of amalgamation and the ravages of competition reduced the total to only 121 in 1910.[1] In 1868 36 of the 43 dailies were morning papers (83 per cent), but the proportion was reduced to under 50 per cent in 1880 by the emergence of the evening press in the 1870s, and by 1885 to about 42 per cent. It was then held fairly steady until a drop to 38 per cent in 1910. At first the mornings had been concentrated in towns of established press activity, six of them in 1868 with three each, and Liverpool with five. There were only seven evening papers, however, in the whole of the English provinces. Only six towns had both morning and evening papers, nine had only a morning, and one had only an evening. By 1874 the change was already noticeable. Nine towns had three or more mornings, but now 15 had at least one evening, with 12 having both morning and evening papers. By 1880, and still more by 1885, the evening press had reached a dominant position in terms of numbers. By the latter date 11 towns had three or more mornings, 8 had three or more evenings, while 25 had just an evening paper. Competition between more than two evening papers, a feature of the 1880s, was a short-lived phenomenon.[2] (See Table 25.)

These changes seem to have affected neither party very greatly in terms of numbers. In 1868 19 of the broadly Liberal papers were mornings (73 per cent). This proportion rose in 1874 to 80 per cent, but had fallen by 1880 to 56 per cent, and steadily thereafter to 31 per cent in 1900, recovering slightly to 35 per cent in 1910. After the 1870s the Conservatives caught up on the evening front, in that marginally more of their papers were evenings than was so on the Liberal side. (See Tables 26 and 27.) In absolute terms, although the extent of their domination did not survive the 1870s, the Liberals maintained a good lead over the Conservatives in the morning and in the halfpenny evening press. They may have done rather worse than these figures suggest, because the so-called 'independent' and 'neutral' papers began swamping the overtly partisan ones in the 1890s, and it is possible that a majority of them were Conservatively inclined. The parties argued over the allegiance of these papers, however, and there has been as yet no analysis of them to determine their political character. It is worth noting none the less that even this large pool of possible Conservative support did not outweigh the quantity of Liberal dailies until 1900.

Tables 28 and 29 show the political distribution of all English papers, provincial and metropolitan, from 1837 to 1887. In London, where 'independent' and 'neutral' papers must be disregarded, as they were mostly 'class and trade' papers, the Liberal lead was narrowest in 1842, at 26 to 22. By the time the stamp had been repealed, however, there were more than twice as many Liberal as Conservative papers. The London press was notoriously against the Liberals in 1874, but even so they maintained a lead of 16, and by 1877 had restored the two to one ratio, and managed to keep this until 1881. The Conservative revival then began to bite, with the Liberals losing over 15 and the Conservatives gaining eight papers by 1883. This, it is important to note, was before the split over Home Rule, which narrowed the gap again, to eight in 1887. In the provinces the lead was always more substantial in absolute terms, but the proportions remained much the same. Liberal papers succeeded in outnumbering the Conservatives by two to one only after the repeal of the stamp, and maintained it only into the 1870s. They kept a lead of some 100 to 150, however, until at least 1887.

If we now look at the distribution in terms of the shares taken by each party of the morning and evening press, we see that until 1895 the Liberals succeeded in holding 50 per cent or more of the morning press, as against the Conservatives' 31 per cent in 1885 and 1886, and an average of 20 per cent to 30 per cent. In the evening press the Liberals managed to increase their share from around 43 per cent in the 1870s and 1880s, to about 50 per cent in the 1890s and 1900s. The

Conservatives, despite their anxiety about their position in that year, never did so well as in 1880, when they held 36 per cent of the evenings. (See Tables 26 and 27.)

It seems clear, then, that in numerical terms the decline of Liberal press representation between the 1860s and the 1900s was slight. The clear Liberal domination of the 1860s and 1870s had been due largely to the lack of a Conservative press, and the development of this in the 1880s and after served to obscure somewhat the fact that the Liberal press shared about equally in the general expansion of those years. (See Table 24.)

Finally, as a measure of quality and type of influence, there was the distribution of papers according to price. (See Table 26.) Reputedly the weightiest journal was the penny morning, the monarch of the golden age. There were never less than 30 of them after 1874, and at most 38 in 1874 and 1886. Until the latter year the Liberals had more than half of them, and always held more than a third. The Conservatives, on the other hand, never managed to obtain a third. From twenty or so in the 1870s, the Liberals came down to only a dozen in 1906, but the Conservatives only ever had as many as eleven, in 1885 and 1886, and were down to eight by 1900. The evening press was mostly a halfpenny press, but here too the Liberals reigned, with over half of them in the 1890s and 1900s, while the Conservatives managed less than a third in 1892, and only a quarter in 1910. Excluding the Infield chain of the 1890s and early 1900s, the Liberals also led the Conservatives in the small halfpenny morning provincial press.

It is difficult in these figures to detect the catastrophic decline in the Liberal press which contemporaries claimed in the 1900s. To understand this view it is necessary to look more closely at the individual papers.

II The Liberal Supremacy

The Conservatives traditionally looked upon the provincial press with suspicion and anxiety. It was admitted on all sides to be dominated by political Liberalism. Since 1836, when the reduction in the stamp duty had resulted in a spate of new papers, most of them Liberal, the tide had run heavily in the Liberal favour.[3] As Liberals were wont to do, they tended to regard this as in the nature of things. The political premises upon which the cheap press had been built were, after all, essentially Liberal premises, and as an economic enterprise it was equally Liberal in motivation. The extension of the franchise, the redistribution of seats in favour of the urban areas, the provision of universal elementary education, and an unmistakably more prosperous country, all of which were essential to the development of a large cheap press, were all seen to be changes favourable to the Liberals. It was natural they should also achieve supremacy in the press.

In London in 1870 the Liberals had the *Daily News* and the *Daily Telegraph* (the two leading dailies in terms of circulation), the new *Daily Chronicle,* the halfpenny *Echo,* the penny evening society paper the *Glowworm,* the twopenny evening *Pall Mall Gazette* and the threepenny *Morning Advertiser,* still Liberal, though less radical than previously. In 1869 they had lost the radical *Morning Star* which had closed, and the *Globe* which had been sold to Conservatives. The evening edition of the *Daily News,* the *Express,* also closed in that year. Ranged against them on the Conservative side were the penny morning *Standard,* two threepenny mornings, *The Times* and the *Morning Post,* the penny evening *Globe,* and the evening edition of the *Standard.* The Conservatives had lost the *Morning Herald* which had closed in 1869. *The Times,* despite its 'independent' tag, counted for much, but it was past the height of its power, and the soaring circulations of the *Daily News,* the *Daily Telegraph* and, a little later, of the *Daily Chronicle,* plus a marked Liberal advantage in the evening press, made the London of 1870 journalistically a Liberal capital.

The supremacy was even plainer in the provinces, as the previous section of this chapter has shown in some detail. In the 16 towns with daily papers in 1868 there were returned twenty-six Liberal MPs, eight Conservatives and one Liberal-Conservative. By 1874 the 29 towns with dailies returned 27 Liberal MPs, 18 Conservatives, one Liberal-Conservative and one Radical. There was in 1874 no Conservative daily paper in Birmingham, Huddersfield, Darlington, Hull or Leicester, and they were outnumbered by three to one in Liverpool and Leeds. If the weekly press is included in the picture, there were only 294 ostensibly Conservative papers, plus 66 Liberal-Conservative ones, against 489 Liberals. If it was true that as the Conservatives claimed 'independent' usually indicated a Liberal paper, then the domination would have been only that much more complete.

It was somewhat ironical, then, when in the year in which the Liberals had the greatest lead in the press that they had ever had or were ever to have, Gladstone was defeated at the polls. Similarly in 1906, just when Liberals were most anxious about their press, their party ironically came to power in a landslide. These famous instances of the divergence of journalistic and political fortune are salutary reminders that quantity was not everything. If more were known of the circulations involved, particularly for the provincial press, it might be easier to establish what the connections were, but such information is extremely elusive. Instead it is proposed to examine the state of the press in the localities before 1890.

The North East

Here was a stronghold not only of Liberalism but of republicanism and Chartism. Newcastle, Sunderland, Darlington and the Shields provided one of the most secure political bases for Liberalism in the whole country until the end of the century, and there was a Liberal press of appropriate strength. In Newcastle there were two penny morning papers of substance on the Liberal side, the *Northern Daily Express* and the *Newcastle Daily Chronicle.* The first was founded by John Watson in 1855, taken over by a wealthy grocer, W.C. Marshall, and had a flourishing career in the late 1850s and early 1860s. In 1865 a company was established by William Saunders and Edward Spender, together with some of their relatives, and a group from Hull including William Hunt, editor of Saunders and Spender's *Eastern Morning News,* and A.K. Rollit, solicitor and later mayor and MP for Hull. The company ran the *Express* until in the 1870s it was sold to Thomas Hedley, a Northumberland colliery owner. The paper survived until Hedley's death in 1886, mainly on the earnings of its monopoly evening edition.[4] The *Chronicle* was founded by Joseph Cowen, a radical politician and a good businessman, Liberal MP for Newcastle from 1874 to 1886. The paper's manager was R.B. Reed, secretary of the National Reform Union, while W.E. Adams, a republican, edited the weekly edition. From 1874 to 1877 the talented Scots journalist James Annand edited the daily paper, but then departed over a conflict with Cowen over the Eastern Question. Cowen's Russophobia was to lead him and his paper away from the party fold in the 1880s, a movement reinforced by Cowen's opposition to Gladstone's Irish policy and to the Egyptian campaign.[5] It was hardly surprising either that he should have retired from politics in 1886, or that other more orthodox Liberal papers have arisen to challenge the *Chronicle.* In 1869 William Hayward, later editor of the *Northern Daily Express,* and William Brignall had started a radical temperance evening paper, the *Newcastle Daily Telegraph,* but this closed in 1872. Newcastle had to wait until 1885 for another attempt to found a radical rival, when the colliery owner James Joicey, Liberal MP for Chester-le-Street 1885-1906, purchased the *Northern Weekly Leader,* then edited by James Annand at South Shields, and brought it out as a daily paper.

This was a direct answer to Cowen's apostasy, Annand editing it as a consistently radical Gladstonian paper until 1895 when , for the second time in his career, he came into conflict with his proprietor and resigned.[6]

South Shields had boasted a halfpenny evening Liberal paper since 1855, the *South Shields Gazette,* but this had only been a telegraphic sheet until 1864. Then J.C. Stevenson, a member of a large local chemical manufacturing family, mayor of South Shields in 1867, and Liberal MP 1868-95, turned it into a more substantial paper. In the same year R. Whitecross and H.A. York left the paper to found a halfpenny Liberal evening paper on the other bank of the Tyne in North Shields, the *Shields Daily News.* The *Gazette* was probably the stronger of the two, and claimed to have the second largest daily circulation in the north-east in 1873. Its political weight was slight, however, until James Annand became editor from 1877 to 1885, when it grew to be an important local radical voice.[7]

In 1873 Samuel Storey, mayor of Sunderland 1876, 1877 and 1880, its Liberal MP 1881-95, and chairman of the Durham County Council 1894-1905, successfully established with the help of other local Liberals the halfpenny morning *Sunderland Daily Echo.* In 1884 he managed to buy the Conservative *Northern Evening Mail* in West Hartlepool, and seriously damaged the Conservative press in Durham by so doing. Storey was best known for his co-operation with Andrew Carnegie in founding a Liberal newspaper syndicate in the 1880s, but this is discussed more fully in a later section.[8]

The Liberal press in Darlington in the 1860s had been run by Henry King Spark, proprietor of the weekly *Darlington and Stockton Times.* In 1870, however, a Scot, J. Hyslop Bell, was invited by a rival Liberal group, led by the Peases, to establish a competitor, and the halfpenny morning *Northern Echo* was founded, soon to be edited by the young W.T. Stead. Bell already owned the weekly *South Durham Mercury,* but, under Stead until 1880, the *Echo* was probably the most impressive provincial newspaper in the country, and when the Eastern Question flared up Stead made it a voice to be reckoned with far beyond the confines of South Durham, and in opposition to Cowen's *Chronicle.* For the next twenty years the paper was less dramatically edited by John Marshall, and by 1887 was making a loss. Bell sold it to a company, of which he became a director.[9]

Yorkshire

The major Yorkshire Liberal daily was the *Leeds Mercury,* the 'orthodox' paper of the Baines family. It had become a daily in 1861, the delay being due to the Baines's reluctance to accept Sunday working.[10] The Baineses were very active in local politics, and from 1859 to 1874 Edward Baines was Liberal MP for Leeds. From 1870 to 1887 the editor was T. Wemyss Reid, an enterprising and politically minded journalist, a pioneer of Lobby reporting, and after 1876 a leading member of the Leeds Liberal Association. He was in close contact with the national party leaders, and having imbibed the Baines's style of Liberalism, adhered closely to Gladstonian policy. He remained suspicious of the 'new journalism', and the *Mercury* always toed a strongly Nonconformist line on issues such as sport and the theatre. By the 1890s it had begun to decline as a business, and efforts to rescue it by Reid and the local Liberals failed, vain appeals having been made to Herbert Gladstone.[11]

Against the moderate Leeds Liberals represented by the *Mercury* there was the *Leeds Express,* founded in 1857 by a group of Liberals including W.E. Forster. It was soon in the hands of the journalist F.R. Spark, who was also a local councillor, and the ex-Chartist R. Meek Carter, MP for Leeds 1868-76, and president of the Radical Reform League. It ran into financial difficulties in the 1870s, having become an evening paper in 1867, and was taken over entirely by Spark until he disposed of it in 1892. At about the time of Meek's departure the Leeds Liberals resolved their differences, and in consequence the papers ceased to represent rival factions. This was just as well, for ranged against them was perhaps the strongest Conservative provincial daily, the *Yorkshire Post,* and the only evening paper in the city, Mackaskie's *Leeds Daily News* (1872-).[12]

In Bradford there was less formidable opposition to the Liberals. William Byles had founded the *Bradford Observer* in 1834, with the assistance of local Liberals, including the uncle of the famous local politician Alfred Illingworth. It became a daily in 1868, the delay here being due to the absence of competition in Bradford. Three rival Liberal papers appeared in the city between 1858 and 1872, but none seriously threatened the *Observer.* In 1872 Byles used it to support the local MP, W.E. Forster, against radicals who were dissatisfied with the latter's Education Act. The radicals tried unsuccessfully to buy Byles out, and then to start their own paper, which lasted but a few months. By the end of the decade these divisions had healed, and in 1884 the Bradford Liberal Club gave a celebratory dinner to the paper.[13]

Joseph Woodhead took over the *Huddersfield Examiner* in 1852 from a company of local Liberals, and made it into an important

exponent of Nonconformist Liberalism. In 1871 it became an evening
paper. Woodhead had been elected to the council in 1868, was mayor
in 1876, and MP for Spen Valley from 1885 to 1892. His main rival
was the Conservative George Harper, proprietor of the *Huddersfield
Daily Chronicle,* who was not active politically, but was more
prominent in journalistic circles than Woodhead, becoming president
of the Provincial Newspaper Society in 1868.[14]

The Liberal press in Sheffield was in the hands of the Leader family,
proprietors of the *Sheffield Independent* since 1829. During the last
half of the century the editor and proprietors were R.E. and J.D. Leader,
the former the founder of the local Liberal Association. Theirs was a
Liberalism comparable to that of the Baineses in Leeds, but they were
much less politically active.[15] Sheffield radicals, the leaders of
temperance and Nonconformity, had been dissatisfied with the tone
of the *Independent* since the early 1870s. Hyslop Bell characterised the
situation in 1874 as 'too much Leng and Leader', Leng being the
proprietor of the Conservative *Sheffield Daily Telegraph.* It should
rather be, he thought, 'an embodiment of Truth, Courage and Christian
Patriotism'.[16] No radical alternative materialised, however, The
Independent ran into financial difficulties in the 1890s, and was sold to
a company headed by a couple of radical journalists from Lincolnshire,
with but little and grudging assistance from the leaders of Sheffield
radicalism.[17]

Hull had no daily paper until William Saunders established the
'independent', but decidedly Liberal, *Eastern Morning News* in 1864,
under the direction of William Hunt, a West Country journalist. Hunt
quickly managed to mop up some of the older weeklies, and in 1870 he
started an evening paper. Not until 1884 was a rival halfpenny morning
established by J.A. Cooke, a Liberal proprietor of long standing in Hull,
and even then the *Eastern Morning News* continued to be by far the
weightiest local daily, to which ample tribute was paid in 1878 by local
dignitaries at its fourteenth anniversary dinner. Hunt himself, while
active with local public work, always refused to enter politics. The
paper had been made a limited company in 1872, but Saunders
remained chairman and chief proprietor until his death in 1895. He
had by the 1880s become a devoted disciple of Henry George, and was
closely associated with Joseph Chamberlain in the election campaign of
1885, when he himself won East Hull. In London Saunders, the
founder of the Central Press agency, helped Michael Davitt and Helen
Taylor found the radical *Democrat.* His nephew, J.A. Spender, later the
famous editor of the *Westminster Gazette,* was editor of the *Eastern*

Morning News from 1886 until 1891, which continued within
Saunders's lifetime at least to be a radical paper of some note.[18]
   The only other Yorkshire towns to have Liberal dailies of note were
Middlesbrough and York. In 1859 H. Gilzean-Reid began the halfpenny
North Eastern Daily Gazette. He was an energetic Aberdonian, an
active Liberal of radical inclinations, who extended his newspaper
interests with great success in the latter part of the century, incidentally
participating in the Storey-Carnegie syndicate of the 1880s. He was
briefly Liberal MP for Aston Manor 1885-6, but more prominent in the
upper reaches of journalism, especially in the Institute of Journalists
which he had helped to found. In York William and John Hargrove
turned their old *York Herald* into a penny morning paper in 1874, and
brought out the halfpenny *Yorkshire Evening Press* in 1882. They had
no serious rival or opponent, although in 1884 the Conservative weekly
Yorkshire Gazette became a morning paper for some ten months, and
reputedly lost £20,000 in the process. One of the family, A.E. Hargrove,
president of the Provincial Newspaper Society from 1857 to 1858, was
also a JP, mayor of York in 1869, and chairman of the Liberal Election
Committee.

Lancashire

This was the most populous English county, the heartland of the
industrial revolution, containing the largely Conservative port of
Liverpool and the largely Liberal city of Manchester, both before the
end of the century the centre of large conurbations. Even at the mid-
century it was a key county, politically speaking. If Liberals were
traders and manufacturers this was where to find them.
   The first substantial morning paper to be established in Manchester
was Alexander Ireland's *Manchester Examiner and Times,* in 1855 at a
penny. The *Manchester Guardian* followed two weeks later, at twopence
until 1857. The *Examiner,* edited by A.C. Paulton, was a radical paper,
backed by John Bright and other free traders. The *Guardian,* on the
other hand, was never a 'party' paper in that sense, and its policy has
been characterised as a broader one of the 'cross-bench mind'. Its
proprietors from 1826 had been J.E. Taylor and J. Garnett. By 1861
Taylor's son, and his brother-in-law Peter Allen, were in charge of what
was by then a very profitable business. In 1868 they began to publish
the ostensibly 'independent' halfpenny *Manchester Evening News.* The
Examiner lost some of its identity with the decline of the old
Manchester School, and after some initial hesitation over Home Rule
began rapidly to decline in the later 1880s. It was sold to Unionists in

1889, and eventually wound up in 1894, which left the *Guardian* a free field on the Liberal side in the local press, as well as a substantial niche in the 'national' press. The Conservatives had T.S. Sowler's *Manchester Courier,* made into a penny daily in 1864. In 1874, despite the *Guardian* and the *Examiner,* the Liberals lost two of the three Manchester seats, and in the same year Sowler launched the halfpenny *Manchester Evening Mail.* The *Guardian*'s proprietors had little to do with local politics. Garnett had been a vigorous opponent of the radical 'machine' in Manchester in the 1840s and 1850s, and in 1857 he and Taylor had helped finance two Palmerstonian candidates who had defeated the sitting radical MPs, Milner Gibson and Bright. Such local divisions, however, were healed by the time Taylor's nephew, C.P. Scott, became editor in 1872, and Taylor played no part in either local or national politics after this. But Scott entered public and political life in the 1870s, and eventually became the MP for Leigh from 1895 to 1906.[20]

The merchants of Liverpool were more Conservative than the manufacturers of Manchester, but this did not prevent a Liberal press from flourishing there. It was indeed the home of the earliest provincial daily, Charles Willmer's Liberal *Northern Daily Times* (1853-61).[21] In 1855 Michael Whitty, proprietor of the weekly *Liverpool Journal,* and Chief Constable of the city 1835-48, founded the *Liverpool Daily Post,* the chief organ of Liverpool Liberalism for many years. Shortly after Whitty's death in 1873 the editor, an ex-*Morning Star* leader writer, Edward Russell, became joint proprietor with A.G. Jeans, a member of a family with important Scottish Liberal newspaper interests. Russell was briefly a Liberal MP, Glasgow (Bridgeton), 1885-7, and became a political confidante of Lord Rosebery.[22] Another 'more moderate' Liberal paper had been started by the Egerton Smiths, the *Liverpool Daily Mercury,* a daily since 1858, and edited in the 1880s by an ex-manager of the Press Association, John Lovell. In 1871 another Liberal weekly, the *Liverpool Albion,* was made into a daily paper by the Bean family. The old Chartist Thomas Frost thought its Liberalism tempered much by local influence and commercial considerations, more Whiggish and less advanced than the *Post.* Indeed, it quickly passed into the hands of the Conservative B.H. Grindley, in 1872, who ran it as an evening paper for ten years, after which it was turned over to a company headed by some leading Conservative politicians. They ran it as a morning paper until it ceased publication in 1885. The most important Conservative paper, however, was Charles Tinling's *Liverpool Daily Courier,* edited by J.A. Willox, a

man prominent in newspaper organisations and Conservative MP for
Everton from 1891 to 1900. Tinling had been the first to produce an
evening paper in the city, the *Liverpool Evening Express* in 1870,
Russell and Jeans's *Liverpool Echo* following in 1879.[23]

The two other most prominent Lancashire Liberal proprietors were
George Toulmin and W.F. Tillotson. Toulmin was from 1860 owner
of the *Preston Guardian,* the paper on which Wemyss Reid of the *Leeds
Mercury* had served his apprenticeship. In 1886 Toulmin began the
daily *Lancashire Evening Post* in Preston, having already with the help
of his brother and 'the cordial support of the Liberal Party', established
the *Blackburn Times* and the *Warrington Examiner.* The *Examiner,*
competed with Mackie's chain of papers in Lancashire and Cheshire,
and spawned a chain of its own before long. Blackburn was later to
boast of a more important paper than the *Times,* when H. Gilzean-Reid
and T.P. Ritzema established the *Northern Daily Telegraph,* edited at
first by Jesse Quail, and then with the assistance of the young
A.G. Gardiner.[24] Toulmin also had interests in Bolton, but this was
really the Tillotsons's territory. In 1867 they had started the first
entirely self-supporting halfpenny evening provincial paper, the *Bolton
Evening News.* The chief proprietor, W.F. Tillotson, was to become
treasurer of the local Liberal Association in 1889, and his son followed
him as treasurer, and also became its secretary. The first editor was an
uncompromising Nonconformist, William Brimelow. The Tillotsons
married into the wealthy Lever family, and were in close association
with the Thomassons, a rich spinning family with unimpeachable
Liberal-radical connections. The Tillotsons were also good businessmen,
and were foremost in the provinces in exploiting the evening and
sporting press.[25]

The Midlands

The *Birmingham Daily Post* was begun in 1857 by a radical Irishman,
J.F. Feeney, and a Scot, J. Jaffray. From 1862 until 1898 it was edited
by an active local Liberal, a founder of the National Liberal Federation,
J. Thackeray Bunce. When Feeney died in 1869 his son had already
been in charge for six years, and in due course he became treasurer of
the National Liberal Union, making the *Post* an important ally of
Joseph Chamberlain. Jaffray had, meanwhile, stood unsuccessfully for
Parliament in 1873. In 1870 the partnership established one of the
early halfpenny evening papers, the *Birmingham Daily Mail.*[26]
Birmingham had had an earlier and more radical morning paper, the
Birmingham Daily Free Press (1855), edited by the radical preacher

George Dawson. This was amalgamated with another radical journal in 1857, the *Birmingham Daily Mercury,* but both ceased in 1858. Dawson entered journalism again in 1871, when he became editor of the *Birmingham Morning News.* He carried on for a couple of years, but the paper was stopped in 1875 when 'its capitalist proprietors gave it up in disgust'.[27] After Home Rule had split the Liberals Gilzean-Reid and Ritzema founded the *Birmingham Daily Argus* in 1891, which was united with the old *Birmingham Gazette* in 1903. Also in 1891 George Cadbury had apparently bought and successfully turned to the Gladstonian cause four weekly papers. But the Unionist *Daily Post* understandably remained pre-eminent in the capital of Unionism.[28]

Nearby Coventry also had a predominantly Liberal press. The oldest example was the weekly *Coventry Herald.* There had been a considerable struggle between moderate and radical Liberals in the 1860s, in which the radicals were worsted. The first Coventry daily did not appear until 1891, when the Iliffe family founded the *Coventry Daily Telegraph.*[29] In Wolverhampton a Scot, Thomas Graham, had established the *Wolverhampton Evening Star* in 1874 with the help of local Liberals. Graham was himself a councillor, and secretary and treasurer of the Staffordshire Liberal Association. In 1878, with the assistance of Andrew Carnegie, he bought three rival papers, and in 1884 played a major part in the Storey-Carnegie syndicate. Finally, at Hanley there was Thomas Potter's *Staffordshire Sentinel,* founded in 1873, and from 1881 run by the radical William Moody.[30]

As so often, the mending of splits within the local Liberal party helped to strengthen the Liberal press in Leicester, by making possible the merger of the moderate *Leicester Chronicle* and the more 'advanced' *Leicester Mercury* in 1864. The radicals continued to have the *South Midlands Free Press,* a weekly founded in 1859. In 1872 William Bradshaw began the first daily paper in the city, the *Leicester Daily Post.* This was followed in 1874 by James Thompson's *Leicester Daily Mercury,* an evening paper, and by the short-lived *Leicester Evening News* (1875-7). The *Mercury,* and in 1883 the *Post,* were bought by Francis Hewitt, a councillor, mayor in 1882, and vice-president of the Leicester Liberal Association. Hewitt also established a number of local weeklies in this area on behalf of the North Leicester Liberals.[31]

In Northampton, the ancient weekly *Northampton Mercury* was the most important journal. It was until 1885 the property of T.E. Dicey, and edited from 1831 to 1871 by the radical G.J. de Wilde. De Wilde eventually found Dicey's Liberalism too mild, and in 1871 started the *Northamptonshire Guardian,* which, however, was soon taken over by

a leading Liberal councillor, S.S. Campion. Meanwhile the *Mercury*
pursued an anti-radical, anti-Bradlaugh Liberalism. On Dicey's death in
1885 Campion bought the paper, after some unsuccessful negotiations
with the Storey-Carnegie syndicate. In 1880 the town was the scene of
a fierce newspaper battle. Its first daily had appeared in 1878, Arlidge's
penny *Midland County Times* (1878-81). In 1880 Campion tried
unsuccessfully to start a rival, the *Northampton Evening Mail,* and an
ex-editor of the *Mercury,* D.A. Peachey, successfully founded the
Northamptonshire Daily Reporter as a halfpenny evening paper. Taken
over in 1884 by Dicey, the latter fell into Campion's hands in the
following year. Meanwhile the Conservatives had started the
Northampton Evening Herald, which lasted only until 1881, and the
more successful *Northampton Daily Chronicle.* When the dust had
cleared, however it seemed that the Liberals had been left clearly
dominant.[32]

In Nottingham the Liberals had the advantage of the first daily in
the city, the *Nottingham Daily Express,* run by J.W. Jevons, who was
later to be a councillor. It was always a rather radical and strongly
Nonconformist paper, and gradually absorbed other local Liberal
journals; in 1870 Charles Sutton's weekly *Nottingham Review;* in 1887
the *Nottingham Daily Journal,* started in 1864 by W. and A. Bradshaw.
For the Conservatives Thomas Forman continued the weighty
Nottingham Daily Guardian, started in 1861. The *Express* was sold to
E. Rennals in 1888, and edited on rigorous and radical Nonconformist
principles under the editorship of John Derry from 1891 to 1895. The
Guardian, in 1878, and the *Express* and the *Journal* in 1885, each
established an evening paper.[33]

The West Country

This was one of the original strongholds of the provincial press, and
despite challenges from the expanding industrial areas to the north it
remained during this period the home of several leading provincial
journals. Thomas Latimer's radical *Western Times* in Exeter had the
highest reputation. Latimer was a most active Liberal local politician,
although Exeter was predictably a Conservative city, and never elected
a Liberal mayor. In 1868, however, two years after the *Times* had
become a penny morning paper, with a halfpenny evening edition, two
Liberal MPs were returned.[34]

Plymouth was more Liberal than Exeter, and Latimer's brother Isaac
had been since 1847 editor and proprietor of the weekly *Plymouth
Journal,* founded by local Liberals in 1842. In 1860 he met the

challenge of the new *Western Morning News* by starting the *Western
Daily Mercury,* which he ran until 1892, when he sold it to the
Gladstonian Liberal MP for Launceston, Thomas Owen. Isaac became
mayor of Plymouth in 1871, and chairman of the Plymouth Liberal
Party in 1885.[35] The *Western Morning News* was the idea of William
Saunders and his more Whiggish brother-in-law Edward Spender,
together with a journalist William Hunt, who had hitherto worked only
on Conservative papers. They began it in 1860 as an 'independent'
daily. By 1866 the partners, who were already running dailies in
Newcastle and Hull, founded the Western Morning News Company.
Spender left the paper temporarily in 1862 to edit Saunders' Central
Press agency, and in 1864 Hunt went to Hull to manage the *Eastern
Morning News.* Until his death in 1878, however, the real editor of the
Western Morning News was Spender, which gave it a decidedly Whiggish
tone, and even led it into the Adullamite Cave in 1867. It was anti-
radical, and became anti-Home Rule, but by that time Saunders had
severed his connection with the paper, sometime in the 1870s.[36]

   Bristol was another of the original centres of English journalism. Of
its major weeklies in 1855 three were Liberal, and one Conservative.
Three years later P.S. Macliver, a radical Scots Congregationalist, who
had learnt his journalism in Newcastle, started the *Western Daily Press,*
edited by Walter Reid, and in 1877 he added it to the halfpenny *Bristol
Evening News.* Macliver was the Liberal MP for Plymouth from 1880
to 1885, and in the latter year president of the Provincial Newspaper
Society. In 1859 the Somertons, proprietors of the weekly *Bristol
Mercury,* began the *Bristol Daily Post,* a less radical Liberal paper,
which changed hands in 1884, and added an evening edition in 1899.
Again the Conservatives were very strong, however, having the
prestigious *Bristol Times and Mirror,* a penny daily since 1865, owned
by Leech and Taylor until 1884, and edited in the 1870s by a future
editor of the *Yorkshire Post,* Charles Pebody. The *Bristol Evening Times*
its evening companion, was started in 1894.[37]

   The remaining Liberal papers of note in the West were all weeklies.
In Yeovil Charles Clinker had amalgamated the *Western Gazette* with
the old *Western Flying Post* in 1867. After local Liberals had refused
to buy the paper from him in 1886 he sold it to the Conservatives, and
the Liberals' own foundation the *Western Chronicle* did not prove
successful.[38] In Gloucester T.H. Chance was proprietor (1872-1906),
and editor (1872-89), of the old *Gloucester Journal.* He claimed that
it was 'not aggressively Liberal', but it boasted the services of the two
most accomplished London Letter writers, both on the Liberal side,

Edward Spender and H.W. Lucy. In 1884 he bought out the other local
Liberal paper, Charles Jeynes's *Gloucester Mercury*. Finally, in Hereford
Charles Anthony had established the *Hereford Times* in 1832, with the
support of local Liberals, and it had since been a major ally of the
party. Anthony was elected six times mayor of the city, and stood as a
Liberal candidate for Parliament in 1867.[39]

The Eastern Counties

Norwich was really the only other major centre of Liberal journalism,
and was, as were the western towns, an old centre of the provincial
press. For some years R.M. Bacon had run the *Norwich Mercury* as a
Liberal weekly, but some more radical local Liberals, John Copeman,
J.H. Tillett and J.J. Colman founded their own *Norfolk News* in 1845.
In 1870 both the *Mercury* and the *News* launched morning papers,
respectively the *Eastern Daily Journal,* which lasted only six months,
and the *Eastern Daily Press.* The *News* and the *Press* were quite closely
involved in local politics in a notoriously corrupt constituency. Tillett,
a founder and editor of the *News,* was elected MP in 1870, upon the
unseating of the Conservative by petition. A counter-petition in 1871
removed Tillett, but the Liberals won the new contest in the person of
J.J. Colman. In the election of 1874 Colman was again returned, but
Tillett was defeated, until a by-election of 1875, only to be unseated
again on petition, whereupon the borough was disfranchised until 1880.
Both Colman and Tillett were then returned without trouble, Colman
continuing to represent the city until 1895.[40]

Meanwhile, Colman, the mustard manufacturer, had from its
foundation in 1862 been the largest single shareholder in the Suffolk
and Essex Newspaper Company. Part of this property consisted of the
Liberal *Ipswich Express,* and the more radical *Suffolk Mercury.* The
company was wound up in 1870, and Colman got an old director of the
Norfolk News Company, and subsequent editor of the *Chester and
Birkenhead Observer,* F.W. Wilson, to help T.R. Elkington manage the
both papers. The *Express* was stopped, and in 1874 the *Eastern Daily
Times* was established, and remained the dominant daily in the area
until the end of the period. Wilson rose to high position in the
journalist establishment, and became Liberal MP for Mid-Norfolk from
1885 to 1900. In 1885 the price of the *Daily Times* was reduced to a
halfpenny, and Elkington put in charge of a new halfpenny evening, in
Ipswich, the *Star of the East.* Colman, Wilson, Elkington and others of
this group were also instrumental, as we shall see, in establishing the
London evening *Star* in 1888.[41]

The Liberal press was predictably weakest in the south and south-east of the country, mostly agricultural areas destitute of large towns and industry, traditional Conservative territory. There was no major daily here, and the Liberals did not control the evening press. In Lincolnshire the *Lincoln, Rutland and Stamford Mercury* was usually on the Liberal side, although ostensibly 'independent'. A few attempts were made by local Liberals to found newspapers in their interest, but none were very successful.[42] In Wiltshire there was the old *Salisbury and Winchester Journal,* Liberal until 1889 when it became Unionist, and the *Salisbury Times and South Wiltshire Gazette,* started in 1868, and sold to the mayor and the secretary of the local Liberal association in 1883. In 1876 the Marquis of Lansdowne, Lord Fitzmaurice, Sir Thomas Grove, the Rt. Hon. E.P. Bouverie, and G.R. Fuller founded the *Wiltshire Times* in the Liberal interest, and in 1878 this was amalgamated with the Liberal *Wiltshire Advertiser.*[43] In Southampton Palmerston helped found the *Hampshire Independent* in 1835, and the local Liberals sold it to T.L. Harmer in 1841. In 1860 the radical *Southampton Times* was started.[44] Finally, in Hertfordshire R. Alston ran the Whiggish *Hertfordshire Mercury* from 1834 to 1884.[45]

There were probably other such papers, but the above at least gives a fairly accurate picture of the strengths of the Liberal press, and of where there was serious Conservative opposition until the 1890s. Until then the Liberal domination was not merely numerical. It was a domination both weighty and qualitative, and gave the Conservatives much to worry about.

III The Conservative Challenge

It was possible to claim that 'the balance of newspaper *power* is uncontestably in favour of the Conservative party' in 1836, with reference only to the London press, and after the split of 1846 it ceased to be the case even there.[46] At a time when the protectionist aristocracy was declining to help C.E. Michele buy the *Morning Post* for £25,000, Disraeli complained that the 'state of our Press is deplorable'.[47] In an attempt to improve matters, he and Lord Stanley tried unsuccessfully in 1850 to buy *John Bull,* and in 1852 Stanley found it necessary to caution Disraeli about making such journalistic forays too public, lest they were accused of using secret service money for the purpose.[48] In May of the following year, however, they did manage to start a sixpenny weekly, *The Press.* This survived for some five years as more or less Disraeli's own organ, and for a further eight years after he had withdrawn his interest from it.[49] He

had written around in the March for financial support, and the response
was a good indication of the problems facing Conservative journalism
at this time. At least three of the replies pleaded poverty on account
of recent election expenses, and the contributions received were only
of the order of £100 and £200 each. Some scepticism was expressed
about the wisdom of trying to start a new paper, although it was agreed
that the existing Tory press, the protectionist *Morning Herald* and the
Peelite *Morning Chronicle,* were unsatisfactory. One of Disraeli's agents
reported in August that 20 of those approached had refused to
contribute, 13 had failed to reply, and 21 had contributed only £445
between them. Things were brighter by the end of the year, however,
when a further £5,750 had been collected or promised in large sums,
and about £490 in small ones. Weeklies had, after all, survived on less,
but the financial state of the paper was never to be healthy. By the
end of the year there was an accumulated loss of £3,103 on running
costs, plus a capital expenditure of £1,613. In June 1854 Disraeli
seems to have forked out £1,500 of his own money.[50] This was a
high price to pay for '2,000 (circulation) and influence in less than six
months', as Stanley claimed.[51] In October Disraeli had demanded cuts
to bring weekly losses down to no more than £50 by the end of the
year. Stanley thought this unwise, because it could be done only by
increasing advertising revenue, which had fallen from £63 in the first
to £10 in the thirteenth week, and to do this he argued would impair
the quality of the journal, making it less attractive to those who
sought a truly party paper. It would, of course, have been politically
damaging to give the paper up at that stage, so, if losses were
unavoidable someone would have to meet them. 'None of our
magnates are very willing to open their purses for such a purpose',
Stanley could do little, and his father would do nothing. 'Can we not',
Stanley therefore suggested, 'find someone who will take the concern
off your hands, and who for the sake of the power and influence
attaching to the post of a newspaper proprietor will run the risk of
present loss. . .'[52] This was a mixture of wishful thinking and an
appeal for political philanthropy. Fortunately cuts and subventions
enabled *The Press* to continue without such help, but, inevitably,
there was an attempt to improve the management of the paper.

    There had been from the start some conflict about style. E.V.
Kenealy, an Irish barrister, later to achieve notoriety in the Tichborne
case, withdrew from *The Press* venture with the following observations:
'plain English, hard-bottomed judgement, extensive learning, and
critical *genius* (for it requires genius), are what are needed for this

paper, not "double firsts", or University (which is always very small)
renown.'[53] Differences over this issue were further indicated when a
correspondent wrote to Disraeli of the editor Samuel Lucas, that he
'does not appear to me to be in the least conversant with *our world*
— and substitutes slang and nambypambysim for wit and simplicity'.[54]
Lucas's position was not an enviable one. He had cautiously pointed
out to Disraeli at an early stage that a political organ of the type which
The Press was supposed to be could at the very best hope only to break
even financially. He also complained that in order to do even that
more space would have to be found for news, and that he needed
help in putting off party men who had a stake in the paper from
contributing long political articles. In March 1854, when it was plain
that his position was in jeopardy, he repeated that no party paper
was capable of paying its way, and that any reduction in his work
would make *The Press* into a mere party paper. His protestations
were to no avail, and in May he was ousted with the assurance that
no opportunity of advancing his interests would be missed by the
proprietors or the party.[55] It is instructive to follow up Lucas's
subsequent career, which made explicit the area of conflict between
the Conservative Party and the press at this time. Immediately Lord
Derby formed an administration, in 1858, Lucas pressed his claim,
and after nine months of effort he stepped into the still warm boots
of a deceased Stamp Distributor at Derby, with a salary of £1,100
a year. Within six months he was after something better, and this
time he put the case without frills.[56]

> If I am allowed to fall through, without any effort on my part,
> and contrary to my wishes, it will create a serious difficulty with
> the class to which I belong.
>   Journalists as a class are opposed to the Conservative party,
> and one element of their opposition is their common conviction
> that our Party is indisposed to treat them considerately. The
> Whigs can point out their Fonblanques, Gregs, Tom Taylors etc.,
> and all satisfactorily placed, while we have simply *no* cases to
> cite as equivalents.

Nine months later he added, 'the Government have just offered John
Delane the permanent undersecretaryship for India. I don't expect
he will take it, but they will nonetheless improve their reputation for
considerate treatment of their literary allies.'[57] The parallels were
pretentious, but the point was significant, and one to be repeated in

subsequent years.

Lucas was succeeded by D.C. Coulton, a former editor of the *Britannia*.[58] Despite the fact that Disraeli's contributions raised the prestige of the paper considerably, circulation grew by only a hundred or so in the next year. It was then that the stamp duty was repealed, and Coulton was quick to point out to his Conservative proprietors the opportunities thus opened to them. A first-class morning paper, he told Disraeli, would be possible at twopence, with no more than three columns of advertising. It was vital to get an early start, he continued, if possible by anticipating repeal slightly. He reckoned £3 profit per thousand papers sold, say £30 a day, plus £20 from advertisements, a total of £300 a week on a circulation of 10,000. The initial capital would have to be in the region of £20,000, but only £5,000 for the first few numbers. Extra advertisements might, he ventured cautiously, for the proprietors had shown themselves somewhat hostile to them, warrant the expense of enlarging the paper eventually. Finally, the whole enterprise could be run from the existing *Press* offices, making a saving on total overheads.[59] It seems clear that Disraeli was unsympathetic and Coulton was soon offering him arguments against repeal which he could use in the Commons! It was a shortsightedness which well characterised Conservative attitudes to the role and the development of the newspaper at the time.[60]

Coulton died in May 1857, and Disraeli retired from active association with the paper in the following year. Its new editor was a man named Haydon, founder of the *New Quarterly Review*. It was sold in 1858, however, to the Protestant publisher Newdigate, with John Seeley's father as editor. In 1866 it was eventually merged with the *St. James's Chronicle*.[61]

It was most probably Haydon who raised the whole question of the Conservative press again in 1860. He asked 'whether the moment has not arrived to improve and develop those organs which, in trying and difficult times, have had the courage to maintain constitutional principles?'[62] The Liberal domination had arisen, he argued, from the fact that extremism was more profitable in politics than Conservatism. He also echoed Lucas in claiming that the Liberals had used their power and position to succour their press, whilst the Conservatives had either been unable or unwilling to do the same. The consequence was 'public opinion, especially in the electoral districts, was gradually weaned from sound Conservatism'. The only remedy, he went on, was to make 'the press a paying property to capitalists who would be disposed to speculate'. Conservatives had also to *'advertise in their own organs'*, and the quality of the papers must be raised, while still aimed at the Ten Pounders. The party's should also be circulated systematically to Reading Rooms, institutions and all public buildings, filled at the moment only with Liberal literature. Finally, and not least important, these steps should be taken with the existing papers. Make them pay and *'private* enterprise will do the rest'. This was a strong hint to the party not to set up papers in competition with proprietors already friendly to the cause.

Of the political worth of the press Haydon had no doubts. 'The Conservative feeling in the country must indeed be deeprooted, which, despite an excess of two hundred newspapers in favour of Liberalism, could return in the present Parliament three hundred members to support the government of Lord Derby.' This feeling had to be tapped. One might easily have concluded, of course, that such a result indicated that the party, under the existing system, had little need of the press, but it was still affirmed that opinion became 'most rabidly Radical' in the absence of a Conservative press.[63] The fact was that even Conservative journalists adhered to a basically liberal ideology according to which the press was, as if by definition, an indispensable political weapon.

This was demonstrated again in 1867 when some Conservative journalists in league with the Adullamite Whigs began a new 'constitutional' daily, the *Day*. Richard Hutton of the *Spectator* had agreed to set it in motion, given £6,000, and W.H. Smith was willing to distribute it, although he more realistically put the cost at about £50,000 for a morning paper, and £15,000 for an evening one. Lord Elcho wrote to Lord Spencer that 'Grosvenor and some of us are striving to fight the battle of the Constitution. . . An organ in the Press is said, and we believe rightly said, to be essential to this purpose.' In the event the paper was no more successful than its cause.[64]

At about the same time the *Globe* had come on to the market, and Robert Lowe had been keen for the Adullamites to get it. It was, however, bought in 1869 by Conservatives. Managed from 1871 by George Armstrong, it became a valuable piece of political and journalistic property, with a modern style and typography, and a wide coverage of constituency politics.[65] In 1867 the Conservatives had also added to their stable the evening *Pall Mall Gazette,* and so by 1870 the ranks of Conservative journalists, at least in London, were hardly inferior in quality those of the Liberals, and included

Escott, Kebbel, Hannay, Traill, Mudford, Percy Greg and J.F. Stephen. On 24 April 1873 yet another attempt to improve the party's morning press was made when D.M. Evans, city editor of the *Standard,* founded the *Hour.* It was a disastrous failure, costing him some £20,000, before it was sold to Captain Hamber, the original proprietor of the *Daily Telegraph,* under whom it led a fitful existence until 1876.[66] In the following year the *Daily Express,* another Conservative London daily, was begun, but closed after only a few weeks.[67] The most successful Conservative London daily was undoubtedly the *Standard,* edited and owned since 1876 by W.H. Mudford. John Gorst, the Conservative agent, had worked very closely with the paper in the early 1870s, but after Disraeli's defeat in 1880 it became unpopular with both parties by giving too much space to Liberals, and especially to Chamberlain.[68]

In the provinces there had, of course, been papers established for the party, notably during the struggle against free trade. The *Lincolnshire Chronicle* and the *Essex Standard* were examples, and Robert Farrant had bought the *Wiltshire County Mirror* to make into a Conservative organ.[69] Berkshire Conservative clubs had reputedly celebrated the gaining of an old Liberal seat in the 1850s by hanging up silk copies of the *Berkshire Chronicle,* and it was not unusual for Conservative papers to appear in blue ink at elections.[70]

The Conservatives, however, were late in joining the cheap press. The first penny Conservative daily paper seems to have been the *Nottingham Daily Guardian* in 1861. The *Birmingham Daily Gazette* followed in 1862, the *Liverpool Daily Courier* and the *Manchester Courier* in 1863, together with the halfpenny *Exeter Daily Telegraph.* The *Bristol Daily Times* appeared in 1865, and then, on 2 July 1866, the first number of the *Yorkshire Post and Leeds Intelligencer* was published by a company led by the Leeds banker William Beckett-Denison. They had purchased the old *Intelligencer* from Christopher Kemplay, and installed John Ralph as editor, helped by T.E. Kebbel in London. The board of the company included George Lascelles, Charles Tennant and Lord Nevill, and the paper was to prove one of the most successful of Conservative provincial newspapers.[71] Indeed, it seems to have been the last Conservative provincial penny morning paper to be founded until the short-lived *Manchester North Times* in 1882.[72] In the evening press, however, the Conservatives could claim 13 of those started between 1870 and 1880, plus a further three halfpenny ones. Many of them were in traditional Conservative territory in the south; Bath, Gloucester, Worcester, Cheltenham and

Brighton, but they were also in Birmingham, Bolton, Bradford, Manchester, Newcastle, Northampton, Oldham and Sunderland.

The Conservatives had also been anxious to secure a good weekly press. In 1865, for example, G.H. Whalley, a Conservative MP, helped found a newspaper company in Peterborough. In 1868 the editor purchased it, promising to keep it Conservative, but his dissatisfied creditors sued him in the following year for failing to do so.[73] Similarly in 1867, the editor of the *Bacup and Rossendale News* seems to have been paid by local Conservatives to bring the paper over to their side.[74] More ambitiously in the same year, a Devon advertising agent and local Conservative councillor, Charles Wescombe, planned a Conservative syndicate in the West Country, where ten years earlier he had bought the *Exeter and Plymouth Gazette.* He obtained some support from London, but when he left to go to the London *Globe* in 1868, he sold out to G.T. Donisthorpe, sometime proprietor of the *Bridgewater Mercury,* and W. Brodie. Donisthorpe gained the ear of Mark Rolle, High Sheriff of Devon and High Steward of Barnstaple, whose brother had been the Conservative county Member until 1868. Rolle enthusiastically contacted Sir Stafford Northcote, and was ready with £200 of his own money for the scheme. Northcote, however, seems to have let the matter drop, although these machinations might possibly have been behind the short-lived rival to the Whig *Western Morning News,* the *Western Daily Standard* (1869-70).[75] In 1869, in fact, there had been a crop of Conservative weeklies launched, and there may have been a syndicate operating in the Newcastle area in 1870.[76] The 1870s were a much quieter period, and only in the 1880s, it seems, were party papers founded again for electoral purposes, in Lincolnshire and Hertfordshire, for example.[77] The pattern was also true of the foundation of Conservative newspaper companies: 19 of the 26 self-styled 'Conservative' or 'Constitutional' companies founded between 1870 and 1890 were founded after 1880.[78]

It was quickly realised that the news agencies, after the take-over of the telegraphs by the Post Office, were of strategic importance for journalistic politics. They were, to use the modern term, 'gatekeepers' across the wires that carried the 'latest news', and in addition they supplied almost everything which a provincial newspaper could want in the form of stereotyped leaders, features, London Letters and so forth. As the *Globe* put it in 1874, 'the provincial and suburban Press will do well to look to its doings or its days may be numbered in favour of a vicious centralisation.'[79]

The politics of the agencies was complicated. The first agency had been a Liberal one, the Central Press, established in 1863 by the proprietors of the *Western Morning News,* William Saunders and Edward Spender. In 1870, under circumstances which remain rather obscure, it was sold to some Conservatives, while Saunders, apparently in breach of the sale agreement, founded another agency, the Central News. The significance of the change was not immediately appreciated. by some subscribers to the CP. The editor of the Liberal *Eastern Daily Press,* E.D. Rogers, came to suspect the political credentials of the CP only in 1872. His suspicions confirmed, he suggested to his proprietor, J.J. Colman, that a new Liberal agency be formed. Either ignorant or dismissive of the new CN, Colman financed a new agency, helped by Edward Spender and the Liberal Chief Whip, Lord Wolverton. In January 1873 Rogers found himself managing the National Press Agency.[80]

The CP had now become the acknowledged Conservative agency, and in August 1873 began to publish Alexander Mackie's daily *Town and Country Newspaper,* a title changed in October to the *Sun.* This was really a partly printed sheet giving out the party line.[81] Towards the end of 1873 Major Keith-Falconer, secretary of the Central Conservative Registration Association, confessed to Disraeli that 'the past two years have been a time of the greatest anxiety to me in regard to the Central Press, but I think I see land at last.'[82] It seems that in 1871[83] the Party had purchased the CP, plus 'the old "Sun",' It had been decided with a view to retaining Liberal clients, two-thirds of the old subscribers, to continue the *Sun* as 'independent'. By 1872, however, Liberal clients, including presumably Rogers, were becoming disturbed at the influence which the CP's 'moderate tone', as Keith-Falconer put it, was having on their papers. They had thus launched the NPA, which was a considerable blow. The CP, however, continued to supply partly printed sheets, and, more importantly, began 'to afford facilities for starting new papers and improving existing journals which through lack of capital might otherwise fall through'. Subsidies were out of the question, but the CP managed to provide some credit, and kept its prices to the minimum compatible with economic viability. The situation had been made worse, however, by the competition of Saunders's CN, and, therefore, Keith-Falconer was looking in 1873 to buy the bankrupt *Weekly Dispatch* for £11,000. He had Mackie's support and pointed out to Disraeli that 'if we could secure (the *Dispatch*) and amalgamate it with the "Sun" and the CP under one management we should form the basis of a sound commercial undertaking, irrespective of its great political value'. Mackie had already agreed to the venture, and was largely responsible for raising the money, £3,000 of it his own. They now had to tap the resources of 'the rich manufacturing classes in Lancashire'. £25,000 was required to carry out the scheme, including the purchase of the *Dispatch,* but not of the *Sun,* which Keith-Falconer and Mackie seemed hopeful of selling to the new company when it was formed. They looked forward to a circulation for the *Dispatch* of 250,000 and to a halfpenny London edition of the *Sun* to compete with the Liberal *Echo.* If all went well the new CP might force the NPA out of existence, he told Disraeli, as it was already 'working at an enormous loss'.[84]

All did not go well, however. The *Dispatch* was not bought, although the London edition of the *Sun* did appear, with Mackie coming out of retirement to manage it.[85] Keith-Falconer left Central Office and severed his connection, it seems, with the CP, but before he left he made an interesting suggestion to Disraeli's secretary Montagu Corry. He recalled 'the extreme difficulty we had in creating anything like cordial relations between the Conservative provincial press and ourselves' when the CP was taken over. Those relations had, however, improved. 'Most of our friends' had been admitted to the government advertising list, and perhaps there now could be an even better system of distributing government information to the press. Why not, he suggested, establish an Intelligence Department to liaise between government departments and the CP? The CP would exercise no restriction on the distribution of information, but no other agencies would be supplied with it. Mackie had ascertained that more than thirty proprietors, including two Liberals, favoured the idea. Nothing formal seems to have come of it, but it was widely believed that Disraeli's government did foster the press very carefully during the 1870s.[86]

The most important agency for the provincial press, however, was the Press Association, founded originally as a protective body for proprietors against the extortionate demands of the independent telegraph companies. From its foundation in 1868 it was ostensibly a non-partisan body, but representing a predominantly Liberal press, it was inevitable that it should be charged with showing Liberal bias. It had been accused of this even before it had properly been constituted, and the charge was made periodically thereafter. In 1880 things came to a head when a report of a private Conservative meeting did much to alienate Conservative opinion. A Conservative reviewer, in the same year, admitted that such charges were without foundation, but they were renewed nine years later by H. Byron Reed, a 'progressive' Unionist MP (Bradford East), and director of the Northern Counties Constitutional Newspaper Company, which ran the *North Star* and *Northern Standard* in Darlington. He was supported by the editor of the *Yorkshire Post,* but a Press Association committee claimed that they had found no substance in the charge. Indeed, most of the complaints had been of a Conservative bias, which, considering Liberal papers still outnumbered Conservative ones, was hardly surprising.[87]

The victory of 1874 had temporarily allayed anxieties about the state of the Conservative press, but defeat in 1880 re-awakened them. The provincial press was pinpointed as a major weakness in the party's armour by a sympathetic critic in 1880. Cheap provincial Conservative papers were needed to counter radical scurrility.[88]

> We don't plead for a multitude of such local papers; but for large papers with correspondents everywhere, with ample telegraph and general news, and with skilled editors and leader writers. It is impossible to suppose that a wealthy and cultured party like the Conservative party cannot find both the men and the money to organise such an enterprise, and we believe that even from a purely financial point of view, the scheme promises a brilliant success.

A month later the issue was raised at the National Union of Conservative Associations annual conference, where the weight of opinion favoured public speaking and lecturing against the newspaper, but the matter was not allowed to drop there. The next year Ashmead Bartlett's prestigious weekly *England* and the new Sunday *People* were warmly praised, but concern was still evident over the Liberal domination.[89] It was complained that party men had failed to support party papers, either at national or at local level. In 1883, for example, a meeting of Conservative provincial proprietors and editors was arranged with party officials, to mark the opening of the new Constitutional Club. Those who attended felt the atmosphere decidedly cool, and regarded Stafford Northcote's absence as a definite snub, the more so, perhaps, when five months later the same minister was to found in Wales urging Conservatives to do more to develop their own press.[90]

Conservative journalists were also concerned that the party had taken little interest in the burgeoning evening press. Byron Reed's *North Star* was conceded to have won a seat, but it was claimed that the Sheffield situation, where nothing had been done, was the more usual. 'Neutral' or 'independent' papers were widely felt to be 'enemies in disguise'.[91]

The central organisation of the party offered little assistance, being more disposed to a self-help policy, including the formation of companies in which working men could buy low-value shares.[92]

In 1884, however, the National Union resolved to set up a committee to obtain information for further action, the beginning of a protracted struggle to get the leadership to take the matter seriously. (The committee was not even mentioned in that year's annual report.)[93] In 1885 Byron Reed returned to the matter. Reminding delegates of the effect of the 1870 Education Act, he affirmed that 'the Reading public will read newspapers. . . give them news first and political information will follow'. He claimed that insufficient was spent on the party's press, and that what there was had been mis-spent. He instanced a case of £23,000 lost on a daily which lasted less than a year. An exorbitant purchase price had been paid, extravagant costs had been incurred, and a drunken editor employed. In another case £100,000 had been spent in sending 'a stream of diluted articles' to the weekly provincial press without much effect. When Conservatives did employ the right men, he went on, they underpaid them, and he sensed 'a disposition upon the part of our leaders to underrate and despise the newspaper man'. Clearly, Reed was talking as a journalist as much as a Conservative here, and it is hardly surprising that such attacks brought about a somewhat defensive reaction from the delegates, who wished neither to condemn their party press, nor to sap party morale. There was unanimous support however, for the setting up of the committee mentioned the previous year. Supporters of Reed were predictably inclined to base their arguments on particular cases. 'I come from a constituency where we are suffering from a Radical Press — namely the Borough of Birmingham,' declared one. Another claimed that the lack of a Conservative paper in Hackney had led to the defeat of a strong candidate 'by some unknown gentleman'. There was the smell of the scapegoat and the alibi in these arguments. In another instance, in Somerset, the party had refused to provide £800 for the support of an established Conservative paper which had now passed to the Radicals.[94]

Before the next conference the Liberals had won one election and the Conservatives the other. These contests provided more ammunition for the disgruntled journalists. Sir Albert Rollitt, now a Conservative, claimed that a seat had been lost in 1885, and had been recovered, together with an additional one after a Conservative paper had been established in the constituency in 1886. Meanwhile, the committee had actually been set up, its machinery put into motion, questionnaires distributed, and information had started to flow in. The process was on such a large scale, however, that the Home Counties and the metropolitan boroughs reports had each taken six weeks to deal with, and the survey would not be complete for some time, delegates were told. The emphasis of the debate tended still to be on party subvention of newspapers, however, the example of a successful purchase in South Wiltshire being used in support of the policy. It was a lone voice which reminded the conference that the papers had to be popular papers if they were to attract sufficient advertising to stand on their own feet.[95] Understandably enough the 1887 conference showed some impatience over the failure of the committee to report in that year. Some of course, used it as a means of getting at the leadership of the party, and its failure to keep in touch with the rank and file. Yet by this time some of the heat had been taken out of the situation by the fact that some of the large dailies had become Unionist, in fact if not in name, and it was astutely observed that the poorer voter would be able to afford only a weekly paper in any case.

Unfortunately, neither the grand survey, nor the minutes of the conferences or annual reports of 1888 and 1889 survive, and it is therefore, not known what became of the committee, or what its findings were. In all probability it was reduced to making further encouraging noises. Certainly no major scheme for the assistance of the party press was carried out. There are a few references to cases in which the party and its supporters were less than helpful in their attitudes. In Byron Reed's constituency, for example, the *Bradford Daily Chronicle and Mail* seems to have been neglected, and Frank Harris has recounted how he met a refusal of help in 1885 to establish a new Birmingham morning paper. As to the *Evening News,* which had been looked to as a reply to the *Echo* in London, Harris's account makes it clear that there was little or no enthusiasm in the party for the project.[96] What party efforts there were ironically met with a critical response from Conservative journalists and proprietors, as, for example, when the Primrose League Printing and Publishing Company was founded in 1887, directed by the Duke of Norfolk, Lord Folkestone, Thomas Gibson Bowles and others. This company established the *Primrose Gazette,* and although Lord Harris denied that it was funded by the League itself, it aroused much anger amongst existing proprietors, not least because they thought it was being supplied with exclusive party news.[97]

By the end of the 1880s, therefore, it was evident that there was general agreement on the Conservative side that the press was an influence upon electoral behaviour, although it was a view held less firmly by those closest to electoral organisation, and most strongly by certain candidates and journalists. Support was to be found within the party both for the help of existing papers, and for the provision of new ones, although both journalists and party men were much less enthusiastic about the latter than about the former. What financial support there was came not from the centre but from the local associations, often from the Conservative aristocracy, as in Chester and Hertfordshire.[98] There was also a greater willingness to accept the lessons of the 'new journalism', that papers had to be made attractive, and that they ought to be financially sound. As late as 1891 it was claimed to be well known that Conservative papers were financially less sound than Liberal ones, and some found it necessary to spell out the lessons that politics were not necessarily a good way to gain political influence for a newspaper, especially if they were partisan politics, and that any good paper had to be made to pay.[99] It was claimed in 1886 that the hope for Conservative journalism in the future lay in the fact that 'journalists like other people, become Conservative when they become possessed of what corresponds to a typical cow; and journals tend in the main to become Conservative as they become prosperous in a prosperous community'.[100] If they learnt their lessons, then, and went with the tide, the Conservatives would necessarily overcome the Liberal domination which had oppressed them for almost four decades.

IV The End of the Golden Age

It has been shown so far that, while Liberal domination of the English provincial press was maintained up to and through into the 1890s, in terms of numbers, the extent and weight of that domination was, and was felt to be, diminishing. From the beginning of the 1880s the Conservatives were engaged in a battle to wrest press power from the Liberals, who found themselves fighting a largely defensive campaign. The struggle was carried on under two assumptions; that the press was a powerful political weapon, and that politics still counted for as much in the press as it had done in the 1860s and 1870s. These assumptions, however, were being increasingly undermined. The old journalism, even in its transformed style of the 1870s, was geared essentially to the old politics, but

neither were compatible with the 'new journalism'. The older
connection can be seen in the careers of two working journalists,
a Liberal, George Gilbert Armstrong, and a Conservative, H.J. Palmer.
Armstrong made a remarkable tour of the most distinguished
politically Liberal papers between 1889 and the 1920s, beginning with
the *Liverpool Daily Mercury,* and moving in succession to the
Nottingham Daily Express, the *North Eastern Gazette* (Middlesborough),
the *Bradford Observer,* the *Bolton Evening News,* the *Morning Leader,*
the *Northern Echo* (Darlington), and the *Daily News.*[101] Less
Odyssean was Palmer's career, beginning at the *Sheffield Daily
Telegraph* in the 1870s, thence to the *Birmingham Daily Gazette,* and
finally to the *Yorkshire Post* in 1890, where he died thirteen years
later, aged fifty.[102] Of similar political purity were the careers of the
Liberals John Derry and James Annand, and of Palmer's predecessor
at the *Yorkshire Post,* Charles Pebody. By the end of the century
this pattern was becoming rarer. The claim that 'the reporter has
nothing to do with the political role of his newspaper' would have been
widely endorsed by the working journalists of the 1890s, the majority
of whom anyway worked for non-political papers.[103] The author of
the statement freely switched from a Liberal paper to a Conservative
one and back again, seemingly without ill-effects either to himself
or to the papers. Such flexibility was commoner amongst younger
journalists, who could not afford principles, and might end up either
converted to the appropriate politics, or transformed into political
eunuchs. C.E. Montague's humorous characterisation of this
situation in *A Hind Let Loose* (1910) was exaggerated, but it is
difficult not to conclude that journalism was by then a career
increasingly likely to encourage cynicism. Some even switched horses
at the highest level, like George Gratwicke, who left Latimer's *Weekly
Times* at Exeter to become the managing editor of the Conservative
Exeter and Plymouth Gazette in 1885.[104]

Political conflict between editor and proprietor is a subject which
must be returned to later, but it may here be observed that Liberal,
and especially radical, journalists did seem affected more than others
by the new trend in proprietorship towards financial success as the
overriding goal. This was mainly because anything of a radical nature
was likely to frighten timid proprietors and advertisers. Commercial
considerations usually dictated conservative politics. The security
of Liberal and radical journalists, therefore, especially before the
formation of the NUJ in 1907, tended to be much less than that of
their colleagues. An extreme example of this was A.E. Fletcher's

resignation from the *Daily Chronicle* in 1894.[105]

> I have not left the Chronicle but I have told my proprietors that I
> cannot continue to be responsible for the publication of betting
> odds. I regard this as the curse and shame of journalism, and
> although it is a very serious step for me to take, as I have heavy
> family responsibilities, I have decided to resign rather than be
> liable to the charge of perpetuating that curse.

Now Fletcher was a sensitive man, and this was an outburst rather of
Nonconformist than of radical conscience, but the two were not
easily separated, and the 'new journalism' pricked them both.

It was argued at the time that the impact of the 'new journalism'
on the Liberal press was accentuated by political developments, which
meant that Liberal splits over Ireland, Empire and Labour were
reflected in a divided and demoralised press. One observer, commenting
on the achievement of the Liberal press in the nineteenth century,
claimed, 'the position was entirely reversed in 1886.'[106] Such a view
was common, and natural at a time when Ireland so dominated
British politics, when Gladstone used Home Rule as an issue to test
his party, when Liberal Unionism was born, when Joseph Chamberlain
defected. How could an issue which had so divided the party fail to
have divided its press? Irish Home Rule as an issue in British politics
is now more soberly appraised by historians, who draw attention to
deeper and stronger forces engendering changes in Liberalism and
politics in the 1880s, who claim that in 'high politics' Ireland was but
another counter in an infinitely devious and utterly complex game.
Nevertheless, Ireland was the issue by which men indicated their
political position, and by its very nature the press was an important
medium for communicating such indications. The dramatic changes
in the London press, with the defections of the *Daily Chronicle* and
the *Pall Mall Gazette,* and in the provinces, with those of the
Birmingham Daily Post, the *Western Morning News* and the *York
Herald,* not to mention the losses in Scotland and Ireland, convinced
many observers that Home Rule had dealt the Liberal press a
considerable blow. Moreover, Liberal Unionism was often only a
step on the road to Conservatism. In 1896 the Conservatives reckoned
that only four mornings and four evenings had become Unionist
without having become Conservative in the whole of the United
Kingdom.[107] Liberal Unionism after all was never very strong, and
with the exception of Birmingham and Glasgow what support it had

was in rural rather than in urban areas, precisely where the Liberal press was weakest anyway.[108] If the split did do much damage to the Liberal press, however, it was not immediately obvious. In the north-east, for example, it seems to have had few immediately deleterious effects, and circumstances combined to keep the papers in Leeds and Bradford Gladstonian, at least for the 1890s.[109] Weaknesses may have resulted in so far as the issue divided Nonconformity, which was an important element in the life of the Liberal provincial press, but it is difficult to point to any prominent Liberal paper, renowned for its Nonconformism, which became Unionist in the 1880s and 1890s. The *York Herald* is a possible candidate, but like the *Western Morning News,* it always was rather Whiggish, and would have been drawn towards Unionism for other reasons than Home Rule. In the press, as in Liberalism generally, Home Rule probably served as an indicator of pre-existent political affiliations and attitudes, rather than as an originator of them.

Much the same may be said of 'imperialism'. Imperial expansion after the 1870s was ideally suited to exploitation by the 'new journalism'. It provided wars sufficiently distant as not to be too distressing, but successful enough to sustain confidence, with occasional setbacks to maintain tension. It provided opportunity for sometimes vastly imaginative tales of foreign lands, disguised as news. It provided the thrills and passions associated with the possibility of clashes with other great powers. 'We never allowed the peoples at home to forget the magnificent heritage they enjoyed through the valiance and self-sacrifice of their fathers', recalled one of the founders of the 'new journalism'.[110] For Liberals, however, it was another wedge driven into their already splintering flank. The old-guard Gladstonians who remembered John Bright and cheered John Morley, saw in the imperial policy of the 1880s and 1890s the antithesis of what they understood by 'a Liberal state'. Yet there was another equally traditional Liberal view, held by those who wished to civilise, to educate, to save less fortunate people than themselves. The Empire provided an instrument for this purpose. E.T. Cook, the editor of the still Liberal *Pall Mall Gazette,* then of the *Westminster Gazette,* and finally of the *Daily News,* wrote in his last leader for the latter paper on 10 January 1901, 'our object, then, has been to keep steadily in view the larger interests and duties of the country as an Imperial Power, and to sink, in some measure, mere party considerations in the face of national emergencies.'[111] The Conservative T.H.S. Escott noted in 1897 that, from 1886 'newspaper

criticism of men and measures has practically ceased. With a few
exceptions, signally that of the *Daily Chronicle,* the paramount task
of the press. . .is to support a combination of groups rallied not under
a party flag, but an Imperial banner.'[112] The broader concept of
Empire was a more powerful one than that of a continued union
between Britain and Ireland; it raised fewer questions of ambivalence;
it encountered at that time much less organised opposition; it
raised greater hopes of reward; and it seemed, unlike Unionism, not to
conflict with social radicalism at home. The Boer War merely served
to intensify such feelings, at least until it began to turn sour mid-way
through 1900.

Anxieties, therefore, about the condition of the Liberal press
after 1886, which increased during the Tory domination from 1895
to 1906, tended to be anxieties about the condition of the more
radical wing of that press, and were inevitably bound up with
contemporaneous difficulties and changes in radical politics. Economic
and technical changes in the newspaper industry were also weakening
the older journalistic basis of that radicalism. Older radical papers
had catered for a much smaller constituency than could now be aimed
at for financial viability. They had either to find external support or
compete by lowering prices. External support was not always
forthcoming or steadfast, and price reduction usually meant a
reduction in sales revenue uncompensated for by increased advertising
revenue. While the older radical politics may in some sense have
reached a peak in the 1890s,[113] survival for the newspaper had come
increasingly to involve compromise, to necessitate a bid for the middle
ground, to entail the loss of party character, and the eschewal of
party allegiance. Such, at any rate, was the assessment of the plight
of the Liberal press in 1902 by H.J. Palmer, and in its defence Sir
Edward Russell, editor of the *Liverpool Daily Post,* could only agree
that the times were indeed non-political, and that the Liberal press
would have to make the best of the situation.[114]

The broader questions of political involvement are examined in
the following chapter, but it is necessary first to describe the process
by which the 'decline' occurred.[115]

In London the two Liberal giants, the *Daily News* and the *Daily
Chronicle,* went into the storm strong and confident. The *Daily News*
had been a penny paper since 1868, and had absorbed the defunct
Morning Star in 1869.[116] From then until 1871 Edward Dicey was
editor, succeeded by F.H. Hill, who remained for the next fifteen
years. In 1886 H.W. Lucy, the paper's famous parliamentary

correspondent, took over for a brief period, but stepped down in 1887 in favour of P.W. Clayden, a radical Nonconformist.[117] He was succeeded in turn in 1896 by the Roseberyite editor of the *Westminster Gazette,* E.T. Cook, a change occasioned by the withdrawal by Henry Labouchere of his quarter share in the paper, held since 1868. He did not want to be associated with 'Birmingham imperialism', and instead reaped a considerable profit from the sale. At that time the other main proprietors were Arnold Morley, an ex-Chief Whip for the Liberals and son of the old Samuel Morley, who had been a founder of the *Morning Star;* the banker Henry Oppenheim; and the industrialists Lord Ashton and Thomas Brassey. Cook's 'imperialist' tone, however, only led to further disagreements amongst the proprietors, at least one of whom, Ashton, became a pro-Boer in 1899. Sir John Robinson, manager of the paper since 1868, also considered resigning, and circulation fell by more than a third within a few months of the outbreak of the war. Ever since its triumphant coverage of the Franco-Prussian War the *Daily News* had been a very valuable property. In 1872 Robinson had been told that his job was secure as long as he continued to provide shareholders with twenty per cent dividends. Sam Morley was 'almost disappointed. I went into the *Daily News* not to make money, but to advocate principles', but most of his fellow proprietors must have been well-satisfied.[118] Now it was a different story, and financial and political problems resulted in the sale of the paper to a group of pro-Boers led by Lloyd George, but financed by George Cadbury, J.P. Thomasson and others.[119] It was a radical coup of some proportions, but before long the new owners became divided over policy, and Cadbury was left with most of the property and the losses. The editing was soon put in the hands of a committee, until Cadbury, whose first choice was the young academic and journalist L.T. Hobhouse, decided, in the face of the latter's reluctance, to appoint the editor of the *Blackburn Weekly Telegraph,* A.G. Gardiner. For good measure, the proprietor of that paper, (and joint proprietor of the *Northern Daily Telegraph,)* T.P. Ritzema, was made manager of the *Daily News.* Under such direction it became a leading exponent of what was coming to be known as the 'new liberalism'. It favoured increased state provision of welfare, as well as land reform and the political accommodation of Labour. In practical terms it was active in support of strikers and the unemployed, as well as lending its support to Labour candidates in by-elections.[120] Cadbury and Ritzema, however, also accentuated its Nonconformist tone, the former insisting that

there should be no betting news, and the latter that there should be
no liquor advertising. Both policies were probably financially injurious,
particularly so when in 1904 the paper was forced to imitate the
Daily Chronicle and reduce its price to a halfpenny, for this increased
its dependence on advertising revenue. Cadbury stood the losses, but
it had really ceased to be a commercially viable newspaper. This was
not changed by the brave decision to publish simultaneously in
Manchester and London in 1908, although it did raise the circulation to
over 400,000.[121]

Part of the *Daily News's* trouble was the competition of its rival,
the *Daily Chronicle*. In 1866 the *Clerkenwell News* had become a
halfpenny daily, and in 1869, at a penny, it took the title of the
London Daily Chronicle. Edward Lloyd bought it in 1876 for £30,000,
and spent some £150,000 in making it into a close competitor of the
Daily Telegraph in terms of circulation. Its politics were on the
moderate side of radical. Whereas the *Daily News* had been unwaveringly
Gladstonian until 1895, the *Daily Chronicle* had taken a Unionist
line in 1885, until 1890, when A.E. Fletcher succeeded R.W. Boyle
as editor. Under Fletcher, and after 1895 under Massingham, the paper
became the most radical in the London mornings, a spokesman of
an emerging 'progressivism'. In 1899, however, Massingham was
persuaded by his editorial colleagues to make the paper into an
anti-war organ, and resigned when told by the proprietors that
criticism of the government's war policy must cease during the
hostilities. His place was taken by W.J. Fisher.[122] How this affected
the circulation of the paper is unknown, but it certainly demoralised
radicals, and robbed them of what had been their strongest journal.
The situation was retrieved in part in 1904, when Robert Donald, an
original member of the staff of the *Star,* became editor, reduced the
price to a halfpenny, and made a remarkable success of running a
more or less orthodox Liberal morning, until its sale to Lloyd
George in 1918.

In the 1870s and 1880s, of course, both the *News* and the *Chronicle*
were journalistically outmatched by the *Daily Telegraph,* but since
its proprietor E.L. Lawson had swung it round to a pro-Turk policy
in 1879, the occasion of a libellous attack on Lawson by Labouchere,
which referred to the former's holdings of Turkish bonds, the paper
had become much less than Liberal, and opposed Home Rule from the
beginning.[123]

In 1892 Sir Frederick Wilson, J.J. Colman, Sir John Brunner,
and other Liberal industrialists, founded the *Morning Leader,* a

halfpenny radical journal edited by Ernest Parke, formerly a sub-editor of the *Echo*. One of the directors was James Stuart MP, secretary of the London Liberal and Radical Union. He and Parke ensured the paper kept to a radical line, and it was claimed to circulate amongst lower-paid clerks and working men, attracted, apparently, by the cricket reporting. Whilst both the *News* and the *Chronicle* were lost to the radicals during the Boer War, the *Leader* was not, and, subsidised by Cadbury, it was widely distributed outside London at that time.[124]

It was closely linked to the evening *Star,* begun in 1888 by Brunner, Colman, Thomas Lough MP, Wilfrid Blunt and others. One of the prophets of the 'new journalism', T.P. O'Connor, was made editor, and he proclaimed from the outset its radical intent. He soon quarrelled with the proprietors, however, who turned first to Massingham, under whom the paper gained a certain notoriety for publishing Fabian and socialist views. He too quarrelled with the proprietors, and in 1891 Parke took over, and ran both the *Leader* and the *Star* from 1892 to 1912. Both followed a radical line, the *Star* having the privilege of being burnt upon the Stock Exchange during the Boer War. From 1904 they were run in close association with the *Northern Echo* which had just been bought by the Rowntrees, but in 1910 the two London papers were transferred to the Cadburys, and in 1912 the *Leader* was swallowed by the *Daily News.*[125]

The *Echo* was an older evening paper, purveying an older style of Liberalism, albeit with strong republican overtones, omitting betting news, and relying heavily on the philanthropy of J. Passmore Edwards, who had bought it in 1875. Two-thirds of it he sold to, and then bought back from, the Storey-Carnegie syndicate in the early 1880s, and he finally sold it to a group of Liberals in 1896, including Thomas Lough. They found they could not make a success of it, and in 1901 F.W. Pethick Lawrence was persuaded to buy it. He gathered round him some radicals of a more modern sort, H.N. Brailsford and Percy Alden, with contributions from J.R. MacDonald, but despite further subsidies from the Sheffield Liberal MP H.J. Wilson in 1902, commercial pressures forced its closure in 1905.[126]

The *Pall Mall Gazette* had been founded in 1865 by a Liberal, George Smith, but was edited by Frederick Greenwood as a Conservative paper until 1880. Smith then gave it to his son-in-law, H.Y. Thompson. Greenwood refused to turn it into a Liberal paper at Thompson's behest, and went instead to the new *St. James's Gazette*, founded by a Conservative banker, H.H. Gibbs. John Morley

succeeded him at the *Pall Mall,* until in 1885 he entered Parliament,
and his place was taken by his young assistant W.T. Stead. Stead,
naturally, sought to make the paper an organ of the 'new journalism'
as he understood it. The resultant disruption together with financial
difficulties, for Stead's brand of 'new journalism' was not very
profitable, led to his replacement by E.T. Cook in 1890. After two
years Thompson, apparently piqued at having been ignored politically
by his party, sold the paper to the Conservative, W. Astor, who hoped
to further his own political career by the purchase. His new editor,
Henry Cust, edited it somewhat too 'progressively' for his liking, but
Astor kept it in the Conservative camp thereafter.[127] The exiles of
1892, however, Cook, J.A. Spender, and some others, were helped
by the proprietor of *Tit-Bits,* George Newnes, to found a rival
evening paper, the *Westminster Gazette.* Newnes told Cook, 'I
think the scheme would find favour with the leading men of the
Party.' It cost him between £35,000 and £45,000 in the first two
years, but he received his knighthood in 1895, and in the following
year Cook left for the *Daily News.* His place was taken by J.A.
Spender, who retained control until it became a morning journal in
1921. Under his guidance in the 1890s and 1900s the *Westminster
Gazette* was established as a heavyweight Liberal paper, in the style
of the golden age, but leavened with the art of F.C. Gould and the
satire of H.H. Munro, and acting politically as a bridge between the
Liberal factions. Nevertheless, its 20,000 circulation and £40,000 a
year advertisement revenue were insufficient to spare Newnes a loss
of £5,000 to £10,000 a year. He sold it in 1908 to a Liberal syndicate,
headed by Sir John Brunner in a deal arranged, it was said, by the
Liberal whips. Despite the pooling of resources with the *Daily
Chronicle,* however, the losses continued.[128]

Such, then, were the misfortunes of the major London Liberal
dailies after the 1880s. Liberalism was also represented in the
Sunday press, but this was usually dismissed as politically less
important. Still, qualitative judgements apart, the strength of J.H.
Dalziel's *Reynold's News,* still a radical paper under the editorship
of W.M. Thompson, *Lloyds Weekly News,* edited from 1906 by
Robert Donald, and George Riddell's *News of the World,* with a
probable combined circulation of more than 4,000,000 should not
easily be disregarded. The only Conservative competition of note was
the *People,* and in terms of prestige the *Observer,* when owned by
Northcliffe and edited by J.L. Garvin.

The Liberals did make some attempts to fight back. Massingham and some leading Liberals tried to start a new paper after the defection of the *Chronicle* in 1899, but without success.[129] The purchase of the *Daily News* in 1901 made up for this, but more was needed, and in 1904 one of the participants in that deal, J.P. Thomasson, died and left several hundred thousand pounds to establish a new Liberal daily. *The Tribune,* as it was called, appeared on 15 January 1906, conceived as an organ of opposition to the old Conservative regime, but destined to play the more difficult role of sympathetic guide to the new Liberal one. In two months circulation fell from 239,000 to 52,000, however, and its defiance of the trend towards halfpenny papers (it was a penny), its imprudent advertising policy, some bad management, and the failure to secure support other than from Thomasson's son Franklin, led to its demise in January 1908. Its radical period had been quite short, and after the departure of many of its brilliant editorial staff, a more old-fashioned individualistic Liberalism was evident in its pages.[130] It was perhaps the most spectacular example of the way in which commercial, journalistic and to a lesser extent political pressures were making it impossible for the journalism of the golden age to survive, or be revived in the 1900s.

Turning to the provinces, we find here too that the old journalism was under considerable pressure.[131] The crucial period from the 1880s up to the 1900s, however, began with an impressive scheme for strengthening the radical wing of the Liberal press. It was ominous for the old believers that the scheme both in conception and execution tended towards the 'new journalism', but it was at least thought of in terms of 'influence' and 'opinion'. The Scots-American steel magnate, Andrew Carnegie, had long dreamt of controlling a newspaper, and disseminating through it his own republicanism and radicalism, and in 1881 the chance arose. He met an old Scots friend, the Wolverhampton merchant Thomas Graham, together with Samuel Storey, the radical MP for Sunderland, and proprietor of the *Sunderland Echo,* and its newer stable-mate the *Tyneside Echo.* The meeting led to the formation of what came popularly to be known as the Storey-Carnegie Syndicate, although in fact it seems to have been a number of separate arrangements between Carnegie and some proprietors. The first move seems to have been for Graham, secretary and treasurer of the Staffordshire Liberal Association, and part founder with other local Liberals of the *Wolverhampton Evening Star,* to buy up, with Carnegie's help, the Conservative group of the *Wolverhampton Chronicle,* the *Midland Counties Express,* and its evening companion,

the *Evening Express*. In 1883 Graham became chairman of the new
Midland News Association, and in the following year the *Express* and
Star were amalgamated into one paper.[132] Meanwhile Storey brought
in his *Echos*, but retained personal control of them. The Syndicate
also bought the weekly *Hampshire Telegraph*, and turned it into an
evening paper, and quickly added the rival *Portsmouth Evening News*.
They were also joined by Hugh Gilzean-Reid, who added his *North
Eastern Daily Gazette* (Middlesborough), but, like Storey, retained
personal control of it. In 1884 Storey purchased the Conservative
Northern Daily Mail (Hartlepool), and Carnegie bought two-thirds of
the London *Echo* from Passmore Edwards. Other ambitious moves
were made, for the *Northampton Mercury* and the *Shields Gazette,*
but these were unsuccessful. In Birmingham, however, Gilzean-Reid
established a new paper, the *Midland Echo*. By the end of 1884 the
Syndicate, therefore, owned eight dailies and about ten weeklies.
Their biggest hope, perhaps, was pinned on the London *Echo*.
Carnegie told Storey to turn it into a London *Petit Journal*.
Passmore Edwards retained a third share of the paper, but it seems
to have been managed by Storey, with Aaron Watson, a north-eastern
journalist of some repute, as editor. Watson claimed that he was given
a free hand editorially, and that it was run independently of the
provincial papers. That may have been true, (and it was obviously
in Watson's professional interest to say that it was so), but it does
seem that the provincial papers were 'fed' a great deal of material
from the *Echo*. This, of course, was not unusual, and even independent
provincial papers were apt to lift a lot from their metropolitan
counterparts. With the Syndicate, however, the lifting seems to have
been rather too standardised, and was claimed to have reduced the
attractiveness of the papers.[133] A junior member of the staff of the
paper, M.L. Hawkes, the son of the republican journalist and lawyer
Sidney Milnes Hawkes, wrote a novel, *A Primrose Dame* (1886), with
the *Echo* as a backcloth.[134] Hawkes claimed that the proprietors
fell out over the effect of Storey's ('Holt's') radicalism on advertisers.
The following fictional exchange between Passmore Edwards
('Paralysis Agitans'), and Hawkes ('Linnell') epitomises the dilemma
which all radical papers faced.[135]

'The word Radical', here interjected Mr. Paralysis Agitans, 'ought
never to be used, Mr. Gripper, in public or in print. In public it
alarms property; in the press it loses advertisements.'
'True', said Linnell; 'but this is not a financial enterprise, I

understand, Mr. Agitans, These papers are to promote the *cause.*'
    'The papers are the cause, sir,' reported Agitans. 'If the papers
succeed, the cause prospers; if not, not. I am a Radical, but I call
myself a Liberal. The papers must be Radical, but they need not use
the word.'

It seems, indeed, that financial difficulties caused the Syndicate to be
wound up, after its biggest effort in supporting the 1884 Reform Bill.
Carnegie first suggested combining all the papers into one, but Passmore
Edwards refused to co-operate, and besides Storey and Gilzean-Reid
would never have relinquished control of their own papers. Carnegie
put most blame on Graham, whose Wolverhampton papers were the
greatest loss-makers. Eventually, on Gladstone's defeat in 1886,
Carnegie decided to put an end to it all, selling the London *Echo* back
to Passmore Edwards at a substantial profit, and leaving Storey, Graham
and Gilzean-Reid to take their own papers, plus any they had acquired
through the Syndicate, but retaining a share in their companies for a
number of years. He subsequently refused many requests for help in
newspaper ventures, his experience with the Syndicate having
thoroughly disillusioned him. There had unduoubtedly been a wish on
his part to have the papers edited on the same political lines, and James
Annand was even asked to be editor of the London *Echo,* and to
manage the political direction of all the other papers.[136]
Characteristically he refused, and co-ordination was reduced to a matter
of stereotyped copy. The failure was evidence that capital alone was
insufficient without management and journalistic flair. Carnegie was
just not willing to go as far as other far less wealthy men in subsidising
the losses of politically congenial papers. 'Money no object as
compared with power' he told Storey, but he realised that money alone
could not create power. As his reference to *Le Petit Journal* indicated
he realised that it was success that bred power, and that commercial
rather than political considerations were fundamental to the success of
a newspaper.
    In Leeds a different situation prevailed. The city was important
both for the Liberal Party and for its press in the 1880s. The
splits of the previous decade, occasioned largely by the Forster
Education Act, were healed, and in 1886 the president of the
Leeds Liberal Association, James Kitson, who was also that year
president of the NLF, led the NLF to reject an anti-Home Rule
resolution, and, thereafter, the Leeds Association and the
Leeds Mercury were at the fore on the Gladstonian side
in the Home Rule struggle. In addition the *Mercury's* local rival the

Yorkshire Post was probably the strongest Conservative provincial daily in the land. Unfortunately for the former paper, however, Leeds was to lead Liberalism for only a brief period, for the Home Rule split led to the transfer of the party organisation from Birmingham to London, and not to Leeds. This probably had a serious effect on the political status of the *Mercury,* although it was no reason why it should, on its own, have led to the decline of the paper. The West Riding was still an important Liberal area.[137]

The *Mercury's* position had been established in the early nineteenth century, had changed little in the middle of the century, and had been improved in the 1870s after Wemyss Reid had become editor, and Edward Baines Jr. had mitigated the paper's Nonconformist temper. After the mid-1870s, also, the radical rivalry of the *Leeds Express* diminished with a change of proprietors. The *Express* continued on the rather old-fashioned radical lines of the *Echo,* whereas the *Mercury,* although more staid, and even 'imperial' in tone, began to orientate itself towards the newer problems of reform and of Labour. Journalistically, under Reid, the *Mercury* was amongst the leading provincial journals of its time, being the first, in co-operation with the *Glasgow Herald,* to establish a London office, and was amongst the most enthusiastic supporters of the 'Lobby'. Reid himself was intimate with many of the Liberal Party's national leaders, particularly with Herbert Gladstone.[138] He and the Baineses were always hostile to Chamberlain, ever since his education campaign of the 1870s, and although initially unenthusiastic about Home Rule, they accepted it as a means of defeating the men of Birmingham. The split, the removal of the centre of Liberal activities back to London, and the departure in 1889 of Reid, however, all worked against the paper, just at a time when the *Yorkshire Post* was doing increasingly well. Journalistically it fell behind modern developments, making little attempt to follow a sound commercial policy, or to initiate typographical change. Thomas Baines the younger, whilst not actually controlling the paper, had loosened the family's links with Nonconformity, by marrying, first, into an Ulster Liberal family in 1879, and, then into the High Church family of a Conservative MP. This was damaging to the image of the *Mercury,* and, anyway, by 1900 the financial position had become critical. Reid told Herbert Gladstone in October 1900 that the war had endangered its prospects by increasing costs. This had practically exhausted the Baines's resources, so could, Reid wondered, Gladstone or the Party help? Evidently some negotiations followed, but in November Reid wrote again to Gladstone, emphasising significantly the commercial-political dilemma.

> I thought (between ourselves) that our friends this afternoon looked
> too much at the purely financial and too little at the political side
> of the question we were discussing. After all it will be a blow to
> Liberalism in Yorkshire if the L.M. either goes under or goes over.[139]

In the following month Sir James Kitson told Gladstone that he was
willing to find £10,000 in aid, if others would do likewise. Neither he,
Reid, Gladstone nor their colleagues were able to save the *Mercury*,
however, and in 1901 it was sold to the Liberal Imperialist Leicester
Harmsworth, who turned it into a halfpenny 'news picture paper' in
1902.[140] Its capitulation to the Conservatives was not to come until
1923, when it was sold to the *Yorkshire Post,* but in 1901 it had
relinquished all claim to be reckoned with the remaining Liberal giants
of the golden age, whose ranks it had hitherto graced. There was, later,
some small consolation in the fact that a company of Liberals managed
to buy the Conservative halfpenny evening paper the *Leeds Daily News,*
in 1906, but it was no adequate replacement, in the eyes of most
Liberals, for the old *Mercury.*[141]

The forces which in Leeds had the *Mercury* as a mouthpiece, chiefly
temperance and Nonconformity, found in Sheffield Liberalism in the
1870s, industrialists for the most part, like Frederick Mappin MP, Batty
Langley MP and H.J. Wilson MP, were radicals, but they lacked a radical
paper. The *Sheffield Independent,* a penny daily since 1861, and run by
the Liberal Leader family, was insufficiently radical for the others'
tastes, particularly over the Contagious Diseases Acts, temperance and
education. As in Leeds, the split in the Liberal ranks was healed in the
mid-1870s, with Robert Leader the chairman, and H.J. Wilson the
secretary of a new Liberal Association. Wilson's hostility to the
Independent, however, had already led him to seek an alternative
outlet.

It had first been the idea to start a rival paper, but after the advice
of the successful proprietor of the *Northern Echo,* J.H. Bell, had been
sought, and the ground surveyed, the suggestion of a new halfpenny
morning paper, like the *Echo,* did not attract Wilson, or his brother
John Wycliffe Wilson. The report they had had, for example, had
claimed that the *Independent* had not been more successful because it
had pushed its principles too far, whereas the Wilsons considered that
its fault lay precisely in its want of principle! Financial considerations
were also important, the Wilsons being unwilling to lay out a fortune,

and failing to get much outside support, even from Alfred Illingworth, who was admittedly concerned about the state of the press in his own Bradford, where the local *Observer* had come out in support of Forster. Nothing came of these activities in Sheffield, and the reconciliation of 1875 seems to have put off any further attempts to replace the *Independent.* Moreover, in the 1880s there was a considerable Conservative effort to establish a successful rival paper. A halfpenny evening, the *Sheffield Daily Mail* (1884-6), and the *Sheffield Morning Guardian* (1887-9), both led brief lives, as did the Independent halfpenny evening *South Yorkshire News* (1886-7). A halfpenny evening independent, the *Sheffield Evening Post* (1880-7), had fared slightly better, but then in 1888 the Liberal *Sheffield Evening Star and Times* disappeared. Meanwhile the *Sheffield Daily Telegraph* was doing very well for the Conservatives. These were not years in which to rock the boat, but the challenges seemed over by the 1890s, and radicals everywhere were by then recovering their voices, muted somewhat by Home Rule. The *Independent* was by then in financial difficulty. J.D. Leader had already considered selling the *Star and Times* to Leng, proprietor of the *Telegraph,* in 1888, as it was losing £2,000 a year, and the *Independent* itself was hardly profitable. By 1892 it was rumoured that it was for sale, and in 1894 J.W. Wilson was approached by a ·'newspaper broker' about the property. Predictably, however, he objected to the suggestion that it could be made to pay if run on the lines of the *Leeds Mercury,* for he regarded the *Mercury* as a purveyor only of milk-and-water Nonconformity. Had he known it, of course, the *Mercury* at this time was hardly a financial success. Efforts were made, but the now moderate Liberal MP Sir Frederick Mappin declined to become involved on grounds of age (he was seventy-three), and of price. H.J. Wilson's children were willing to contribute out of their future share of the family fortune, but were as severe as their uncle on the terms. They demanded that the policy be Liberal, anti-gambling, but neither anti-Christian, nor opposed to Labour, and for temperance, social purity and disestablishment. The stumbling block which prevented outside collaboration was always the problem of betting news, not because others were confirmed gamblers, but because the publication of betting news was almost universally accepted as a necessary part of any newspaper which sought to make a profit. In 1895 the sons agreed to co-operate with a new group, including the temperance leader Batty Langley, and with the Baptist editor of the *Nottingham Daily Express* as editor. Reluctantly, and only after soliciting Joseph Rowntree's advice, and having rudely interrogated the new editor, John Derry, as to his Nonconformist credentials, H.J. Wilson did agree to invest £500. Derry and Joseph Cooke ran the paper from then until 1907, with the grudging support of those Derry called 'the Sheffielders'. By 1907 H.J. Wilson was already referring to the paper as 'Roseberyite', although it claimed to be 'an exponent of the New Liberalism'. In that year a new company was formed by two local industrialists, who put up £22,000 between them. They required more than this, however, and Wilson negotiated cannily so that in 1909 they left the field clear for him to make his own arrangements. He tried unsuccessfully to recruit Sir Christopher Furness, the Liberal proprietor of the *North Mail* (Hartlepool), and then the Scotts of the *Manchester Guardian* suggested approaching James Stuart of the *Morning Leader*. J.R. Scott added significantly that 'if the Whips were more in sympathy with our end of the party they would be the natural people to approach'. They had in fact, as we have seen, just secured the transfer of the *Westminster Gazette* to Mond. Wilson did manage to find support from Stuart and the *Star-Morning Leader* group, still owned by the Rowntrees, together with assistance from Liberal Associations and MPs. He also got the expert and invaluable advice of Starmer and Parke. The new paper, at a halfpenny, and with accounts of prize fights, but without betting news, appeared on 4 October 1909. The old radicals had at last, and surely too late, paid the price of a new 'progressive' paper. As it was the *Independent* had never matched the prestige, or probably the circulation of the Conservative *Telegraph,* and the struggle in Sheffield had been largely an internal one for the soul of Liberalism. Without this enduring conflict it is possible that the compromises of 1909 would have been made in 1894. Whether they would have produced a stronger Liberal press in the town, however, is another question.

Both Manchester and the north-east have been studied in some detail by David Ayerst and Maurice Milne, and may therefore be treated quite briefly here.[143] Manchester did not resume its place as a stronghold of political Liberalism until 1906, but the *Manchester Guardian* was amongst the handful of leading, and one of the very few profitable provincial morning papers. As J.R. Scott had put it, the test was 'to make readable righteousness remunerative', and the *Guardian* made a very good job of it. It was hard hit by its anti-war stand in 1900, and continued to lose circulation until 1907, but it was still the leading Manchester paper, despite the fact that Northcliffe had subsidised the Conservative *Manchester Courier.* The radical *Manchester Examiner* had been sold to the Unionists in 1889, but had folded altogether in

1894. In addition to the *Guardian* there was its stable-mate the
Manchester Evening News, ostensibly 'independent', but obviously
sympathetic. The proprietors had not meddled in local politics since
the 1850s, but the editor C.P. Scott was active, and sat as MP for Leigh
from 1895 to 1906, and then became president of the Manchester
Liberal Federation. The main danger to the paper came from inside,
after J.E. Taylor's death in 1905. The struggle for the proprietorship
lasted almost a year, and when eventually the Scotts secured it, the
paper was reckoned to be in financial danger until 1910. Having
weathered this storm, however, the *Guardian* grew stronger, and
remained the leading radical provincial paper in the country.

Liverpool, which did not undergo Liberalisation after 1906 as
Manchester did, was less well served in the matter of a Liberal daily,
but until 1905 there were still two Liberal morning papers, the
Liverpool Daily Post, and the *Liverpool Daily Mercury,* and when they
were merged in that year the position of the former seemed very
healthy. Over the previous five years it had shown an average annual
profit of over £40,000, while the *Mercury* had shown one of nearly
£11,000 over the same period.[144] The Conservative rival, the *Liverpool
Courier,* the property of J.A. Willox MP, was almost certainly inferior
both politically and commercially to the more prestigious properties
of the Liberal Sir Edward Russell and A.G. Jeans.[145]

It was in the north-east that the struggle between the old and the
new, and between Liberal and Conservative was the fiercest.[146] The
area had been since the 1870s a Liberal one, and it was claimed in 1874
that 'it would have been hopeless for any Liberal candidate to come
forward without Mr Cowen's approval'. Cowen had bought the
Newcastle Daily Chronicle at the end of 1859, and by 1873 it was
claiming a circulation in excess of 45,000. He had recruited a radical,
not to say republican staff, and in 1874, on his election to Parliament,
he appointed James Annand as editor. The two men soon fell out,
however, over Cowen's long-standing Russophobia, and Annand left in
1879 to edit J.C. Stevenson's *Shields Gazette,* which he made into a
strong Liberal organ. Cowen's increasingly hostile attitude towards
Gladstone's foreign policy eventually led him out of Parliament, and
already, by 1881, Newcastle Liberals were trying to establish a new,
more orthodox paper. They helped Samuel Storey and the Syndicate
buy the *Tyneside Echo* in that year, and then got Annand to start the
Northern Leader in 1884. When in 1885 Joicey took over the *Leader,*
with Annand as editor, the ensuing battle between the Newcastle dailies
saw the end of the old Liberal morning paper, the *Northern Daily*

Express, in 1866, and of Storey's more recent *Tyneside Echo,* in 1888.
During the 1890s a Lib-Lab paper, the *Newcastle Evening News,* was
published by a new independent Liberal company in 1899, the Morning
Mail Company, whose papers, however, were becoming increasingly
Unionist. In 1901 the company and its papers were bought by the
proprietor of the *Daily Express,* C.A. Pearson, and the new Unionist
North Mail appeared. Worse was to come when Joicey tired of the
radicalism of Watson, editor since 1895, sacked him in 1901. Two
years later he sold the paper to the *North Mail.* Meanwhile the
Newcastle Daily Chronicle had veered increasingly towards Unionism,
which left Gladstonians in Newcastle without a journal.

They had to look to the *Northern Echo* in Darlington.[147] Under
W.T. Stead's editorship this had been perhaps the most successful of
provincial papers, but in 1887 Bell sold it to a company of local
Liberals, including the industrialists Christopher Furness and Alfred
Pease. In 1895 they in turn relinquished control in favour of
E.D. Walker, who engaged the young Charles Starmer as managing
editor, and this proved a master stroke. By 1903 the winds of political
change might easily have toppled the *Echo,* but Starmer approached
Joseph Rowntree, and in 1904 through the Rowntree Social Service
Trust, the North of England Newspaper Company was formed to run
the paper, with the advice of Ernest Parke of the *Star* and *Morning
Leader.* A Newcastle office was opened, and close relations were
established with the Newcastle Liberals. Both Walker and Starmer had
been mayors of Darlington, and Starmer was himself secretary of the
Darlington Liberal Association. G.G. Armstrong succeeded Cox Meach
as editor, and, a little later, succeeded to Starmer's secretaryship. It was
Starmer's management, however, which seems to have ensured the
paper's success, and the maintenance of a Liberal press in the area,
albeit one geared to the new journalism, which the older giants had
spurned.

Elsewhere in the north-east the picture was gloomier. The
Sunderland Echo had for long reflected the increasingly idiosyncratic
course of Storey, through to his adoption of Protection in 1903. His
Northern Daily Mail (Hartlepool) was kept on a more even Liberal keel
by the influence of one of his co-proprietors, Furness, and it was,
indeed, Furness who managed to buy the *North Mail* from a
disillusioned Pearson in 1906. This was an important capture, but it did
not go unnoticed that the surviving papers, like the *Echo* and the *Mail*
were halfpenny evenings. The days of the penny morning were quite
obviously almost gone.

When looked at in local detail, therefore, the anxieties expressed by Liberals about the state of their press at the turn of the century are seen to have had some foundation. The *Sunderland Daily Post,* a Conservative paper, observed on the demise of the *Newcastle Daily Leader* in 1903 that 'there will not be a single penny morning liberal paper between Dundee and Manchester'.[148] This was not strictly true, as it ignored the *York Herald* and the *Bradford Observer,* but the import of the observation was accurate enough. The heavy artillery had indeed virtually ceased to function. It was perhaps a little disingenuous of the *Post,* however, not to point out that the Conservatives had only the *Yorkshire Post* and the *Newcastle Daily Journal* in this category in England, and in Scotland south of Dundee only the *Scotsman* and the *Glasgow Herald,* both of which were rather Unionist than Conservative papers. In 1904 W.J. Fisher went even further, claiming that the Liberals had no paper, presumably of any sort, between Glasgow and Bradford. Again the penny morning *York Herald* was missed, and in addition the halfpenny morning *Northern Echo* and six other halfpenny evenings in England alone. And again on the Conservative side there were only the two penny mornings mentioned above, two halfpenny mornings, the *North Star* and the *North Mail,* and two halfpenny evenings in Sunderland and Scarborough. The Liberal position, therefore, relative to the Conservatives was not disastrous. What was serious was the decline in the position of the Liberal press relative to that which had existed in the golden age. This was a trend adverse not only to the Liberal press, but to the penny morning press as a whole, and even to a small extent to the halfpenny morning press.

To put Liberal anxieties in perspective it should be remembered that there was equally frantic activity to secure a good press on the Unionist side. Joseph Chamberlain, who had always been adept at press relations, secured first the backing of Alfred Harmsworth with the *Daily Mail,* the *Evening News* and the *Daily Mirror,* and then of C.A. Pearson, proprietor of the *Daily Express,* in the pursuit of his Tariff Reform campaign from 1903.[149] Pearson was the more closely involved, as he was from July 1903 chairman and a most active member of the Tariff Reform League.[150] His influence, however, was exerted at a personal and organisational level, rather than through his newspaper. Not for nothing had Chamberlain called him 'the greatest hustler I have • ever known'.[151] His journalism was probably less effective than his management of speaking tours and press campaigns at local level, and the manipulation of agents.[152] On the business side of the press, however, he did make some important contributions. In 1903 he

bought the *St. James's Gazette,* and in November 1904 he purchased
the ailing *Standard* and the *Evening Standard* from the Johnstone
family for £300,000. He told Chamberlain that

> 'the Standard' has from the point of view of newspaper influence
> done far more to impede the course of Tariff Reform than any
> other paper. It has still a great hold among the sober thinking classes
> and particularly among businessmen, for its commercial intelligence
> has always been looked upon as the very best.[153]

The Liberal press, of course, attacked the transaction as an example of
improper control of the free press, but in the first instance at least only
the editor, Byron Curtis, was removed, with S.H. Jeyes remaining as
assistant editor. By 1905, however, the Free Food Unionists were
claiming that the Cecils had been working through Jeyes to set up a
newspaper favourable to them.[154] H.A. Gwynne had succeeded Curtis,
with his cousin William Woodward taking over the *Evening Standard.*
    By this time Pearson also controlled the Midland Express Company,
which ran the *Midland Express;* the *Birmingham Daily Gazette,* which
he had bought in 1904; the *Birmingham Evening Dispatch,* which came
to him with the *Standard* from the Johnstones; the *Leicester Evening
News,* which folded in 1905; the *Newcastle Weekly Leader,* which he
had bought from James Joicey in 1903; and the *North Mail,* which he
had founded in Newcastle in 1901.[155] This was an impressive list, and
it has been calculated that the Unionists in London in 1905 could reach
1,605,000 readers to the Liberals' 550,000, and that most of the
leading provincial papers were Unionist.[156] It was hardly surprising,
then, that Campbell-Bannerman lamented during the 1906 election that
'the newspaper press had largely (and he thought it was a great
misfortune) got into the hands of combinations of capitalists and
others.'[157]
    From the Unionist point of view, however, the crucial point was
that the party was divided, and that the strength of Tariff Reform in
the London press served only to exacerbate the division. Iwan Muller,
a leader writer for the *Daily Telegraph,* had in 1905 expressed his
concern to Balfour at the lack of a Unionist evening halfpenny paper
outside Leeds and Birmingham, and in a post-mortem on the 1906
result made it plain to the Unionist leader that the Unionist press had
only served to publicise the internal divisions of the party.[158] Balfour,
indeed, had lacked press support, with the exception of the less than
dependable *Times,* which had offered Arthur Elliot, a Free Food

Unionist, a column and a half three days a week to put his case! The offer was declined, and had probably been made in the hope of forestalling the establishment of a new Free Food Unionist paper, but it was hardly witness to the steadfastness of *The Times*.[159] In the provinces Balfour could count on the *Yorkshire Post,* often the *Pall Mall Gazette,* and possibly the *Scotsman* and the *Liverpool Daily Post*.[160] The Unionist Free Traders had to rely on the weekly *Spectator.* They tried to buy their way into the *Manchester Courier,* but were outbid by Harmsworth, and failed to find finance for the new paper that had been rumoured. In January 1905 they made Cadbury an offer for the *Daily News,* a desperate and inevitably unsuccessful bid.[161]

The Unionist Free Traders were a weak group, but it is more remarkable that the massed guns of the Tariff Reform press had so little effect in 1906. Party divisions were important, but the failure is also indicative, as was the surprising victory of the Liberals, that electoral results were not to be explained by the balance of the press alone. The continued failure of a strong Protectionist press in the ensuing years adds strength to this view. Harmsworth picked up the *Observer* in 1905, and *The Times* in 1908, and Pearson, suffering from early blindness, relinquished the *Standard* and the *Evening Standard* in 1910 to Davison Dalziel, and the *Daily Express* in 1912, partly to the Conservative Party, under the charge of R.D. Blumenfeld, and eventually to Max Aitken. The *Standard* continued to decline, *The Times* and the *Observer* brought little financial reward to Northcliffe, and although the *Express* held up, none of these papers seems to have benefited from their Protectionist leanings, or to have exercised much influence that way either on the voters or on the politicians. This failure, perhaps even more than the decline of the old Liberal press at the same time, was due witness to the advent of both a 'new journalism' and a 'new politics'.

Matters of 'influence' will be left to the next chapter, but it is convenient to conclude this section with a look at the situation in terms of circulation. After all, the mere number of titles on the one side and the other might be no indication of their true strengths. Unfortunately one is immediately confronted with almost insuperable difficulties. Evidence as to circulations before the First World War, with the exception of a few large papers which published audited net sales certificates, is very scarce, and invariably unreliable. Advertising lists habitually used 'peak' figures as if they were averages, or spoke of the number of 'readers' rather than the copies sold. Most papers, faced with stiffening competition, were also reluctant to divulge such valuable information, even to their advertisers.

Table 30 gives an idea of the sort of circulations involved, although the figures happen to relate in the main to Liberal papers. It seems likely, however, that after the 1880s a provincial daily was viable on a circulation of over 20,000 (perhaps something more like 40,000 for an evening paper). The most successful were pushing to the 50,000 mark. In the 1870s the crucial level may have been about 15,000. Interestingly enough, this meant that even in the 1880s some provincial weeklies had larger circulations than the dailies. The *Newcastle Weekly Chronicle,* for example, was up to 38,000 in 1875, and the *Western Gazette* (Yeovil), was up to 30,000 in the 1880s.[162] If it is assumed that the readers of the dailies were more or less the same day after day, this would give the edge to at least some of the weeklies in terms of coverage. However, the balance was somtimes redressed by the increased Saturday circulations of the dailies. In 1872, for example, the *Sheffield Daily Telegraph* printed 16,000 on Saturdays instead of the usual daily 8,000-9,000, and its rival the *Independent* printed 25,000 instead of 6,000-7,000.[163] This is, unfortunately, a very rare example of a case where Liberal and Conservative papers can be compared and little or nothing can be said, as yet, about the national picture.

In London, however, at least a reasonable guess may be hazarded. By 1910 there is no doubt that the Conservatives had a big lead in the morning press, albeit that the press was no more united than its party. The Conservatives had more papers and larger ones. Using what must again be stressed are unreliable figures for individual papers, at least an overall pattern may be discerned. The Conservative morning press, that is the press which was not admittedly Liberal, had something like 2.5 million circulation compared to the Liberals' 0.8 million. In the evening press the Liberals had the *Star,* and if the *Advertisers' A.B.C.* figure of 300,000 is used for the Conservative *Evening News,* the Liberals may have had 0.3 million to the Conservatives' 0.6 million. It is well attested, however, that the *News* was up to 0.8 million in 1898, and if this is assumed to have been maintained, then the Conservative advantage would have been nearer four than two to one.[164] Only in the Sunday papers did the Liberals have a clear lead, with something like 4.75 million to the Conservatives' 0.6 million, assuming the latter's *People* had reached 0.5 million by that time. The morning and evening proportions, however, would have been inconceivable in the golden age of the 1870s, and even the 1880s.

Finally, and perhaps more importantly, there had by 1910 already

been a large degree of concentration of ownership. Table 31 shows
the position for the London press, where two-thirds of the morning
and four-fifths of the evening circulation was controlled by the same
three proprietors, or groups, and four-fifths of the Sunday circulation
was shared by only four proprietors. (If the *Evening News* is credited
with its previously recorded 800,000, this would raise the share of the
top three proprietors in the evening circulation to nearly 90 per cent,
with the *News* itself accounting for more than 55 per cent of it.) It
was this process, possibly even more than changes in political
complexion, that was most significant. Even the Liberal press was
caught up in the vortex of monopolisation. This was especially true
in the provinces, for while both Northcliffe and Pearson had extended
their empires there by 1910, the Liberals had probably done so more
successfully. In 1910 the Cadbury Trust, which owned the *Daily
News*, absorbed the *Morning Leader* and the *Star* from the Rowntrees'
Northern Newspaper Company, which was left, however, with the
Northern Echo, and the successor of the weekly *Speaker,* the *Nation.*
By 1910 also the company, led by Starmer, had control of the
Sheffield Independent and the *Birmingham Gazette,* thus laying the
foundations of one of the large post-war chains, the Westminster Press.
Some members of the *Morning Leader* company had also old
connections and interests in the two leading East Anglian Liberal
dailies. Ritzema of Blackburn had long been in association with
Gilzean-Reid in Middlesborough, and had been brought into the *Daily
News* in 1902. In 1905 J.E. Taylor had been unsuccessfully urged to
obtain a controlling interest in the *Leeds Mercury* and the *Yorkshire
Observer.*[165] Economic pressures thus forced the old Liberal patrons
ineluctably together in their fight to preserve a Liberal press, and they
were successful only at the price of increasing concentration of
control. Fewer proprietors also meant fewer genuine alternatives. By
1910 the number of towns having at least one daily paper had been
reduced to 57, from a peak of 71 in 1906. Even discounting the effect
of the Infield chain, which disappeared in that year, the trend was
clear, the number of daily papers in England having been reduced
from 139 in the hectic year of 1886 to 121 in 1910. It was to be
further reduced to 106 by 1921.[166] What all this meant in terms of
the political role of the press is the subject of the next chapter.

6 DEMOCRACY AND THE PRESS

I A Question of Influence

The Liberal vision of the press as a vehicle of political education depended, as we have seen, on the development of education in general, and on the effects of this on literacy, readership and politics. This development, however, was slow, and although education and literacy had improved by the 1880s this was not the miraculous result of the Forster Education Act. The advances were on the whole technical in nature, and were certainly not guarantees of an 'educated democracy'. The physical expansion of the press after the repeal of the stamp was also a largely technical achievement, resulting in more and cheaper newspapers, owned and run by men who were entrepreneurs and businessmen, and made by journalists whose status had changed from earlier disrepute, through a 'professional' to a 'tradesman' stage, parallel with the expansion of the industry. Against these technical advances the Liberal domination of the press by the 1880s had begun to be eroded, partly by the growth of a Conservative press, and partly by a decline in the institution of the 'party newspaper'. Changes in the political structure and process also encouraged changes in the structure and nature of the press, and in its relation to politics, such that the older liberal theory of the political role of the press became less and less tenable. It is that political role which remains to be discussed.

The problem raised at the beginning of this essay was precisely that of the relationship between the press and politics, but then as now it was put in such a way as to go beyond the rather restricting framework of functional analysis.[1] Quite rightly the Liberal vision extended to the whole socio-political context of the press, and it was in the light of this vision that the development and decline of the Liberal, and of the liberal idea of the press was watched and criticised, and even deplored during the rest of the century. The technical, social and economic parts of the problem have now been examined, and it is possible to focus upon the political part as such. What were the political functions of the press? How did the 'fourth estate' relate to the 'governing classes'? Did it perform, or seek to perform the functions foreseen for it by its earlier advocates?

Before the repeal of the stamp there were some, like Henry

Brougham, who looked to the newspaper as the only way of
expressing public opinion until the course of parliamentary reform
had been run. That course was run slowly, and in the meantime it
became accepted that the press was no mere temporary expedient,
but a permanent if informal part of the constitution. If few politicians
conceded the typical journalists' claim that the press was, indeed, a
'fourth estate', at least by the 1870s it was almost universally
acknowledged that it did have a valuable political function, namely, that it
helped politicise in an acceptable way those who were in increasing numbers
being brought within the political pale. What the young Joseph
Chamberlain said in defence of the party caucus would have been quite
happily accepted as applicable to the press by many politicians and
journalists: 'every institution which assists the political
education of the people, which increases their interest in public affairs,
which tempts them to take their share in moulding the destinies of the
nation, everything, in short, which helps the people to govern themselves,
is a contribution (to democracy)'.[2] The only difference would have been
that it seemed likely that the press might thus further political education on
a larger scale than the deliberately exclusive party caucus. The *Leeds Mercury*
in 1872 claimed that the burgeoning of the provincial press had in fact been
a response to the demand for information created by recent political change.[3]
Yet claims such as these, so frequently made, had always in our period
to remain speculative, partly as will be seen because no attempt was
made to test them empirically, and partly because it was only after
the effects of the Reform Acts and Education Acts had had time to
work through, that a system open enough to accommodate such a view
of the press's role could develop. They were claims, if made precise,
which had to be couched in terms of political influence, claims which
touched the issues of the efficacy of elections, the responsibility of
governments and political power.

Analytically a distinction may be made between the influence
actually exercised by the press, together with its strength, its various
forms, and its effectiveness, and the influence which it was thought to
possess or exercise. It is clear, however, that there must always be
interaction between these aspects of influence. What people do and say
is affected by what they think, directly or indirectly, even if what they
think happens to be mistaken. A political system controlled by those
who believe the press a valuable weapon in political warfare will provide
evidence of attempts by politicians to use the press for political ends.
That such attempts might prove fruitless does not detract from the fact
that they have been made. Money poured into newspapers, and

pressures put upon journalists might be quite ineffectual against an impervious and incorruptible press, but the money and the pressures are, after all, evidence that not everyone believes that they will be ineffectual. And one need not, of course, impugn the motives of those who seek to use the press for political ends. It is the Liberal premise that this is what the press should be used for. It was precisely the depoliticisation of the press, in party terms, that so exercised Liberals at the turn of the century. To appreciate their concern it is necessary first to look briefly at some aspects of the political system after the 1860s.

It is now accepted that the electoral reforms of 1867, and of 1884 and 1885 did not make the system radically democratic. By 1911 still only some 59 per cent of the adult male population was enfranchised, a proportion effectively reduced by plural votes, registration difficulties and uncontested elections.[4] The change, however, from a close community-based politics of the mid-Victorian period, to the more nationally class-based politics of the twentieth century was already under way by the 1880s, and was substantially advanced by 1910.[5] This meant that local pressures were of declining political significance, and although this trend should not be exaggerated in this period, it was one inevitably deleterious to the status and power of the provincial daily. Moreover, there was a change of 'political morality' which legitimised the practice of using social policies to 'buy' or win votes. The reformed electoral system was increasingly recognised to have given power to the electorate at elections, and, through a reasonably cohesive two-party system, to have ensured majorities in Parliament to the winners of elections.[6] These developments tended to concentrate the vulnerability of governments, but less so of parties, in elections, usually, of course, at times of their own choosing. This, as we shall see, had a considerable effect on the political role of the press. If, now, the electorate was a greater force to be reckoned with, the political elite was still oligarchical and self-generating. A few politicians held enormous power by virtue on the one hand of party organisation, and on the other of the increasing power of the Cabinet in relation to Parliament.[7] There were some who saw in this a tyranny of 'the party system', and connected with it a decline of 'the free press'.[8] In a political system thus organised, it was claimed, the press became at best a 'party press' without either power or influence. Whether or not this was a legitimate claim, it was one which focused attention on the crucial question, namely the political influence of the press. It suggested that the press had not been able to cope with the political changes which had occurred since the 1870s, not at least in a way which enabled it to continue as a 'fourth estate' of the realm.

There is some case for dispensing altogether with the catch-all concept of 'influence'. People living in the same society cannot, after all, help 'influencing' each other, if only by occupying a space which, therefore, cannot simultaneously be occupied by anyone else. If there is to be any communication whatever between individuals, and if there is none there can be no society, then such communication must in some way, 'influence' or 'condition' the thought and behaviour of those involved. The concept, therefore, needs to be considerably narrowed to be of any operational use. It must not, however, be narrowed so much that, for convenience, some activities are arbitrarily segregated from others, or examined over too short a span of time.[9] It is not sufficient, for example, merely to examine the ways in which politicians formally 'influence' electors at elections, for this would neglect important conditioning processes, and the social and political contexts of voting. Modern studies of political change have gone some way in the direction or providing a more comprehensive understanding of such activities, although there is still a tendency to stop the process in order to dissect it, and thereby to lose its character.[10] Fortunately the additional difficulties of the historian oblige him to widen his vision. There is no way of discovering what 'influence' newspapers may have had upon the political opinions and decisions of the electorate before 1914.[11] No opinion polls or readership surveys were conducted, and even the basic data about the press is fragmentary and suspect. It remains virtually impossible even to gauge the exposure of the electorate to the press at this time, let alone to assess what the effects may have been.[12] We must, therefore, rely on more indirect methods of inference, and for these to be at all plausible they must be closely related to the wider social and political context of the problem. It is also important to remember that contemporaries were as much in the dark as we are about such matters. Election canvasses were made, but they were highly localised, and few survive. Party organisers had usually to rely on intuition and experience, and the use of rules of thumb about the voting propensities of occupational and religious groups. Such evidence, then, will necessarily be largely impressionistic. So too were the opinions of contemporaries about the place of the press, but it is as important to understand what men have thought to be the case as it is to understand what it actually was.

In what follows press 'influence' is examined as exercised firstly upon the electorate, and secondly upon what the Victorians termed 'the governing classes'. This distinction has also been put in terms of the direction of 'influence', so that the relationship between the press and the electorate is in the nature of a vertical process connecting the electorate to the politicians, while that between the press and the governing classes is more of a horizontal process connecting different groups and individuals within the governing classes, including the press itself.[13] In the Liberal vision it had been the first which had been emphasised, but in practice the horizontal process was equally if not more important than the vertical, especially in this period, when journalists and proprietors were often active politicians themselves, or were at least in intimate contact with them. It was not that there was not room in the Liberal pantheon for such relationships. Indeed, they came very near to what some of the democratic elitists like J.S. Mill would have desired. But Mill had never shared the more democratic aspect of the Liberal vision of the newspaper press. Radicals, on the other hand, had always distrusted liaisons between journalists and politicians, as tending to corrupt if not deprave the journalist, whilst putting a powerful weapon in the hands of the unscrupulous politician. This conflict of view was heightened by political and journalistic changes after the 1870s.

II The Press and the Electors

The ultimate test of political opinion in the British political system is the election, and it is tempting to follow common sense, and to expect that if the press, either in a particular place or over the whole country, was of a certain political hue, then the majority of the electorate concerned would vote accordingly. Even if the press did not directly affect the voters, it would seem likely that, at least in its own interest, it would reflect their views. The problems of the composition both of the electorate and of readership, and of the complexities of the working of the system, are easily put to one side in favour of a simple demonstration of 'influence'. The first use of such arguments on a national scale came with the defeat of Gladstone in 1874. Three years previously he had praised the provincial press for expressing the real opinion of the country, as against the London papers of the clubs and 'the powerful classes'.[14] In 1874 he attributed his defeat to the temporary apostasy of the provincial press, and the continued conservatism of the metropolitan. It was a view he was long to maintain. The point was taken up by Wemyss Reid after Gladstone's return to power in 1880, this being a sign, Reid thought, that public opinion was indeed reflected in the provincial rather than in the London press.

A Conservative politician concurred in this view, and Randolph
Churchill used similar reasoning in 1890 when he forecast Gladstone's
return in 1892.[15] The thesis continued to flourish until 1906, when the
result was considered to be so aberrant in relation to the political
deployment of the press that the simple provincial/metropolitan
dichotomy was clearly insufficient to explain the Liberal victory.
J.A. Spender later reflected that the press had been correct in reporting
the political interests of its readers and advertisers as Conservative. The
majority of the newspaper-reading public, he thought, had been
Conservative. The important fact was, however, that they no longer
constituted the majority of the electorate.[16] There were nearly eight
million potential electors in 1911, all of them adult males. It is
unlikely that the total circulation of the daily press, plus the popular
Sundays, came near this figure, and whereas fewer women and children
may have been newspaper readers than men, there was no law
prohibiting them from the activity, so it is reasonable to assume that
not more than half of this circulation would have had the vote, and that
something under half the electorate may have been newspaper readers.
(If circulation is boosted by a multiplier of two or three to account for
multiple readership, there would still be an excess of newspaperless
electors, and some at least of the total circulation would have
represented sales of more than one paper to the same individual.) Thus
Spender's argument was plausible. Furthermore, it was not a happy
admission for a Liberal journalist of the old school to have to make, for
its corollary was that the press was relatively uninfluential, because a
great many electors did not read newspapers, or at least did not seem
to glean their politics from them. What was left of the Liberal vision of
an educated democracy when a Liberal government was elected with a
huge majority by illiterate or politically apathetic voters? Some face
could be saved by pointing out that in terms of votes cast, the Liberals
received only 6 per cent more than the Conservatives, the 'landslide'
being in part due to the way in which the system magnified the effect
of small majorities, and diminished that of large ones.[17] But there was
no escaping the fact that Liberals and Labour seemed to have done
disproportionately well in relation to the state of their press. As we
have seen, the state of the Liberal press, at least in the provinces, was
not as parlous as some liked to maintain, but even a degree of erroneous
pessimism does not explain the problem away completely. Those most
closely involved, and those in contact with the machinery of electoral
politics were probably less surprised than the 'higher' journalists or the
national politicians. In the course of his study of party organisation

Ostrogorski

> frequently had occasion to note that in a locality where the Press of
> a party is prosperous, where for instance the latter has three papers
> with a good circulation to one of the opposite political persuasion,
> the party is beaten at the elections, sometimes badly beaten. I have
> noticed similar facts in Yorkshire, in Lancashire and the Midlands, in
> manufacturing towns as well as in rural districts.

He also noted that the secretary of a local caucus had remarked to him
that 'while the only newspaper of our political opponents exists simply
on the subsidies of the party, we have three and all doing well, but I
will make a bet that these three papers have not secured us three
votes'.[18] Allowing for some exaggeration, it is likely that this was not
an untypical view of local experts. Of course, no agent was actually
going to refuse financial support in the form of contributions to the
running of the local paper, and connections with proprietors were
always worth having, as was anything in the nature of publicity. The
work of A.F. Stephenson, the proprietor of the *Southport Visiter,* was
well thought of by local Conservatives, although the paper seems to
have been of little political value.[19] The fact remained, however, that
efforts to control the local press were often very disappointing.
Manchester Conservatives, for example, gave a cool reception to
Northcliffe's injection of £50,000 into the *Manchester Courier* in the
1900s.[20] London Conservatives also seem to have been sceptical of the
utility of newspapers, and spent more on hoardings and placards than
on press advertising, or on other means of supporting friendly papers.[21]

Many acknowledged that the important role of the newspaper was
rather in the keeping than in the winning of votes. It might be that, as
Dr Johnson had put it a couple of centuries earlier, the newspaper
'affords sufficient information to elate vanity, and stiffen obstinacy,
but too little to enlarge the mind into complete skill for
comprehension',[22] but whatever the cause the effect had often been
noted. Ostrogorski found that

> if the voter does not take his party politics from the paper, it
> confirms him in his party preferences or prejudices, and by an action
> analogous to that of water dripping on a stone, keeps him loyal to
> the party; in any event the newspapers provided the parties and their
> organisations with a highly effective means of publicity.[23]

Modern studies of the effect of the press on party preferences have
echoed this view, in Britain and elsewhere.[24] Newspapers, when they
did preach, almost always did so to the converted, for it is usually only
the converted who will abide being preached to. There may be
occasions, as David Butler and Donald Stokes have suggested in the case
of Britain's applications to join the EEC in the mid-1960s, where
conversions and apostasies take place amongst those most exposed to
sources of information such as the press, and it might be that historians
will be able to demonstrate a similar process in relation to the complex
issues of unemployment insurance and old age pensions before 1914,
as well as for the more obviously divisive issues such as Irish Home Rule
and Tariff Reform, but that is not the case as yet. Butler and Stokes
found that change and 'influence' occurred amongst the committed
when their usual framework for understanding political issues proved
inadequate, because those issues were too complex or too novel, and
this was hardly the case with either Home Rule or Protection.[25] It
remains fairly certain that the press's role has lain largely in the erosion
of well-established patterns of prejudice, and not in Damascene
conversions.

The old liberal point, of course, had been that the provision of a
framework of understanding was precisely the proper role of the
newspaper, to help its readers reach their conclusions in the light of a
sustained and informed commentary, but Ostrogorski was not alone
in his scepticism about the effectiveness of the political education
given by the press.[26]

A good many representatives of the Associations hold that the Press
explains political questions to the electorate so completely and
satisfactorily as to make it unnecessary for them to take any thought
for political education. In reality it is only as a channel of political
information that newspapers contribute to the enlightenment of the
public, and even this statement requires qualification. But as for
improving the political judgement of their readers, the great
majority of the newspapers utterly fails to do so.

Once again modern studies have supported his analysis. Studies of the
modern provincial press in particular have demonstrated the failure of
papers to inform or to educate their readers, over whom they now
exercise in the vast majority of cases a monopoly on matters such as
planning and education.[27]

Diachronic comparisons must be used cautiously. Readership, the electorate and the very means of mass communications have changed greatly since 1914. There were fewer newspaper readers, no women voters, and no radio or television, apart altogether from the other social changes which have altered the entire environment of the press, and of politics. Yet there is no reason to suppose that the sort of 'influence' that was exercised by the newspapers of the 1900s was greatly different from that exercised by those of today. The trend since at least as far back as the turn of the twentieth century has been away from newspapers as political educators, in the old sense of the term. Thus the disappointment of the older journalists, especially those who held to the Liberal vision, can better be understood. The aim of the old journalism had been, indeed, not to preach to the converted, but to convert, to improve, to educate, to perform a responsibly critical role outside the party system if necessary. By the end of the century this was a role increasingly confined to a weekly press of 'opinion', and, with notable provincial exceptions, absent from the everyday newspaper. J.L. Garvin claimed that this type of serious journalism, given a large circulation, could rule a democracy, but even with Northcliffe's backing he could not attain that size of circulation for the *Observer*.[28] The aim was, in the classic phrase of J.R. Scott of the *Manchester Guardian,* 'to make readable righteousness remunerative'.[29] To the 'new journalism' if not to the new politics the righteousness of the activity was hardly a consideration.

There were some who put the blame for the decline in the political status and quality of the press at the feet of the readers, who were somehow unsuited to the political education provided by the best papers. More radical critics, concurring in the fact of the decline, blamed the papers themselves for the dereliction of their political duty. This last argument could be given a keener edge, by Graham Wallas, for example, who saw in the modern press an example of his theme of the increasingly non-rational structure of modern society, in which newspapers had only a temporary and emotional effect, and succeeded in divorcing their readers from reality, in providing substitutes for thought, and in replacing coherence by discontinuity.[30] This was certainly to exaggerate the virtues of the golden age press in order more deeply to damn that of Wallas's own time, but as we saw above, there was ample reason to believe that this was indeed the tendency of the 'new journalism'. Having failed to establish, or to manufacture a consensus from above, the 'new journalism' had instead sought to give the illusion of a greater contribution from below, from the 'public'. It was an illusion because the relationship of the reader, or the 'public', to the paper, and to other readers, was increasingly distorted by the demands of the market. The informed letter writer of earlier years who plagued local and national authorities found it more and more difficult to get a hearing, while the larger newspapers depended more and more upon selling space dearly to advertisers, and lived in too much fear of the libel laws to give the 'public' much rein.[31] Concentration of ownership and the growing scale of newspaper enterprise made entry to what had been looked upon as a public market place much more difficult, even for journalists. Radicals were, therefore, understandably chagrined at this blunting of what they had always reckoned as their most dangerous weapon, a free, cheap press.

There can have been few, if any, who argued the exactly contrary case, that Northcliffe and company had been a positive social or political benefit. The Conservatives were as angry as the radicals at his swift elevation to the peerage. Commenting on the honours of Wandsworth, Michelham and Harmsworth, the *Saturday Review* asked 'why should the British aristocracy allow impecunious party whips to thrust into their chamber scandalous journalists and Jewish moneychangers?'[32] It was, however, argued that the decline of politics as a partisan pursuit was to be welcomed, and that 'independence' and non-political matters were mercifully characteristic of the post-golden age press. The *Spectator* explained that the 1860s were gone; there were no longer the old Ten Pounders who could be addressed as a cohesive group, and when newspapers had more room for politics and for style. 'Readers have ceased to wish that the journals they prefer should agree with them in sentiment.'[33] The *Spectator*, however, was not very enthusiastic about the change. In 1904 it forecast a surprise result at the next election, and it lamented the old Ten Pounders.

> The householders have often (since then) shown complete
> independence of the Press; and the classes to which halfpenny papers
> appeal ask, or are supposed to ask for very different intellectual food
> from anything that John Delane or his colleagues have consented to
> supply.[34]

Independence of the press was, of course, for most journalists a dubious virtue, although it may have been true that some editors had sought to inculcate a critical attitude into their readers. Democratic Scotland, for example, was claimed never to have been ruled by the newspaper.[35] More important from the journalists' point of view was the press's independence of party. O'Connor of the *Star* said 'we believe that

the reader of the daily journal longs for other reading than mere
politics', and yet there was no lack of political material in the *Star.* It
was party politics that he meant.[36] Warnings of dependence on party
came from both ends of the political spectrum. Frederick Greenwood,
one of the most respectable of Victorian journalists, and a Conservative,
warned against papers losing their freedom of action to 'the political
machine', and H.W. Massingham, the young radical journalist, then
writing for the *Daily Chronicle,* claimed in 1892 that 'journalism, new
and old, is after all too dependent on the party machine'.[37] These were
views expressed at the end of the divisive 1880s, however, and
increasingly after that overt partisanship began noticeably to decline.
The socialist H.M. Hyndman was trying to cheer his supporters after the
electoral failure of 1895 when he called the claim of newspapers to
influence elections 'just so much rubbish and rhodomontade. . .
Newspapers are read nowadays for their news, not for their views', but
it was an observation which was receiving growing contemporary
support.[38]

The political implication of 'independence' or 'neutrality' was that
the press became a potentially less radical institution than before. A
recent study of the English provincial press in the 1960s has
demonstrated that a non-political stance is invariably a conservative
one. News of disorder in society is used to reinforce the reader's
confidence in the ability of his community to cope with it. 'The
provincial press is essentially a conservative medium.'[39] One notorious
radical journalist, Henry Labouchere, proprietor and editor of *Truth,*
argued that 'so long as there are grievances the newspaper will be a
radical agent',[40] but *Truth* was a metropolitan weekly, not unlike *The
Week* or *Private Eye* of later generations, and was in no way typical of
the press as a whole, even of the radical press. Indeed, it has been
argued that through the reporting of scandals the press has become
one of the most important vehicles of 'organised hypocrisy', and is used
to define and legitimise the existing social and political structure.[41]
There is a sense, moreover, in which a non-political press can be neither
radical nor critical, for political judgement is always involved here. In a
politically pluralist view this would apply even to the exclusion of
'mere' party politics. However, at the turn of the nineteenth century
it was a question of a tendency towards the non-political, and not of
the annihilation of the political, a tendency magnified by comparison
with the high degree of political partisanship of the previous thirty or
forty years.

Some claimed that depoliticisation also reduced the power of the large proprietors, because they could not profitably disseminate their views in a political form.[42] This was to ignore the facility they had for subsidising loss-making political papers which would do the job for them, and if the public's disenchantment with politics did keep them accepting a paper's political line, it did nothing to stop future press barons from using their papers to enhance their political power, however unsuccessful this policy may have been in practice.

None of these doubts about the effectiveness of the newspaper as a political weapon, none of the criticisms of the press for its failure to perform its proper political duties, none of the claims about the decline of party politics, deterred journalists and politicians from trying to use the press for political, usually party political, ends. The attempt to influence voters through newspapers was also related to other ways of influencing them. Before the Ballot Act and the extension of the franchise 'influence' had usually been personal, and perhaps secret, physical and corrupt. There had been little the press could do about this, except to 'expose' such practices, particularly at local level, but financial prudence, personal involvement and the fear of the libel laws usually restricted such activities to short-lived satirical sheets. The enlarging of the electorate, the greater secrecy of the proceedings, and the changing climate of political morality noted above undoubtedly widened the scope for newspaper influence on electors. At first, naturally, there were some cases of the press being used to continue corrupt practices which had become illegal or too expensive, and there was never to be agreement as to how far a newspaper might go in the latter direction. In the notoriously corrupt borough of Norwich it has been claimed that the Liberal *Norfolk News* partly concealed the extent of the very large expenses incurred in the 1874 election by the Liberal candidates, who were respectively proprietor and editor of the paper.[43] Shortly before this, in Macclesfield, the Conservative candidate was found to have spent £1,750 in advertising in the *Macclesfield Advertiser,* a paper said to have been 'brought out. . .by a section of the party. . .as much for the 1868 election as anything else'. In 1873 the Liberals established and subsidised the *Macclesfield Guardian,* and its successor, the *Macclesfield Chronicle,* was found to have received in 1880 substantial payments from the Liberals during the election, which were omitted from the returns of election expenses.[44] The line was a fine one between prior subsidisation and illegal election expenditure. Straight subsidies to party papers were, as we have seen from the Conservative Party's debates of the 1880s, an accepted practice. Edward Clarke, later to be Attorney-General, claimed that he had spent

£500 of his own money during an election, by way of subsidising the *Southwark Mercury*.[45] Provided such expenses did not exceed the legal limit, however, it was difficult to see how such practices could be stopped. In 1886 a case was brought against R. Gent-Davis, the Conservative MP for Kennington, claiming that his purchase of the *South London Standard* before the election should be chargeable to his expenses, but, while the judge accepted that the paper had been bought for the purpose of assisting Gent-Davis at the election, he found that it was not an illegal practice, as he had bought the paper before the campaign had started.[46] Such activity as this may well have been widespread, although in most cases it would be difficult to identify. In 1909 E.T. Powell, a supporter of more open government, suggested that the practice of papers publishing anything and everything about the candidates free of charge, with the exception of the election address, contravened the spirit of the Corrupt Practices Act, more particularly in cases where the paper was owned or controlled by the candidate in question.[47] He suggested some intricate rules to put an end to such practices, but practical difficulties and lack of political will ensured that it never became a matter for legislation. The 1883 Corrupt Practices Act had, in fact, made no mention of newspapers, nor did it touch any expense arising from the promotion and dissemination of party, as distinct from candidates', opinions. Sir Stafford Northcote did point out, however, that the restrictions on the use of placards worked slightly in favour of newspapers as a medium.[48] In 1895 the Act was amended to take cognisance of the libel laws, making it illegal to publish false statements about candidates. This was necessary because of the practice of publishing false statements so near to the actual poll that the ordinary law of libel could not provide adequate redress. It now became a petitionable offence, and several actions were pursued under the Act, including one against the editor of the *Eastern Post* in 1896.[49] It was, however, a very small restriction, and apart from it, and the ordinary law of libel, the law continued to exercise virtually no control over the activities of newspapers as newspapers, at election or any other time.

If the older morality lingered on, a newer one was quickly taking its place, one which continued to condemn the actual purchase of votes, but condoned and even encouraged the use of policies and programmes to obtain the approval and, therefore, the votes, of particular groups of the electorate. It was possible, of course, to look at this in the old terms of the intellectual market place, in which policies were openly offered, not for purchase, but for discussion and debate. Yet the process by which these policies were brought to the market place made the whole thing seem less intellectual than commercial in inspiration and control. The subsidisation of the press thus came to be seen by some, particularly particularly radicals, as not far removed from old fashioned borough-mongering.[50] Ironically it was the radical press which received most benefit from this political subsidisation. Indeed, it could not have survived without it.

The relationship of the press to the politicians and to the government itself will be examined in the next section, but arising from the argument about the influence of the newspaper on electors, and consequently about the control and use of the newspaper, was the more general debate about the press and the nature of government it was best suited to. Perhaps the best and most perceptive discussion of this problem came at the end of the period in R. Scott-James's *The Influence of the Press* (1913). There he pointed out that the modern state would not have been possible without the aid of printing, but that printing tended to encourage devolution rather than centralisation of government and of power, and thus simultaneously created a major problem for the state. Printing had, on the one hand, provided the opportunity and the means of obtaining and retaining political power, of 'making society articulate', whilst, on the other, through commercialisation, it had also demoralised society, blurred the distinction between falsehood and truth, trivialised, sensationalised and derationalised. What was wanted was decentralisation plus reason (his book was published by the Guild Socialist 'New Age' press), and the only real way of avoiding, or dealing with the danger of demoralisation was education, which would create a demand for an intellectually responsible and democratically useful press, in the form of the political and literary weeklies, presenting a continuous and informed discussion of the news.[51]

This was to reject the 'Barnum 'n' Bailey show' of the 'new journalism' with a vengeance, and it was a criticism characteristic of intellectuals, and one of long standing. Fitzjames Stephen voiced it in 1862, and in 1905 Edward Dicey deplored the way in which the 'new journalists' pandered to the demands of 'the newspaper reading public of today (who) want to be assured, not instructed. They like to have their mental food in minces and snippets, not in chops and joints.'[52] There were some who had held out against the trend. J.A. Spender in the *Westminster Gazette* and J.L. Garvin in the *Observer* had both tried to put forward connected analyses of the news, but had to fight against the new journalistic ethic which put facts and novelty before understanding, heat very much before light. Such editors were few, and the criticism, if arguably unhelpful, was not ill-founded.

It was a criticism which also led back to the issue of 'independence', for despite claims of 'neutrality' it was plain to many that the news itself in its selection and presentation was used as 'subtle propaganda for suggestion'.[53] The journalist, so Spender claimed, became 'so other-minded. . .(he) ceased to have a mind of his own'.[54] The position had changed by the turn of the century from what it had been even thirty years previously, when newspapers were glad to claim 'influence' because it was thought that would increase their circulation amongst the newspaper-reading public who were concerned with politics.[55] Clearly there was a difference between influencing readers who had opinions, and influencing readers whose only opinions had already been culled from a cursory acquaintance with the papers themselves. With parliamentary reform in mind J.B. Kinnear had complained in 1867 of the extent to which readers were slaves to their papers, and it was claimed in 1893 that the leading journals 'pander to the most ignorant prejudices, and make their miserable capital out of the vices or the passions of the classes which they profess to educate'.[56] These were partial views, but they represented an important strand of contemporary criticism, and drew attention to a particularly sensitive area, namely the effect of the 'new journalism' on the working classes.

The main line of this argument remained almost unchanged after 1870. The lower classes were regretfully too easily satisfied with literary trash. Abel Heywood, the Manchester printer and newsagent, pointed out in 1876 that there was little point in altering the tone of a paper with a view to improving its readers, because the paper would then attract a different readership, an argument that was sudden death to the whole Liberal conception of the press as an educational instrument.[57] The only effect of the 1870 Education Act, it seemed to many, was an increase in the number of 'junior clerks and such like' who had become the audience of the new weeklies of Harmsworth, Pearson and Newnes.[58] 'In this twilight of the lower middle-classes all the cats are grey.'[59]

Yet this sort of 'influence' was, as Escott shrewdly pointed out in 1880, more social than political. It affected the way in which people lived their lives, and only indirectly how they made their political decisions. One of the most obvious instances was the way in which people derived their style of language and vocabulary from the newspapers, both in written communication and in conversation.[60] As we have seen, with the 'new journalism' the newspaper came to play an increasingly important part in the leisure life of its readers, in some cases such as football and horse-racing transforming the very activities themselves. The more numerous, the more 'mass' the press became, the more its 'influence' in this sense grew. Fox-Bourne thought the newer press of the 1880s was more dangerous than that of the press of the golden age, because it now tended to foment rather than mollify 'jealousies of race, religion and class'.[61]

There had long been complaints about the way in which the press allegedly inflamed industrial unrest, from the agricultural disturbances of the 1830s to the Welsh mining conflicts of the 1850s, and so on.[62] The changing climate of labour relations after the 1860s, however, with greater attempts being made to foster the support of 'Labour', saw some of the largest papers in London and in the provinces take up labour grievances. It has been claimed that Joseph Arch and his Union benefited greatly from the coverage of the *Daily News* in the 1870s, and after the 1880s the radical press at least became very closely involved in disputes, and often, by thorough and sustained reporting, usually sympathetically, they lent strength to the workers involved.[63] As the employers continued to get their usual coverage, it might have seemed, indeed, that the press was exacerbating class 'jealousies', but it was probably and usually an unintentional consequence of the reporting of real conflict, of real 'jealousies'. These are questions, however, which have as yet been insufficiently studied to yield many answers. The effect of the structure and nature of the press upon the incorporation of the working class is clearly a crucial issue, as is its effect upon the condition of women, who being without the franchise, or economic power for the most part, had to rely upon men and the press to represent them.[64] Whatever the reality may have been, there is detectable towards the close of the century an air of increasing cynicism about the press and its relationship with its readers, and with the electorate. The old Liberal vision was fast fading, and it was giving way to a spectre of demagoguery and jingoism, of mob rule and unreason. G.M. Trevelyan, a Whig intellectual, wrote at the height of the Boer War of the 'White Peril', namely the flood of newsprint that was threatening to envelope the whole of rational society.[65] Others were less hysterical, but no less pessimistic. L.T. Hobhouse, one of the brightest intellectual leaders of the 'new liberals', wrote in 1909 that 'the Press more and more the monopoly of a few rich men, from being the organ of democracy has become rather the sounding-board for whatever ideas command themselves to the great material interests.'[66]

It is in this area of 'the great material interests', and more particularly in the relationships those interests had with politics and government, in the socially and politically 'horizontal' plane of communication, amongst the 'governing classes' themselves, that the discussion of the political place of the press must conclude. If the Liberal vision of a press-enlightened electorate was fading, it was still hoped that the influence of enlightened journalists might be exerted more directly, through the advice and information they could provide, either indirectly through their papers, or personally through direct contact with political decision-takers.

III The Press and the Politicians

We have seen how the status of the journalist and of the press had changed during the nineteenth century. Those who worked for respectable papers were by the third quarter of the century received as 'Gentlemen': their job had acquired the *cachet* of a profession; the law's hostility had been mollified, if not by any means removed; and political recognition was in the process of being granted. And yet the function of the newspaper and of the journalist remained ambiguous. Bagehot voiced a common view in 1851 that modern journalists were akin to the old 'vagabond speculators' and the Greek Sophists. They catered for the popular demand for gossip and speculation, and were paid for doing so.[67] In an acute article some sixty years later T.H.S. Escott returned to this point. He noted that the older view of the Sophists as either corrupters of Athenian democracy, or the product of an already corrupt society, should be altered in favour of the philosophical-radical view of George Grote, who had argued that they were really a sort of established clergy, who through their arguing reinforced rather than undermined the accepted morality of the age. Socrates liked to represent himself as the hammer of the Sophists, but they, like him, defended the worst argument until it was broken down, and it was this process which buttressed the established system of values. This, as we have seen, was the classical liberal argument for freedom of speech, and Escott claimed that it provided a close parallel with modern journalism. 'The average journalist like the average Sophist, the average statesman and the average man of business, accepts the recognised rules of his calling. . .and plays a more or less essential part in the complicated machinery of government', especially in a system of politics organised around the institution of rival parties.[68] This was, however, by the time that Escott was writing, to exaggerate the political nature of the press, and to neglect the progressive withdrawal of the newspapers from distinctive political argument. The Sophists

were now to be found not in the leading columns, the voice of the
newspaper, which in Delane's time had been a major source of news as
well as the sole expression of opinion in the paper,[69] but in the work
of the political columnists and commentators. The question of
'influence' would become much more complex when papers started to
employ columnists of the opposite political hue from that recognised
to be their own, and it is arguable that it became profitable to do such
a thing partly at least because politics had ceased to play an important
part in the running of the paper.

There was always, however, a small but important audience for
political news and opinion, namely those who lived by and for politics.
If the Sophist-journalists were speaking to anyone it was to the
politicians. This was what Stead had had in mind when he wrote of
'government by journalism', and it was referred to by one of Stead's
favourite authors, James Russell Lowell, when he spoke of 'the
pluralising in his single person, by the Editor of the Newspaper, of the
offices once divided amongst the Church, the University and the Courts
of Law'.[70] Ironically Delane had built up the power of *The Times* by
refusing to become beholden to politicians, even to those with whom
he was friendly, and on relinquishing the editor's chair to Chenery in
1877, he had feared that the paper would, indeed, become too much
of a ministerial organ.[71] The question of the sort of relations between
journalists and politicians which could be considered proper was to
remain of great importance in determining the changing role of the
press.

Political journalists and other editorial staff were always liable to
decamp into either academia or politics. Most of them, perhaps, were
recruited from the same social strata that produced the intellectual and
political elites, and, therefore, felt comfortable enough amongst those
elites, if not quite of them. The careers of many Liberal journalists
exemplified this relationship; those of L.T. Hobhouse, J.L. Hammond,
C.F.G. Masterman, for example. A spell on the editorial staff of a
London, or large provincial daily was quite a common entree for the
young intellectual into politics, or back again, from university, into
academic life. The connections do not appear to have been so close on
the Conservative side, possibly on account of the rather less open
nature of that party, and of the lack of an intellectual ginger group such
as the Liberals had after the 1880s.

Many journalists led double newspaper/political lives. George
Armstrong, editor of the *Northern Echo* at Darlington, became
secretary of the Darlington Liberal Association, and stood for

Parliament in 1910. Harold Spender, successively of the *Daily News,*
the *Manchester Guardian* and the *Morning Leader,* became in 1909
secretary of Lloyd George's Budget League. C.P. Scott, whilst
continuing editor of the *Manchester Guardian,* was an MP for twelve
years, and President of the Manchester Liberal Federation.[72] In the
provinces the local contact of journalists and politicians was vital to
both journalists and politicians, even after the opening of the Lobby
in 1878, which was for long still a very formal arrangement. Joseph
Chamberlain himself acknowledged William Harris, the editor of the
Birmingham Daily Post, to have been 'the father of the caucus', while
J.F. Feeney, the proprietor of the paper, was briefly treasurer of the
National Liberal Federation. Austen Chamberlain maintained the
connection with the paper through Sir Alfred Robbins. Herbert
Gladstone, as we have seen, had a similarly close relationship with
Wemyss Reid and the *Leeds Mercury.*[73] Such political associations
frequently led to Parliament itself,[74] and there was an increasing
number of professed 'journalists' in the Commons after the 1880s.
This was partly due to the fact that journalism was still a very handy
occupation for an impecunious MP, hence the large proportion of Irish
and Labour MPs identified as 'journalists'.

As working journalists became better organised, there were
complaints against Labour MPs who wrote regularly for newspapers
whilst in the House.[75] Only unionisation could overcome this problem,
and even then issues of freedom of speech would be raised. Meanwhile,
Labour MPs continued to practise journalism as Liberal and
Conservative MPs continued to practise law, whilst sitting Members of
the House of Commons. This makes it difficult to tell how well-
represented the profession of the press was in Parliament, but Table 32
shows how the numbers increased, particularly up to 1906, and how
overwhelmingly Liberal they were. By 1906, journalists, according to
J.A. Thomas, were the third largest occupational group in the Commons,
after the law and the services.[76]

Such representation and associations were not guarantees of
'influence', and in some cases astute politicians were the masters of
naive journalists, but the connections were important, both for the
politicians and the government, who were provided with convenient
outlets for information and ears for its collection, and for journalists,
who were given access to information, and opportunity for
communicating their own ideas direct to the politicians. This last point
was seized upon by the radicals, especially it seems after the 1880s, as a
way of exerting pressure from within.[77]

How such pressure was brought to bear, how 'influence' was exercised, and how effectively it was done is problematical. The familiar processes of erosion may have played a part, and within the political strata the effects of this would have been much more highly concentrated than on the public at large. Some politicians became very angry about the alleged influence of men like H.W. Lucy, whose London Letters were syndicated through a large part of the provincial press,[78] and this suspicion continued to be an important characteristic of political reactions to the press, a suspicion, it seems, greater than had existed in the mid-century, when more aristocratic politicians had written widely for the press themselves. On the other hand, there were other, usually younger and more adventurous politicians, who a assiduouslycultivated and used the press for their own ends. Before 1914 both attitudes were to be encountered. An American observer commented in 1903 that

> 'the governing class' in England holds journalism and journalists suspect, instead of following the American example and welcoming the Fourth Estate as an ally. That is one of the reasons why from time to time the 'governing class' contrives to run full-tilt against the almost unanimous opinion of the country.[79]

Some leading politicians never read newspapers, either from indolence, disinclination, arrogance, or, in the case of the ageing Gladstone, as a result of deteriorating eyesight.[80] Sometimes it appeared that little attention was given to the cultivation of the press as a possible asset, so that the manager of the *Daily News* complained that no attempt was made to keep him informed of Cabinet policy during Gladstone's second administration, even while a Cabinet Minister was a director of the paper.[81] Campbell-Bannerman maintained a patrician disdain for the press, whether politically friendly or not, and Winston Churchill took to rallying Liberal support in 1909 by dismissing the importance of a press hostile to the Government, with the dubious assertion that the platform was in any case more powerful.[82] Churchill, however, was astute enough in getting his own speeches fully and promptly reported to realise that the platform now depended heavily on the press for its impact.

Deep-seated suspicion and outward aloofness did not prevent politicians from using what outlets the press provided for them. Gladstone in the 1880s became very sensitive to political commentary and news, and developed a keen nose for conspiracies. These there may have been, at a time when political knives were flashing. Chamberlain, Gladstone's chief suspect, later admitted that there was considerable contact between Cabinet ministers and the press.

At one of these Cabinets (in November 1880) there was a warm discussion on the subject of communication between Cabinet ministers and the press, and this question was revived from time to time afterwards. The fact was that several of the ministers were in intimate connection with Editors of newspapers. Thus, Forster was continually communicating with Chenery of *The Times,* and I believe with Mudford of the *Standard.* Dilke was intimate with Hill of the *Daily News,* and I was in constant intercourse with Morley, Editor of the *Pall Mall Gazette,* and Escott who was a writer at that time on the *Standard.*[83]

Not the least interesting point about this list is the extent to which the contacts made were cross-party, a point which particularly riled Gladstone. Chamberlain saw nothing reprehensible in it, although it often led to misplaced blame for 'leaks', and he did, he said, disapprove of Morley using the *Pall Mall Gazette* to put pressure on Forster to resign. Nevertheless,

it was pointed out (in Cabinet) that without special intercourse it was impossible to secure in the press an adequate defence of the decisions and policy of the Government. Whether the confidence made in any case overstepped what was right must be a matter of opinion, but as far as myself I know nothing underhand or unfair was done by any member of the Government.[84]

Reginald Brett's later observation to Balfour, that 'all the disasters of 1880-5 came from the Government of the day allowing themselves to be swayed by the newspapers', is hardly a sustainable judgement, but it does seem that this period of political infighting gave the press a political prominence that it lacked at other times.[85] The temptation to leak information or misinformation was very great. The most notorious case, of course, was the Hawarden Kite, but the practice was not at all unusual.[86] E.W. Hamilton suspected Chamberlain and Forster in 1880 of 'curious leakages' to the *Standard,* and Gladstone himself was concerned in 1881-2 about leaks on Irish matters, which were thought to stem from Forster's private secretary.[87] By May 1881 Hamilton was eager to get rid of Forster because of the persistent leaks. Later

H.C.E. Childers, the Home Secretary, primed the editor of the *Scotsman* about Home Rule, and used that paper as a vehicle of opposition to Gladstone on the issue.[88] Chamberlain had also been suspected of leaks on the Land Bill in 1881, but was cleared at a Cabinet meeting, after which suspicion devolved on the unfortunate Forster.[89] In 1882 Granville complained of Chenery having published in *The Times* papers on Egyptian policy which should have been secret, and here too mention was made of an unnamed Cabinet Minister.[90] Leaks of minor matters also abounded. In 1881 the *Morning Post* published advance news of the granting of an honour; in 1883 the name of the new Speaker was published before the official decision had been taken; in 1884 a memorandum on the Redistribution Bill was being touted around the newspapers for £10.[91] Questions were asked in Parliament about the continuing leaks, and by the end of 1884 the problem had become so acute that it must have had some effect on the way matters were discussed in private.[92] Not least damaging to the government was the general atmosphere of paranoia that resulted. The situation did not return to the point it had reached in 1878, however, when Cabinet ministers actually recounted to the Commons what had been said in the Cabinet, in the discussion of the Treaty of San Stefano![93] The methods of leaking information varied, from direct personal contact and letters, to the flourishing of documents in one's club. In the House it was easy for an MP to leave a document behind 'by accident', which would later be returned to him by a conscientious journalist.[94] Some leaks, however, were not inspired, but the result of deliberate theft. Some of the trouble in 1881, for example, was due to a reporter stealing some letters from a counsel during an Irish trial.[95] Not many such incidents were discovered, or admitted, and there was no clear policy as to what action should be taken in the event of such a thing happening. The law was vague. William Hudson Guerney was acquitted of larceny in 1858 for taking and then giving to the *Daily News* some Colonial Office dispatches, which were then published. Charles Marvin was acquitted on the same charge twenty years later when he probably sold details of the Anglo-Russian agreement to the *Globe*. Guerney and Marvin were both civil servants, and the latter case led the Civil Service to amend its rules of conduct and service, although this did not enable then to control civil servants who left the service before the actual offence, or, presumably, before the prosecution. When the bland Official Secrets Act of 1889 was passed it related almost exclusively to matters of defence and security, was rarely used, and hardly touched the press.[96]

Yet other leaks were what might be called 'official', in that they stemmed from the government, and were used as instruments of government policy, and not for the particular interests of any individual members of it. Gladstone thought that Disraeli had been in continuous contact with the press, but admitted that he himself was very bad at managing it. Granville replied that he was no better.[97] Nevertheless, they both used the press. Gladstone leaked the government's decision to legislate to allow an MP to make a declaration instead of taking an oath, after the Bradlaugh case.[98] Granville claimed that Chenery of *The Times* would usually co-operate in publishing information on a government brief.[99] In 1890 Gladstone sought to correct statements made by Parnell by seeing Charles Morley and E.T. Cook of the *Pall Mall Gazette,* and Stuart of the *Star,* whilst Herbert Gladstone read out a copy of his father's reply to Parnell to assembled reporters.[100] For the Conservatives Balfour, then responsible for Ireland, declared his intention, privately, to use *The Times* as a channel of government propaganda in Ireland, a decision unfortunately made at the very time of the disclosure of the Piggott forgeries![101]

The press was also used by government to guide opinion on difficult subjects, but this could be embarrassing if discovered. In 1883 it was revealed that it was the normal practice of the War Office to pass information to *The Times* before it was given to Parliament, because the paper was the only one which devoted serious attention to the topic, and it needed time in which to digest the material.[102] The disclosure did not prevent the practice from continuing, however, and in 1904 J.S. Sandars, albeit reluctantly, 'manipulated' the press over the War Office Report of that year.[103] The use of the press by departments of government was not new, although Gladstone had stopped Trevelyan using it in the cause of civil service reform in the 1850s.[104] By the 1870s it was pointed out that 'there was not a department in the State which did not make use of the press for the purpose of replying to attacks which could not conveniently be answered in the House of Commons'.[105] The Treasury at this time kept a list of newspapers which were to be favoured with government advertisements.[106]

Government intervention could also be censorious. In 1884 Gladstone was seeking support for the Egyptian Crown against its dissident ministers, and claimed that he had 'snuffed out an arrangement under which Dicey was to receive £1,000 a year for writing up the (ministers) in the English press'.[107] The rather casual way in which Gladstone referred to this suggests that it was not an unusual course of

action, even if the press in Britain was in no way as responsive to or
controlled by the government as was the case in Germany or France.
The greatest control was traditionally exercised in Ireland, and Lord
Spencer at this time was said to have got the government 'to gag the
Press lately' about reports concerning the whereabouts of Irish
informers.[108] British newspapers, however, had been known to have
been in the pay of other governments, such as the *Morning Post* in
1852 (France), and in 1855 (Turkey).[109] If the government wanted to
take action against the press after 1870 it could still resort to the law
of sedition and of seditious libel, but it did not find it expedient to
censor or ban a major newspaper until the First World War. The editor
of the anarchist *Freiheit* was imprisoned for enthusing over the
assassination of Alexander II, and earlier in 1870 Zia Bey was prevented
from advocating the assassination of the Turkish Grand Vizier in his
paper *Huriet*.[110] Generally, however, it was felt that more harm than
good would come of such actions.[111]

Only a country where prior censorship did not exist would have any
trouble with unauthorised leaks. As Dicey pointed out, Britain had no
law or code to safeguard the liberty of the press, excepting the ordinary
law of the land, which in almost every case applied only to offences
actually committed, the only important exception being the Theatres
Act of 1843.[112] It is possible that there were cases where injunctions
were sought and granted against the publication of certain matter, but
if so none seems to have attained the status of a *cause célèbre.* Indeed,
in 1874 the position of the journalist engaged in disclosing information
was strengthened by a case in which John Vaughan, editor of the
Liverpool Leader, successfully defended the right of a journalist not to
disclose the sources of his information in a court of law.[113]

Such latitude at times made politicians, and Parliament as a whole,
rather touchy. A long debate on breach of privilege ensued in 1893
after the publication of an article in *The Times* criticising the supposed
financial dependence of Irish MPs upon the Liberal Party and the
government. Gladstone predictably supported the view that this was a
breach of privilege, but the cooler Balfour warned the House not to be
too sensitive about such things. In the end the article was found to be
in breach of privilege, but no punitive action was taken.[114] A few days
later J.W. Russell MP got the House to condemn an article by
H.W. Massingham which referred to Russell as a 'tireless mercenary of
Unionism'.[115] In this case a warning was sent to the editor of the *Daily
Chronicle,* who promptly published it, and the embarrassment so
caused probably meant that such tactics were not used again.[116]

It seems in general that after 1870, when the last remnants of the
old security system were abolished, the Government was reluctant to
use the stick to the press, and even when it wished to do so it found it
difficult without prejudicing its own position. This was plainer after the
1880s with the amendment of the libel law and the opening up of the
Commons to the press. If the stick was a tactic to be used with care,
however, so too was the carrot. The most successful way of doing this
was by the provision of information, and by making certain journalists
feel at home within the 'governing classes', and even within the political
system. J.A. Spender, J.L. Garvin, H.A. Gwynne and Robert Donald
were examples of such politicised journalists, but others, particularly
proprietors, were often after more obvious signs of grace. Towards the
end of the century the award of honours became a matter of some
contention, and newspaper honours were no exception. John Easthope
was probably the first man to receive an honour, a baronetcy, for
political services which included the purchase and running of a
newspaper, the *Morning Chronicle,* in the Tory interest. This was in
1841, but for the next forty years there appear to have been none
given for services of an obviously, or overtly, journalistic nature. As we
have seen this caused some bitterness amongst the higher ranks of
journalists, particularly the Conservative ones, who were always
complaining that their party gave them an insufficient share of
government patronage when they were in power. Patronage when it was
given, even by the Liberals, was at a much lower level. Disraeli was
responsible for the first honour directly given for newspaper enterprise,
when he knighted the proprietor of the *Morning Post,* Algernon
Borthwick, in 1880. In 1887 Salisbury made him a baronet, although
by this time he was more politically active, being the chairman of the
Metropolitan Unionist MPs. In 1895 he was raised to the peerage, again
by Salisbury, and again not ostensibly for newspaper work. In 1885
Gladstone had knighted the journalist William Hardman, and Salisbury
made George Armstrong a baronet in 1892 for services to the
Conservative Party, which included his proprietorship of the *Globe*
since 1875, and of the *People* since 1882. This was perhaps somewhat
generous to a man whose paper had leaked the Salisbury-Schouvaloff
Treaty in 1878! Henry H. Gibbs, founder, and until 1888 proprietor
of the *St. James's Gazette*, was made a baron in the same year as
Armstrong, but he was best known as a banker and as a leading
Conservative City politician. Also in 1892 Gladstone gave John Jaffray,
editor and proprietor of the *Birmingham Daily Post,* a baronetcy, one
supposes as either a sop or a consolation to Chamberlain.

It was precisely at this time that Yates Thompson sold the *Pall Mall Gazette* to Astor, apparently in a fit of pique at not having received an honour from Gladstone.

> As for the Party I feel no compunction at all. They have never done anything for me, though I did a real service for them in 1880 by turning the paper round. They despise the Press. Mr. Gladstone might easily have kept the *Chronicle* and probably the *Telegraph* if he had baroneted Lloyd and Lawson; if they had done anything for me I don't suppose I should be selling now.[117]

In fact the last number of the *Pall Mall Gazette* with E.T. Cook as editor, before Astor took over, appeared about a week after the news of Lawson's baronetcy, from Gladstone.[118]   Thompson was probably right, however, for it had been Lawson, son of the founder of the *Daily Telegraph,* and sole proprietor since 1885, who had swung the paper around to a pro-Turk policy in 1879, and it was never to return wholly to the Liberal fold. Gladstone's gesture had been too late. It was to be **Balfour who made Lawson a baron in 1903.**

Rosebery was sensitive to the potential power of the press, and had close connections with journalists, and in 1893 he was responsible for honouring the first provincial newspapermen, John Leng of the *Dundee Advertiser,* Hugh Gilzean-Reid of the *Northern Daily Telegraph* amongst other papers, and Rosebery's own friend, Edward Russell of the *Liverpool Daily Post,* all Liberal papers. At the same time he knighted John Robinson, manager of the *Daily News.* In 1894 came Wemyss Reid, then retired from active journalism, and in 1895 the venerable *Times* war correspondent W.H. Russell. In 1895 also a baronetcy was given to George Newnes for political services which included the establishment of the *Westminster Gazette.* This eventually provoked Harmsworth to write to Lord Onslow in 1897:

> My opponent and friend Sir George Newnes started the *Westminster Gazette,* and Lord Rosebery promptly recognised his journal by a reward that in the formation of his company this year proved of enormous advantage to him. On our side owners of newspapers of comparatively slight influence are rewarded, and my predecessor in the *Evening News* received recognition, though the journal was a failure.
>
> However, I would rather say nothing more on the subject; the Party leaders are no doubt quite ignorant of the revolution which

the *Daily Mail,* in its infancy at present, is making in London journalism. They have never even enquired as to the new provincial offshoots I am preparing.[119]

Thompson never got his reward, but Harmsworth did, and his biographers suggest that 'he had been in close touch with Balfour and other leaders of the administration about the future of the *Manchester Courier,* and his investment in the newspaper group at Norwich represented a similar readiness at co-operation. His *Southern Daily Mail* venture may have come into the reckoning.'[120] His meteoric rise started with a baronetcy in 1904, a barony in 1905, and a viscounty in 1917. This provoked much criticism at the time, as there was a suspicion that contributions to party funds were involved. Campbell-Bannerman protested that party money was entirely an affair of the whips, and he seems to have restrained Whitely, his Chief Whip, from extorting payments for honours. Herbert Gladstone also denied that payments were tied to honours, although he expressed disappointment when on two occasions no money was forthcoming.[121] But newspaper proprietors were in a good position to contribute indirectly to party funds, by financing new or ailing papers, or by ensuring the loyalty of their own papers. Harmsworth was said to have put £50,000 into the *Manchester Courier,* for example. In general it is probable that there was little money involved in newspaper honours, although newspaper proprietors who were well up in either party would be expected as a matter of course to contribute to party funds.

Asquith for one did not welcome what had become an established practice. He wrote to J.A. Spender in 1909:

> There is nothing gives me so much trouble, (or I may well add such profound disgust) as the allocation of honours. In the case of the smaller fry I am obliged to act mainly on the advice of the whips and other such experts. The man you mention (I think his name is Riddell) was strongly recommended to me on the ground (amongst others) that his paper the 'News of the World' had become definitely Liberal, and was a valuable party asset. I am disposed to agree with you that it would be better if journalists should neither seek nor accept such distinctions; but that unfortunately is the way of the world in which we live.[122]

In 1912 it was Northcliffe, no less, who through Churchill put it to Asquith that he should do more to recognise leading journalists, men

like Massingham, Spender and Scott. Yet none of these men would
have accepted such honours. E.T. Cook only accepted a knighthood in
retirement. Acceptance would have merely endangered their
independence. In any case Asquith remained unsympathetic. 'To
Massingham I shall certainly not offer (recognition)', he told Churchill,
referring to the journalist who had been the government's chief critic
over foreign policy.[123]

   Asquith's unconcealed disgust was compensated in some measure
by Lloyd George's enthusiasm. He had early in his career co-operated
with Samuel Storey in an attempt to set up a new daily in South Wales,
and had been party to the deal over the *Daily News* in 1901, and was
shortly afterwards involved in an attempt to re-invigorate the ailing
Echo.[124] He was a close friend of Riddell, whom he had supported in
Cardiff, and had used him as an industrial negotiator, Riddel for his
part providing Lloyd George with a house. It was most probably Lloyd
George who had recommended Riddell to Asquith for an honour in
1909. Lloyd George also kept in very close contact with Liberal
newspaper proprietors and editors, meeting them regularly over
breakfast. These connections were accompanied by the efforts of the
Liberal whips to cultivate good press relations, and the employment of
Sir Henry Norman as an unofficial press agent for the party.[125] There
does not seem to have been such a network on the Unionist side, where
perhaps only Gwynne and Garvin, with perhaps Blumenfeld, enjoyed
such intimate political relationships.[126]

   The men discussed above were almost all journalists, or proprietor-
journalists, but by the 1880s those who were proprietors without really
being journalists at all had won a certain degree of political acceptance.
We have seen how the proprietor won a place in public life by the
1870s, with access to the Bench and the local Council. The expansion
of party organisation had also opened out further opportunities, and
by the 1880s an impressive number of proprietors were to be found in
Parliament itself. There are difficulties in quantifying such a change in
status, but the available figures do make the situation somewhat clearer.
They probably err on the low side, as MPs with multiple interests would
usually only bother to record the major of them, and many may even
have sought to conceal their connections with newspapers. Yet even on
the crude figures derived from Dod's *Parliamentary Companion*
(see Table 34), by 1885 there were twenty-two proprietor MPs, ten
Liberals, three Conservatives, three Radicals and six Irish Nationalists.
The preponderance of Liberals in the list is at once obvious, and
naturally the greatest gap between the Liberal and the Conservative

proprietors was in 1906, with the Liberal landslide. But, as with the
journalist MPs, by 1910 the gap was drastically reduced, with the
Liberals losing nine by December 1910, and the Conservatives gaining
three. Numbers prove nothing about the influence of these men, of
course, but they do suggest that the press, provincial as well as
metropolitan, was in closer proximity to the reins of political power
than might otherwise be thought. The proprietors were inevitably
carriers of news and gossip to their papers, and sometimes wrote regular
London Letters or Parliamentary Sketches for them. On their side the
party leaders could use them as channels through which to approach
the press. Compared to the mere journalist, the proprietor was in a
stronger position when in Parliament, as a working journalist could not
continue in a full-time job whilst an MP, whereas the newspaper
proprietor, like other capitalists, found the two occupations perfectly
compatible. Few issues came before the House which directly affected
the press as an industry, so there were few occasions when the press
interest could have acted concertedly, and even over the Libel and
Registration Act of 1888 there were divisions in the ranks. Nevertheless,
there can have been few large newspaper companies who lacked a
parliamentary representative, and to this extent the newspaper industry
resembled other successful Victorian industries, and like those other
industries the press had to a considerable degree become integrated into
the political system by such a process.

This chapter has examined what has been throughout the distant focus
of this essay, namely the political functions and functioning of the press
during the last quarter of the nineteenth and the first decade of the
twentieth centuries. Ironically, by the turn of the century the once
triumphant Liberals were deploring the way in which the political role
of the press had developed in practice since the repeal of the taxes on
knowledge and the extension of elementary education. Politics had
always been central to the Liberal idea of the press. The aim was to
achieve what later came to be termed an 'open society' on pluralist
lines, civilised, healthy, wealthy and wise. This was what politics was
about, for utilitarians and their Liberal critics alike, and the function
of the press was to advance towards this political goal. In narrower
'democratic' terms this meant that it had to enlighten and to inform,
to educate the masses towards democracy under the leadership of the
most intelligent, whilst all the time safeguarding the liberty of the
individual and the public good. This last was also the most immediate,
and supposedly the easiest function to fulfil. Men of various political

philosophies concurred in their praise of the newspaper as a public
watchdog. For Herbert Spencer 'this marvellous appliance' had
succeeded in spite of state intervention and hostility, so that it now
(1871) gave 'to the ministers news in anticipation of their dispatches. . .
to members of Parliament a guiding knowledge of public opinion,
enables them to speak from the House of Commons' benches to their
constituents, and gives to both legislative chambers a full record of their
proceedings'.[127] Lord Salisbury had more directly, in the early years of
the cheap press, stressed the independent dimension of the press, which
was he thought, 'one of the surest guarantees by which (governmental)
efficiency can be secured'.[128] In his extravagant essay on 'Government
by Journalism' in 1886, which had prompted Arnold's attack on the
'feather-brained' new journalism, W.T. Stead had concluded by speaking
of the press as 'the great inspector'.[129] Each in their own way, then,
accepted the role of the press as the guardian of the guardians. Such a
claim might lead Stead into sensationalism, which both Spencer and
Salisbury abhorred, but they were agreed that in principle such a role
was an honourable and necessary one, and few would have questioned
the claim by the 1880s. The improvement in the status of the
newspaper proprietor and of the working journalist, the easing of the
libel laws, and the gradual opening up of government to the press,
particularly at local level, were all indications that the press's claim to
be a public watchdog was an acceptable one.

This admission did not necessarily make the governors themselves
much more amenable to being watched, but certainly relations between
leading politicians and leading journalists became if anything closer
after the 1870s, as they found such association to be mutually
beneficial. It was soon learned, if it had ever been forgotten, that the
best way of meeting press criticism was through the good offices of
one's own press friends. The expansion of political activity resulting
from the extensions of the franchise and the organisation of modern
parties further stimulated close working relations between the press
and politicians so that by 1914 the framework at least of the modern
system had emerged.

At the same time the 'new journalism' had helped to depoliticise the
press, compared to the golden age of the 1860s and 1870s. It can be
argued that after the 1880s society was in any case less politically
enthused, less concerned and less involved, as a result of the so-called
'nationalisation' of political organisations and issues, of the replacement
of sectional by class interests, of the increasing role of the state in social
and individual life, and so on. If so, then the new journalism can be

seen reflecting this deeper change of mood, and not merely manipulating the public into it for its own commercial ends. In this, the press, as other institutions, had already become the prisoner of the economic system of which it was a part.

As far as the press was concerned, however, there was another aspect of depoliticisation. The golden age had been a time when there were two distinct parties in rivalry for political power. This was the stuff of the old Liberal ideal, shared even by the Conservatives, who tried in pursuit of it to establish their own party press. After the 1880s, however, party lines became increasingly confused, and party politics to some extent discredited. This did not mean the end of political conflict, of course, but the lines of cleavage began to shift, and they shifted in a way which made it difficult for the press, according to the old and established model, to follow. In the golden age a prosperous proprietor and an eminent journalist could run a commercially sound newspaper, whether Liberal or Conservative. It was true that the Liberals tended to be better at it, but the point was that there was nothing in the system working against the establishment of either Liberal or Conservative papers. Social conflict could be contained within the bounds of that system, even to the extent of the overwhelmingly middle-class press catering for the artisan or labouring reader. After the 1880s a combination of economic logic within the newspaper industry, and of the appearance of a more distinct class politics, meant that radical and Labour sympathisers found either that they had no press, or that that which they had was forced to and beyond the limits of commercial viability as a result of the increasing power of advertisers, and of the seduction of the politically uneducated reader by newspapers which set out to amuse rather than to inform or to instruct. This meant that the economic and the political context which had nurtured a strong political press was vanishing. So while government and party relations with the press improved, while they came to terms with each other, the assumptions on which those relations were based were changing. The press was becoming less overtly party political, and although politicians liked to foster journalistic connections, they did so less as a flag-waving exercise than as an attempt to keep their end up within their own fairly restricted political circles. This change reflected some consciousness at least of the sometimes embarrassing incongruity between the political spectrum of the press and that of the electorate. Gladstone's defeat in 1874 could plausibly be laid at the door of rebellious Liberals who happened to control the party press, but the 1906 Liberal landslide could not conceivably be explained away in terms of press-induced error. The 1906 result also emphasised how much the constituency of the press had changed since the 1860s. Arguably since 1885 the daily press had spoken to a fairly narrow stratum of the 'governing classes', just as novelists, critics, poets and scientists had spoken to much the same stratum of the educated classes. Until the 1880s the universe of political discourse was tolerably well-known and understood, its vocabulary and conceptual store were common change. The widening of the electorate and of newspaper readership meant that this helpful symmetry no longer obtained. The mechanical expansion of the electorate and of readership did not guarantee a concomitant expansion of political interest and knowledge.

Now the answer to this problem from a Liberal point of view was more of the same. The process of education had to continue. The press should still cultivate the old political circles, but it should continue to try to 'educate democracy'. Here there was a problem, for the expansion of elementary education, together with the development of the technical capacity to reach mass audiences, were obstacles to the sort of political education which had been at the centre of the old Liberal vision. Now a Gresham's law of reason seemed to be working itself out, whereby the cheap and the tawdry, the trivial and the sensational, kept out of the market place the valuable, the authentic, and the serious. This was the gravamen of the Liberal charge against the new press, although it was a charge not exclusively the possession of Liberals, but of those who had been brought up to adhere to the Liberal idea which had dominated in the golden age. What did this charge amount to? How well-founded was it? What alternatives were considered to a continuation of the 'Barnum 'n' Bailey show'?

7 DISILLUSION

In January 1905 the Liberal Chief Whip Herbert Gladstone and the radical journalist H.W. Massingham met on their respective ways to Biarritz. Massingham observed to Gladstone with his customary gloom that it was 'an open question whether the 1*d* papers are not played out'.[1] For Massingham and his contemporaries such a prospect was indeed deeply depressing. The penny daily was for those who had grown up, say, between 1860 and 1890 a symbol of respectability and and insurance of political security and well-being. Liberalism and progress itself were somehow identified with the continued existence and prosperity of the penny daily, almost if not equally as much as they were identified with the doctrine of free trade. In defiance of the trend which Massingham had correctly perceived, the following year saw the launching of a new penny daily, a Liberal London one at that, with the backing of a deep purse and a staff of brilliant journalists. Within two years the *Tribune* was dead, although everyone had agreed what an excellent and masterly paper it had been. Some argued that it had been too good a paper, and been done down by the halfpenny trash which was more attractive to the mass of readers which it needed in order to be able to compete with its rivals. Its crash, it was said, was ample witness to the truth of the fears which pervaded Liberal, radical and progressive circles during the dark years of Unionist rule — but was it? Did it really die because it was too good? And even if that were true what did that mean for the survivors like the *Manchester Guardian* or the *Daily News,* which were also very 'good'? How adequate a critique was that put forward by the 'new' and some of the old liberals, and shared by many conservatives, radicals and men of labour?

The ideal against which the reality was compared was the familiar one set out earlier in this essay, and put simply by the Unitarian radical W.J. Fox in 1846: 'the press is an open place where anyone may bring counsel for his fellows.'[2] It was an ideal closely pursued by many radicals after the mid-century, and most firmly if ultimately unsuccessfully put into practice by the *Morning Star,* a joint attempt by the Peace Society and free traders to demonstrate after the repeal of the taxes on knowledge what newspapers should be like.[3] The ideal was often, as in the case of the *Morning Star,* pursued as a goal of political philanthropy. John Bright could without anxiety advise its second editor Justin McCarthy that 'I would think only of what was right and just', for he, Bright, had no financial stake in the paper, but there were some at least of its backers who seemed to have agreed.[4] Sam Morley, for example, who after the demise of the *Star* became a director of the *Daily News,* was disappointed that that paper was proving so profitable.[5] Nor was this an attitude confined to the radical elite. Robert Donald reminded his fellow journalists in 1913 that the old proprietors had preferred less profit to any compromise over principle, and as we have seen few of them seem to have considered running their businesses as means of maximising profits.[6] The *Leeds Mercury,* the *Manchester Guardian* and the *Newcastle Daily Chronicle* were certainly cases in point. Whether Conservative papers such as the *Sheffield Daily Telegraph,* the *Manchester Courier* or the *Yorkshire Post* were equally jealous of their principles is difficult to tell, for their principles were less dogmatically held, and less likely to provoke conflicts of interest, but there is no reason to suppose that they were necessarily, as a consequence of their politics, more mercenary. The editor of the *Yorkshire Post,* H.J. Palmer, was in no doubt that he 'would rather see newspaper proprietors suffering from their fidelity to newspaper ideals than that their properties should be handed over to the dividend hunters who care only for a return on their money'. He added that 'fidelity to the public interest (lies) at the root of (newspaper) prosperity.'[7] Whether true or not this observation makes it quite clear what Palmer's own view was. Whether his proprietors agreed or not was in this case irrelevant, for the *Post* was a very profitable venture. Indeed, as we have seen, the happiest situations were, as here, and with the *Manchester Guardian,* the *Daily News* and the *Daily Telegraph,* where politics and profits proved compatible. In the golden age this was quite often the case, partly as a result of a high level of political interest, partly because this was a period of rapid growth in the industry. Political philanthropy, however, had always been evident, and as the industry developed and the process of depoliticisation set in, it became more frequent and more necessary.

Direct subsidisation by political parties, or more usually by individual, or groups of, supporters of parties, seems to have been most common in the 1880s, as the Conservatives increased their efforts to compete with the prevailing Liberal domination. Depoliticisation in the 1890s and after made it a less attractive activity. There was a movement of feeling against 'party'. J.J. Colman, proprietor of Liberal and radical papers in East Anglia and London, stated in 1894 that he 'never believed in papers which require to be permanently subsidised by political parties. . .independence on the part of journals and journalists is the only sound basis to go upon'.[8] The papers Colman was associated with do not seem to have received party subsidies, but they almost certainly benefited from the financial support of their industrialist proprietors. The choice was between patronage of some sort, party or not, and the running of the paper as a commercially viable concern. Patronage was a traditional means of support, but even political philanthropists of the scale of Cadbury and Thomasson were not capable of unlimited subsidies. Andrew Carnegie had once spoken of 'money no object', but the *Echo* project had soon made him see that it was. Spenser Wilkinson told the young Liberal William Beveridge, who was going to contribute to the Conservative *Morning Post,* that Lord Glenesk, the proprietor, was a businessman first and a Conservative second. In practice Liberal proprietors took much the same attitude, although they were usually too sensitive to admit it.[9] Cadbury rationalised his newspaper commitments as follows:[10]

> I had a profound conviction that money spent on charities was of
> infinitely less value than money spent in trying to arouse my fellow
> countrymen to the necessity of measures to ameliorate the condition
> of the poor, forsaken and downtrodden masses which can be done
> most effectively by a newspaper.

But it is to be noted that it was money which would otherwise have been destined for charities. The Rowntrees held similar views, stipulating that the *Northern Echo* and other papers taken over by their Social Service Trust 'must pay their own way — though it was not necessary that they should show a large profit'.[11] Sometimes, as when the Wilsons bought the *Sheffield Independent* in 1909, or when Cadbury took over the *Star* and the *Morning Leader* in 1910, principles had to be tempered, and priorities allotted. Betting news was accepted in these papers, against the previous policies of the new proprietors, because 'there are not so many daily newspapers willing to take the unpopular side, and to make a brave fight for national righteousness even to the extent of opposing the leaders of their own political party, that the country can lightly dispense with one of them.'[12]

Behind these attitudes lay a continued faith in the intellectual influence of the press. In vain was H.J. Wilson advised in 1874 that 'the Daily Telegraph thought and wrote *with* the people, the Morning Star *to* the people. . . Men are not courted by argument; they are swayed by interest and sympathy.'[12] This was indeed the message of the 'new

journalism', even of W.T. Stead's version of it, but it differed radically
from that of the old, in which journalism had been regarded as a
profession to be ranked with other professions, at least potentially, and
to be followed according to the middle-class ethic of public service. By
the mid-1880s, as we have seen, to all intents and purposes such
recognition had been accorded, and the newspaper proprietor and
journalist had captured the status of the professional man, at least in
the upper echelons. Yet already in other fields the professional was
being undermined by the business ethic with which it had for long
compromised, and this process began to affect journalism as well. In
1897 Escott observed that whereas Delane had been 'the interpreter of
middle class English thought', modern journalists had become 'the
custodians of a commercial interest'.[14] This was the nub of the matter.
How far had economic development encroached upon and sullied the
old ideal? How far did commercial considerations result in political sails
being trimmed to a financial wind? There is, of course, no simple causal
answer. Political change and economic development, within and outside
the industry, were mutually reinforcing processes, and if it was not by
1914 clear how the interaction would work out, there was a wide
measure of agreement that the press would continue to increase in size,
that its ownership would continue to become concentrated in fewer
and fewer hands, and that politics would play a smaller and smaller part
in its contents. Interest and sympathy were indeed replacing argument.

The *Daily News* found it necessary to give a glimpse of the obvious
in 1909 in an attack on Northcliffe: 'it is (the wealthy men) who own
newspapers.'[15] Robert Donald made this his theme in his presidential
address to the Institute of Journalists in 1913. 'The proprietorial
system has almost disappeared', he complained. 'Nine tenths of the
leading daily and evening newspapers belong to limited companies,'
with shares dealt in on the Stock Exchange. 'The nationalising of
London newspapers' with earlier deadlines, special trains and
simultaneous publication in London, Manchester and Glasgow, had
sapped the advertising revenue of provincial papers and had presented
them with stiffer competition. Journalistically 'the administrator is
becoming the dominant power', ousting the old 'writing editor'. The
papers themselves, he admitted, were now better written, more
readable, more attractive and better informed, but they were fewer. He
foresaw that the trend would continue until papers with circulations of
less than half a million would cease to rank seriously; local papers
would take on a more 'national' look; the nationals would improve
their typography and their distribution system. The competition of

other news services, the cinema and the gramophone, would make
people 'too lazy to read, and news will be laid on to the house or office
just as gas or water is now', with machines in the hall giving forth
newspapers column by column like tape machines.[16] Edward Bellamy,
William Morris and H.G. Wells had foreseen similar developments, but
Donald was too knowledgeable about his subject to consider these
things in a utopian spirit. He was sure that they would come to pass,
and like many of his contemporaries he deplored the prospect. There
was, deep behind the Liberal vision of the press, a puritan urge to have
people strive for what they sought. The effort, the struggle was part,
perhaps the major part of the exercise. Spoon-feeding the public 'what
it wanted' was precisely what liberal-minded critics objected to in the
new press. The driving force behind these changes was, as Donald noted,
an economic one. After he too had become a victim of newspaper
corporatism in 1918, when he was ousted from the editorship of the
Daily Chronicle, which had been purchased for political, not economic,
ends by Lloyd George and his friends, he began to think quite radically
about what was to be done. By 1921 he was even suggesting that
newspapers should be included in any scheme to control trusts, an idea
unthinkable to pre-war generations of Liberals.[17]

Nevertheless, the argument that the press was a capitalist institution
had received widespread support before 1914, from men as far removed
in politics as Campbell-Bannerman and Keir Hardie.[18] In 1900 Ramsay
MacDonald, soon to be secretary of the Labour Representation
Committee, explained the Labour point of view, complaining that the
benefits of the cheap press had been diminished because access to it had
been restricted.

The press has been gradually passing out of the control of the reader,
and has been becoming the organ of the advertisers and the
convenience of the capitalist. The newspaper so characteristic of the
democratic movements on the Continent and not unknown in this
country, which depends altogether upon its opinions for its
circulation is being crushed out of existence.[19]

The notion that the press, or at least any but a very small part of it, had
ever been under the control of the reader was a romantic distortion of
the facts, but MacDonald's other observations were tolerably accurate,
and the situation gave rise in 1908, at a congress of socialist journalists
in Stuttgart, to the complaint that the British Labour Party had no
daily newspaper.[20] The LRC had been talking about starting one since

1903, but only came to the point in 1912, with the *Daily Citizen.* [21]
The delays had been largely due to the difficulty of finding financial
backing. The example of the failure of the weekly *Cooperative News* to
obtain a circulation of 100,000, including Scotland, was hardly
encouraging — the membership of the Cooperative Union was then
about two and a quarter million.[22] The difficulty of establishing a
distinctly Labour national daily emphasised the fact that the golden
age had been an aspect of the assumption of social power by the middle
classes, that its political role had been as an anti-aristocratic weapon.[23]
A crucial phase in the appearance of a labour movement had been
accompanied by the appearance of a radical working-class press, but
after the 1840s this faded away, never again reaching the extent or
status it had had in the 1820s and 1830s. The Sunday papers quickly
became forerunners of the post-1918 mass press, but they too had
become less radical after 1850, and were as much a part of the new
journalism as of an authentic working-class press. On the radical side
the *Morning Leader* and the *Star,* and on the Conservative side the
Evening News catered for post-1880 working-class readers, but they
were, of course, all halfpenny papers. Attempts on all sides to revive the
the old political press met with no success. Press economics had by
1900 become self-restricting, in the manner of other major industries.
The logic was to the larger and the fewer, whereas in the Liberal vision
the size of each component should have remained small or medium, and
the aggregate number should have remained large. The Liberal case had,
ironically, been put forward in the Conservative *Blackwoods' Magazine*
in 1834, where it was claimed that the press, given half a chance, would
deny influence to property and wealth, and pay heed to mere numbers.
Whether property, wealth or intelligence were at stake, there was little
disputing that the economic logic at this time was indeed a logic of
numbers.[24]

It was a logic which also had its effect upon the relations between
the working journalist and the proprietor. Several notorious instances
of these relations breaking down, with editors being sacked by their
proprietors for differences over policy, have already been noted. James
Annand fell out with Joseph Cowen in the 1870s, and in 1886 is to be
found preaching the pure gospel of the old, independent journalist.

> The chief glory of a newspaper is that it shall go straight, that it shall
> keep business interests entirely apart from public policy, that its
> advocacy shall be kept for public purposes and not for the
> furtherance of private interests, and whatever may be in its

advertising columns, that it shall keep its news columns free from all influences that would corrupt, and its editorial columns free from the bias that comes from narrow self-interest.[25]

Put like this, the rules seemed clear enough, and were evidently so for Annand, but when did an interest cease to be public and become private? Certainly the Anti-gambling League, in common with other organisations of militant Nonconformity at this time, did not regard their interest as 'private', very much the reverse. So in 1891 when pressure was put upon Annand to exclude betting news from the *Newcastle Daily Leader* there was an open conflict. Annand argued that such a step would not abolish gambling, and that in fact his paper pursued and proclaimed an anti-gambling policy in its leading columns. 'A newspaper is not like a church, or chapel, or even anti-gambling society'; it had, unlike them, to be commercially sound.[26] Annand's proprietors were not bigots, and agreed broadly with his arguments, but his defeat in the 1892 general election was partly due to the organised opposition of the Newcastle Social Purity League.[27] It was an indication that a Liberal editorship was much like living in a glass-house at this time, an experience, it must be added, which many of the occupants obviously greatly enjoyed.

An even more famous 'dissenting' journalist was H.W. Massingham, and in April 1900, four months after relinquishing the editorship of the *Daily Chronicle* because of his disagreement with the proprietors over imperialist policy, he reflected upon 'the Ethics of Editing' in the Conservative *National Review*. The modern newspaper, he observed, depended heavily upon its advertisers, and it was in the interest of the advertisers to please the mass of readers, and in the proprietors' interests to please the advertisers. The result was

conventional opinion on all subjects. . .opinion believe(d) to be congenial to the mass of people in England who own property, and go to the more costly seats in theatres and opera houses, and accept, without question, most English institutions as they exist. It is clear that the ideas of these people are in the main shared by less wealthy classes, the similarity of views among Englishmen, rich and poor, being one of the sources of our national strength.

This, he thought, applied equally to matters of private taste and of public concern. Certain papers carried ideas but 'the ideas are those of the average man or woman, shaped in view of the necessities of a

political party, and. . .as a rule the editor must not overstep these
ideas,. . .he must not be "excessive" even in the expression of them'.
Massingham, in contrast, much preferred the personal political
journalism of the French. In England he was sure that the trend was,
as Donald was later to remark, for the editor to be replaced by the
administrator. 'Capitalism, unifying its control, will gradually abolish
real, as opposed to artificial, distinctions of political opinion.'[28]

Massingham's points were well put, but his argument was flawed,
and his suggestions hardly realistic. In a tart rejoinder A. Shadwell
argued that what Massingham seemed to want was the patronage of
an uninterested Midas, which was, to say the least, a mildly utopian
idea. Some of the great newspaper philanthropists had in fact been
very interested indeed in furthering their interests. Even if such a
blissful state of 'independence' were achieved, however, Shadwell
argued, 'independence' of the 'mass of people', of 'the average man
or woman', it would be an empty victory if no one were to listen to
what was published, and, of course, if they were to listen, then the
paper would be a commercial proposition, and Midases would be
redundant. This was a disingenuous argument though, for what
Massingham and others were after was a guarantee of access to the
press. No one can choose not to listen to those denied speech, for
whatever reason they are denied it. For Shadwell the only alternative
to the market, and to an unlimited supply of neutral Midases, was
state subsidisation, and he rightly doubted whether Massingham would
countenance that.[30] The 'independence' that people wanted, he
concluded, was not independence of the reader, but of party. What
they also demanded was more news and less opinion. Massingham
was consequently wrong in thinking of the newspaper only in terms
of opinion, as an agent of conversion and salvation. As Shadwell put
it, 'freedom of speech and the liberty of the press. . .do not mean a
right to be listened to', but the Liberal assumption had always been
that people should listen, and that if they were given the opportunity
and the education then that is what they would do. The cause of
Liberal disillusion now, such as Massingham's, was precisely that fewer
people, proportionately at least, seemed to be listening, and this was
the result not of their rejection of the ideas put forward, but of the
concentration of the control of the press into a few 'capitalist' hands.
Ironically the old idea of free competition of ideas in the market place
had now to contend with the reality of newspapers being sold as any
other commodity, by proprietors who were first and foremost not
educators, or public servants, but grocers, as Massingham repeatedly

pointed out.[31]

In 1921 he looked back with longing to the time 'when papers were organs of opinion, (and) Fleet Street was more or less a habitation of the human mind'.[32] Towards the end of our period a number of alternatives were suggested and discussed, as a means of restoring that 'habitation', of turning journalism from what it was, a trade, into what it had been, a profession.

Massingham never seems to have considered the idea of public ownership or control, and the idea does not seem to have been seriously discussed before 1914. Ideological hostility to state intervention may have been diminishing in the face of the increasing expansion of the state into social life, but state interference with the press required a shift of opinion almost of a different order of magnitude. Even the protagonists of 'national efficiency' do not seem to have contemplated it. The sale of the *Daily Chronicle,* as we have mentioned, spurred Donald to think of controlling newspaper trusts, but the more typical response came from J.H. Dalziel, when asked about the affair in Parliament. 'Really, is it a matter for the House of Commons that they should sit down seriously and discuss my business operations?'[33] The answer was in effect no, and perhaps the question would not have arisen had not the war necessitated Parliament's concern over the behaviour of the press, and with the relationship between it and the government.

The concept of state control or ownership was, naturally enough, taken up by the left, but without enthusiasm. H.G. Wells pointed out in 1908 that the place of the press under socialism had hardly been discussed.[34] Annie Besant had broached the subject in her Fabian essay in 1889. She suggested that the 'commune', a unit based on the then new county councils, should delegate to its 'printing committee' the power of deciding what and what not to print, including newspapers. Anybody refused facilities would, she claimed, be sufficiently affluent in the new socialist society to pay the Committee to have it printed.[35] This facile plan managed to evade not only the difficulties facing the press under capitalism, but also the problem of providing real safeguards for what even socialists accepted as part of their Enlightenment heritage, and fundamental to any socialist society, the freedom of speech. Wells thought the opportunity for people to pay for their own publication was a dubious guarantee of that freedom, but his own faith in the competitive virtues of municipalisation does not seem to be greatly different from Besant's idea.[36] He did allow, however that anyone should be permitted to establish himself as a printer and

publisher should he so wish. The dangers of another capitalist system
being kindled from this surviving ember of the old was to be avoided
by giving the state complete control of the system of distribution.[37]
How this would avert the dangers of what Wells himself termed 'a
bureaucratic mandarinate', and of 'authoritative interference with
opinion', is not clear, except that in a vague way, people would be
educated out of the instinctive desire to suppress adverse opinion.

In 1919 two socialists sketched a much fuller scheme for demo-
cratising the press, even before the socialist dawn. Their basic assumption was that what democracy really needed was not so much a free
press on the old lines, but an educated people, and that the press
should be treated first and foremost as an instrument in this education.
Editorial anonymity would be abolished, responsibility would be
encouraged amongst journalists through 'national guilds' of journalists,
and there would be a 'Truthful Press Act'.[38] In addition to the
extension of state control which these measures would have meant, the
authors proposed that the front and back pages of every newspaper
should be put under the control of 'an Aristocracy of Merit', consisting
of 'anyone who had achieved distinction from a University degree to
a Victoria Cross'. In this way serious matters would always be on the
front page, and cultural and social news on the back page. 'A few
determined leaders' as in Japan or Germany, they claimed, would
invigorate the people so that they did desire and would work for
freedom, instead of being content to be amused and excited.[39] Here,
breaking through the paeans for democracy was the tinkling of the
authentic Liberal impatience to suffer fools, not merely gladly, but
at all. It was not so much the capitalist system that was being
attacked as the ignorance of those who helped it to survive.

Such views, contradictory and inconsistent, may not have been
typical of the time, or have had a wide following, but they were
expressed with the intention of stimulating debate, and in this met
with some success. In his pamphlet *The Press and the Organisation
of Society* in 1922, Norman Angell accepted many of the authors'
arguments, but crucially insisted that more attention should be given
to state control, particularly, he added a decade later, along the lines
of the BBC.[40] This aspect had been much muted in the work of
Hayward and Langdon-Davies, reflecting an almost total neglect of
the issue before 1914, when the suggestion of a public press corporation
would have been even less welcome than that of a monopolies commission, which some of the 'new liberals' and perhaps most of the
Labour supporters would have gladly accepted. The idea of a 'press

law', such as that introduced in France in 1881 was anathema, while a commitment to the freedom of speech and of the press, as in the First Amendment to the American Constitution, was of no relevance in Britain where even the majority of Liberals were happy that there was no written constitution.[41]

A more frequently canvassed alternative to the 'capitalist' or commercialised press was the cultivation of what Hilaire Belloc termed 'a Free Press'. This had been foreshadowed by some remarks in Belloc and Cecil Chesterton's *The Party System* in 1911. The press, they had argued, was an adjunct of 'the Party System', and as a consequence had lost much of its old influence, for the public really wanted papers 'independent' of party. In any case the 'system' had ceased to benefit from a party press, and would soon cease to subsidise it. In 1918 Belloc expanded on what for him was at root a capitalist conspiracy for the control of the press, which only a few papers, like his old *Eye Witness,* and G.K. Chesterton's *New Witness,* had succeeded in defying. Like the Liberals, Belloc the 'distributivist' was anxious to preserve a press of opinion, a press which allowed the discussion of real issues in a genuinely informed manner. The modern press was merely a commercial enterprise, and, echoing Massingham, the newspaper proprietor was 'exactly the same kind of man' as those who had bought a peerage from the profits of music halls, or who had cut their throat after their financial speculations had failed.[42] Widening his line of attack, Belloc then turned to the advertisers who had enabled newspapers to be sold at below-cost price, thus creating public expectation of cut-price newspapers, which made it impossible for other, 'independent' newspapers to exist. The alternative was, he claimed, a 'Free Press', founded upon a desire to disseminate certain ideas and doctrines, upon indignation against falsehood, and against arbitrary power. The Free Press was economically weak, small in size, and suffered from fissiparous tendencies, but it was read carefully, and by the right people, those through whom ideas spread in society, a return in effect to the good old days of Delane. Belloc's book has to be treated with caution, of course. Much of it was special pleading, such as his attacks on the libel laws and libel lawyers, and upon politicians indiscriminately. The resort to the cumulative effect of the minority press to defeat the purposes of the mass popular press, however, was an attractive one to those of various political persuasions.[43] Radicals had always to resort, perforce, to this tactic, and the *Nation,* the *Westminster Gazette* and the *Spectator,* no less than the *New Witness,* were examples of what Belloc was seeking.

The Free Press, however, was less an alternative to than an evasion

of the problem. It was rather an intellectualist-cum-populist response
to political disillusion. The signs had been there in W.T. Stead's
unsuccessful *Daily Paper* of 1904, 'the paper of the Home' as he styled
it.[44] Some of the confidence in a new 'free press' was well-founded, as
witnessed by the continued success of the *Nation,* the *Westminster
Gazette* and the *Spectator,* albeit only the latter was not heavily
subsidised, and managed to survive the 1920s. There was some truth
in the view that 'the report that God is on the side of the Big Battallions
is propaganda put out by the Big Battallion commanders. They hope
thereby to spread alarm and despondency among the smaller forces.'[45]
The era of the real mass press had yet properly to begin, although
glimpsed in the Sundays. A reasonable assessment of the circulation
of the London dailies and Sunday papers in 1910 would be at most
9 million. By 1930 it was nearly 25 million.[46] Nevertheless this sort
of expansion was only a matter of time, and was not in the power of
the 'free press' to stem. The real problem was not the eradication of
popular ignorance, or even the enlightenment of the few. Nor was it
the perpetuation of a parochial party press. The problem was that the
old liberal theory to which almost everyone clung no longer fitted the
facts of modern industrial capitalism, in which literacy, technology and
the demands of the market had made the press into a major industry,
and in which it was called upon to play an important integrating role
in the structure of power. As an industry it depended upon the
continued and smooth functioning of the economy, and as a political
institution it had become legitimised since its early days of dubious
status. In the fourth quarter of the twentieth century this may have
the ring of cliché about it, but this was the time when it was a
comparatively fresh realisation, and even contemporaries who were
aware of the changes were reluctant to draw very appropriate conclusions from them. If this were the path of future press development
after all, then either one had to change it, by adapting society to the
old theory, an extreme voluntarist notion which few embraced, or to
find a new theory, and this, by 1914 at least, was an intellectual task
which had yet to be accomplished.

The dilemma which liberals faced becomes even clearer if it is
shown that it was not merely a British problem. Even the briefest of
comparisons with the development of the press in France and the
United States will serve to show that this was the case. First, some
general points of comparison will provide perspective. Both France
and the United States were more politically democratic in the nineteenth
century than Britain, albeit that there were severe restrictions on

liberty in the Second Empire, that the American blacks were effectively disfranchised, and that political corruption was the commonplace of politics in both countries to an extent which it was not in Britain even before the legislation of 1872 and 1883. The effect of greater democratisation was that in those countries it was rather a question of how many voters were newspaper readers, than as in Britain of how many newspaper readers were voters. Literacy and education varied widely both between and inside the countries themselves, and it is as difficult to measure there as we have seen it to be in Britain. Roughly measured, however, rates seem to have been similar in all three countries, with perhaps greater regional variations in France and the United States than in Britain by the turn of the century.[47] The political and legal framework within which the press had to operate in these countries obviously varied in well-known ways, reflecting tradition, economic change, institutional development, intellectual heritage, and so on. None of these differences, however, seems to have radically interfered with the development of the press as an industry, as was the case, for example, in Germany.[48] The major differences seem to have arisen from the different rates of economic growth and associated differences in economic structure. In this context French press development was slightly slower than in Britain, and in Britain than in the United States. But such variations were predictable, and the most striking aspect of the development of the press in these three countries was their similarity, especially, as in other technological fields, in a shared store of technical ideas and innovations. Economic conditions favourable to the growth of the newspaper industry in all three countries appeared at approximately the same time, and in the same sequence. Technological advances were transported rapidly from one to the other; each experienced a marked growth in population, France less so than Britain, Britain less so than the United States; an expanding market was being created in all three, which in turn created a vast advertising potential; the pattern of amalgamation and integration in industry was a common one, and applied equally to newspapers, but again less so in France; there was a common improvement in the status of the journalist, concomitant with the expansion of the professions and 'middle classes' in each country; employers' and employees' associations developed simultaneously in each country; the expansion of cheap communication facilities was a common feature, first with the railways and then with the telegraphs; the price of paper started to fall at about the same time in each country; and so on.

Built on top of these common factors it was hardly surprising that the development of the press and journalism in each country was very similar. In France there had been a long tradition of political newspapers, but the cheap daily made its appearance with Girardin's *La Presse* in 1836, closely followed and for a while outstripped by *Le Siècle*.[49] The success of *La Presse* encouraged Girardin to introduce the stereotyping process in 1852. Meanwhile in 1846 *La Patrie* had been the first paper in the world to use the Hoe rotary press. The French newspaper stamp, however, meant that the web rotaries of 1865 could not be used in France until the repeal of the stamp in 1872. By the 1860s when there was some relaxation of Napoleonic controls, *Le Petit Journal* was selling over a quarter of a million copies a day, the largest circulation in the world. Already agencies had been formed to exploit advertising, and the press was becoming big business, with *Le Siècle* making over half a million francs a year in the 1850s. Thereafter advertising developed less quickly than in the United States and Britain. In 1869 Kastenbein composing machines were introduced, followed in 1880 by the more sophisticated Thorne machines, and in 1886 by linotypes, three years ahead of Britain, but only finally accepted by the unions in 1900, some years after this had happened in Britain. The railways and the telegraphs had come in the 1840s and 1850s to France, as to Britain and the United States, and as early as the 1860s the Havas news agency was being accused of monopoly practices. It continued regardless, and in the early 1890s successfully fought off a challenge from the Scot Davison Dalziel. The 1870s saw the temporary appearance of the tabloid in France, but by the 1890s even the 'petit' press changed over to broadsheet. In the 1870s too, as in Britain and the United States, there was the foundation of the evening press, to capture, it was said, 'a new class of readers'. The total number of papers published rose to some 2,000 in 1900, and then began to decline, with provincial dailies falling from 257 in 1892 to 242 in 1914. Towns with at least one paper, usually an evening, continued to increase, however, from 62 in 1874 to 94 in 1914. The process of integration and amalgamation in France did not go so far as in Britain or the United States, but was compensated for financially by hidden subsidisation.

By this time newspaper business in France was on a smaller scale than in the other two countries, and somewhat less profitable, thanks partly to the smaller size of papers, and a lower average circulation. Distribution was as in Britain in the hands of agencies with 'Maison Hachette' comparable to W.H. Smith's. France had no 'national' papers, but it is arguable that, at least before the development of simultaneous publication of dailies in different centres in Britain, the Parisian papers had a similar status as London papers in Britain and New York papers in the United States. Indeed, the French provincial press was less independent of the centre than was the case in the other countries. It was economically weak, and prone to be very 'national' in style and content. The large Parisian dailies in the nineteenth century found from a third to a half of their circulations in the provinces, and by 1914 *Le Petit Parisien* was selling 80 per cent of its production in the provinces. The provincial papers themselves usually took their editorial line from one or other of the Parisian papers. The 1881 Press Law had tended to stimulate political papers, but many of these, which so attracted Massingham, were 'newspapers without readers', produced by politicians to establish their names and ideas. The weekly press also became more political after the liberalising law of 1881, but the development of the larger circulation paper, and the emergence in France of the 'new journalism' around 1902 began a trend towards depoliticisation which was to continue and increase after 1918. By 1914 the Parisian dailies, like their London counterparts, looked for their influence more with the executive and in the corridors of power than with the legislative or the electorate. Political reporting, as in Britain, declined in quantity and quality, to a level at which interest rather than understanding was the prime object. Perhaps more than in Britain, however, there were close political-journalistic ties, especially on the left. Journalists in France had organised themselves at much the same time as their British counterparts, with the Syndicat de la Presse Républicaine des Départements in the 1870s corresponding roughly to the Provincial Newspaper Society; and the Association Syndicale Professionnelle des Journalistes Républicaines Français in 1880 corresponding to the Institute of Journalists. As in Britain and the United States, the emergence of a strong cheap press in France after 1870 was closely associated with liberalism and in France's case republicanism, the conservative papers in France in the 1870s being as aware as the conservative press in Britain at that time of its inferior position to the republican papers. Moreover, the reaction against this domination was not in the form of a conservative renaissance, but, again as in Britain, in the form of an increasingly non-party-political press.

Commercialisation started sooner in the United States, but as in the other countries it proceeded for some time alongside a strong party-political press.[50] The polemical excesses of the earlier nineteenth-century United States newspapers were, as we have seen, notorious, and played

some part in the debate over the desirability of a cheap press in
Britain. There were Americans, however, who were also critical, and
some blame was laid at the door of the English journalists of the time,
like Cobbett, for setting a bad example. The early difficulties which
the Republic had experienced over the freedom, or licence of the press,
however, had been overcome largely by 1830, and the press there did
not labour under the legal disabilities which existed in France and
Britain. Only the abolitionist press before the civil War was seriously
interfered with, both by governments and by private individuals.

The first penny daily was the New York *Sun,* which by 1835 was
making some $20,000 p.a. By 1837 34 dailies had been started in
New York City alone, including the New York *Herald* in 1835. The
Herald was outselling the *Sun* by 1860, both having circulations in
excess of 50,000. Both were reformist, anti-corruption and even anti-
party papers. Cheapness was not everything. The railways and the
telegraphs had resulted in agencies being formed in the 1840s, the
most powerful of them the New York Associated Press in 1848,
followed by the rival Western Associated Press in 1862. Postal rates
were reduced after 1850, but paper prices were still relatively high,
and gathering and publishing the news was, as was being found in
Britain and France, an expensive activity. In the United States, however,
the growth in population, the increased urbanisation and the general
economic growth of the country meant that the *Herald* in 1836 and
the New York *Tribune* in 1842 had been able to raise their prices to
two cents without losing circulation. They were raised again after the
costly Civil War, again, in most instances, without losing circulation.
By the 1840s, as in France and Britain, advertising agencies had
appeared to exploit chaotic advertising rates. By the 1870s display
advertising was becoming the rule in the dailies, which had mostly
banished advertisements from the front page. The 1870s was also the
decade in which the 'new journalism' was ushered in, with the spread
of the 'interview' and the development of the sports and evening
press. By 1880 there were more evening papers than morning ones,
and by 1890 two-thirds of all the dailies were evening papers. Their
development was helped further by the lowering of postal rates in the
1870s and of telegraphic rates in the 1880s. The end of the 1870s
and the beginning of the 1880s saw the 'new journalism' come of age
with Joseph Pulitzer's New York *World,* a nice blend of sensation and
editorial weight and quality, much like the *Pall Mall Gazette* was to
become under W.T. Stead. The political press had remained strong in
the United States until the Civil War, in the form of the great

subscription dailies, the Whig ones subsidised by the wealthy mercantile families, the Democratic ones by successive governments. The war and the break-up of the Whig party, together with the development of the cheap press, resulted in a decline of this political press. By the 1880s most new foundations claimed to be non-political, and by 1890 one-third of those papers listed in the directories claimed to be so. In the country areas, as in Britain, many papers were in fact partly printed sheets, with a total of 3,000 of them in 1890. Until Pulitzer and his emulator and rival W.R. Hearst developed their own 'independent' style of journalism in the 1880s and 1890s, however, most papers still had identifiable party allegiances. By the 1870s, as in Britain, the empirical basis of these attachments was being undermined, for it had become clear that press support was no guarantee of votes, with presidential candidates in 1876 and 1880 having had the clear support of the press, and yet having failed to gain a majority of the popular vote. As in France there were no national papers in the United States, and New York did not dominate even so much as Paris did in the regional press, thanks partly to the larger scale of the country, and one might suggest to the federal tradition and structure of the United States as opposed to the heavily centralised prefectorial system in France. American dailies tended to have smaller circulations than their British counterparts, but were more numerous, New York having 17 in 1864, and Cincinatti, the fifth largest city in the 1850s, with 10 dailies. As in Britain and France, the aggregate of all papers probably peaked at or before 1914. The process of amalgamation started earlier than in the other countries, and individual specialised sections of the industry grew larger more quickly. The new agencies, formed by groups of large newspaper proprietors, like but not as general as the British Press Association, reorganised in 1892, after the monopoly power of the New York Associated Press had been successfully challenged by the independent United Press. In 1900 the new Associated Press was 'busted' under the anti-trust laws, but immediately arose in another guise to compete with the agency of the Hearst organisation. Distribution was usually by post in the country areas, and by the papers themselves in the cities, unlike either France or Britain. This led to violent clashes between the papers' employees in the cities before 1914. The 'new journalism' was carried furthest by Pulitzer in his *Sunday World,* Sunday editions of daily papers having been accepted in the United States since sabbatarian opposition had been overcome in the 1840s. The *World* tended to be a liberal, pro-labour anti-corruption paper, as did the chain of evening papers set up by E.W.

Scripps, and, for a time at least, the *Sun,* under the editorship of
Charles Dana. The *Tribune,* on the other hand, once the radical organ
of Greely, had become by the 1880s under Whitelaw Reid anti-labour
and protectionist, and Hearst's New York *Journal* was similarly
inclined. It was competition between the *World* and the *Journal*
which resulted in the creation of 'yellow journalism', between 1896
and 1902. Characterised by scare headlines covering the front page,
more or less deliberately fraudulent stories, masses of 'human interest'
and 'pseudo-science', combined with a clear identification with the
underdog, 'yellow journalism' culminated in the notorious war-
mongering of both papers in 1898, and in the assassination of
President McKinley, which act the *Journal* had openly incited. It
was a form of journalism not imitated in either France or Britain,
at least not until after 1918. Sobered by the excesses of 1901, the
American press returned to the development of the 'new journalism'
proper. Hearst had lost millions of dollars in that hectic period, and
even Pulitzer's phenomenally successful *World* had begun to lose
money. Now advertising improved, and the industry began to conform
to more orthodox financial standards. Symbolic of this was the
success of the previously ailing *New York Times* under its new
proprietor Adolph Ochs. Run as a good quality penny daily it made
Ochs twenty-five million dollars in twenty-five years, with a
circulation rising from about 150,000 in 1910 to 300,000 in 1920.
Proprietors had organised themselves in the American Newspaper
Proprietors Association, and the United Typothetae of America
in 1887, partly in response to the decision of the International
Typographical Union to join the American Federation of Labour in
the previous year. The printing unions, however, had been encouraged
by some of the New York dailies, in contrast to the attitude of British
proprietors. Journalists had also organised, in the same year as those
in Britain, 1884, and with an organ with the same title as the British
one, the *Journalist.* Politically there were close connections between
politicians and journalists, with some proprietors becoming politicians
on the strength of their papers. As in the other two countries there
was by the turn of the century more inclination to exercise influence
upon the executive than upon the legislature or upon the electorate.
The 'muckraking' of the 1900s made the unearthing of corruption a
profitable business, although there was an undoubtedly political,
'progressive' aspect of it.

    Just as it would be a mistake to imagine that all British newspapers
at the end of our period were like the *Daily Mail,* so it would be

mistaken to imagine all French ones like *Le Petit Parisien,* or all American ones like the *World.* Nevertheless, they were the most profitable papers, and in the van of technical and stylistic advance. Certainly they provoked similar and generalised criticism in all three countries. The French condemned a worsening quality of journalism, which put facts before ideas, and attributed it to 'americanisation'. As early as 1873 Albert Sorel was lamenting that 'our trumpery newspapers are the newspapers that pay'.[51] Americans themselves had complained of the sensationalism of their own press in the 1840s, and towards the end of the century criticism increased of the new readership which had created, it was claimed, 'a mental and moral chaos'.[52] Ochs's *New York Times,* and even the *World* before Pulitzer succumbed temporarily to the pressures of Hearst, and *Le Petit Parisien,* all managed to maintain themselves profitably whilst remaining, in part at least, informative and serious newspapers. With these examples it was clearly possible to produce an acceptable 'liberal' paper under the conditions of advanced capitalism. It is significant, however, that the *New York Times* remained comparatively small, and that the *World* and *Le Petit Parisien* did succumb to commercialisation in the end.

There were then certain discrepancies in the development of the press in these three countries, but it is the similarities and parallels that remain most striking. Some are accounted for by the spread of technology and the communications revolution of the nineteenth century. Educational advance and increasing wealth per head helped create a growing market for advertisers. In all three countries such expansion was helped in turn by a gradual process of national unification and depoliticisation, a slow eclipse of the provinces and regions and a growing distrust of party politics. Indeed, where a party political press flourished longest, the industry grew most slowly, in France. In all three countries the expansion of the cheap press was associated with a liberal ideology. In France and Britain it was a broadly liberal press which seemed to suffer most from commercialisation, although this was not so in America, where before 1914 a new and profitable blend of liberalism and populism, in its wider sense, emerged. In all three countries the subsidisation of the press by politicians and political parties continued, but in all three political influence seems to have been sought in the horizontal, political plane, rather than in the vertical one between the people and the politicians. In all three countries news increasingly replaced ideas and opinions, which brought liberal protests in each case.

What these comparisons show most clearly is that in each country
the conditions necessary to maintain a press based upon the old
liberal ideal were rapidly disappearing. In each country there was a
brief flowering of such a 'liberal press', from the 1830s to the 1880s,
perhaps, in the United States; from the 1880s to the 1900s, perhaps,
in France; and from the 1850s to the 1890s in Britain. To ask for a
return to these conditions, as Belloc was doing in the 1910s, even a
personalised and idealistically motivated muckraking form of
'liberal press', was to ask for the reversal of a trend which itself
depended upon greater forces than the development of journalism
only. These comparisons also show that it was not really a matter
of parochial party politics that was involved, except that it was the
early domination of the Liberal papers which of necessity bore the
brunt of the attack, whilst the new 'independent' or 'neutral' papers
tended towards conservatism. Nor was it a matter of peculiar defects
in the British political, educational or economic systems. Britain
shared her failings with at least two other advanced industrial
countries. In the simplest of terms, the press had become a business,
not only first, but increasingly a business almost entirely, and a political,
civil and social institution hardly at all. The old liberal theory was not
capable of adapting to this change.

Not until the vicissitudes of the 1930s were over, and had had
remarkably little adverse effect on the economic position of the
largest papers, while removing many more of the smaller ones, was
a liberal approach to the new conditions clearly formulated. In 1947
the publisher Henry Luce financed a Commission on the Freedom
of the Press, which in its report set out a version of what has come to
be known as 'the social responsibility theory' of the press.[53] It was
an attempt to meet the shortcomings of a press in a society which
imposed economic restrictions and distortions upon the proper
functioning of the press, as that was understood in a broadly liberal
sense. Unfortunately the 'theory' was founded upon a notion of 'the
moral right to free expression', and was avowedly an appeal to
conscience and duty. While this would have harmonised admirably
with the thought of T.H. Green, it did not explicitly at least make
the application of the politics of conscience to the problem of the
press. Yet even had they done so the real issue would have been
evaded, for the American formula was as empty as any formula
must be which is based purely on an appeal to 'duty' *per se,* for
which duty, and who is to decide which duty, are crucial unanswered
questions. A further example of the difficulty the Commission found

in arriving at a theoretical formulation on liberal principles was their attempt simultaneously to defend and to limit the right to err. The Commission, and the British Royal Commission which came a little after it, could only rely on exhortation, backed up in Britain by a weak watchdog institution, the Press Council. When in America the Supreme Court acted against the concentration of ownership in the mass media it was a case in which the press and radio were involved.[54] In Britain references to the Monopolies Commission were eventually made, but they failed to stem the process of concentration.

The 'social responsibility theory' also looked to a greater degree of professionalisation, not only in the older sense of meeting certain standards of behaviour and living up to a publicly bestowed status, but also in the more modern and more American sense of becoming technically more proficient, and of following the principle of 'objectivity'. It lies beyond the scope of this essay to enter into a discussion of the validity of the theory of 'objectivity', but it is relevant to relate it to the general liberal theory with which most people worked before 1914. There had since perhaps the 1860s been an increasing tendency for news to be valued more than opinion, and in the twentieth century for it to replace opinion. Even C.P. Scott of the *Manchester Guardian* was insisting that 'fact is sacred'. Apart from the deeper epistemological problem of whether any 'fact' can stand alone, however, there were obvious shortcomings in practice;[55] not even the voluminous American papers could really print '*all* the news that's fit to print', as Ochs boasted of the *New York Times*. Neither the American nor the British commissions made much headway against difficulties such as these.

The crisis of the liberal press before 1914 was one of vanishing opinion and diminishing numbers.[56] There existed a cheap press; a democracy was emerging; and the schoolmaster had long been abroad in the land, and yet the 'fourth estate' was developing along lines much different from those envisaged for it at the time of the repeal of the taxes on knowledge. Its 'golden age' in liberal terms had been all too brief, while the future was bleak, and the alternatives unattractive. The old vision had been rendered obsolete by the forces of social, economic and political change. The vision of an order in which the press enjoyed an enduring and unchanging role was fast disappearing, and the bitter lesson of 'plus ça change, moins c'est la même chose' had to be learned.

SELECT BIBLIOGRAPHY

Place of publication is London, unless otherwise stated.

I *Manuscript sources cited in the Notes*

Board of Trade, Companies Registration Office, B.T.31, PRO.
H. Campbell-Bannerman Papers, British Library.
Disraeli Papers, National Trust, Hughenden Manor.
Viscount Gladstone Papers, British Library.
F.C. Gould, MS Autobiography, House of Lords Record Office.
Home Office, Correspondence and Papers, Domestic and General,
    (Registered Papers), H.O. 45, PRO.
Lord Iddesleigh Papers, British Library.
National Union of Conservative and Unionist Associations, Annual
    Conference Minutes.
E.R. Pease Collection, British Library of Political and Economic Science.
Sir Edward Russell-Lord Rosebery Correspondence, Liverpool University
    Library.
J.A. Spender Papers, British Library.
Lord Wemyss Papers, National Register of Archives (Scotland).
H.J. Wilson Papers, Sheffield Central Library.

II *Theses cited in the Notes*

Hooton, J.F., 'Libraries in Hull in the Nineteenth Century', Library
    Association, 1967.
Jones, D.M., 'The Liberal Press and the Rise of Labour...1850-95',
    Leeds Ph.D., 1973.
Russell, A.K., 'The General Election of 1906', Oxford D.Phil., 1962.
Strick, H., 'British Newspaper Journalism, 1900-1956', London Ph.D.,
    1957.

III *Parliamentary Papers cited in the Notes*

Betting, Sel. Cttee.H.L. Rep., 1902 (389) viii.
Corrupt Practices in the Borough of Macclesfield, R.Com.Rep.,
    C.2853 (1881).
Electric Telegraphs Bill, Sel.Cttee Rep., 1868 (435) xi.
Illiterate Voters, 1883 (327) liv.
Joint Stock Companies, Parliamentary Returns, 1845-1907, for
    details see General Index of Parliamentary Papers.

Justices of the Peace, Returns of names and occupations, 1875 (388)
lxi,397; 1886 (13-SessI) liii,237; 1888(356) lxxxii, 193.
Justices of the Peace, R.Com.Rep., Cd.5358 (1910).
Law of Libel, Sel. Cttee Rep., 1878-79 (343) xi.
Law of Libel, Sel. Cttee Rep., 1880 (284) ix.
Newspaper Stamps, Sel. Cttee Rep., 1851 (558) xvii.
Parliamentary Reporting, Sel. Cttee Rep., 1878 (327) xvii.
Post Office (Telegraphic Department), Sel.Cttee Rep., 1876 (357) xiii.
Press. R.Com. Rep., Cmd. 7700 (1949).

IV *Works cited in the Notes more than once*

'Advertisements', *QR* (1855), xcvii, pp.183-225.
'Conservative Journalism', *NQR* (1860), ix, pp.385-96.
'English Country Newspapers', *Temple Bar* (1863), x, pp.128-41.
'The Fourth Estate', *GM* (1894), cclxxvii, pp.40-9.
'How News is Distributed', *Congregationalist* (1871), i, pp.673-81.
'Journalism of the Provinces', *Colburn's* (1836), xlviii, pp.137-49.
'Lament of the Leader Writer', *WR* (1899), clii, pp.656-64.
'Liberal Newspapers – Effects of the Reduction of Stamp Duty',
    Tait's Magazine (1836), iii, pp.685-92, 799-808.
'London Morning Newspapers', *CJ* (1849), xii, pp.85-90.
'The L.S.D. of Literature', *GM* (1874), n.s., xii, pp.713-30.
'My Newspaper', *AYR* (1864), xi, pp.473-6.
'The Newspaper Press', *WR* (1829), x, pp.216-37.
'A North Country Worthy', *RR* (1894), x, pp.85-6.
'Our Special Wire', *CJ* (1868), xlv, pp.433-6.
'Penny Newspapers: I and II', *LPCPN,* 15 Jun., 16 Jul. 1866.
'The Press in the Nineteenth Century', *Eclectic Magazine* (1853), xxviii,
    pp.289-305.
'The Provincial Newspaper Press', *WR* (1830), xxiii, pp.69-103.
Altick, R.D., *The English Common Reader* (1963).
Andrews, A., *The History of British Journalism* (1859).
Armstrong, G.G., *Memorieş* (1944).
Aspden, H., *Fifty Years a Journalist* (Clitheroe, 1930).
Aspinall, A., 'The Social Status of Journalists at the Beginning of the
    Nineteenth Century', *Review of English Studies* (1945), xxi,
    pp.216-32.
Ayerst, D., *Guardian. Biography of a Newspaper* (1971).
'B', 'English Journalism', *Nation* (NY), 22 Jul. to 14 Oct. 1880.
'B', 'The Conservative Provincial Press', *NR* (1885), v, pp.634-45.
Bahlman, D., ed., *The Diaries of Edward Walter Hamilton, 1880-85*

(Oxford 1972).

Baines Jr., Edward, *Life of Edward Baines* (1851).

Ball, W. Valentine, *The Law of Libel as Affecting Newspapers and Journalists* (1912).

Banks, J.A., *Prosperity and Parenthood* (1954).

Bateman, C., 'A great speech distributing agency', *Young Man* (1904), xviii, pp.217-22.

Baylen, J.O., 'The "New Journalism" in Late Victorian Britain', *Australian Journal of Politics and History* (1972), xviii, pp.367-85.

Bell, Lady, *At The Works* (1907).

Bellanger, C., *et al.*, eds., *Histoire Générale de la Presse Française* (Paris, 1969-74).

Belloc, H., *The Free Press* (1918).

Billington, M.F., 'Women in Journalism', *Sell's* (1891), pp.58-62.

Booth, C., *Life and Labour of the People in London* (1903), 2nd.s., iv.

Breed, W., 'Social Control in the Newsroom: a functional analysis', *Social Forces* (1955), xxxiii, pp.326-35.

Brett, R., *Journals of Viscount Esher* (1934).

(G.H. Burton), 'Lincolnshire Newspapers', *Lincoln, Rutland and Stamford Mercury*, 20 Mar. and 17 Apr. 1914.

Byles, F.G., *William Byles* (Weymouth, 1932).

Catling, T., *My Life's Pilgrimage* (1911).

Chamberlain, J., *A Political Memoir*, C.H. Howard, ed. (1953).

Chilston, Viscount, *W.H. Smith* (1965).

Clarke, P.F., *Lancashire and the New Liberalism* (Cambridge, 1971).

Coleman, D.C., *The British Paper Industry, 1495-1860* (Oxford, 1958).

Collett, C.D., *History of the Taxes on Knowledge* (1933 ed.).

Colman, H.C., *J.J. Colman* (1905).

'A Conservative Journalist', 'Why is the Provincial Press Radical?' *NR* (1886), vi, pp.678-82.

Cook, E.T., *Delane of The Times* (1915).

Cooke, A.B. and Vincent, J., *The Governing Passion* (Brighton, 1974).

Cox, H. and Morgan, D., *City Politics and the Press* (Cambridge, 1973).

Curtiss Jr., L.P., *Coercion and Conciliation in Ireland* (1963).

Dark, S., *Life of Sir Arthur Pearson* (1922).

Dawson, J., *Practical Journalism* (1885).

Dicey, A.V., *An Introduction to the Law of the Constitution* (1939 ed.).

(E. Dicey), 'Provincial Journalism', *St. Paul's Magazine* (1868), iii, pp.61-73.

Dicey, E., 'Journalism New and Old', *FR* (1905), lxxxiii, pp.904-18.

Escott, T.H.S., *England: its people, polity and pursuits* (1880).

Escott, T.H.S., *Social Transformations of the Victorian Age* (1897).

Feuchtwanger, E.J., *Disraeli, Democracy and the Tory Party* (1968).

Fox Bourne, H.R., *English Newspapers* (1887).

Frost, T., *Reminiscences of a Country Journalist* (1886).

Fyfe, H., *T.P. O'Connor* (1934).

Gardiner, A.G., *Life of George Cadbury* (1923).

Gibb, M. and Beckwith, F., *The Yorkshire Post. Two Centuries* (1954).

Gollin, A., *The Observer and J.L. Garvin* (1960).

Grant, J., *Travels in Town* (1839).

Grant, J., *The Newspaper Press* (1871).

Greenwood, F., 'The newspaper press', *BM* (1897), clxi, pp.704-20.

Hadley, W.W., *The Bi-centenary Record of the Northampton Mercury, 1720-1920* (Northampton, 1920).

Harris, F., *My Life and Loves* (1964 ed.).

Haslam, J., *The Press and the People* (Manchester, 1906).

Hatton, J., *Journalistic London* (1882).

Havighurst, A.F., *Radical Journalist* (1974).

Hayward, F.H. and Langdon-Davies, B., *Democracy and the Press* (Manchester, 1919).

Hennock, E.P., *Fit and Proper Persons* (1973).

History of the Sheffield Independent (Sheffield, 1892).

History of The Times, ii, (1939).

(J.F. Hitchman), 'The Newspaper Press', *QR* (1880), cl, pp.498-537.

Hobhouse, L.T., 'The Contending Forces', *English Review* (1909), iv, pp.359-71.

Hodgson, G.B., *From Smithy to Senate* (1908).

Hollis, P., *The Pauper Press* (Oxford, 1970).

Howe, E., *Newspaper Printing in the Nineteenth Century* (1943).

Howe, E., *The London Compositor* (1947).

Humphrey, G., 'The Reading of the Working Classes', *NC* (1893), xxxiii, pp.690-701.

Hunt, W., *Then and Now* (Hull, 1887).

Hurt, J., *Education in Evolution* (1972 ed.).

Innis, H.A., *The Bias of Communication* (Toronto, 1951).

Isaacs, G.A., *The Story of the Newspaper Printing Press* (1931).

Jeffries, R., *Hodge and His Masters* (1880).

Jephson, H., *The Platform* (1892).

Johnston, W., *England As It Is In The Middle of the Nineteenth Century* (1851).

Jones, K., *From Fleet Street to Downing Street* (1919).

Jones, M., *Justice and Journalism* (1974).

238 *Select Bibliography*

Kebbel, K., *Lord Beaconsfield and Other Tory Memories* (1907).
Kellet, E.E., 'The Press', *Early Victorian England*, G.M. Young, ed.
(1934).
Kieve, J., *The Electric Telegraph* (Newton Abbot, 1973).
Kinnear, A., 'The trade in great men's speeches', *CR* (1899), lxxv,
pp.439-44.
Kinnear, A., 'Parliamentary Reporting', *CR* (1905), lxxxvii, pp.369-75.
Kinnear, J.B. 'Anonymous Journalism', *CR* (1867), v, pp.324-39.
Knight, C., *The Old Printer and the Modern Press* (1854).
Knight, C., *Passages in a Working Life* (1864).
Koss, S., *Sir John Brunner: Radical Plutocrat* (1970).
Koss, S., *Fleet Street Radical* (1973).
Lambert, R., *The Cobbett of the West* (1939).
Lee, A.J., 'Franklin Thomasson and "The Tribune"', *HJ* (1973), xvi,
pp.341-60. (I).
Lee, A.J., 'The Management of a Victorian Local Newspaper',
Business History (1973), xv, pp.131-48. (II).
Lee, A.J., 'The Radical Press', *Edwardian Radicalism*, A.J.A. Morris,
ed. (1974).
Lee, J., *Social Leaders and Public Persons* (1963).
Linton W.J., *Memories* (1894).
Lockwood, D., *The Blackcoated Worker* (1958).
Lucas, R., *Lord Glenesk and the Morning Post* (1910).
Ludlow, J.M. and Jones, L., *Progress of the Working Classes, 1832-1867*
(1867).
Lytton, Lord, *England and the English* (1833; 1874 ed.).
McCarthy, J., *Reminiscences* (1899).
MacDonagh, M., *The Reporters' Gallery* (1912).
Mackintosh, J.P., *The British Cabinet* (1968 ed.).
Mansfield, F.J., *Gentlemen. The Press!* (1943).
Massingham, H.W., *The Daily Press* (1892).
Massingham, H.W., 'The Ethics of Editing', *NR* (1900), xxxv, pp.256-61.
Mayhew, H., *London Labour and the London Poor* (1851; 1967 ed.).
(Gibbons Merle), 'Weekly Newspapers', *WR* (1829), x, pp.466-80.
Mills, J.S., *Sir Edward Cook* (1921).
Milne, M., *Newspapers of Northumberland and Durham* (Newcastle,
1972).
Moneypenny, W.F. and Buckle, G.E., *Life of Benjamin Disraeli* (1914).
Moore, D.C., 'Political Morality in Mid-Nineteenth Century England',
VS (1969), xxiii, pp.5-36.
Morison, S., *The English Newspaper, 1622-1932* (Cambridge, 1932).

Morley, J., 'Anonymous Journalism' *FR* (1867), viii, pp.287-92.

Morley, J., *Life of Richard Cobden* (1896 ed.).

Morley, J., *Life of Gladstone* (1908 ed.).

Mott, F.L., *American Journalism: a history 1690-1960* (NY, 1962 ed.).

Musson, A.E., *The Typographical Association* (1954).

Musson, A.E., 'Newspaper Printing in the Industrial Revolution', *EcHR* (1957-58), 2nd.s., x, pp.411-26.

Nicoll, W.R., *J. Macdonell, Journalist* (1890).

Nowell-Smith, S., *The House of Cassell, 1848-1958* (1958).

O'Boyle, L., 'The Image of the Journalist in England, France and Germany, 1815-1848', *Comparative Studies in Society and History* (1968), x, pp.290-317.

One Hundred Years of the Shields Gazette (Shields, 1949).

Ostrogorski, M., *Democracy and the Organisation of Political parties* (1901).

Parris, H., *Constitutional Bureaucracy* (1969).

Pebody, C., *English Journalism* (1882).

Plummer, J., 'The British Newspaper Press in 1875', *British Almanac and Companion* (1876), pp.63-86.

Porritt, E., 'The value of political editorials', *Sell's* (1910), pp.508-13.

Pound, R. and Harmsworth, G., *Northcliffe* (1959).

Pratt-Boorman, H.B., *Your Family Newspaper* (Maidstone, 1968).

Progress of British Newspapers in the Nineteenth Century (1901).

Ramm, A., ed., *The Political Correspondence of Mr Gladstone and Lord Granville, 1876-1886* (Oxford, 1962).

Reader, W.J., *Professional Men* (1966).

Registrar-General's *Annual Report,* 1858, 1861, 1867.

Reid, A., 'How a provincial newspaper is managed', *NC* (1886), xx, pp.391-402.

Reid, T.W., 'Our London Correspondent', *MM* (1880), xlii, pp.18-26.

Reid, T.W., *Memoirs,* S.J. Reid, ed. (1905).

Reid-Smith, E.R., *Parliament and Popular Culture in the Early Nineteenth Century* (1969).

Rempel, R.A., *Unionists Divided* (Newton Abbot, 1972).

Rendel, Lord, *Personal Papers* (1931).

Richardson, H., 'The Newspapers of South Wiltshire', *Wiltshire Archaeological and Natural History Magazine* (1922), xli, pp.53-69, 479-501.

Roberts, A.W., 'Leeds Liberalism and Late Victorian Politics', *Northern History* (1970), v, pp.131-56.

Roberts, R., *The Classic Slum* (Manchester, 1971).

Robinson, J., *Fifty Years of Fleet Street* (1904)

Rogers, E.D., *Life and Experiences* (1912).

Ruskin, J., *Collected Works*, E.T. Cook, ed. (1903-1912).

Russell, A.K., *Liberal Landslide* (Newton Abbot, 1973).

Russell, P., *The Author's Manual* (1891).

Sala, G.A., *Twice Around the Clock* (1859; 1971 ed.).

Sala, G.A., 'The World's Press – what I have known of it', *Sell's* (1897), pp.80-94.

Salmon, E.G., 'What the working classes read', *NC* (1886), xx, pp.108-17.

Sampson, H., *A History of Advertising* (1875).

Schofield, R., 'The measurement of literacy in pre-industrial England', *Literacy in Traditional Societies*, J.R. Goody, Ed. (Cambridge, 1968).

Scott, G., *Reporter Anonymous* (1968).

Scott, J.W.R., *The Story of the Pall Mall Gazette* (1950).

Seymour-Ure, C., *The Political Impact of the Mass Media* (1974).

Shannon, H.A., 'The First Five Thousand Limited Companies', *EcHR* (1932), ii, pp.396-424.

Siebert, F.S., Peterson, T. and Schramm, W., *Four Theories of the Press* (Urbana, 1969 ed.).

Simonis, H., *Street of Ink* (1917).

Sinclair, A., *Fifty Years of Newspaper Life, 1845-1895* (Glasgow, 1897).

Singleton, F., *The Tillotsons of Bolton* (1950).

Spark, F.R., *Memories of My Life* (1913).

Spender, H., *The Fire of Life* (1926).

Spender, J.A., *The Public Life* (1925).

Spender, J.A., *Life, Journalism and Politics* (1927).

Starmer, C., 'The Story of the Birmingham Gazette', *World's Press News,* 17 Oct. 1929.

Stead, W.T., 'Government by Journalism', *CR* (1886), xlix, pp.653-74.

(Stephen, J.F.), 'Newspaper English', *SR* 9 Aug. 1856.

(Stephen, J.F.), 'Journalism', *CM* (1862), vi, pp.52-63.

Stephenson, W.H., *Alfred Frederick Stephenson* (Manchester, 1937).

Symon, J.D., *The Press and its Story* (1914).

Taylor, H.A., *Robert Donald* (1934).

Thompson, G.C., *Public Opinion and Lord Beaconsfield, 1875-1880* (1886).

Thompson, H., *The Choice of a Profession* (1857).

'Theta' (J.S. Mill), 'Taxes on Knowledge', *Monthly Repository* (1834), p.109.

Trevelyan, G.M., 'The White Peril', *NC* (1901), 1, pp.1043-55.

Tylecote, M., *The Mechanics Institutes of Lancashire and Yorkshire Before 1851* (Manchester, 1957).

Vernon, A., *A Quaker Businessman: Life of Joseph Rowntree, 1836-1925* (1958).

Watson, A., *A Newspaperman's Memories* (1925).

Webb, R.K., 'Working class readers in early Victorian England', *EHR* (1950), lxv, pp.333-51.

Webb, R.K., *The British Working Class Reader, 1780-1848* (1955).

Weir, W., 'London Newspapers', *London,* C. Knight, ed. (1843), v.

Wells, H.G., *New Worlds for Old* (1909 ed.).

Western Morning News, Supplement, 3 Jan. 1910.

Whates, H.R.G., *The Birmingham Post, 1857-1957* (Birmingham, 1957).

Whorlow, H., *The Provincial Newspaper Society, 1836-1886* (1886).

Whyte, F., *Life of W.T. Stead* (1925).

Wickwar, W.H., *The Struggle for the Freedom of the Press, 1819-1832* (1928).

Wiener, J., *The War of the Unstamped* (1969).

Williams, D.G.T., *Not in the Public Interest* (1965).

(Wilson, J.F.,) *A Few Personal Recollections by an Old Printer* (1896).

Wood, B., 'The Bradford Newspaper Press', *The Bradford Antiquary* (1906), pp.49-67.

Yeo, H., *Newspaper Management* (Manchester, 1891).

Yorkshire Observer, Centenary Supplement, 6 Feb. 1934.

NOTES

CHAPTER ONE

1. F.S. Siebert, T. Peterson and W. Schramm, *Four Theories of the Press*, (Urbana, 1969 ed.). Note, however, the authors' distinction between a 'libertarian' and a 'social responsibility' theory. I have used 'liberal' when referring to the general principles of 'liberalism', and 'Liberal' when referring to the political party or its connections.
2. W.J. Fisher, 'The Liberal Press and the Liberal Party', *NC* (1904), lvi, p.201.
3. G.M. Trevelyan, 'The White Peril', *NC* (1901), 1, p.1047.
4. L.T. Hobhouse, 'The Contending Forces', *English Review* (1909), iv, p.365.
5. This was not exclusively a liberal claim. Carlyle, for example, wrote, 'literature is our Parliament too. . .the nation is governed by all that has tongue in the nation', *Heroes and Hero Worship* (1902 ed.)-, pp.199f. Nevertheless, Carlyle was quoted in the main on the subject of the press by 'liberals'.
6. Cf. D.C. Moore, 'Political Morality in Mid-Nineteenth Century England', *VS* (1969), xxiii, pp.5-36.
7. R.G. Collingwood, *The Idea of History* (1961 ed.), p.260.
8. C. Bellanger *et al.,* eds. (Paris, 1969-72).
9. H.D. Lasswell, 'The Structure and Function of Communication', *The Communication of Ideas,* L. Bryson, ed. (N.Y., 1948).
10. M. Burrage, 'Two Approaches to the Study of the Mass Media', *Archives Européenne de Sociologie* (1969), x, pp.238-53.
11. C. Seymour-Ure, *The Political Impact of the Mass Media* (1974), pp.41ff. See also W. Breed, 'Social Control in the Newsroom: a Functional Analysis', *Social Forces* (1955), xxxiii, pp.326-35.

CHAPTER 2

1. Notably by the sometime editor of the *Morning Advertiser,* James Grant, in *The Newspaper Press* (1871), i, p.vi, and ii, pp.455-60.
2. A. Andrews, *The History of British Journalism* (1859), i, p.6.
3. 'The State of the Press', *Edinburgh Review* (1821), v, pp.366-7. For further instances of the use of the mechanical metaphor see E.E. Kellet, 'The Press', in *Early Victorian England,* G.M. Young, ed. (1934), ii, pp.3-6. The sheer scale of things tended to overwhelm. 'The combined issues for a single day of the "Times", "Telegraph", "Standard" and "Daily News" if placed end to end would form a continuous line of nearly 600 miles, or about the distance between London and Berlin'. For America it was calculated that nearly 1.2 million miles of paper were used for newspapers each year, (J.F. Hitchman), 'The Newspaper Press', *QR* (1880), cl, pp.508-9. Cf. also *AYR* (1864), xi, p.476.
4. 'Newspapers', *WR* (1824), ii, p.210.
5. Lord Lytton, *England and the English* (1833; 1874 ed.), p.198.
6. W. Mckinnon, *On the Rise, Progress and Present State of Public Opinion in Great Britain and Other Parts of the World* (1828), p.1.
7. Ibid. pp.6-7.

8. F. Siebert, *Freedom of the Press in England, 1476-1776* (1952), p.192.
9. Jeremy Bentham in the 1780s, quoted in C. Bay, *The Structure of Freedom* (1958), p.41.
10. F.L. Mott and R.D. Casey, eds., *Interpretations of Journalism* (1937), pp.56-7.
11. S. Bailey, *Essays on the Formation and Publication of Opinions* (1826 ed.), p.165. Cf. W.H. Wickwar, *The Struggle for the Freedom of the Press, 1819-1832* (1928), pp.246-7.
12. J. Mill, 'The Liberty of the Press', *Essays* (n.d. (1824), pp.21-8).
13. S. de Sismondi, *Political Economy,* trans, and ed. M. Mignet (1847), pp.333-4.
14. J.S. Mill to G. d'Eichthal, 7 Nov. 1829, *The Earlier Letters of John Stuart Mill, 1812-1848,* F. Mineka, ed. (1963), pp.38-9.
15. J.S. Mill, 'Civilisation', *Mill's Essays on Literature and Society,* J. Schneewind, ed. (1965), p.165, and cf. also p.168.
16. A. de Tocqueville, *Democracy in America,* J.P. Mayer, ed. (1968), i, (1835), pp.22ff, ii, (1840), p.906. The American press provided a shining example to British radicals, G. Lillibridge, *Beacon of Freedom* (1955), pp.9ff, and J. Wiener, *The War of the Unstamped* (1969), p.8. The case for (QQ.614ff, 640ff, 2542ff), and against (QQ.694ff, 2115-16) the American press was given to the Select Committee of 1851, The French press, which was also used as a mirror, was usually regarded as an instrument of revolution, although France was recognised as a country where the journalist had a high social status, Kellet, op.cit., p.12, and L.O'Boyle, 'The Image of the Journalist in England, France and Germany, 1815-1848, *Comparative Studies in Society and History* (1968), x, p.300. J.S. Mill's opinion of it was unfavourable, see letter cited in note 14 above.
17. H. Brougham, *Works* (1856 ed.), xi, pp.109-100.
18. B. Disraeli, *Coningsby* (1844; 1948 ed.), pp.119, 315.
19. Cf. G. Watson, *The English Ideology* (1973), pp.161-2; J.H. Burns, 'J.S. Mill and Democracy', *Mill,* J. Schneewind, ed. (1969), pp.280-328. For a similar diagnosis of the state of the American press by an American conservative, see D.P. Crook, *American Democracy in English Politics 1815-1850* (Oxford, 1965), p.115, quoting Alexander Hamilton.
20. Wiener, op.cit., pp.115-36; P. Hollis, *The Pauper Press* (Oxford, 1970), pp.10-25.
21. Wiener, op.cit., p.118.
22. Ibid., pp.30-1.
23. For example, Lytton, op.cit., p.200 n.*; C. Knight, *The Old Printer and the Modern Press* (1854), pp.295ff; and, a French view, E. Alletz, quoted in O'Boyle, op.cit., p.301.
24. *SCNS,* evidence of Collett, Q.980, and Spencer, Q.2369.
25. *SCNS,* evidence of Knight Hunt, Q.2353; 'Theta', (J.S. Mill). 'Taxes on Knowledge', *Monthly Repository* (1834), p.109. Cf. also M. Jones, *Justice and Journalism* (1974), p.24.
26. S. Smiles, 'What are the people doing to educate themselves?', *People's Journal* (1846), i, p.230.
27. Speech to the Association for the Promotion of the Repeal of the Taxes on Knowledge, *The Times,* 9 Feb. 1854.
28. Mrs Bayley, 'The influence of public opinion on the habits of the working classes', *Trans NAPSS,* 1863, p.695. On the same point see *SCNS,* evidence of Whitty, QQ.603-4, and Hogg, Q.1035; Cobden, quoted in R.K. Webb, 'The Victorian Reading Public', *From Dickens to Hardy,* B. Ford, ed. (Harmondsworth, 1958), p.209; C.D. Collett, *History of the Taxes on Knowledge* (1933 ed.), p.49.

29. J. Hurt, *Education in Evolution* (1972 ed.), p.62.
30. J.M. Ludlow and L. Jones, *Progress of the Working Class, 1832-1867* (1867), pp.181, 187-8.
31. 'Theta', op.cit., p.105; *SCNS,* evidence of W.E. Hickson, Q.3254.
32. Andrewes, op.cit., ii, p.189.
33. Registrar-General's Reports, 1861, 1867.
34. Collett, op.cit., p.78.
35. E.R. Reid-Smith, *Parliament and Popular Culture in the Early Nineteenth Century* (1969), p.6.
36. *SCNS,* Q.2364.
37. Kellet, op.cit., p.66. Cf. also a Mechanics Institute petition against the newspaper taxes in 1831, quoted in Reid-Smith, op.cit., p.5.
38. *SCNS,* Q.2174.
39. (J.F. Stephen), 'Journalism', *CM* (1862), vi, pp.57-8.
40. Edward Baines Jnr., *Life of Edward Baines* (1851), p.44; M. Whitty, evidence in *SCNS,* QQ.600-04; W. Weir, 'London Newspapers', *London,* C. Knight, ed. (1843), v, p.337.
41. W.T. Stead, 'The London Morning Dailies that are and are to be', *Sell's* (1892), p.107.
42. For example, Charles Booth in 1903, quoted in W.H.G. Armytage, 'The 1870 Education Act', *British Journal of Educational Studies* (1970), xviii, p.132; E. Dicey, 'Journalism New and Old', *FR* (1905), lxxxiii, p.917; and J. Haslam, *The Press and the People* (Manchester, 1906), p.3.
43. R.K. Webb, 'Working class readers in early Victorian England', *EHR* (1950), lxv, p.349. Elsewhere Professor Webb has estimated that in the early nineteenth century the average literacy rate in England was more than 50%, and that in Scotland there was almost universal adult literacy, *The British Working Class Reader, 1790-1848* (1955), p.22. It should not, of course, be supposed that illiteracy was confined to the working classes. In 1854 some 2% of teachers in dame schools signed the register with a mark, not all of whom would have done so merely in deference to the deficiencies of their husbands, 1851 Census Report, *Education* (1854), p.xxxiii. For a detailed discussion see R.D. Altick, *The English Common Reader* (1963 ed.), pp.141-72. For continuities in educational provision and organisation see J. Hurt, op.cit.
44. W. Hunt, *Then and Now* (Hull, 1887), p.70, emphasis added. G.A. Sala also thought it was unjust to put so much emphasis on 1870, 'The World's Press – what I have known of it', *Sell's* (1897), p.87.
45. T. Wright, 'On the possibilities of a popular culture', *CR* (1881), xl, p.26.
46. D.C. Coleman, *The British Paper Industry, 1495-1860* (Oxford, 1958), p.209; *Driffield Times,* 21 Jan. 1860; Ludlow and Jones, op.cit., p.150. In case Jackson's claim seems exaggerated it should be noted that the East Riding had high rates of literacy: 82% of men and 68% of women signed the marriage register in 1858, Registrar-General's Report, 1858. Cf. also W.P. Baker, *Parish Registers and Illiteracy in East Yorkshire* (1961).
47. In any case, such questions asked in France are thought to have yielded very dubious results, *World Illiteracy at the Mid-Century* (Paris, 1957), chapter 2.
48. Webb, op.cit. (1955).
49. G. Simmons, *The Working Classes* (1849), pp.149-50.
50. R. Roberts, *The Classic Slum* (Manchester, 1971), p.49.
51. Illiterate Voters, *PP* 1883 (327) liv. This uses the 1880 election registers , and the 1881 census. Only 6.4% of the English counties' population were registered electors, and less than 1% of these were illiterate. 12.8% of the English boroughs' population were registered, and 1.4% of these were illiterate. Of counties where all seats were contested only Monmouthshire

had over 2% illiterate electors. Of contested boroughs over 100,000 population, Blackburn had more than 6% of illiterate electors, and eleven others had more than 2%.

52. A systematic analysis of these is being conducted at Cambridge. The figures used here are drawn from the annual reports of the Registrar-General, and are meant only to indicate broad trends.

53. Registrar General's Report, 1861, p.vii; L. Stone, 'Literacy and education in England, 1640-1900', *P&P* (1969), no.42, p.99. Dr. Schofield, 'The Measurement of Literacy in Pre-Industrial England', *Literacy in Traditional Societies,* J.R. Goody, ed. (Cambridge, 1968), p.324, accepts the Reigstrar's point, but cf. Webb, op.cit. (1950), p.336.

54. Schofield, op.cit., p.322.

55. W.E. Hickson thought that three or four years was as long as the skill of reading usually lasted after leaving school, in his experience as an inspector, *SCNS,* Q.3240.

56. Registrar-General's Report, 1861.

57. M. Sanderson, 'Literacy and social mobility in the industrial revolution in England', *P&P* (1972), no.56, pp.75-104.

58. H.J. Wilson was surely correct in questioning Collard Ellis' opinion, given him in 1874, that 'the population of Sheffield will not be a reading population to the same extent of populations engaged in woolen or cotton factories', *HJW,* MD 5999, p.4

59. V.A. Hatley, 'Literacy at Northampton, 1761-1900', *Northamptonshire Past and Present* (1971-72), iv, p.379, and Registrar-General's Reports.

60. It is, however, a dubious argument that anything which maintains and improves the skill of reading, whether it be comics, betting news or posters is by dint of that alone beneficial. It might be asked in what sense it is desirable for people to read the blandishments and deceits of those who seek to exploit them, before, and indeed instead of, anything which would fortify them against such dangers? This was a problem inherent in the liberal model. For a defence of the argument, however, see Roberts, op.cit., pp.129-34, and, a less committed view, Hollis, op.cit., p.115. On the importance of oral communication at this time see E.E. Kellet, *As I Remember* (1936), pp.37-8, and M. Springhall, *Labouring Life in Norfolk Villages, 1834-1914* (1936), p.70.

61. Schofield, op.cit., p.313; Roberts, op.cit., p.127

62. Webb, op.cit. (1955), p.32; Altick, op.cit., p.323

63. C.M. Smith, *The Working Man's Way in the World* (1857 ed.), p.188; E.G. Salmon, 'What the working classes read', *NC* (1886), xx, p.109; Lady Bell, *At the Works* (1907), p.145.

64. Estimates of multiple readership vary. W.H. Smith reckoned a London daily was read three or four times, *SCNS,* Q.2832. The author of 'Journalism in the provinces', *Colburn's* (1836), xlviii, pp.141-2, reckoned between ten and twenty; (Gibbons Merle), 'Weekly Newspapers', *WR* (1829), x, p.477, went up to thirty. So great was the demand for newspapers in pubs before repeal that 'a placard was generally hung up in the bar requesting gentlemen not to monopolise the current paper for more than (five minutes)', (J.F. Wilson), *A Few Personal Recollections by an Old Printer* (1896), p.11. The *Morning Advertiser,* organ of the Licensed Victualllers, was, of course, taken by every pub. Next to it in frequency were the *Weekly Dispatch* and the *Morning Chronicle, Journal of the Royal Statistical Society* (1838), 1, p.486

65. J.F. Hooton, 'Libraries in Hull in the Nineteenth Century. . .', unpublished Library Association thesis (1967), pp.66, 90, 103, 134, 139; Freebody's *Hull* (1851).

66. Reid-Smith, op.cit., p.25

67. (Gibbons Merle), op.cit., p.476; (J.F. Stephen), op.cit., p.63; Capt. St. Clair Ford, 'Coffee Taverns', *Trans NAPSS* (1879), pp.641-42.
68. For a more sympathetic view of the achievement of the Institutes as working-class institutions see E. Royle, 'Mechanics Institutes and the Working Classes, 1840-1860', *HJ* (1971), xiv, pp.305-21.
69. M. Tylecote, *The Mechanics Institutes of Lancashire and Yorkshire Before 1851* (Manchester, 1851), pp.114-16; W.H. Chaloner, *The Social and Economic Development of Crew, 1780-1923* (Manchester, 1950), pp.233-5. The Hull Mechanics Institute spent £25 p.a. on 'approved periodicals', J. Greenwood, *Pictures of Hull* (1835), pp.125-8.
70. *SCNS*, QQ.1036, 1065; Tylecote, op.cit., p.116.
71. *SCNS*, QQ.1040-41.
72. *SCNS*, Q.1067.
73. 'The Labourers' Reading Room', *Household Words* (1851), iii, pp.583ff. For a favourable report on the six working men's reading rooms in Carlisle in 1861, and for a clear exposition of what were felt to be the differences between them and the Mechanics Institutes' rooms, see R. Elliott, 'On working men's reading rooms as established in 1848 at Carlisle', *Trans NAPSS* (1861), pp.676-9.
74. J. Hole, *An Essay on the History and Management of Literary, Scientific and Mechanics Institutions* (1853; 1970 ed.), pp.72-4.
75. J.D. Mullins, 'Our Newsrooms', *Library Chronicle* (1884), i, pp.37-9.
76. N. Rowe, 'The English Press: I', *Continental Monthly* (1864), cv, p.104; W.H. Stephenson, *Alfred Frederick Stephenson* (Manchester, 1937), p.91; 'Readers', *BM* (1879), cxxvi, p.242.
77. 'Penny Newspapers: II', *LPCPN*, 16 Jul. 1866, pp.9-10.
78. G.A. Sala, op.cit. (1897), p.82.
79. R. Jefferies, *Hodge and his Masters* (1880), pp.198ff, 202. Cf. also *SCNS*, QQ.1429, 2689.
80. 'The Press in the Nineteenth Century', *Eclectic Magazine* (1853), xxviii, p.305.
81. 'B', 'English Journalism: IX English Provincial Journalism', *Nation* (N.Y.), 12 Aug. 1880.
82. Ibid., 'VII The Evening Newspapers', 7 Oct. 1880.
83. Dicey, op.cit. (1905), pp.915-16.
84. H.W. Massingham, *The Daily Press* (1892), p.10.
85. G.R. Humphrey, 'The reading of the working classes', *NC* (1893), xxxiii, p.694.
86. J. Leigh, 'What do the masses read?', *Economic Review* (1904), xiv, pp.166-7. His article is a valuable discussion of the methodological problems of such a survey.
87. Haslam, op.cit., a survey apparently made with a view to starting a new working-class paper in Manchester.
88. Cf. L. James, *Fiction for the Working Man* (1963), chapter 2.

CHAPTER 3

1. H.R. Fox Bourne, *English Newspapers* (1887), ii, p.226.
2. Ibid., p.113.
3. On the 'unstamped press' see Wickwar, op.cit., Wiener, op.cit., Hollis, op. cit. For the post-1836 period see Collett, op.cit., which has to be supplemented by Fox Bourne, op.cit., ii, pp.112ff, and *History of The Times* (1939), ii, pp.193ff.
4. Collett, op.cit. p.33.

5. 'The Journals of the Provinces', loc.cit., p.149. For a detailed survey of the provincial press after the Act see 'The Liberal Newspapers — Effects of the Reduction of the Stamp Duty', *Tait's Magazine* (1836), iii, pp.685-92, 799-808. *NPD* is unreliable for this period, but gives UK totals of 295 in 1831, and 472 in 1841.
6. Andrewes, op.cit., ii, p.189; *SCNS*, Q.2856, evidence of W.H. Smith.
7. Collett, op.cit. pp.44-5.
8. On Collett see G.J. Holyoake, *Byegones Worth Remembering* (1905), p.269.
9. Collett, op. cit. pp.49-50
10. Ibid., pp.112-13.
11. For Moore see W.J. Linton, *Memories* (1894), p.30.
12. Fox Bourne, op.cit., ii, p.211.
13. For Hickson see Linton, op.cit., p.59.
14. *The Times*, 9 Feb. 1854. Cf. also Collettt, op.cit., pp.111, 113, and J. Morley, *Life of Richard Cobden* (1896 ed.), ii, p.421.
15. *SCNS*, pp.x-xi.
16. Collett, op.cit., p.105
17. *SCNS*, QQ.2037ff.
18. *History of The Times,* ii, p.198 n.1.
19. Ibid., p.207.
20. Ibid., pp.207-10
21. *The Times,* 14 May 1855.
22. E.de Fonblanque, *Life and Times of Albany Fonblanque* (1874), p.458.
23. *SCNS*, QQ.1812ff.
24. The APRTK again complained of favour shown to *The Times* in 1870, when the postage rate was reduced to a halfpenny, regardless of weight, Collett, op.cit., pp.205-6.
25. Henry Vizetelly wrote of a complementary Newspaper and Periodical Press Association for Obtaining the Repeal of the Duty, in 1858, with M. Gibson as president, J. Francis as treasurer, and Vizetelly as secretary. It was supported financially by Edward Lloyd, Edward Lawson and others, and concentrated mainly on the conversion of MPs, H. Vizetelly, *Glances Back Through Seventy Years* (1893), ii, pp.42-4. H.J. Nicoll has this Association as the direct successor of the earlier committee to repeal the advertisement duties, *Great Movements* (1881), p.269. There was also a Constitutional Defence Association, chaired by James White, MP, formed to fight the House of Lords resistance to the repeal of the paper duty, J.F. Ritchie, *British Senators* (1869), pp.143-4.
26. These included the proprietor of the *Morning Post,* T.B. Crompton, R. Lucas, *Lord Glenesk and the Morning Post* (1910), pp.64-5.
27. Fox Bourne, op.cit., ii, p.231.
28. Morley, op.cit. (1896), ii, pp.496-504.
29. Holyoake, introduction to Collett, op.cit., pp.ix-x.
30. 'The Cheap Press', *Tait's Magazine* (1855), xxii, p.229.
31. D.J. Rowe, ed., *London Radicalism, 1830-1843* (1970), Appendix to document 105, (c.1838).
32. 'English Country Newspapers', *Temple Bar* (1863), x, p.129.
33. NPD; (G.H. Burton), 'Lincolnshire Newspapers', *Lincoln, Rutland and Stamford Mercury,* 17 Apr. 1914.
34. The Lawsons of the *Daily Telegraph* and the Lloyds of the *Daily Chronicle* should be mentioned here.
35. 'Legal and Fiscal Trammels of the Press', *WR* (1833), xviii, pp.474ff.
36. G. Cranfield, *The Development of the Provincial Newspaper, 1700-1760* (1962), pp.50, 193-4, 249ff. For nineteenth-century examples see H. Richardson, 'The Newspapers of South Wiltshire', *Wiltshire Archaeological*

and Natural History Magazine (1922), xli, pp.63-4. A rough check of NPD (1855-73), shows some 56 proprietors of weekly papers who were also 'patent medicine vendors', or the like.

37. K. Jones, *From Fleet Street to Downing Street* (1919), p.175. The contemporary estimate of £20,000 given in Webb, op.cit. (1958), p.222, seems exaggerated, but there were men willing to lose large sums. *The Representative,* for example, was said to have lost £26,000 in six months in 1825, *Sell's* (1896), p.27.

38. (J.F. Hitchman), op.cit., p.502.

39. *SCNS,* QQ.631ff.

40. W. Hindle, *The Morning Post, 1772-1937* (1937), p.177.

41. 'The provincial newspaper press', *WR* (1830), xxiii, p.79.

42. E. Baines Jr., op.cit., p.46; *Yorkshire Observer Centenary; D.* Ayerst, *Guardian. Biography of a Newspaper* (1971), p.21; *Stockport Advertiser Centenary,* chapter 10; *NPP,* Feb. 1871.

43. *NW,* 19 Aug. 1939; H. Whorlow, *The Provincial Newspaper Society, 1836-1886* (1886), p.88.

44. *SCNS,* QQ.631ff.

45. M. Milne, *Newspapers of Northumberland and Durham* (Newcastle, 1972), p.44.

46. *NPP,* Sep. 1869; H.B. Pratt-Boorman, *Your Family Newspaper* (Maidstone, 1968), pp.154-5.

47. Ayerst, op.cit., pp.145-6.

48. *DNB; Boase.*

49. *Modern Mayors of Derby* (Derby, 1909); *NPD* (1903), p.31.

50. There were two other organisations mentioned in the late 1860s, when trade was depressed: the Newspaper Proprietors Defence Association, and the Newspaper Proprietors Protection Society, both of which seem to have been responses to the problem of defaulting advertisers, *NPP,* Dec. 1870, and Feb. 1867. The London and Provincial Press Protection Society was established in 1874 to give protection against vexatious libel suits, *NV,* Feb. 1874.

51. Whorlow, op.cit., p.23.

52. Ibid., pp.53-5.

53. *NPD* (1846), p.104.

54. Ibid., p.3. Whitty, in contrast, drew the attention of the 1851 Committee to the fact that there were four editors in the US Senate, and another four in the House of Representatives, *SCNS,* Q.615.

55. Andrewes, op.cit., ii, pp.266ff.

56. *SCNS,* QQ.2196, 2198, 853, and 1019.

57. 'London Morning Newspapers', *CJ* (1849), xii, p.85.

58. The following is based on G.A. Isaacs, *The Story of the Newspaper Printing Press* (1931), and E. Howe, *Newspaper Printing in the Nineteenth Century* (1943). See also A.E. Musson, 'Newspaper Printing in the Industrial Revolution', *EcHR* (1957-8), 2nd.s., x, pp.411-26, which refers especially to the *Manchester Guardian.*

59. Only newspapers used this size of sheet, and were, therefore, a leading sector in the development of printing technology, G. Pollard, 'Notes on the Size of the Sheet', *The Library* (1941), n.s., xxii, p.135, and E. Howe, *The London Compositor* (1947), p.68.

60. *A Centenary History of the Staffordshire Advertiser* (Stafford, 1895), p.14; R.S. Lambert, *The Cobbett of the West* (1939), p.97.

61. There had been patents before this, including one by Rowland Hill in 1835. For *La Patrie* see Bellanger, op.cit., ii, pp.146, 259. Hoe also sold a rotary to the Philadelphia *Public Ledger* in 1846, Musson, op.cit. (1957-58), p.416.

62. For interesting contemporary accounts of the stereo process see 'How we get our newspapers', *CJ* (1865), 4th.s., ii, p.771, and (J.F. Hitchman), op.cit. pp.507-8.
63. Howe, op.cit. (1943), p.31.
64. For prices of machines in the 1860s see A.E. Musson, *The Typographical Association* (1954), p.93. Steam presses were more widespread than Musson allows for, however, and one must add to his list at least those at Reading, Exeter and Newcastle-under-Lyme. By 1890 a small Victory could produce 12,000 eight-page papers an hour, W.J. Gordon, 'The Newspaper Printing Press of Today', *Leisure Hour* (1890), xxxix, p.266.
65. *DNB,* entry on Edward Lloyd; *NV,* 1 Oct. 1873.
66. Coleman, op.cit., pp.212-22; J. Evans, *The Endless Web* (1955), pp.88ff; A. Sinclair, *Fifty Years of Newspaper Life, 1845-1895* (Glasgow, 1897), pp.28-31.
67. *The Times* used the Kastenbein machine from 1872, but it was never very satisfactory. For a description of earlier machines see 'Contemporary Literature: Newspaper Offices', *BM* (1879), cxxvi, pp.481ff.
68. The typographers spoke of themselves as the 'aristocracy of the working-classes', Musson, op.cit. (1954), p.25. It was claimed, however, that black compositors in India worked well with the help of two or three Europeans, even though they could not read English, 'The Provincial Newspaper Press', loc.cit., p.79.
69. Howe, op.cit. (1947), pp.490-9.
70. *Printers Register,* 6 Jan. 1880; Musson, op.cit. (1954), pp.226, 186-7, 190.
71. Howe, op.cit. (1947), pp.490-9.
72. Musson, op.cit. (1954), p.209.
73. Isaacs, op.cit., p.72.
74. 'Penny Newspapers: I', *LPCPN,* 15 Jun. 1866, pp.9-10.
75. 'New Forces in Journalism', *Sell's* (1921), p.24.
76. It seems, however, that pigeons were often shot, Sel. Cttee Rep. on the Electric Telegraphs Bill, *PP* 1868 (435) xi Q.1537.
77. 'Anecdotal history', *Sell's* (1897), pp.55-6. Cf. B. Redivivus, 'Special Newspaper Trains', *Railway Magazine* (1899), p.41, where the time from London to Berwick in 1848 is given as 8 hrs. 2 mins.
78. (E. Dicey), 'Provincial Journalism', *St. Paul's Magazine* (1868), iii, pp.63-4; J. Plummer, 'The British Newspaper Press in 1875', *British Almanac and Companion* (1876), p.82; (J.F. Hitchman), op.cit., p.506.
79. Viscount Chilston, *W.H. Smith* (1965), pp.4-5; Ayerst, op.cit., pp.93-4; *SCNS,* QQ.2822-6. For newspaper trains at the end of the century see Sinclair, op.cit., pp.99ff, and C.A. Cooper, *An Editor's Retrospect* (1896), chapters xiv and xviii.
80. G.A. Sala, 'The Press — what I have known of it', *Progress of British Newspapers in the Nineteenth Century* (1901), p.205.
81. J. Kieve, *The Electric Telegraph* (Newton Abbot, 1973), pp.47-71.
82. Sel. Cttee Rep. on the Electric Telegraphs Bill, loc.cit., Q.1308. Cf. also C. Knight, *Passages in a Working Life* (1864), iii, p.158 n*.
83. 'Our Special Wire', *CJ* (1868), xlv, p.434.
84. W. Hunt, op.cit., chapter 10; Ayerst, op.cit., pp.142-8. For descriptions of the machines and offices see 'My newspaper', loc.cit., p.475; 'How News is Distributed', *Congregationalist* (1871), i, pp.680ff; 'Our Special Wire', loc.cit., p.433f; Knight, op.cit. (1864), iii, pp.159ff.
85. This was the first recommendation of the Special Report of the Sel. Cttee on the Electric Telegraphs Bill. See also Kieve, op.cit., chapters 7 and 8.
86. G. Scott, *Reporter Anonymous* (1968), pp.27ff.
87. These were the *Eastern Morning News* of Hull, and the *Northern Whig* of

Belfast, see Hunt, op.cit., pp.118ff, and Sel. Cttee Rep. on the Electric Telegraphs Bill, QQ.1450ff.

88. Kieve, op.cit., chapter 9; 'How News is Distributed', loc.cit., pp.674-80.
89. Kieve, op.cit., chapter 11.
90. Sel. Cttee Rep. on the Post Office (Telegraphs Department), PP 1876 (357) xiii, QQ.4371, 4179.
91. On the question of the telegraph as an instrument of decentralisation it has been claimed that in the United States it 'destroyed a centrally directed government', H.A. Innis, *The Bias of Communication* (Toronto, 1951), p.170.
92. There had been considerable interference by the government with the railways from the 1840s, mainly over matters of safety and charges, but the 1867 Royal Commission nevertheless rejected the principle of public ownership. Intervention continued to increase thereafter, with power being given the government to take over in time of national emergency, and in the 1880s the railway rates question proved a source of political embarrassment. At the time of the take-over of the telegraphs, however, the railways were not blatantly exploiting a monopoly advantage, as the telegraph companies undoubtedly were. H. Parris, *The Government and the Railways in Nineteenth Century Britain* (1965), esp. pp. 212-25.
93. *SCNS,* Q.1790.
94. Sel. Cttee Rep. on the Electric Telegraphs Bill, QQ.1509ff.
95. Ibid., QQ.1374ff.
96. Fox Bourne, op.cit., ii, p.284.
97. Idem, 'The Cheapening of Journalism', *Sell's* (1899), p.25.
98. J. Grant, *Travels in Town* (1839), i, pp.306-8; *SCNS,* Q.1839.
99. J.W.R. Scott, *The Story of the Pall Mall Gazette* (1950), pp.111-12; G.A. Sala, *Twice Around the Clock* (1859; 1971 ed.), p.54.
100. (J.F. Wilson), op.cit., p.29.
101. For example, Sala, op.cit. (1859), p.53; 'Our Modern Mercury', *Once a Week* (1861), iv, pp.160-3; 'How We Get Our Newspapers', *CJ* (1865), 4th.s., ii, pp.772-3; 'How We Get Our Newspapers', *AYR* (1875), n.s., xv, pp.305-9. The best inside story, however, is Sean O'Casey's description of a Dublin newsagents at the turn of the century, *Pictures in the Hallway* (NY 1963 ed.), pp.325ff.
102. Knight, op.cit. (1864), iii, pp.150-1; T.H.S. Escott, *England: Its People Polity and Pursuits* (1880), i, pp.309-10.
103. Weir, op.cit., pp.347-8; (T. Wright), *Some Habits and Customs of the Working Classes* (1867), p.222; Andrewes, op.cit., ii, p.203; H. Mayhew, *London Labour and the London Poor* (1851: 1967 ed.), i, p.289; G. Sturt, *A Small Boy in the Sixties* (Cambridge, 1927), pp.97ff.
104. T. Catling, *My Life's Pilgrimage* (1911), p.184; J. Grant, op.cit. (1839), pp.315-17.
105. G. Sala, op.cit. (1859), pp.232-5; 'The Newsboy's Day', *CJ* (1853), xix, pp.305-8.
106. Mayhew, op.cit., pp.289-92; Sinclair, op.cit., p.88; Catling, op.cit., p.65; *NPP,* Jan. 1869.
107. H. Friederichs, *The Life of Sir George Newnes* (1911), p.70.
108. *NV,* 1 Sep. 1873.
109. H. Sampson, *A History of Advertising* (1875), p.31.
110. Catling, op.cit., p.43.
111. *NV,* 1 Apr. 1874.
112. *NV,* 1 Oct. 1873, 1 Mar. 1874. See also *Jt,* 1889, *passim.* For a description of a street newsboy's good day see 'Street Newsboys of London', *CJ* (1974), li, pp.113-15. It was harder in the 1880s, 'Sixteen Years of the Kerbstone and Gutter', *Pall Mall Gazette,* 3 Jan. 1887.

113. J.D. Symon, *The Press and its Story* (1914), pp.55-9.
114. *Manchester Guardian*, 26 Apr. 1901.
115. *NV*, 1 Oct. 1873. Cf. Booth's picture of the older sellers, *Charles Booth's London*, A. Fried and R. Elman, eds. (1971), p.133.
116. *NPP*, Oct. 1870.
117. H. Fyfe, *Sixty Years of Fleet Street* (1949), p.107.
118. For early Scottish dailies see R.M. Cowan, *Newspapers in Scotland, 1815-1860* (Glasgow, 1946), pp.283ff, and *Notes and Queries* (1899), 9th s., iv, pp.357, 425.
119. D. Dixon's valuable *Local Newspapers and Periodicals of the Nineteenth Century* (Leicester, 1973), a list of the holdings in major provincial libraries, will be a great aid in obtaining a fuller picture, as will the University of Leicester's forthcoming bibliographical study of nineteenth-century periodicals.
120. *NPP*, Nov. 1868. Cf. also Collett, op.cit., p.134.
121. As it happened they were right, but this consideration did not prevent the government from prosecuting Bradlaugh while the repeal of the security system was on the way in 1868, Collett, op.cit., pp.208ff.
122. There had been a penny evening paper founded in August, the *Evening News*, but it appears to have been short-lived.
123. Andrewes, op.cit., ii, p.342. For a short history of the London local press see W. Wellsman, *The Local Press of London* (1898).
124. *May's British and Irish Newspaper Press Guide* (1874). For further discussion of this see chapter 5 below.

CHAPTER 4

1. *SCNS*, Q.990. Cf. also Hickson, ibid., Q.3196, and Whitty, ibid., Q.616, on the advantages of a regional press.
2. 'B', 'English Journalism: I', *Nation* (NY), 22 Jul. 1880, p.59. Gladstone said the London press reflected 'the opinions of the Clubs rather than the opinion of the great nation', *The Times*, 4 Sep. 1871. Cf. J. Morley, *Life of Gladstone* (1908 ed.), ii, p.76, and J.P. Mackintosh, *The British Cabinet* (1968 ed.), pp.101ff.
3. The development of the British provincial press in this period was in many respects similar to that of the French, J. Kayser, 'La Presse de Province sous la Troisième République', *Revue Françaises de Science Politique* (1955), v, pp.547-71, and Chapter Seven below. On the decline of the provinces, D. Read, *The English Provinces c.1760-1960* (1964), pp.207ff.
4. 'B', 'English Journalism: I', loc.cit., p.59; J. Hatton, *Journalistic London* (1882), p.40.
5. Quoted in M. Gibb and F. Beckwith, *The Yorkshire Post. Two Centuries* (1954), p.34.
6. C. Pebody, *English Journalism* (1882), pp.88-9, 157.
7. 'B', 'English Journalism: IX', *Nation* (NY), 28 Oct. 1880, p.303.
8. W.R. Nicoll, *J. Macdonell, Journalist* (1890), pp.126-7. Cf. 'English Country Newspapers', loc.cit., p.141.
9. (J.F. Hitchman), op.cit., p.519.
10. Jeffries, op.cit., pp.198, 202. Cf. also Plummer, op.cit., p.80.
11. A. Reid, 'How a Provincial Newspaper is Managed', *NC* (1886), xx, pp.391-3. See also W.T. Stead's claim for the *Pall Mall Gazette*'s influence on the local press, *RR* (1893), vii, p.150.
12. W.E. Adams, *Memoirs of a Social Atom*, J. Saville, ed. (1968), p.17, n.24, referring to the *Newcastle Weekly Chronicle*.
13. Milne, op.cit., p.9.
14. H. Perkin, *The Origins of Modern English Society, 1780-1880* (1969),

pp.221ff; J. Vincent, *The Formation of the Liberal Party* (1966), p.258.
15. *PP* 1878-79 (343) xi 261ff, Q.145.
16. Ibid., Q.145.
17. Ibid., QQ.251, 260.
18. 137, *H.C. Deb.* 3s. 26 Mar. 1855 col.1147.
19. S. Coltham, 'The Bee-Hive Newspaper: its origins and early struggles', *Essays in Labour History*, A. Briggs and J. Saville, eds. (1960), pp.174-204.
20. W. Shepherdson, *Starting a Daily in the Provinces* (1876), pp.19-20.
21. Fox Bourne, op.cit., ii, p.369.
22. 'The Provincial Dailies: their present position', *Bookman* (1891), i, pp.32-3.
23. J. Saville, 'Sleeping Partnerships and Limited Liability, 1850-56', *EcHR* (1956), 2nd.s., viii, pp.418-33.
24. D. Fraser, 'The Press in Leicester, c.1790-1850', Leicester Archaeological and Historical Society *Transactions* (1966-67), xlii, pp.53f; *idem,* 'The Nottingham Press, 1800-1850', Thoroton Society *Transactions* (1963), lxvii, pp.46ff; W.W. Hadley, 'Rochdale Newspapers', Rochdale Literary and Scientific Society *Transactions* (1906), ix, pp.8ff; F. Byles, *William Byles* (Weymouth, 1932), pp.24ff.
25. The following is based largely on a study of the Parliamentary Returns of Joint-Stock Companies. The author is presently engaged in examining the actual returns made by newspaper companies to the Registrar, which will reveal much more about the structure and personnel of the companies.
26. The early caution was well-founded, for the earlier limited liability company invariably made a business loss, H.A. Shannon, 'The First Five Thousand Limited Companies', *EcHR* (1932), ii, p.419. A similar, and, of course, related expansion of joint-stock enterprise began after 1855 in the printing industry, but there too a great majority of firms remained private businesses, Musson, op.cit. (1954), p.92.
27. It is not always possible to find out, even from the actual returns to the Registrar, whether a company was founded for the purpose of running or setting up a newspaper, hence the totals are not to be treated as exact. Certain differences in categories account for discrepancies between these figures and those given by H.A. Shannon, 'The Limited Liability Companies of 1866-1883', *EcHR* (1933), iv, pp.396-401.
28. By 'infant mortality' is meant the proportion of companies returned as having been wound up or in the process of dissolution in the return recording their formation.
29. Shannon, op.cit. (1932), pp.422-3.
30. Ibid., pp.407-8, and G. Todd, 'Some Aspects of Joint-Stock Companies, 1844-1900', *EcHR* (1934), iv, pp.68-9. Early companies tended to continue long after they should have wound up, in the hope that the creditors could be landed with some of the losses, and that some of the high costs of winding up could be avoided. Many companies were never, in fact, wound up officially until the Registrar took action in the 1880s. The results of these delays were usually large losses, Todd, op.cit., p.58, n.2.
31. *PRO*, BT.31/69 Pt.2, 5070.
32. All figures refer only to the first year of the company.
33. In some papers shares were kept within the firm by selling them to employees, see *Western Morning News,* 3 Jan. 1910, supplement, p.2.
34. *Economist* (1886), xliv, p.266. See also J.B. Jefferys, 'The denomination and character of shares', *EcHR* (1946), xvi, pp.44-5.
35. *NPP,* Jul. 1867.
36. R. Pound and G. Harmsworth, *Northcliffe* (1959), pp.148, 290. In 1898 it was reckoned that £3.32 million of newspaper shares were on the open market, valued at £6 million, L.H. West, 'Newspaper Companies as Investments', *Sell's*

(1898), p.136.
37. B. Wood, 'The Bradford Newspaper Press', *The Bradford Antiquary,* (1906), p.66.
38. *Census of Production* (1907).
39. 'The Modern Newspaper', *British Quarterly Review* (1872), lv, p.375; Pebody, op.cit., p.138.
40. *DNB.*
41. 2 Sep. 1887, *PP* 1887 (121) lxxv; H. Fyfe, *T.P. O'Connor* (1934), p.145; ⹁ S. Koss, *Sir John Brunner: Radical Plutocrat* (1970), p.158.
42. Pound and Harmsworth, op.cit., p.170.
43. S. Nowell-Smith, *The House of Cassell, 1848-1958* (1958), p.120.
44. Milne, op.cit., p.124.
45. A. Reid, op.cit., pp.394, 397.
46. *NPD* (1903), p.31; A.J. Lee, 'The Management of a Victorian Local Newspaper', *Business History* (1973), xv, pp.137, 140.
47. H. Yeo, *Newspaper Management* (Manchester, 1891); W. Sidman, *A Treatise on Newspaper Bookkeeping* (1887), pp.1-2.
48. *HJW,* MD 5999, C. Ellis Report, p.8.
49. Cf. A.J. Beresford-Hope, 'Newspapers and Their Writers', *Cambridge Essays* (1858), iv, p.3.
50. F.V. Wright, *A Hundred Years of the West Sussex Gazette, 1853-1953,* (Arundel, 1953), p.15
51. A.J. Lee, op.cit. (1973), (2), p.136.
52. Whorlow, op.cit., pp.1ff.
53. H.R.G. Whates, *The Birmingham Post, 1857-1957* (Birmingham, 1957), pp.49-50, 51.
54. 'How to make a paper pay', *Jt.,* 24 Feb. 1888, pp.4-5
55. W.L. Andrewes, *Yorkshire Folk* (1935), p.41.
56. *LPCPN,* 15 Aug. 1867.
57. A. Reid, op.cit., p.395.
58. Richardson, op.cit., pp.495-6.
59. F. Presbrey, *The History and Development of Advertising* (NY, 1929); Sampson, op.cit.; 'Advertisements', *QR* (1855), xcvii, pp.183-225, esp. p.212. It is significant that no example from an ordinary newspaper is included in J. Laver and L. de Vries, *Victorian Advertisements* (1968). For the *Courier,* see B.B. Elliott, *A History of English Advertising* (1962), pp.171-2.
60. Kellet, op.cit. (1934); S. Morison, *The English Newspaper 1622-1932* (Cambridge, 1932), p.269; Plummer, op.cit., p.67; G. Dibblee, *The Newspaper* (1913), p.125.
61. Plummer, op.cit., p.67; Sampson, op.cit., pp.502ff.
62. 'Advertisements', loc.cit., pp.223ff; Sinclair, op.cit., p.8; A.J. Lee, 'Franklin Thomasson and The Tribune', *HJ* (1973), xvi, p.350.
63. Sinclair, op.cit., p.93.
64. F. Knight Hunt, *The Fourth Estate* (1850), ii, pp.196-204.
65. *HJW,* MD 5998, paper by J. Fillingham, 3 Jul. 1872.
66. *HJW,* MD 5999, Report by Collard Ellis, pp.6,9.
67. *HJW,* MD 5999, J.R. Beckett to Wilson, 28 Jan. 1875.
68. W.H. Stephenson, op.cit., p.39
69. 'The Journals of the Provinces', loc.cit., p.146.
70. Ayerst, op.cit., pp.132, 152, 301.
71. *Biograph,* Nov. 1907, p.9.
72. *Sell's* (1905), p.125.
73. Escott, op.cit. (1880), ii, pp.474-5.
74. Hatton, op.cit., p.75.
75. A.G. Gardiner, *Life of George Cadbury* (1923), p.222.

76. *Boase,* 'J.M. Levy'; *Sell's* (1891), p.80.
77. 'The British Newspaper: the penny theory and its solution', *Dublin University Magazine* (1863), lxi, p.364.
78. *NPP* (1867-1872).
79. (J.F. Hitchman), op.cit., p.504.
80. F. Harris, *My Life and Loves* (1964 ed.), p.319.
81. *Sell's* (1905), p.124.
82. *Sell's* (1897), p.106; Hunt, op.cit. (1887), pp.170-1.
83. *Printers' Register,* 6 Jun. 1883, p.204; Knight, op.cit. (1864), iii, pp.143ff. *NPD* gives twelve papers in receipt of Knight's sheets, but there is evidence of at least two more.
84. *The Globe,* 12 Jan. 1874. The *Printers' Register,* 18 Feb. 1874, p.6, pointed out that those sheets printed almost entirely in London only existed where original papers could not have survived. Cf. also *LPCPN,* 18 Feb. 1874, *Printers' Register,* 6 Jun. 1883, and Plummer, op.cit., p.81. When William Saunders took over the *Northern Daily Express* in 1865 he proposed to run it as a partly printed paper, much to the disgust of its editor, who confided to a Liberal journalist of the 'old school', 'under (Saunders) the Express will have no creed, no principles, no anything, but a sneaking determination to pay', Nicoll, op.cit., pp.108-9.
85. (J.F. Hitchman), op.cit., p.529; Yeo, op.cit., p.9; *Progress of British Newspapers in the Nineteenth Century* (1901), p.79; 'The Lament of a Leader Writer', *WR* (1899), clii, p.662, n.1.
86. See p.61 above, and pp.153-5 velow.
87. *PRO* BT.31/1054, 1849c; *The Times,* 20 January 1868.
88. Baxter, (q.v. below), had been brought to court for such practice, and had been let off with a warning, *NPP,* 1 Apr. 1867. For a case in Cheshire see H. Aspden, *Fifty Years a Journalist* (Clitheroe, 1930), p.11.
89. *NPP,* Mar. 1867, pp.73ff. A similar judgement on limited newspaper companies was made by 'a Conservative Journalist' in 'Why is the Provincial Press Radical?', *NR* (1886), vi, p.682.
90. Pratt-Boorman, op.cit.
91. 'The Newspaper Press', *NQR* (1861), x, p.88.
92. 'The L.S.D. of Literature', *GM* (1874), n.s., xiii, p.727. School inspectorships were not in fact the subject of patronage.
93. *NPP,* Sep. 1868.
94. J. A. Thomas, *The House of Commons, 1832-1901* (1955).
95. *NPP,* Nov. 1870; *NW,* 1 Jul. 1939; J. Lee, *Social Leaders and Public Persons* (1963), p.36.
96. *Yesterday, Today and Tomorrow* (The Newspaper Society, 1948).
97. *Collected Works* (1903-12), E.T. Cook, ed., xxviii, p.639, ('Fors Clavigera', 1876).
98. Collett, op.cit., pp.190-9, 208-18; *NPP,* Aug. 1868; 32 & 33 Vict. Ch.24. The Home Office expressed regret at the inconvenience caused by the introduction of an optional system, *PRO* H.O./O.S, 8420.
99. In Ireland the press remained less free, in Scotland more so. As far as Ireland was concerned this was proved most dramatically in 1881 when the government suppressed *United Ireland,* and in 1887 when Arthur Balfour tried to tighten restrictions on the Irish press. His failure was due to the combined effects of political and legal advice against the policy, and an outraged English public opinion. It was, therefore, found more expedient to use *The Times* as an organ of anti-nationalist propaganda, L.P. Curtiss Jr., *Coercion and Conciliation in Ireland* (1963), pp.210-15.
100. *NPP,* Aug. 1868 and Mar. 1870. This sort of activity was linked to attempts to stop the sale of newspapers on Sundays, which offence was punished with

fines of 2s 6d in 1869, *NPP*, May 1869. Cf. also the Lord's Day Observance Society's 3rd Annual Report, 1834, p.viii, quoted in P. Fryer, *Mrs Grundy* (1965 ed.), p.129. The case against a Hull lad in 1887 for selling papers on a Sunday was dismissed, but only because he was considered to be an errand boy, and not a bona fide newsvendor, *Eastern Morning News*, 19 and 21 Apr. 1887.

101. 137 *H.C. Deb.* 3s. 23 Apr. 1855 cols. 1679, 1982.

102. 233 *H.C. Deb.* 3s. 11 Apr. 1877 col. 935.

103. 137 *H.C. Deb.* 3s. 30 Apr. 1855 cols. 2009-10, 2013.

104. Newspaper Registration Bill, *PP* 1876 (64), v, 259.

105. 233 *H.C. Deb.* 3s. 11 Apr. 1877 cols. 923-30.

106. Ibid., col.921.

107. On the principles and precariousness of this privilege in the magistrates' courts, M.Jones, op.cit., pp.46, 61ff.

108. R. Brett, *Journals of Viscount Esher* (1934), i, p.23; G. Scott, op.cit., pp.75-7.

109. Wason v. Walter (1868), *Law Reports*, 4 Q.B. 73.

110. M. Jones, op.cit., pp.37-8, 60; E.D. Rogers, *Life and Experiences* (1911), p.17.

111. *Jt.,* 27 May 1887, 16 Nov. 1888.

112. Ibid., 1888, *Passim.*

113. G. Gibbon and R.W. Bell, *History of the London County Council, 1889-1939* (1939), pp.140-1; R. Burke, *The Murky Cloak* (1970), pp.5-8. There was another side to the matter, however. Joseph Cowen, proprietor of the *Newcastle Daily Chronicle,* deplored the offer made his paper by the Town Clerk to attend Standing Committees, because it would make too much work for the paper,and would hinder the councillors at their business. He even urged them to go into sub-committees! *Jt.,* 20 Jan. 1888.

114. W. Valentine Ball, *The Law of Libel as Affecting Newspapers and Journalists* (1912), p.119.

115. 44 & 45 Vict., Ch.60; 261 *H.C. Deb.* 3s. 11 May 1881 cols.218-30, 13 May 1881 cols.503-12, 2 Jun. 1881 cols.1978-83; Law of Libel, Sel. Cttee Rep., *PP* 1878-9 (343) xi 261; Law of Libel Sel. Cttee Rep., *PP* 1880 (284) ix 301.

116. W.F. Finlayson, 'The Law of Libel as to Newspapers', *NPD* (1888), pp.5-8; *idem, NPD* (1891), p.11; *idem, NPD* (1892), p.10; Ball, op.cit., pp.103ff; Whorlow, op.cit., Chapter 5.

117. A.V. Dicey probably exaggerated its effect on the legal status of the press, *An Introduction to the Law of the Constitution* (1939 ed.), p.240 n.1.

118. Ball, op.cit., pp.34ff.

119. *Jt.,* 13 and 20 Jan., 16 Nov. 1888.

120. *Jt.,* 30 Dec. 1887, 15 Nov. 1889. For an allegation of collusion between a proprietor and a Chief Constable over publication of a local council discussion of the conduct of the police see ibid., 30 Dec. 1887.

121. *PRO* H.O./10024, 8566985.

122. E.O. Tuttle, *The Crusade Against Capital Punishment* (1961), pp.30, 32, 34-5. Cf. D. Cooper, *The Lesson of the Scaffold* (1974), p.174 n.+

123. Whorlow, op.cit., pp.55-6; Public Health (Members and Officers) Act, 48 & 49 Vict. Ch.53, section 4.

124. *NPP*, Oct. and Sep. 1869.

125. Return giving the names and professions of all Justices of the Peace in the various boroughs and cities on 1st day of March 1875, *PP* 1875 (388) lxi 397; ibid. . . . .for the Counties of England and Wales on 1st day of June 1887, *PP* 1888 (356) lxxxii 193; Gibb and Beckwith, op.cit., appendix.

126. 278 *H.C. Deb.* 3s. 26 Apr. 1883 col. 1153; Viscount Gladstone Papers, Add MS 46,041, f.54, Reid to Gladstone, 23 Jul. 1883.

127. See note 125 above.
128. H.R. Pratt-Boorman, *Newspaper Society's 125 Years of Progress* (Maidstone, 1961), p.165.
129. Justice of the Peace, R.Com.Rep. 1910 Cd.5358, xxxvii, Q.123.
130. J.A. Spender, *The Public Life* (1925), ii, p.116.
131. K. Jones, op.cit., p.173.
132. G. Weill, *Le Journal* (Paris, 1934), pp.245ff.
133. O'Boyle, op.cit., pp.290-317.
134. *London Review*, 1835, quoted in A. Aspinall, 'The Social Status of Journalists at the beginning of the nineteenth century', *Review of English Studies* (1949), xxi, pp.219-20.
135. Weir, op.cit., p.352.
136. The decision in France in 1861 to require signatures for all political articles had no effect upon English practice, although it was discussed.
137. (E. Dicey), op.cit. (1868), p.65.
138. 'The L.S.D. of Literature', loc.cit., p.721.
139. W.F. Moneypenny and G.E. Buckle, *Life of Benjamin Disraeli* (1914), iv, p.518, emphasis added.
140. *NV*, Nov. 1873.
141. Cf. A. Helps, *Friends in Council* (1859), 2nd.s., ii, p.77.
142. E.P. Hennock, *Fit and Proper Persons* (1973), pp.317-18.
143. G.A. Sala, *America Revisited* (1882), p.77.
144. Lord Lytton, op.cit., p.210.
145. W. Johnston, *England As It Is In The Middle of the Nineteenth Century* (1851), p.237.
146. H.B. Thompson, *The Choice of a Profession* (1857), p.339.
147. 'It is not one of the recognised professions', 'The L.S.D. of Literature', loc.cit., p.721.
148. (E.C.G. Murray), *The Press and the Public Service* (1857), p.257. See also 'The Press and the Public Service', *FM* (1857), lv, pp.649-62, and Fox Bourne, op.cit., ii, p.301.
149. T.H.S. Escott, 'English Journalism in 1832 and 1874', *Belgravia* (1876), xxviii, pp.39ff.
150. J. Morley, 'Anonymous Journalism', *FR* (1867), viii, p.292.
151. Morley, op.cit. (1896), ii, p.438.
152. Morley, op.cit. (1867), p.290.
153. J.B. Kinnear, 'Anonymous Journalism', *CR* (1867), v, pp.324-5.
154. 'The Press in the Nineteenth Century', loc.cit., p.302.
155. 'Annonymous Journalism', *St. Paul's Magazine* (1868), ii, pp.229-30.
156. T. Hopkins, 'Anonymity?', *New Review* (1889), i, pp.516-17.
157. J. Robinson, *Fifty Years of Fleet Street* (1904), pp.221ff.
158. 'The Newspaper Press', *WR* (1829), x, p.223; 'The Provincial Newspaper Press', loc.cit., p.78; Grant, op.cit. (1871), ii, p.450; *NPP*, 1 Nov. 1869.
159. J. Dawson, *Practical Journalism* (1885), p.112; B.L. Crapster, 'A Lost Editor', *Victorian Periodicals Newsletter* (1974), vii, pp.7-8.
160. Dawson, op.cit.3 p.112; 'The L.S.D. of Literature', loc.cit., pp.720-1.
161. *NV*, 4 Aug. 1875.
162. K. Jones, op.cit., p.185.
163. 'The Newspaper Press', loc.cit., p.233; 'The Provincial Newspaper Press', loc.cit., p.78; *One Hundred Years of the Shields Gazette* (South Shields, 1949); *SCNS*, Q.670; Dawson, op.cit., p.111.
164. F.Whyte, *The Life of W.T. Stead* (1925), i, p.34.
165. 'The L.S.D. of Literature', loc.cit., p.720; Ayerst, op.cit., p.141; Dawson, op.cit., p.111.
166. Johnston, op.cit., p.228.

167. T.M. Cornock, 'The newspaper editor', *People's Journal* (1858), iv, p.6;
     D. Lockwood, *The Blackcoated Worker* (1958), chapter 1.
168. J.A. Banks, *Prosperity and Parenthood* (1954), p.108; W.J. Reader,
     Professional Men (1966), p.201.
169. 'Sub-editing a London newspaper', *CJ* (1879), lvi, p.744.
170. *NPP*, 1 Nov. 1869; C. Booth, *Life and Labour of the People in London*
     (1903), 2nd s., iv, chapter vi; P. Russell, *The Author's Manual* (1891), p.126.
171. Dawson, op.cit., p.111; J.B. Mackie, *Modern Journalism* (1894), pp.82-3.
172. F.J. Mansfield, *Gentlemen. The Press!* (1943), pp.20-2.
173. Lockwood, op.cit., p.27; Banks, op.cit., p.226; Reader, op.cit., p.192.
174. Sala, op.cit. (1859), p.327; M. MacDonagh, 'In the sub-editor's room',
     NC (1897), xlii, pp.999-1008.
175. *History of The Times,* ii, p.125; Ayerst, op.cit., p.238.
176. *Jt.,* 19 Nov. 1886.
177. (J.F. Stephen), op.cit., pp.55-6.
178. H. Spender, *The Fire of Life* (1926), p.18; T.E. Kebbel, *Lord Beaconsfield
     and Other Tory Memories* (1907), pp.171-2.
179. J. Grant, *The Great Metropolis* (1838), ii, p.204; Aspinall, op.cit., p.230
     n.5.
180. 'The Newspaper Press', loc.cit., pp.222-3; Booth, op.cit. (1903), Chapter
     6; Russell, op.cit., p.22; 'The Fourth Estate', *GM* (1894), cclxxvii, p.47;
     A. Kinnear, 'Parliamentary Reporting', *CR* (1905), lxxxvii, p.373. The
     ailing *Observer* was fortunate in obtaining H.W. Lucy for only £5 a week,
     but Lucy profited from the syndication of his work, A. Gollin, *The Observer
     and J.L. Garvin* (1960), pp.151-2.
181. F.S.A. Lowndes, 'Journalism for University Men', *CR* (1901), lxxx, pp.814-
     22.
182. *NPP*, 1 Nov. 1869; Booth, op.cit. (1903), p.154; K. Jones, op.cit., p.185.
     The Press Association reporters received from thirty to fifty shillings a week
     in 1871, G. Scott, op.cit., p.67.
183. F.R. Spark, *Memories of My Life* (1913), p.63.
184. Ayerst, op.cit., pp.63, 81-2; Robinson, op.cit., p.17; *One Hundred Years of
     the Shields Gazette;* Mansfield, op.cit., p.23.
185. 'Family Budgets: II', *CM* (1901), n.s., x, p.657; 'The Fourth Estate',
     loc.cit., p.47.
186. M.F. Billington, 'Women in Journalism', *Sell's* (1891), p.59. Cf. also T. Frost,
     Reminiscences of a Country Journalist (1886), pp.326-8.
187. Lockwood, op.cit., p.27; Banks, op.cit., p.106; Reader, op.cit., p.202;
     A. Tropp, *The School Teachers* (1957), p.133.
188. T. Frost, *Forty Years Recollections* (1880), p.241.
189. H. Strick, 'British Newspaper Journalism, 1900-1956', unpublished London
     Ph.D. thesis, 1957, p.251; H.A. Taylor, *Robert Donald* (1934), p.275.
190. 'The Newspaper Press', loc.cit., p.234; Knight, op.cit. (1854), p.280.
191. 'London Morning Newspapers', loc.cit., p.88. This was not a situation
     unique to England. In France smaller papers paid their contributors in
     kind, and one Frenchman compared the lot of some French journalists with
     'the picture of poverty that one only encounters in England', Bellanger,
     op.cit., ii, pp.342-3.
192. Mansfield, op.cit., p.23.
193. *Clarion,* 10 Aug. 1906, quoted in Strick, op.cit., p.249.
194. Lytton, op.cit., p.217.
195. E. Dicey, op.cit. (1905), p.908; Kebbel, op.cit., p.176.
196. *SCNS,* Q.3049. For a Conservative defence of 'Bohemia' see F. Greenwood,
     'The Newspaper Press', *BM* (1897), clxi, p.706.
197. 'London Morning Newspapers', loc.cit., p.87.

198. See the novels of Thackeray, Trollope. Dickens, Gissing, C.E. Montague amongst others.

199. *Law Reports,* xvii, n.s. 1867, p.179; *Jt.,* 27 Jan. 1888 and after. Chipchase, the city editor of the *Day,* had previously successfully sued for £63 arrears of salary on the closure of the *Morning Chronicle* in 1862, *Law Reports,* vii, n.s. 1862, p.290.

200. A.J. Lee, op.cit. (1973), (1), pp.357-8.

201. Thompson, op.cit., p.341.

202. C. Bateman, 'A great speech distributing agency', *Young Man* (1904), xviii, p.221. Cf. also A. Lawrence, *Journalism as a Profession* (1903), pp.2-4.

203. T.M. Rendle, *Swings and Roundabouts* (1919), pp.38-9; Mansfield, op.cit., p.18; K. Jones, op.cit., p.191; Booth, op.cit. (1903), appendix A, Part I.

204. The Newspaper Press Benevolent Association was established in 1837, and was succeeded in 1864 by the Fund, whose first president was Lord Houghton, *Rules and Regulations of the Newspaper Press Benevolent Association* (1837); *Newspaper Press Fund, 1864-1964* (1964).

205. *Jm.,* Dec. 1887, (Strick, op.cit., pp.102ff, puts the foundation back to 1884, but this seems incorrect); 'The Fourth Estate', loc.cit., p.40.

206. *Jt.,* Mar. 1887 onwards, esp. 30 Dec. 1887, 9 and 16 Mar. 1888, 25 Oct. 1889, 8 Nov. 1889.

207. H.R. Fox Bourne, 'The Institute of Journalists', *Sell's* (1899), p.17.

208. Strick, op.cit., p.167. The Association had established a Parliamentary Committee on the exclusion of the press from magistrates' courts in 1887, *Jm.,* Nov. 1887.

209. Strick, op.cit., p.169.

210. Ibid., pp.165-74; C.J. Bundock, *The National Union of Journalists* (1957), pp.1ff.

211. Strick, op.cit., p.453; 'The Infancy of the Labour Party', LRC Executive Committee Minutes, 18 Dec. 1907, pp.60-1.

212. *NPP,* 1 Sep. 1869; 'A Newspaper Institute', *CJ* (1879), lvi, pp.395-7. It was probably at attempt by Alexander Mackie to provide labour for his Cheshire chain of papers.

213. E. Porritt, 'Newspaper Work when the century was young', *Sell's* (1896), p.25; J. Pendleton, *Newspaper Reporting* (1890), Chapter 5.

214. *Jt.,* 24 May 1889.

215. Booth, op.cit. (1903), pp.156-7.

216. *Jm.,* Mar. 1888. For attempts to dislodge them see *Jt.,* 24 Aug. 1888.

217. Society of Women Journalists, *4th Annual Report* (1898).

218. Booth, op.cit. (1903), p.158. On women's journalism see Billington, op.cit., and L.A. Smith, 'Women's work in London and the Provincial Press', *NPD* (1897), pp.14-15.

219. (Oxford, 1948 ed.), p.665.

220. Reader, op.cit., pp.158-9.

221. 'Up to Easter', *NC* (1887), xxi, pp.638-9.

222. W.T. Stead, 'Government by Journalism', *CR* (1886), xlix, pp.653-74. Cf. J.O. Baylen, 'Matthew Arnold and the Pall Mall Gazette', *South Atlantic Quarterly* (1969), lxviii, pp.543-55.

223. *The Times,* 6 Feb. 1852, quoted in E.T. Cook, *Delane of The Times* (1915), pp.277-8.

224. Cf. J.O. Baylen, 'The "New Journalism" in Late Victorian Britain', *Australian Journal of Politics and History* (1972), xviii, p.372, for a different interpretation.

225. Quoted in Baylen, op.cit. (1972), p.374.

226. Ibid., pp.375, 382-3.

227. Whyte, op.cit., ii, pp.13ff.
228. T.P. O'Connor, 'The New Journalism', *New Review* (1889), i, p.423.
229. For O'Connor's political creed see Fyfe, op.cit. (1934), pp.138ff.
230. Johnston, op.cit., pp.223ff.
231. Ruskin, op.cit., xxviii, p.646; cf. also p.639, and xxix, pp.470-1, 480.
232. 'Newspaper Sewage', *SR,* 5 Dec. 1868.
233. Cf. Q.D. Leavis, *Fiction and the Reading Public* (1934), pp.181-2; R. Williams, 'Radical and/or respectable', *The Press We Deserve,* R. Boston, ed. (1970), pp.14ff.
234. Morison, op.cit., pp.265ff; A. Hutt, *The Changing Newspaper* (1973). *The Globe* was using cross-heads on the front page on 5 Mar. 1874.
235. 'The Jubilee of the "Daily News"', *Spectator,* 25 Jan. 1896, p.132; P. Ferris, *The House of Northcliffe* (1971), p.45; Bell, op.cit., p.168.
236. Kellet, op.cit. (1934), ii, pp.57f; Hunt, op.cit., p.67; 'Newspapers under the Paper Duty', *CJ* (1861), xxxvi, p.309; *SCNS,* Q.1452; H. Spender, op.cit., pp.30ff; H. Herd, *The March of Journalism* (1952), p.37. Weather forecasts had been carried as far back as 1836 in the *Western Times,* Lambert, op.cit., p.98, and daily weather charts appeared about 1875, and were available on stereo from news agencies, 'Modern Newspaper Enterprise', *FM* (1876), xciii, p.711; (J.F. Hitchman), op.cit., p.530.
237. F. Dilnot, *The Adventures of a Newspaperman* (1913), pp.23-4; H.M. Hughes, 'News and the Human Interest Story,' *Contributions to Urban Sociology* E.W. Burgess and D.J. Bogue, eds. (Chicago, 1964), p.272.
238. J.A. Spender, op.cit. (1925), ii, p.101.
239. (J.F. Stephen), op.cit., p.53.
240. E. Dicey, op.cit. (1905), p.1910; 'The Lament of a Leader Writer', loc.cit., p.656.
241. J.A. Spender, *Life, Journalism and Politics* (1927), ii, pp.155ff.
242. 'The Lament of a Leader Writer', loc.cit., p.660.
243. A. Kinnear, op.cit. (1905), p.370.
244. H. Jephson, *The Platform,* (1892), i, pp.546-7; Symon, op.cit., p.84.
245. A. Kinnear, 'The Trade in Great Men's Speeches', *CR* (1899), lxxv, p.439.
246. Ibid., p.441. On the susceptibility of these summaries to political bias see *Sell's* (1906), p.92. Between 1872 and 1879 the Central News agency reported the following speakers at the average lengths of 6,300 words for Gladstone, 5,300, for Bright, 4,500 for Hartington, 3,800 for Stafford Northcote, and 2,800 for W.E. Forster, *Printers' Register,* 6 Feb. 1880.
247. Bateman, op.cit., p.220; A. Kinnear, op.cit. (1905), p.369. Robbins told Bateman, loc.cit., that Chamberlain, Balfour, Rosebery, Devonshire, Campbell-Bannerman, Morley and Harcourt were actually reported verbatim, but this did not mean, of course, that everyone or anyone would want such a report for publication. In the early 1890s the *Westminster Gazette* published an annual class list of politicians according to the length at which they were reported in the previous year's papers. Robert Hudson, secretary of the National Liberal Federation, got Spender, the editor, to stop the practice because it was destroying the nerve of his star performers. Spender obliged, but later commented that the newspapers were already reducing their reporting of speeches drastically, J.A. Spender, *Sir Robert Hudson* (1930), pp.43-4.
248. J.H. McBath, 'Parliamentary Reporting in the Nineteenth Century', *Speech Monographs* (1970), xxxvii, pp.30ff; H.D. Jordan, 'The Reports of Parliamentary Debates, 1803-1908', *Economica* (1931), xi, pp.437-49.
249. Parliamentary Reporting, Sel. Cttee Rep. *PP* 1878 (327) xvii, QQ.886, 916ff.
250. Ibid., QQ.666ff.

251. Ibid., Q.2234.
252. Ibid., QQ.519, 808.
253. Ibid., Q.2107.
254. Ibid., QQ.1343ff, 1153, 1382.
255. C.W. Radcliffe Cook, *Four Years in Parliament With Hard Labour* (1890), pp.34ff.
256. *The Times*, 4 May 1899, and cf. speech reported for 15 Nov. 1899 in *Sell's* (1901), p.175; *British Orations* (1915), pp.330-3, a speech of 12 Apr. 1913.
257. 21 Geo. 3, Ch.49, the rigours of which were mitigated by 22 Vict. Ch.32 (1859), and 38 & 39 Vict. Ch.80 (1875). For prosecutions usually unsuccessful, see *Jt.*, 25 May 1888. For local authority prosecutions for 'crying' Sunday papers see *Jt.*, 13 and 20 Apr. 1888. For Bills against selling them see *NPP*, May 1869, Dec. 1873.
258. Andrewes, op.cit., ii, p.93.
259. Chilston, op.cit., pp.33, 493-4.
260. (J.F. Stephen), 'The Sunday Papers', *SR*, 19 Apr. 1856. By the 1880s only *Reynolds News* was accounted really 'radical', (J.F. Hitchman), op.cit., pp.520-2, and Salmon, op.cit., pp.110-12.
261. They had been mooted in 1889, but met with the strong disapproval of journalists, *Jt.*, 8 Feb. and 22 Mar. 1889.
262. R. Donald, 'How Seven Day Journalism Was Killed in London', *Outlook*, (1899), lxiii, pp.262-4; *The Times*, 4,8,19 and 25 May 1899; 'Over the Grave of Seven Day Journalism', *RR* (1899), xx, p.525; 70 *H.C. Deb.* 4s. 27 Apr. 1899, cols. 705-6; Pound and Harmsworth, op.cit., pp.241-3. The Institute of Journalists was hostile to the idea, *Jt.*, 8 and 15 Feb., 22 Mar. and 5 Apr. 1889.
263. There had been a Scottish one in 1856, the *Edinburgh Bawbee*.
264. *HJW*, Bell to Wilson, 1874, MD 6000, and Ellis Report, 12 Sep. 1874, p.4, MD 5999.
265. 'The Lament of a Leader Writer', loc.cit., p.657.
266. A. Reid, op.cit., pp.395-6.
267. (T.C. Sandars), 'The Sporting Press', *SR*, 9 Feb. 1856; 'How News is Collected', *Congregationalist* (1872), i, p.549.
268. Betting, Sel. Cttee H.L. Rep. *PP* 1902 (389) viii, QQ.1633, 2952ff; 'A North Country Worthy', *RR* (1894), x, p.86. The *Leeds Mercury* took up a similar attitude over the theatre, leaving reports and advertisements entirely to its rival, the *Yorkshire Post*, G.R. Sims, *My Life* (1917), p.111.
269. Harris, op.cit., p.417; *Sell's* (1906), pp.104-5.
270. Gardiner, op.cit., pp.230-3; A. Fry, *A Memoir of the Rt. Hon. Sir Edward Fry* (1921), pp.251-2; G.G. Armstrong, *Memories* (1944), pp.113-18.
271. *HJW*, J.W. Wilson to H.J. Wilson, 17 Sep. 1874, MD 6000.
272. *HJW*, H.J. Wilson to W. Clegg, 7 Sep. 1907, MD 6000.
273. *HJW*, undated cutting on local council discussion of the issue, MD 6002; Betting. Sel. Cttee H.L. Rep. QQ.699-712; 37 & 38 Vict, Ch.15; Betting, Loc.cit., QQ.1831,2123; *Manchester Guardian*, 23 Jan., 7 Nov. and 12 Dec. 1901.
274. A. Cave, 'The New Journalism', *CR* (1907), xci, pp.18-32.
275. Harris, op.cit., pp.572ff.
276. F. Singleton, *The Tillotsons of Bolton* (1950), pp.17ff.
277. *NV*, 1 Aug. 1873; *Jt.*, 11 Jan. 1889.
278. M. Jackson, *The Pictorial Press: its origins and progress* (1885); C.K. Shorter, *C.K.S. An Autobiography* (1927), pp.53ff. For reservations about the beneficial effects of illustration see M. Wolff and C. Fox, 'Pictures from the Magazines', *The Victorian City*, H.J. Dyos and M. Wolff, eds.

(1973), ii, pp.559-80. F.C. Gould, 'Autobiography', unpublished, pp.386-8.
279. (J.F. Stephen), 'Newspaper English', *SR,* 9 Aug. 1856.
280. Greenwood, op.cit., p.717.
281. *Progress of British Newspapers,* p.46; S. Dark, *Life of Sir Arthur Pearson*
    (1922), p.48.

CHAPTER 5

1. It is important to note the effect on these figures of H.J. Infield's chain of
   papers in the south-east, most of them local editions of the *Sussex Daily
   News* (Brighton), and the *Hastings Argus.* A few claimed to be Liberal, but
   most were 'independent' or 'neutral'. A couple reached back to 1868, two
   were started in 1880, and thirty between 1893 and 1901. Three disappeared
   between 1896 and 1897, but in 1906 all but three were discontinued. These
   titles distort the picture considerably from 1893 to 1906 by giving an illusion
   of great growth in the 1890s and a catastrophe in 1906.
2. These figures refer only to the town in which the papers were published. Their
   circulation areas may have been considerably wider.
3. 'The Liberal Newspapers'. loc.cit., p.685; 'Journals of the Provinces', loc.cit.,
   p.144.
4. Milne, op.cit., pp.44, 132-3; *PRO* B.T.31/2138c; *Western Morning News,*
   loc.cit., p.8; *Jt.,* 22 Oct. 1886. For an account of the early days of the
   Express see T.W. Reid, 'Some Reminiscences of English Journalism', *NC*
   (1897), xlii, pp.55-8; Nicoll, op.cit., pp.107ff.
5. Milne, op.cit., *passim.*
6. Milne, op.cit., pp.85-6, 128-30, 170-2; A. Watson, *A Newspaperman's
   Memories* (1925), pp.183-90; G.B. Hodgson, *From Smithy to Senate*
   (1908), *passim.*
7. *NW,* 1 Apr. 1939; Milne, op.cit., pp.45-6, 54-5, 129; Watson, op.cit., pp.168,
   183ff; Hodgson, op.cit., pp.79-89; *One Hundred Years of the Shields
   Gazette.* In 1885 Watson succeeded Annand as editor of the *Gazette,* and
   was himself succeeded by Annand's biographer, Hodgson, when he took over
   the *Leader* from Annand. This type of journalistic incest was a common
   feature of provincial journalism, and often served to lend it consistency and
   strength.
8. *DNB*; Milne, op.cit., pp.117-8.
9. Milne, op.cit., pp.56, 87-8; 'A North Country Worthy', loc.cit., pp.85-6; *HJW,*
   J.B. Hodgkin to H.J. Wilson, 1 Dec. 1891, MD 6000.
10. The problem was resolved eventually by printing the Monday edition on
    Saturday, T.W. Reid, *Memoirs,* S.J. Reid, ed. (1905), pp.91-2.
11. T.W. Reid, op.cit. (1905), pp.102, 312ff; *Sell's* (1896), p.34; Viscount
    Gladstone Papers, Add. MSS, 46,028, 46,041. The best study of the *Leeds
    Mercury* is D.M. Jones, 'The Liberal Press and the Rise of Labour. . .1850-
    95', unpublished Leeds Ph.D. thesis, 1973.
12. Spark, op.cit., pp.173ff; R.Hinton, *English Radical Leaders* (1875),
    pp.86-96; Hennock, op.cit., pp.204, 215-17; A.W. Roberts, 'Leeds Liberalism
    and Late Victorian Politics', *Northern History* (1970), v, pp.131ff; *Sell's*
    (1905), p.124.
13. *Yorkshire Observer Centenary,* loc.cit.; Byles, op.cit., p.28; D.M. Jones,
    op.cit., Chapter 6.
14. *NPD* (1914), p.28; *NW,* 21 Mar. 1939; *NPD* (1898), p.83.
15. *History of the Sheffield Independent* (Sheffield, 1892); Whorlow, op.cit.,
    p.96.
16. *HJW,* J.H. Bell to H.J. Wilson, 15 Sep. 1874, MD5999.

17. *HJW,* MD 1988, 1989, 1900, 6000, 6002, 6003 *passim.*
18. Hunt, op.cit., pp.76ff; *Eastern Morning News,* 22 Apr. 1889; J.A. Spender, op.cit. (1927), i, pp.26ff; H. George Jr., *Life of Henry George* (1900), pp.389-579.
19. *Sell's* (1905), p.124; Whorlow, op.cit., pp.90-1.
20. Ayerst, op.cit., pp.100-2, 125-7, 134, 231-2, 236ff.
21. For an account of the *Northern Daily Times* see J. McCarthy, 'The Birth of the Provincial Daily Newspaper in England', *Sell's* (1907), p.17. Willmer's brother Edward was a pioneer of the parliamentary sketch, and a writer for the *Morning Star, NPP,* Jul. 1869.
22. B.D. White, *History of the Corporation of Liverpool, 1835-1914* (Liverpool, 1951), p.20; *NW,* 25 Feb. 1939; Russell-Rosebery correspondence, 1888-1901; Frost, op.cit. (1886), pp.117ff. Whitty's brother was a pioneer of the London Letter, E.M. Whitty, *St. Stephens in the Fifties,* J. McCarthy, ed. (1906). Jeans's brother, William, acted as parliamentary correspondent for the *Post,* and for the *Dundee Advertiser* for forty-five years, W. Jeans, *Parliamentary Reminiscences* (1912).
23. Armstrong, op.cit., pp.39ff; *Sell's* (1905), pp.125ff; Frost, op.cit. (1886), pp.133-4, 210-11, 310; *Liverpool Courier,* 17 Jun. 1905.
24. T.W. Reid, op.cit. (1905), p.73; Aspden, op.cit., pp.8-9, 11; *Sell's* (1892), pp.47-8; S. Koss, *Fleet Street Radical* (1973), p.20ff.
25. Singleton, op.cit., pp.10, 16ff, 33ff; *NW,* 14 Jan. 1939; Armstrong, op.cit., pp.68ff.
26. Whates, op.cit., *passim; NPD* (1906), p.17. For the *Mail* see H.J. Jennings, *Chestnuts and Small Beer* (1920), pp.76ff.
27. Whates, op.cit., p.45; W. Wilson, *Life of George Dawson* (Birmingham, 1905), p.121; D.C. Murray, *Recollections* (1908), pp.75, 97ff; *idem, The Making of a Novelist* (1894), pp.6ff; T. Anderton, *A Tale of One City* (Birmingham, 1900), p.127.
28. *NW,* 5 Aug. 1939; Gardiner, op.cit., pp.211, 220; C. Starmer, 'The Story of the Birmingham Gazette', *World's Press News,* 17 Oct. 1929.
29. *Coventry Herald,* 10 and 11 Apr. 1908.
30. *NW,* 24 Dec. 1938; *NPD* (1910), p.18; *NPD* (1908), p.14.
31. *Victoria County History of Leicester* (1958), iv, pp.273, 294-5; *NPD* (1898), p.82.
32. W.W. Hadley, *The Bi-Centenary Record of the Northampton Mercury, 1720-1920* (Northampton, 1920), pp.41-2; *NW,* 3 Jun. 1939; R.W. Brown, 'Northamptonshire Printing, Printers and Booksellers', Northants. Natural History Society and Field Club, *Transactions,* (1919), xx, pp.45-56.
33. *NW,* 8 Apr. 1939; R.A. Church, *Economic and Social Change in a Midland Town: Victorian Nottingham, 1815-1900* (1966), pp.216-18.
34. Lambert, op.cit., *passim,* esp. p.189.
35. *Western Daily Mercury,* 2 Jun. 1910; Hunt, op.cit., Chapters 2 and 3.
36. *Western Morning News,* 3 Jan. 1910, supplement; Hunt, op.cit., Chapter 6; *PRO,* B.T.31/3078.
37. *NPD* (1892), p.78; *Sell's* (1892), pp.159ff.
38. *NW,* 22 Jul. 1939; *Jt.,* 22 Oct. 1886.
39. *NW,* 6 May 1939; *NPP,* Jul. 1868.
40. 'M.P.', *The Norwich Post* (1951); H.C. Colman, *J.J. Colman* (1905), pp.23,371.
41. *Souvenir of the East Anglian Daily Times* (Ipswich, 1936); Colman, op.cit., p.371; *NPD* (1911), p.18; *PRO,* B.T.31/85c.
42. R. Olney, *Lincolnshire Politics, 1832-1885* (1973), pp.85-7; (G.H. Burton), op.cit.
43. Richardson, op.cit., pp.479-89.

44. F.A. Edwards, *The Early Newspaper Press of Hampshire* (Southampton, 1889), p.3; A.T. Patterson, *History of Southampton, 1700-1914* (1971), ii, pp.35, 163-4.
45. *Victoria County History of Hertfordshire* (1914), iv, p.262.
46. 'The Morning and Evening Papers', *FM* (1836), xiii, p.620.
47. Lucas, op.cit., pp.29-34; Moneypenny and Buckle, op.cit., iii, p.490.
48. Stanley to Disraeli, 13 Sep. 1852, Disraeli Papers, B.VI.69.
49. For the political history of the paper, see Moneypenny and Buckle, op.cit., iii, Chapter 14.
50. P. Rose to Disraeli, 28 Jun. 1854, ibid., B.VI.48.
51. Stanley to Disraeli, 24 Aug. 1853, ibid., B.VI.7a.
52. *Idem,* 10 Oct. 1853, ibid., B.VI.73.
53. Kenealy to Disraeli, 23 Apr. 1853, ibid., B.VI.26.
54. 'F.V.' to Disraeli, 16 May 1853, ibid., B.VI.29.
55. P. Rose to Lucas (copy), 12 May 1854, ibid. B.XXI.L 86a. For Lucas see *Boase,* and T.H. Ward, *Men of the Reign* (1885).
56. Lucas to Disraeli, 13 Mar. 1858, ibid., B.XXI.L385; *idem,* 12 Jun. 1859, ibid, B.XXI.L408. For Fonblanque see H. Parris, *Constitutional Bureaucracy* (1969), p.59. For Derby's side of the Lucas case see ibid., pp.60-1.
57. Lucas to Disraeli, 23 Mar. 1860, Disraeli Papers, B.XXI.L411.
58. For Coulton see *Boase.*
59. Coulton to Disraeli, 20 Feb. 1855, Disraeli Papers, B.VI.97.
60. *Idem,* 7 Mar. 1855, ibid., B.VI.100.
61. Kebbel, op.cit., pp.217-19. The *Press* seems to have passed to R.H. Patterson until 1865, and from then until its close to G.H. Townshend, both Conservative journalists, *Boase.*
62. 'Conservative Journalism', *NQR* (1860), ix, p.385.
63. Ibid., pp.385-95.
64. Elcho to Spencer, 16 Jan. 1867, Wemyss Papers; *LPCPN,* 15 Oct. 1868. On dissolution the company paid only 9¼d in the pound to the shareholders, *NPP,* Sep. 1868.
65. Fox Bourne, op.cit., ii, p.275. Armstrong had been secretary of the Westminster Conservative Association from 1866 to 1869, *NPD* (1908), p.9. It is possible that it passed to the Conservatives a little earlier than indicated in the text, when Charles Wescombe joined it in 1868. H. Simonis, *Street of Ink* (1917), p.149.
66. *NV,* Jan. and Feb. 1874; Robinson, op.cit., p.226; Fox Bourne, op.cit., ii.p.337; *Boase,* 'D.M. Evans'.
67. Fox Bourne, op.cit., ii, p.337.
68. Hatton, op.cit., p.152; D. Rhode, 'Round the London Press: V', *New Century Review* (1898), i. pp.44-6; E.J. Feuchtwanger, *Disraeli Democracy and the Tory Party* (1968), p.120.
69. (G.H. Burton), op.cit; *NPP,* 1 Oct. 1869, 1 Dec. 1870; *NV,* 1 Apr. 1874.
70. *NW,* 26 Aug. 1939; *NPP,* 1 Oct. 1869, 1 Dec. 1870; *NV,* 1 Apr. 1874.
71. Kebbel, op.cit., pp.225-9; *NW,* 19 Aug. 1939; Gibb and Beckwith, op.cit.
72. Ayerst, op.cit., pp.226-7. In Wales, however, the Marquis of Bute, a local colliery owner, founded the *Western Mail* at Cardiff in 1869, and in Scotland it was later claimed that the Duke of Buccleuch and his friends had spent lavishly on Tory newspapers in Edinburgh, Glasgow and Aberdeen, without avail, Lord Riddell, *The Story of the Western Mail* (Cardiff, 1929); *Boston Evening Transcript,* 12 Jan. 1901; E. Porritt, 'The Value of Political Editorials', *Sell's* (1910), p.509.
73. *NPP,* 1 Sep. 1869, 1 Mar. and 1 Apr. 1870.
74. *NPP,* 1 Apr. 1867.
75. Lambert, op.cit., pp.201, 207; Rolle to Northcote, Aug. 1869, Iddesleigh

Papers, Add. MS 50,038, f.706; *Western Morning News,* loc.cit.; *NW,* 9 Sep. 1939.
76. *NPP,* 1 Apr. 1869; Milne, op.cit., pp.86-7.
77. (G.H. Burton), op.cit., *Jt.,* 7 Jun. 1889.
78. Calculated from the parliamentary returns of companies.
79. *The Globe,* 12 Jan. 1874.
80. Rogers, op.cit., p.41.
81. *NV,* Aug., Sep., Oct. and Nov. 1873, and Mar. 1874; *LPCPN,* 18 Feb. 1874; Feuchtwanger, op.cit., p.120.
82. Keith-Falconer to Disraeli, 31 Oct. 1873, Disraeli Papers, B.XXI.F.5.
83. The date is not specified, but 1871 seems most probable.
84. *NV,* 4 Aug. 1875; Keith-Falconer to Disraeli, 3 Nov. 1873, Disraeli Papers, B.XXI.F.6.
85. *LPCPN,* 18 Feb. 1874. It was sold to Ashton Dilke in 1875, for £11,000.
86. Keith-Falconer to Disraeli, 30 Mar. 1874, and Mackie to Keith-Falconer, 24 Feb. 1874, Disraeli Papers, B.XXI.F9, 9a. William Saunders claimed that 'nearly the whole of the London daily newspapers, and the source of foreign intelligence, had been brought directly under (the Conservative government's) influence', *The New Parliament* (1880), p.200. For an excellent but neglected study of the press during Disraeli's administration see G.C. Thompson, *Public Opinion and Lord Beaconsfield, 1875-1880* (1886).
87. Hunt, op.cit., pp.135-6; G. Scott, op.cit., pp.75,77,80,84.
88. 'Conservative Reorganisation', *BM* (1880), cxxvii, p.809.
89. National Union of Conservative Associations, Annual Conference Minutes, 1880 and 1882.
90. *The Times,* 9 and 12 May, and 24 Oct. 1883; 'B', The Conservative Provincial Press', *NR* (1885), v, p.637. It is not clear whether this was the same meeting as that referred to by a journalist in 1887, at which Salisbury was said to have hinted at assistance. If not, some progress, from the press's point of view, may have been made, *Jt.,* 7 Jan. 1887.
91. National Union, minutes of 1884 Conference.
92. Ibid., 1887; H.J. Hanham, *Elections and Party Management* (1959), p.113; Feuchtwanger, op.cit., p.207; National Union minute of 1884 Conference.
93. National Union, minute of 1884 Conference; 'B', op.cit. (1855), p.634.
94. Ibid., minute of 1885 Conference.
95. Ibid., minute of 1886 Conference.
96. Wood, op.cit., p.66; Harris, op.cit., pp.417-20, 319ff, 572ff. Until Harris took a hand the *Evening News* was losing about £40,000 a year for its proprietors, the banker Coleridge Kennard and Lord Folkestone. By 1914 it was being called 'the vade mecum of the Tory working-man', Symon, op.cit., p.153. Cf. also *Jt.,* 24 Aug. 1888 for description of a Conservative newspaper company in Blackburn,and its management.
97. *Jt.,* 7,14,21,28 Jan. 1887.
98. J.M. Lee, op.cit., p.36.
99. 'B' (1885), op.cit., p.637; 'A Conservative Journalist', op.cit., pp.678ff; *Jt.,* 5 and 12 Apr. 1889.
100. 'A Conservative Journalist', op.cit., p.681.
101. Armstrong, op.cit., *passim.*
102. Gibb and Beckwith, op.cit., pp.50ff.
103. Aspden, op.cit., p.19.
104. *NPD* (1913), p.16. Another example is John Copleston, editor of the *Northern Echo* from 1870 to 1871, and eventually editor of the *Evening News* in 1893, Whyte, op.cit., i, p.29.
105. A.E. Fletcher to H.J. Wilson, 31 Oct. 1894, *HJW,* MD 6003.
106. 'English Journalism', *Outlook* (1901), lxix, p.186.
107. *Constitutional Year Book* (1896). It should be noted, however, as a

further indication of the diminishing importance of politics in the newspapers, that the *Western Morning News* claimed that Home Rulers were still amongst its readers since it had become a Unionist paper, *Western Morning News,* loc.cit., p.10.

108. M. Kinnear, *The British Voter* (1968), p.18.
109. Milne, op.cit., pp.144ff; D.M. Jones, op.cit., pp.196ff,289.
110. K. Jones, op.cit., p.149.
111. J.S. Mills, *Sir Edward Cook* (1921), p.199.
112. T.H.S. Escott, *Social Transformations of the Victorian Age* (1897), p.384.
113. T.W. Heyck, 'The British Radicals and Radicalism, 1874-1895: a Social Analysis', *Modern European Social History,* R. Bezucha, ed. (1972), pp.28-58.
114. Sir Edward Russell and H.J. Palmer, 'The Outlook for Liberal Journalism', *Sell's* (1902), pp.33-6,27.
115. For an account of the radical press after 1900 see A.J. Lee, 'The Radical Press', *Edwardian Radicalism, 1900-1914,* A.J.A. Morris, ed. (1974), pp.47-61.
116. J. McCarthy, *Reminiscences* (1899), i, pp.65, 163-89; *idem,* and Sir J. Robinson, *The Daily News Jubilee* (1896).
117. H.W. Lucy, *Sixty Years in the Wilderness* 1909), pp.129-36. In 1886 Labouchere had offered the job to Reginald Brett, who declined it. Wemyss Reid then became rather bitter because Herbert Gladstone had not done more on his behalf, Brett, op.cit., i, p.123; Reid to Gladstone, 26 Feb. to 12 May 1886, Viscount Gladstone Papers, Add. MS 46,041.
118. Robinson, op.cit., pp.235ff; A.T. Rogers, *Life of Henry Labouchere* (1913), pp.87-8; E. Hodder, *Life of Samuel Morley* (1887 ed.), p.247; Massingham, op.cit. (1892), pp.41ff. Clayden was an executive committee member of the NLF, see *DNB.* Ashton seems to have been Lord Ashton of Ashton, formerly James Williamson, a contributor to Liberal Party funds, and raised to the peerage in 1895, B. McGill, 'Francis Schnadhorst and Liberal Party Organisation', *Journal of Modern History* (1962), xxxiv, pp.30-1.
119. (W.T. Stead), 'The reconversion of the Daily News', *RR* (1901), xxiii, pp.147-53; H. Spender, *The Prime Minister* (1920), pp.122-3; Mills, opcit., pp.192ff. Cf. also Herbert Gladstone's gossipy account of the deal in a letter to Campbell-Bannerman, 15 Jan. 1901; Campbell-Bannerman Papers, Add. MS 41,216, ff.71-3. Gladstone had obviously not been kept informed of the negotiations.
120. Koss, op.cit. (1973), pp.36ff; Gardiner, op.cit., pp.211ff. Cadbury was providing important financial support to the Liberal Party at this time, Gardiner, op.cit., pp.76-7, and T. Lloyd, 'The Whip as Paymaster: Herbert Gladstone and Party Organisation', *EHR* (1974), lxxxix, pp.796, 800; R. Douglas, *History of the Liberal Party, 1895-1970* (1971), p.68.
121. Gardiner, op.cit., pp.211ff; Armstrong, op.cit., pp.101ff.
122. Taylor, op.cit., pp.15ff; A.F. Havighurst, *Radical Journalist* (1974), pp.54-110.
123. E.L. Lawson, *Peterborough Court* (1955), pp.20-6; G.C. Thompson, op.cit., i, pp.435-40.
124. Armstrong, op.cit., pp.75-90; Gardiner, op.cit., pp.216-17; S.L. Hughes, *Press, Platform and Parliament* (1918), pp.21f.
125. Havighurst, op.cit., pp.18-40; *The Story of the Star, 1888-1938* (1938); Fyfe, op.cit., p.138; Koss, op.cit. (1970), pp.131, 157-8; J. Stuart, *Reminiscences* (1912), *passim.*
126. Nowell-Smith, op.cit., pp.117-21; J.P. Edwards, *A Few Footprints* (1906 ed.) pp.37-9; F.W. Pethick Lawrence, *Fate Has Been Kind*

(1942), pp.57ff.
127. (W.T. Stead), 'The "Pall Mall Gazette"', *RR* (1893), vii, pp.135-56;
J.W.R. Scott, op.cit., esp. pp.235ff; *idem, The Life and Death of a Newspaper* (1952), pp.60-150, 260-73.
128. J.A. Spender, op.cit. (1927), i, pp.52ff, and ii, pp.133ff; J.W. Harris,
J.A. Spender (1946), p.28; for the activities of the Liberal whips see Lord
Riddell, *More Pages From My Diary, 1908-1914* (1934), p.14.
129. Havighurst, op.cit., pp.111-12.
130. A.J. Lee, op.cit. (1973), (1), pp.341-60; *Sell's* (1909), pp.132-4.
For *The Tribune's* Russian policy see B. Hollingsworth, 'Benckendorff's
"Bête Noire": "The Tribune" and Russian Internal Affairs, 1906-08',
forthcoming.
131. For a typically gloomy assessment of the provincial Liberal press in 1903
see Harold Spender's series 'Wake up Liberals!', in *Daily News,* Jan. and
Feb. 1903.
132. *NW,* 24 Dec. 1938. For this and the following see B.J. Hendrick, *Life
of Andrew Carnegie* (1933), pp.217-34; J.F. Wall, *Andrew Carnegie*
(1970), pp.429-41; Milne, op.cit., pp.124-7 and *passim; Hampshire Telegraph,*
14 Oct. 1899; *NW,* 1 Apr. 1939; *One Hundred Years of the Shields Gazette;*
Hadley, op.cit., pp.43ff.
133. *Jt.,* 23 and 30 Mar. 1888.
134. For S.M. Hawkes see Watson, op.cit., p.31. For the views of one of the
paper's old radical journalists, who left after Watson became editor on
Edwards' resumption of the proprietorship, on the grounds that it was
espousing socialism, H. Evans, *Radical Fights of Forty Years* (1913), p.97.
135. It is interesting that Watson claimed that he had got the publishers to
withdraw the novel, which he seems to have considered a slanderous travesty,
Jt., 4 Apr. 1888.
136. Hodgson, op.cit., pp.83-4.
137. For the following see D.M. Jones, op.cit.; T.W. Reid, op.cit. (1905);
A.W. Roberts, op.cit.
138. The claim that Herbert Gladstone chose the *Mercury* in particular to
launch the Hawarden Kite, however, seems unjustified, D.M. Jones, op.cit.,
pp.186-7.
139. Reid to Gladstone, 9 and 23 Oct., and 5 Nov. 1900, Viscount Gladstone
Papers, Add. MS 46,041.
140. Kitson to Gladstone, 18 Dec. 1900, ibid,. Add. MS 46,028; Simonis,
op.cit., p.206.
141. *Sell's* (1906), p.91. The price seems to have been £66,000, L.T. Hobhouse
to H. Gladstone, 30 Mar. 1905, and attached newspaper cutting, Viscount
Gladstone Papers, Add. MS 46,062 ff.176-7. It would appear from the
same letter that Byles was also offering the *Bradford Observer* for sale
at the same price.
142. For the following see *HJW,* MD 5998-6007, MD 1988-1997; W.Fowler,
A Study in Radicalism and Dissent: the Life of H.J. Wilson, 1833-1914
(1961); *History of the Sheffield Independent.*
143. Ayerst, op.cit.; Milne, op.cit.
144. *Sell's* (1905), p,125.
145. *Liverpool Courier,* 17 Jun. 1905.
146. Milne, op.cit; Hodgson, op.cit.; Watson, op.cit., pp.29-50, 183-90.
147. Milne, op.cit.; 'A North Country Worthy', loc.cit. pp.85-6; *HJW,* MD
6000, J.B. Hodgkin to Wilson, 1 Dec. 1891; Armstrong, op.cit., Chapter
12; A. Vernon, *A Quaker Businessman: Life of Joseph Rowntree, 1836-
1925* (1958), pp.161ff.
148. Milne, op.cit., p.172.

Notes

267

149. Harmsworth's support faltered in 1904, Pound and Harmsworth, op.cit., pp.289-90.
150. Some thought Pearson's activities actually detrimental to both the organisation and the cause, L.P. Amery, *My Political Life: Before the Storm* (1953), p.239.
151. Dark, op.cit., p.104.
152. J. Amery, *Life of Joseph Chamberlain* (1969), vi, pp.454,512,797; Dark, op.cit., pp.100-20.
153. Dark, op.cit., p.114.
154. R.A. Rempel, *Unionists Divided* (Newton Abbot, 1972), p.149.
155. Starmer, op.cit.; Milne, op.cit., pp.169ff.
156. A.K. Russell, *Liberal Landslide* (Newton Abbot, 1973).
157. Ibid., p.139.
158. Ibid., pp.140, 142-3.
159. Rempel, op.cit., p.150.
160. *Idem.*
161. Ibid., p.149; *Manchester Guardian,* 30 Jan. 1905.
162. *NV*, 18 Aug. 1875; *NW,* 22 Jul. 1939.
163. *HJW,* MD 5998, J. Fillingham to Wilson, 3 Jul. 1872.
164. Pound and Harmsworth, op.cit., p.239.
165. A.J. Lee, op.cit. (1974), p.54.
166. Royal Commission on the Press, Cmd 7700 (1949), p.188.

CHAPTER 6

1. See the critiques of functional analysis in communications research in Seymour-Ure, op.cit., p.42, and H. Cox and D. Morgan, *City Politics and the Press* (Cambridge, 1973), pp.18ff.
2. J. Chamberlain, 'The Caucus', *FR* (1878), xxx, p.741.
3. Quoted in D.M. Jones, op.cit., p.329.
4. N. Blewett, 'The Franchise in the United Kingdom, 1885-1918', *P & P* (1965), No. 32, pp.27-56.
5. P.F. Clarke, *Lancashire and the New Liberalism* (Cambridge, 1971), p.6.
6. Moore, op.cit., pp.5-36; A. Beattie, 'Coalition Government in Britain', *Government and Opposition* (1966), i, pp.3-34.
7. Cf. A.B. Cooke and J. Vincent, *The Governing Passion* (Brighton, 1974), *passim,* and V. Cromwell, 'The Losing of the Initiative of the House of Commons, 1780-1914', *Transactions* of the Royal Historical Society (1968), 5th s., xviii, pp.1-23.
8. H. Belloc and C. Chesterton, *The Party System* (1911), pp.218ff, and H. Belloc, *The Free Press* (1918), *passim.*
9. D. McQuail, *Towards a Sociology of Mass Communications* (1969), p.47; Seymour-Ure, op.cit., p.47.
10. For a critique see Cox and Morgan, op.cit., p.32.
11. It is doubtful, of course, whether such 'influence' can ever be satisfactorily isolated and measured, and almost certainly not without considerably more conceptual refinement.
12. Oral history offers some possibilities for the recent past, but the difficulties of sampling and of overcoming simple amnesia seem overwhelming.
13. R. Rose, *Politics in England* (1965), pp.160-1.
14. *The Times,* 4 Sep. 1871; cf. also *Spectator,* 5 Aug. 1878, pp.949-50. The reference in 1871 was to the opposition to the Army reforms of that year.
15. T.W. Reid, 'Public opinion and its leaders', *FR* (1880), xxxiv, pp.230ff; Morley, op.cit. (1908), ii, p.76; Fox Bourne, op.cit., ii, p.327; J.K. Chapman,

ed., 'A Political Correspondence of the Gladstone Era', *Transactions* of the American Philosophical Society (1971), n.s., lxi, Pt.2, p.17; Robinson op. cit., pp.122-3.

16. J.A. Spender, op.cit. (1925), ii, p.109.
17. F.W.S. Craig, *British Parliamentary Election Results, 1885-1918* (1973), p.576.
18. M. Ostrogorski, *Democracy and the Organisation of Political Parties* (1902), i, p.410.
19. Stephenson, op.cit., *passim*. The leader of the local Conservatives became a director of the paper in 1886, and Stephenson the proprietor subsidised a new local paper in the Conservative interest. In 1898 the new editor of the paper was raised by Central Office, although Stephenson remained in overall charge. Stephenson only received his knighthood in 1920, however, ibid., pp.xiii-vi.
20. Pound and Harmsworth, op.cit., p.296.
21. P. Thompson, *Socialists, Liberals and Labour: the struggle for London, 1885-1914* (1967), p.77. Clarke, op.cit., p.131, also notes that the press was not used extensively for political advertising in Lancashire before 1910. A Conservative plan to distribute one million copies of a special edition of the *Observer* for the December election of 1910 was never carried out, Gollin, op.cit., p.256.
22. *The Collected Works of Samuel Johnson* (1963), ii, p.23
23. Ostrogorski, op.cit., i, p.410. For instances of the same metaphor see Jephson, op.cit., ii, pp.602-3, and F. Taylor, *The Newspaper Press as a Power* (1898), p.18
24. D. Butler and D. Stokes, *Political Change in Britain* (Harmondsworth, 1971), pp.274-6. Cf. also for Norway, S. Rokkan, *Citizens, Elections and Parties* (NY, 1970), pp.42-3.
25. This statement does not mean that either issue was simple, merely that both were debated in simple terms. Some would argue that any issue must be so simplified if it is to be debatable politically.
26. Ostrogorski, op.cit., i, p.410.
27. Cox and Morgan, op.cit., pp.98ff.
28. Gollin, op.cit., pp.17-19.
29. Ayerst, op.cit., p.451.
30. G. Wallas, *The Great Society* (1925), pp.282-3; *Human Nature in Politics* (1908; 1929 ed.), pp.42-3.
31. P.J. Lucas, 'Furness Newspapers in Mid-Victorian England', *Victorian Lancashire* (Newton Abbot, 1974), S.P. Bell, ed., p.92.
32. 'The Traffic in Titles', *SR*, 20 Jul. 1907.
33. *Spectator*, 25 Nov. 1899, p.776, and 25 Jan. 1896, p.132. Cf. also Sala, op.cit. (1897), p.82.
34. *Spectator*, 12 Nov. 1904, pp.731-2.
35. Ibid., and Baron Craigmyle (Thomas Shaw), *Letters to Isabel* (1936), pp.92-4, who remarked that, nevertheless, the *Scotsman's* defection to the Unionists had been a great shock.
36. Fyfe, op.cit. (1934), p.140.
37. F. Greenwood, 'The Press and the Government', *NC* (1890), xxviii, pp.108ff; Massingham, op.cit. (1892), pp.191-2.
38. *The Times*, 31 Jul. 1895.
39. I. Jackson, *The Provincial Press and the Community* (Manchester, 1971), p.278.
40. *Truth*, 30 Nov. 1904.
41. G. Playfair, *Six Studies in Hypocrisy* (1969).
42. Porritt, op.cit., p.514.
43. C. O'Leary, *The Elimination of Corrupt Practices in British Elections, 1868-1911* (Oxford, 1962), p.104, n.1.

44. Rep.. . .into. . . Corrupt Practices in the Borough of Macclesfield, *PP* 1881
    C.2853 xliii, pp.11, 20, and Minutes of Evidence, QQ.1560ff, 2136ff.
45. Sir E. Clarke, *The Story of My Life* (1918), pp.150ff.
46. E.L. O'Malley and H. Hardcastle, *Reports of Decisions. . .of the Trials of
    Election Petitions. . ., iv, (1893), pp.93-5.
47. E.T. Powell, *The Essentials of Self-Government* (1909), p.152. The press,
    however, itself put pressure on candidates. In 1868 the *Manchester City News*
    refused to report the speeches of candidates who had not previously
    advertised their candidature or politics in the paper, and it was common for
    election advertisements to be charged at double the normal rates, A.J. Lee,
    op.cit. (1973), (2), p.136, and W.B. Gwyn, *Democracy and the Cost of
    Politics in Britain* (1962), p.68. Later both Ostrogorski, op.cit., i, pp.439,
    472-92, and A.L. Lowell, *The Government of England* (1926 ed.), i. pp.232ff,
    stressed how difficult it was to enforce the 1883 Act, especially over matters
    of agency, timing, 'nursing', and proof, although neither specified newspapers
    as a means of evasion.
48. *The Times,* 24 Oct. 1883.
49. 'Journalism and the General Election of 1895', *Sell's* (1896), pp.46-7.
50. But it was a view shared by some Conservatives, one of whom considered the
    change a new kind of political immorality which displayed a distinct 'lack of
    manliness', J.A. Bridges, *Reminiscences of a Country Politician* (1906),
    pp.26-7.
51. Pp.29-34, 273-85. Cf. H.A. Innis, *Empire and Communication* (Oxford, 1950),
    and *idem*, op.cit. (1951).
52. (J.F. Stephen), op.cit., p.54; E. Dicey, op.cit. (1905), p.917.
53. J.A. Spender, op.cit. (1925), ii, p.111.
54. Ibid., p.109.
55. *SR,* 15 Mar. 1856, pp.472-3.
56. J.B. Kinnear, op.cit., p.324; Humphrey, op.cit., pp.690-701.
57. A. Heywood, 'Newspapers and Periodicals', *Papers* of the Manchester Literary
    Club (Manchester, 1876), ii, pp.48-9.
58. *SR,* 29 Apr. 1899, p.529.
59. *SR,* 15 Apr. 1899, pp.455-6.
60. Escott, op.cit. (1880), ii, pp.476-7; (J.F. Stephen), op.cit. (1856), p.46.
61. Fox Bourne, op.cit., ii, p.375.
62. See above, p.28 and Johnston, op.cit., p.237 .
63. G.R. Kitson Clark, *Churchmen and the Condition of England* (Cambridge,
    1973), p.246; Baylen, op.cit. (1972), p.376, n.43; A.J. Lee, op.cit. (1974),
    passim.
64. Mrs Humphrey Ward, *A Writer's Recollections* (1918), p.98.
65. Trevelyan, op.cit., pp.1043-55.
66. Hobhouse, op.cit., p.365. Cf. J. Annand's similar comment in 1895, quoted in
    Hodgson, op.cit., p.234.
67. W. Bagehot, 'The French Newspaper Press', (1852), *Collected Works,*
    N. St. John Stevas, ed. (1968), iv, p.71.
68. (T.H.S. Escott), 'John Delane and Modern Journalism', *QR* (1908), ccix,
    pp.524ff; cf. T.H.S. Escott, *Masters of English Journalism* (1911), pp.24ff.
69. Cook, op.cit., p.287.
70. J.R. Lowell, *Collected Works* (1904), p.159.
71. Cook, op.cit., p.286.
72. Armstrong, op.cit., pp.82ff; H. Spender, op.cit.; Ayerst, op.cit., p.328.
73. Whates, op.cit., p.94; A. Briggs, *History of Birmingham* (1952), ii, pp.107-8;
    A. Chamberlain, *Politics from the Inside* (1936), pp.48-9, 201, 446, 461, 636.
74. This had happened much earlier in France, O'Boyle, op.cit., p.300.
75. Strick, op.cit., p.453.

76. J.A. Thomas, *The House of Commons, 1906-1911* (1958), pp.22-3.
77. H.V. Emy, *Liberals, Radicals and Social Politics, 1892-1914* (Cambridge, 1973), pp.10-11.
78. T.W. Reid, 'Our London Correspondent', *MM* (1880), xlii, pp.18ff.
79. S. Brooks, 'The English Press', *Harper's Weekly*, 4 Apr. 1903, p.570.
80. Mackintosh, op.cit., p.228; A. Ramm, ed., *The Political Correspondence of Mr Gladstone and Lord Granville, 1876-1886* (Oxford, 1962), i, p.214.
81. Robinson, op.cit., p.235.
82. J.A. Spender, *Life of Campbell-Bannerman* (1923), ii, p.192; A.K. Russell, op.cit., p.139; Lord Rendel, *Personal Papers* (1931), p.174; Gollin, op.cit., pp.94-5.
83. J. Chamberlain, *A Political Memoir*, C.H. Howard, ed. (1953), pp.9-10. It was pointed out how unusual it was for Mudford, a journalist, to be admitted to the Carlton Club, 'B', op.cit. (26 Aug. 1880, pp.148-9). For Conservative contacts with the *Hour* in the 1870s see 'E', 'Politics and the Press', *FM* (1875), n.s., xii, p.43.
84. J. Chamberlain, op.cit. (1953), p.10.
85. Brett, op.cit., i. p.211.
86. D.M. Jones, op.cit., pp.186ff.
87. D. Bahlman, ed., *The Diaries of Edward Walter Hamilton, 1880-1885* (Oxford, 1972), pp.83, 193, 258 and n.2.
88. Cooke and Vincent, op.cit., pp.397-8.
89. Bahlman, op.cit., pp.125-7, cf. also pp.193, 263. On the Land Bill leaks see Ramm, op.cit., ii, pp.253 n.4, 218 n.6, 231 n.2, 315 n.3. On Chamberlain's use of leaks in 1883 to shatter the Tory-farmer alliance, J.P.D. Dunbabin, 'The Politics of the Establishment of County Councils', *HJ* (1963), vi, p.232.
90. Ramm, op.cit., ii, p.4.
91. Bahlman, op.cit., pp.113, 520, 702.
92. Ibid., p.732; D.G.T. Williams, *Not In The Public Interest* (1965), p.50.
93. *The Times*, 13 Apr. 1878.
94. M. MacDonagh, *The Reporters' Gallery* (1912), pp.63-4. Higginbottom of the *Pall Mall Gazette* claimed that he and W.E. Pitt of *The Times* used MPs leaks quite extensively in the 1900s, F.J. Higginbottom, *The Vivid Life* (1934), pp.150-1.
95. MacDonagh, op.cit., p.62. Wemyss Reid tells of an occasion when a reporter is supposed to have rifled the desk of the Home Secretary, but this sounds a trifle apocryphal, T.W. Reid, op.cit. (1880) *MM*, p.23.
96. D.G.T. Williams, op.cit., Chapter 1. Steps were taken, however, to tighten security in the event of war, to which end a liaison committee was at last established in 1911, with representatives of the newspaper proprietors, the Admiralty and the War Office, D. Hopkin, 'Domestic Censorship in the First World War', *Journal of Contemporary History* (1970), v, p.153.
97. Ramm, op.cit., i, pp.213, 214, and ii, p.290.
98. Ibid., ii, p.23.
99. Ibid., i, p.209. For Granville's relationship with Chenery see *History of The Times* (1939), ii, pp.600-1.
100. Rendel, op.cit., p.76.
101. Curtiss, op.cit., pp.210-15.
102. 279 *H.C. Deb.* 3s. 24 May 1883, cols. 760ff.
103. Mackintosh, op.cit., p.218.
104. M. Wright, *Treasury Control of the Civil Service* (1969), pp.59-61. For earlier examples see Parris, op.cit. (1969), pp.93-8.
105. T.W. Reid, op.cit. (1880) *MM*, p.24. This almost certainly did not hold true for the Foreign Office, which succeeded in ignoring the existence of the press until the First World War, H.A. Taylor, op.cit., pp.151-2, and A.J.P. Taylor,

Beaverbrook (1974), pp.198-209.
106. H.J. Hanham, 'Political Patronage at the Treasury, 1870-1912', *HJ* (1960), iii, pp.80-1.
107. Ramm, op.cit., ii, p.159, and note.
108. Bahlman, op.cit., p.470.
109. Mackintosh, op.cit., p.97; Kebbel, op.cit., pp.218-19. Secret Service money was used to pay the editor of the *World* to ensure its circulation in Irish country districts, H. Maxwell, *Life and Letters of G.W. Frederick, 4th Earl of Clarendon* (1913), i, pp.317-20.
110. Ramm, op.cit., i, p.256; G. Woodcock, *Anarchism* (Harmondsworth, 1963), pp.415-16; *PRO,* H.O. A/38.025.
111. As in the case of *Der Deutsche Eidgenosse, PRO,* H.O., O.S.7914, and L.O.O. 152. Cf. also another case, *PRO,* H.O., L.O.O. 178.
112. 6 & 7 Vict. Ch. 68 section 12. See A.V. Dicey, op.cit., pp.235ff.
113. *NV,* 19 Aug. 1874.
114. 9 *H.C. Deb.* 4s. 13 Mar. 1893 cols. 1866-69.
115. 10 *H.C. Deb.* 4s. 29 Mar. 1893 cols. 1401-06.
116. Ibid., 30 Mar. 1893 cols. 1507-10.
117. Mills, op.cit., pp.115-16.
118. *The Times,* 15 Oct. 1892; *Pall Mall Gazette,* 21 Oct. 1892.
119. Pound and Harmsworth, op.cit., pp.233-4.
120. Ibid., pp.295-6
121. J. Wilson, *'C.B.'* (1973), pp.581-2.
122. J.A. Spender Papers, Add. MS 46,388, letter 11 Nov. 1909. Cf. J.A. Spender, op.cit. (1927), i, p.152.
123. R. Churchill, *The Young Statesman* (1967), companion vol.iii, pp.1628-9.
124. A.J. Lee, op.cit. (1974), p.58; K.O. Morgan, ed., *Lloyd George Family Letters* (1973), pp.88, 126-7, 147.
125. N. Blewett, *The Peers, the Parliament and the People* (1972), pp.303-4.
126. See above, pp.177-8.
127. 'Specialised Administration', (1871), in *Man versus the State.* D. Macrae, ed. (Harmondsworth, 1969), p.301. On parliamentary reporting see above, p.111.
128. (1862), quoted in M. Pinto-Duchinsky, *The Political Thought of Lord Salisbury, 1854-1868* (1967), p.117.
129. Stead, op.cit. (1886), p.673.

CHAPTER 7

1. H. Gladstone to Campbell-Bannerman, 20 Jan. 1905, Campbell-Bannerman Papers, Add. MS 41,216, ff.71-73.
2. W.J. Fox, 'On the duties of the press towards the people', *People's Journal* (1846), i, p.4.
3. H. Richard, *Memoirs of Joseph Sturge* (1864), p.520. For relation of the *Morning Star* and the *Tribune* see A.J. Lee, op.cit. (1973) (1), pp.343-44.
4. McCarthy, op.cit., i, pp.81-2, 185-7.
5. See above, p.163. It was natural that the editor of the *Evening Star,* F.W. Chesson, should be secretary of the Aborigine Protection Society, *T.P. O'Connor's Weekly,* 4 Aug. 1905, p.133.
6. H.A. Taylor, op.cit., pp.266-7.
7. Gibb and Beckwith, op.cit., p.53.
8. Colman, op.cit., pp.371-2.
9. W. Beveridge, *Power and Influence* (1953), p.34. The *Morning Post,* however, was a less successful business proposition than the leading Liberal dailies.
10. Gardiner, op.cit., p. 236.

11. Vernon, op.cit., p.162.
12. Rowntree and Cadbury, quoted in ibid., p.175.
13. *HJW*, MD 5999, Ellis to Wilson, 31 Oct. 1874.
14. Escott, op.cit. (1897), pp.10-11.
15. Gollin, op.cit., p.102.
16. H.A. Taylor, op.cit., p.269. A newspaper facsimile transmission system was demonstrated in Japan in 1970, *The Times*, 17 Dec. 1970, 'The World's Press', p.iii.
17. 'New Forces in Journalism', *Sell's* (1921), p.24. The newspaper industry, however, was never mentioned in the extensive literature on trusts and their control which built up from the 1890s.
18. A.K. Russell, 'The General Election of 1906', Oxford D.Phil. thesis, 1962, pp.421 n.2, 422.
19. 'The People in Power', *Ethical Democracy*, S. Coit, ed. (1900), pp.66-7.
20. P. van der Esch, *La deuxième Internationale, 1889-1923* (Paris, 1957), p.69.
21. 'The Infancy of the Labour Party', E.R. Pease Collection.
22. Cooperative Union, *39th Annual Report* (Manchester, 1907), p.331.
23. For Labour and Socialist local weeklies see A.J. Lee, op.cit. (1974), pp.53-4, 59 n.38.
24. 'The Influence of the Press', *BM* (1834), xxxvi, pp.375-6. For the Liberal reply see *WR*(1834), xxi, pp.498-505.
25. Quoted in Hodgson, op.cit., p.103.
26. Quoted in *Sell's* (1892), pp.33-4.
27. Hodgson, op.cit. pp.115-16.
28. 'The Ethics of Editing', *NR* (1900), xxxv, pp.257-61.
29. 'Proprietors and Editors', *NR* (1900), xxxv, pp.592-601.
30. Massingham had mentioned the possibility of 'associations of small proprietors uniting in the establishment of a paper for common purposes. . .', loc.cit., · p.260, but what he had in mind remains obscure.
31. 'Present Day Problems', *Nation*, 18, 25 Jul., 1, 8, 15, 22, 29 Aug. 1908.
32. 'The Independent Editor', *Sell's* (1921), p.38.
33. *H.C. Deb.* 5s. 15 Oct. 1918 cols. 87-8.
34. *New Worlds for Old* (1909 ed.), p.293. For a useful survey of contemporary socialist discussion of the question see J.T. Stoddart, *The New Socialism* (1909), pp.144-53.
35. 'Industry Under Socialism', *Fabian Essays*, A. Briggs, ed. (1962), pp.193-4.
36. Wells, op.cit., pp.297-8.
37. Ibid., pp.298, 295-6. Cf. also K. Kautsky, 'On the Day After the Social Revolution', (1902 trans; 1916 ed., *The Social Revolution)*, pp.178-9, where trade unions are called upon to perform the same functions as municipalities in Wells's scheme.
38. F.H. Hayward and B.N. Langdon-Davies, *Democracy and the Press* (Manchester, 1919). In connection with the 'Truthful Press Act' they referred to Sir. C. Walston, *Truth: an essay on moral reconstruction* (Cambridge, 1919). Walston's Press Arbitration Court would have been much more powerful and 'independent' than that which emerged in 1949 as the Press Council.
39. Hayward and Langdon-Davies, op.cit., pp.59ff.
40. N. Angell, *The Press and the Organisation of Society* (Cambridge, 1922; 1933 ed., p.69).
41. The 1881 Press Law liberalised the position in France, but in practice it was administered repressively, especially during the anarchist outrages of the 1890s, Bellanger, op.cit., iii, pp.7ff, 240ff. In 1914 an attempt to secure the disclosure of circulation in Britain failed, although in the previous year an American law requiring this had been ruled constitutional by the Supreme

Court, *The Times,* 26 Mar. 1914.
42. Belloc, op.cit. (1918), p.18.
43. See R.A. Scott-James, *The Influence of the Press* (1913), Chapter 17. Scott-James's book was published by the Guild Socialist New Age Press, and he perhaps shared many of Belloc's assumptions.
44. *RR* (1903), xxviii, pp.571-83; (1904), xxix, pp.11-13. *The Majority* was another attempt at a similar enterprise, 14 to 19 Jun. 1906.
45. C. Cockburn, in P. Cockburn, *Years of the Week* (Harmondsworth, 1971), p.10.
46. Royal Commission on the Press, *Cmd.* 7700, pp.190-1.
47. There are few satisfactory statistics, but see C.M. Cipolla, *Literacy and Development in the West* (Harmondsworth, 1969), F.L. Mott, *American Journalism: a history, 1690-1960* (NY, 1962 ed.), pp.304, 507, and F. Furet and W. Sachs, 'La croissance de l'alphabetisation en France xviiie-xixe siècle', *Annales: Economies, Sociétés, Civilisations* 1974, xxix, pp.714-37.
48. Cf. T.S. Hamerow, *The Social Foundations of German Unification, 1858-71* (NY, 1969). pp.282ff.
49. For the following see Bellanger, op.cit., ii, iii; J. Kayser, *La Presse de Province sous la Troisième République* (Paris 1958); R. Manevy, *La Presse de la Troisième République* (Paris, 1955); F. Amaury, *Histoire de Plus Grand Quotidien de la Troisième République. Le Petit Parisien, 1876-1944* (Paris, 1972).
50. For the following see Mott, op.cit., pp.156-89.
51. A. Sorel, 'La Presse Allemande', *Revue des deux mondes* (1873), ii, p.715.
52. E.L. Godkin, quoted in Innis, op.cit. (1951), p.183 n.86. Cf also Siebert et al., op.cit., p.79.
53. *A Free and Responsible Press* (Chicago, 1947); Siebert *et al.*, op.cit., pp.173ff.
54. Mott, op.cit., p.858.
55. For a shrewd study of 'objectivity' in the press see Breed, op.cit., and for a relevant critique of what has become a classic case of investigatory journalism, the *Washington Post*'s reporting of the Watergate affair, see A. Cockburn, 'Propaganda for the Victors', *New York Review of Books,* 28 Nov. 1974.
56. See Table 35.

TABLES

Table 1: The English Provincial Daily Press in 1855

Title	Date Started	Date Ended	Remarks
Northern Daily Times	24 Sep. 1853	1861	Liverpool. 3*d,* reduced to 2*d* 11 Jun., to 1*d* 30 Jun. 1855.
Manchester War Telegraph	20 Oct. 1854	1855	1*d*, raised to 2*d* 4 Dec. 1854, reduced to 1*d* 18 Jun. 1855.
Northern Daily Express	21 Apr. 1855	1886	Darlington. Newcastle from Oct. 1855. 1*d*, Liberal. New.
Birmingham Daily Press	7 May 1855	1858	1½*d*. Liberal. New.
Events	19 May 1855	1855	Liverpool. ½*d*. New. Regularly from 4 Jun. 1855.
Sheffield Daily Telegraph	8 Jun. 1855	. . . .	1*d*. New.
Liverpool Daily Post	11 Jun. 1855	. . . .	1*d*. Liberal. New, but from office of old *Liverpool Journal*
Manchester Halfpenny Express	13 Jun. 1855	1855	½*d*. New, but from old *Manchester Express*
15 June 1855: Royal Assent to repeal of stamp duty			
Manchester Examiner and Times	18 Jun. 1855	1894	1*d*. Liberal. Old.
Sheffield Morning News	19 Jun. 1855	1855	1*d*. New.
29 June 1855: Repeal Act, 18 Vict. Cap. xxvii, comes into force			
North and South Shields Gazette	30 Jun. 1855	. . . .	*Daily Telegraph* ed. 1*d*. Old. Reduced to ½*d*. Jul. 1855.
Manchester Guardian	2 Jul. 1855	. . . .	2*d*. Liberal. Old.
Hull Morning Telegraph	2 Jul. 1855	1880	½*d*. New.
Stevenson's Daily Express	2 Jul. 1855	1856	Nottingham. ½*d*. New.

Note: . . . . indicates still being published
Sources: NPD (1846-); A.E. Musson, 'The First Daily Newspapers in Lancashire', *Transactions* of the Lancashire and Cheshire Antiquarian Society, (1955), lxv, pp.104-31; A.P. Wadsworth, 'Newspaper Circulations 1800-1954', *Transactions* of the Manchester Statistical Society, (1955), p.19; M. Milne, op. cit.; *One Hundred Years of the Shields Gazette* (South Shields, 1949); D. Dixon, op. cit.

274

Table 2: The English Provincial Daily Press 1856-1870

Founded	Title	Ended	Remarks
1856	*Sheffield Daily News*	1862	
1857	*Birmingham Daily Post*	....	1*d*. Liberal.
	Liverpool Daily Mail	1857	1*d*. Conservative.
1858	*Newcastle Daily Chronicle*	....	1*d*. Liberal
	Liverpool Mercury	1904	1*d*. Liberal
	Western Daily Press	....	Bristol. 1*d*. Neutral, Lib.-Ind. 1860
1859	*Sheffield Daily Argus*	1859	
	Western Daily Times	1859	Exeter. 1*d*. Liberal (See 1866)
	Liverpool Morning News	1859	
	Hull Daily Express	1864	1½*d*, ½*d* 1862. Liberal
1860	*Western Daily Mercury*	....	Plymouth. 1*d*. Liberal
	Western Morning News	....	Plymouth. 1*d*. Ind.
	Bristol Daily Post	1909	1*d*. Liberal
	Nottingham Daily Express	....	1*d*. Neutral
1861	*Sheffield Independent*	....	1*d*. Liberal
	Newcastle Journal	....	1*d*. Conservative
	Leeds Mercury	....	1*d*. Liberal
	Nottingham Daily Guardian	....	1*d*.
	Liverpool Journal of Commerce	....	1*d*.
	Liverpool Evening News	1863	1*d*.
1862	*Hull Morning Star*	1862	1*d*. Lib.-Ind.
	Birmingham Daily Gazette	....	1*d*. Lib.-Cons.
1863	*Exeter and Plymouth Gazette, Daily Telegram*	1885	½*d*. Conservative
	Sheffield Daily Advertiser	1863	
	Liverpool Daily Courier	....	1*d*. Conservative
1864	*Shields Daily News*	....	1*d*. Liberal. E.
	Manchester Courier	....	1*d*. Conservative
	Easter Morning News	....	Hull. 1*d*. Ind.
	Eastern Evening News	1867	Hull.
	Nottingham Daily Journal	1887	2*d*., 1*d* 1865. Lib.-Cons.
1865	*Bristol Times and Mirror*	....	1*d*. Conservative
	Sunderland Daily Shipping News	1913	1*d*. Neutral
1866	*Yorkshire Post and Leeds Intelligencer*	....	1*d*. Conservative
	Devon Weekly Times and and Evening Express	....	Exeter. ½*d*. Liberal
	Northern Evening Express	1886	Newcastle. ½*d*. Lib.
	Western Daily Times	....	Exeter. 1*d*. Liberal
1867	*Leeds Evening Express*	1899	½*d*. Ind.-Lib.
	Bolton Evening News	....	½*d*. Liberal
	Hull Morning Times	1867	½*d*.
	Hull Morning Paper	1867	½*d*.
1868	*Western Counties Daily Herald*	1869	1*d*. Conservative
	Bradford Daily Telegraph	....	½*d*. Liberal. E.
	Bradford Observer	....	1*d*. Liberal
	Bradford Daily Times	1872	½*d*. Liberal
	Manchester Evening News	....	½*d*. Ind.
	Brighton Daily News	1880	½*d*. Ind.

Table 2 (Continued)

Founded	Title	Ended	Remarks
1869	*Bradford Daily Review*	1871	½*d*. Neutral
	Sheffield Daily Times	1888	½*d*. Conservative
	Oldham Evening Express	1889	½*d*. Ind.
	Sheffield Evening Star	1888	½*d*. Liberal
	Western Daily Standard	1870	Plymouth. 1*d*. Liberal
	Western Daily Telegraph	1875	Bristol. ½*d*. Cons.
	Middlesborough Daily Gazette	. . . .	1*d*. Ind.
	Leicester Daily Mail	1870	
1870	*Birmingham Daily Mail*	. . . .	½*d*. Liberal
	Northern Echo	. . . .	Darlington. ½*d*. Lib.
	South Wales Evening Telegram	1891	Newport. ½*d*. Lib.
	Bolton Morning News	1870	Liberal
	Bolton Daily Chronicle	. . . .	½*d*. E.
	Evening News	1876	Hull. ½*d*.
	Liverpool Evening Express	. . . .	½*d*. Ind.
	Tidings	. . . .	Penzance. ½*d*. Neutral
	Eastern Daily Press	. . . .	Norwich. 1*d*. Ind.
	Sunderland Evening Chronicle	1871	
	Newcastle Evening Courant	1876	½*d*. Neutral

Notes: Political attribution and price apply to dates of foundation only unless otherwise stated.
. . . . = extant in 1914
Lib. = Liberal. Cons. = Conservative. Ind. = Independent. E = evening paper.

Sources: Main sources have been *NPD* (1846-) and *New Cambridge Bibliography of English Literature* (Cambridge, 1969), iii, cols.1794-98. Numerous other studies have been used to supplement and check these.

Table 3: The Provincial Press and Provincial Cities in 1870

Town	Population in '000s	Number of Dailies	Dailies per '000 pop.
Liverpool	493	5	1 : 100
Manchester	351	4	1 : 90
Birmingham	343	3	1 : 110
Leeds	259	3	1 : 80
Sheffield	239	4	1 : 60
Bristol	182	4	1 : 45
Bradford	145	4	1 : 35
Newcastle	128	5	1 : 24
Salford	124	—	—
Hull	121	3	1 : 40
Portsmouth	113	—	—
Oldham	113	1	1 : 113
Sunderland	98	2	1 : 50
Leicester	95	1	1 : 95
Brighton	90	1	1 : 90
Nottingham	86	3	1 : 29
Bolton	82	3	1 : 28
Norwich	80	1	1 : 80
Plymouth	68	3	1 : 23
North and South Shields	45	2	1 : 22
Middlesborough	35	1	1 : 25
Exeter	34	3	1 : 11
Darlington	27	1	1 : 27
Newport (Mon.)	27	1	1 : 27

Notes: The following towns with populations of between 50,000 and 100,000 had no dailies in 1870 — Preston, Blackburn, Huddersfield, Wolverhampton, Halifax, Devonport, Rochdale, West Ham, Tottenham, Stockport and Bath. Penzance is not included in this Table.

Sources: Table 2, and 1871 Census.

Table 4: English Provincial Dailies in 1870

Towns	L.	C.	IL.	LI.	LC.	I.	N.	O	½d.	1d.	0.	E's	Total
Birmingham	2				1				1	2			3
Bolton	2							1	2	1		1	3
Bradford	3						1		3	1			4
Brighton						1			1				1
Bristol	1	2			1				1	3			4
Darlington	1								1				1
Exeter	2	1							2	1		1	3
Hull						1	1	1	2	1		1	3
Leeds	1	1	1						1	2		1	3
Liverpool	2	1				1	1		1	4		1	5
Leicester							1				1		1
Manchester	2	1				1			1	3		1	4
Middlesborough						1				1			1
Newcastle	3	1					1		2	3		2	5
Newport (Mon.)	1								1			1	1
North and South Shields	2								2			1	2
Norwich						1				1			1
Nottingham				1		2					3		3
Oldham								1	1			1	1
Penzance							1		1				1
Plymouth	2						1			3			3
Sheffield	2	2							2	2		1	4
Sunderland							1	1		2		1	2
Total	26	9	1	1	2	8	8	4	25	30	4	13	59

Notes: This table does not include the *Liverpool Telegraph and Shipping Gazette*, which was established in 1826.
L. = Liberal. C. = Conservative. IL. = Independent Liberal. LI. = Liberal-Independent. I. = Independent. N. = Neutral. O. = Other. E's = Evening papers.

Sources: Tables 1 and 2.

Table 5: Metropolitan Dailies in 1855

Mornings:	*Morning Advertiser,* Liberal 5*d.*
	Morning Chronicle, Liberal-Conservative 5*d.*
	Daily News, Liberal 5*d.*
	Morning Herald, Conservative 5*d.*
	Morning Post, Conservative 5*d.*
	The Times, Independent 5*d.*
Evenings:	*Express,* Liberal 3*d.*
	Globe, Whig 5*d.*
	Standard, Conservative 5*d.*
	Sun, Liberal 5*d.*

Source: NPD (1854). No *NPD* was published for 1855.

Table 6: Metropolitan Dailies in 1870

Mornings:	*Daily Chronicle,* Liberal ½*d.*
	Daily News, Liberal 1*d.*
	Daily Telegraph, Liberal 1*d.*
	Morning Advertiser, Liberal 3*d.*
	The Times, Independent 3*d.*
	Morning Post, Conservative 3*d.*
	Standard, Conservative 1*d.*
Evenings:	*Echo,* Liberal ½*d.*
	Evening Standard, Conservative 1*d.*
	Pall Mall Gazette, Liberal 2*d.*
	Sun, Liberal 4*d.*
	Globe, Conservative 1*d.*

Note: Five commercial dailies have been omitted from this list.
Source: NPD (1870).

Table 7: Metropolitan Parochial Newspapers in 1870

	Liberal	Conser- vative	Neutral	Indepen- dent	Other	Total
½d.	5		5		2	12
1d.	8	4	9	5	2	28
1½d.			1			1
2d.			1	1		2
Total	13	4	16	6	4	43

Sources: NPD (1870), and *The Times Tercentenary Handlist* (1920).

Table 8: Nominal Capitals of Newspaper Companies 1856-1885

	Percentage of companies with nominal capitals of				
	£1 — £499	£500—	£1,000—	£10,000—	£100,000+
1856-65	2.8	2.8	79.0	13.0	1.4
1866-75	0.8	4.0	68.0	23.2	2.0
1876-85	1.7	3.1	60.0	31.5	3.5

Source: Parliamentary Returns of Joint-Stock Companies.

Table 9: Called Capital of Newspaper Companies 1856-1885

	Percentage of Companies giving details	Percentage of Companies giving details with			
		£1—	£500—	£1,000—	£10,000+
1856-65	50	31	17	43	8.5
1866-75	24.8	32	9.6	50	6.4
1876-85	60	32.5	16.2	38.4	12.5

Source: Parliamentary Returns of Joint-Stock Companies.

Table 10: Distribution of Shareholders in Newspaper Companies 1856-1885

	Companies with 7-10 shareholders	Companies with 10+ shareholders
1856-65	30	36
1866-75	89	30
1876-85	118	105

Source: Parliamentary Returns of Joint-Stock Companies.

Table 11: Proportion of Newspaper Companies Registered in London 1856-1885

1856-65	40%
1866-75	25.9%
1876-85	35.3%

Source: Parliamentary Returns of Joint-Stock Companies.

Table 12: New Investment in Newspaper Companies 1856-1885 in £'000s

	Nominal Capital	Called Capital
1856	66.6*	71.0*
1865	63.6	4.6
1875	130.0	13.7
1885	594.0	205.6

Note: *excludes the National Newspaper Company.
Source: Parliamentary Returns of Joint-Stock Companies.

Table 13: Survival of Newspaper Companies Formed 1856-1865

Abortive or small	29
1-3 years	12
4-5 years	9
6-10 years	12
11-15 years	3
16-20 years	2
21-30 years	3
31-40 years	1
More than 40 years	3
Total	74

Source: Registrar-General's returns in PRO.
It should be noted that although calculated from the same returns these figures are not exactly correspondent to the survey conducted by Shannon, op. cit. See above, p.252, n.27.

Table 14: The Political Distribution of English Provincial Dailies, 1868

	Mornings		Evenings		Total
	½d	1d	½d	1d	
Liberal	4	11	4	1	20
Liberal-Independent	—	1	1	—	2
Independent (but Liberal)	1	2	1	—	4
Conservative	1	7	—	—	8
Liberal-Conservative	—	1	—	—	1
Independent	1	—	—	—	1
Neutral	1	6	—	—	7
Total	8	28	6	1	43

Source: NPD.

Table 15: The Political Distribution of English Provincial Dailies, 1874

	Mornings		Evenings		Total
	½d	1d	½d	1d	
Liberal	8	17	4	1	31*
Liberal-Independent	1	1	—	—	2
Independent (but Liberal)	—	3	1	—	4
Conservative	3	6	1	—	12†
Liberal-Conservative	—	1	—	—	1
Independent	1	4	3	1	9
Neutral	3	6	3	—	12
Total	16	38	12	2	71

Note: *includes one 1½d evening.   †includes one 1½d evening, and
                                       one 2d morning.
Source: NPD.

Table 16: The Political Distribution of English Provincial Dailies, 1880

	Mornings		Evenings		Total
	½d	1d	½d	1d	
Liberal	12	16	18	1	48*
Liberal-Independent	—	1	1	—	2
Independent (but Liberal)	—	3	4	—	9†
Neutral (but Liberal)	—	—	1	—	1
Conservative	5	7	14	—	26
Independent (but Conservative)	1	1	—	—	2
Neutral (but Conservative)	—	—	2	—	2
Independent	—	3	14	—	17
Neutral	—	5	4	—	11†
Other	—	1	1	—	2
Total	18	37	59	1	120

Note: *includes one other evening.   †includes two other mornings.
Source: NPD.

Table 17: The Political Distribution of English Provincial Dailies, 1885

| | Mornings | | Evenings | | Total |
	½d	1d	½d	1d	
Liberal	10	16	26	—	53*
Liberal-Independent	—	1	1	—	2
Independent (but Liberal)	1	2	4	1	10†
Neutral (but Liberal)	—	—	1	—	1
Conservative	6	10	18	1	35
Liberal-Conservative	—	—	1	—	1
Independent (but Conservative)	1	1	—	—	2
Neutral (but Conservative)	—	—	1	2	3
Independent	1	2	13	1	17
Neutral	—	4	6	—	12††
Total	19	36	71	5	136

Note: *includes one other evening. †includes two other mornings.
††includes a 2d morning, and a subscription evening.
Source: NPD.

Table 18: The Political Distribution of English Provincial Dailies, 1886

| | Mornings | | Evenings | | Total |
	½d	1d	½d	1d	
Liberal	9	16	27	—	53*
Liberal-Independent	—	1	1	—	2
Independent (but Liberal)	—	3	5	—	10†
Neutral (but Liberal)	—	—	1	—	1
Conservative	6	10	18	1	35
Independent (but Conservative)	1	1	—	—	2
Neutral (but Conservative)	—	—	2	1	3
Independent	1	2	15	1	19
Neutral	—	5	6	—	15††
Total	17	38	75	3	138

Note: *includes one other evening. †includes two other mornings.
††includes one 2d morning and one subscription evening.
Source: NPD.

Table 19: The Political Distribution of English Provincial Dailies, 1892

| | Mornings | | Evenings | | Total |
	½*d*	1*d*	½*d*	1*d*	
Liberal	8	16	30	1	56*
Liberal-Independent	—	—	1	—	1
Independent (but Liberal)	1	1	3	—	7†
Conservative	4	9	20	1	34
Independent (but Conservative	1	1	—	—	2
Neutral (but Conservative)	—	—	1	1	2
Unionist	—	—	1	—	1
Independent	1	2	5	1	9
Neutral	—	6	6	—	14††
Total	15	35	67	4	126

Note: *includes one other evening. †includes two other evenings.
††includes one 2*d* morning, and one subscription evening.
Source: NPD.

Table 20: The Political Distribution of English Provincial Dailies, 1895

| | Mornings | | Evenings | | Total |
	½*d*	1*d*	½*d*	1*d*	
Liberal	11	14	33	1	60*
Liberal-Independent	—	—	1	—	1
Independent (but Liberal)	1	1	3	—	7†
Conservative	4	9	20	1	34
Independent (but Conservative)	1	1	—	—	2
Neutral (but Conservative)	—	—	1	1	2
Unionist	—	—	1	—	1
Independent	2	2	7	2	13
Neutral	1	6	5	—	15††
Total	20	33	71	5	135

Note: *includes one other evening. †includes two other mornings.
††includes two 2*d* mornings and one subscription evening.
Source: NPD.

Table 21: The Political Distribution of English Provincial Dailies, 1900

	Mornings		Evenings		Total
	½d	1d	½d	1d	
Liberal	4	14	41	1	61*
Liberal-Independent	—	—	1	—	1
Independent (but Liberal)	1	1	4	—	8†
Neutral (but Liberal)	—	—	1	—	1
Conservative	3	7	21	2	33
Independent (but Conservative)	2	1	—	—	3
Neutral (but Conservative)	—	—	1	1	2
Unionist	1	—	1	—	2
Independent	14	6	13	2	35
Neutral	5	7	9	1	25††
Total	30	36	92	7	171

Note: *includes one other evening. †includes two other mornings.
††includes one gratis morning, one 2d morning, and one subscription evening.
Source: NPD.

Table 22: The Political Distribution of English Provincial Dailies, 1906

	Mornings		Evenings		Total
	½d	1d	½d	1d	
Liberal	5	11	40	1	58*
Independent (but Liberal)	1	1	2	—	6†
Conservative	3	7	16	1	27
Independent (but Conservative)	2	1	—	—	3
Neutral (but Conservative)	—	—	1	1	2
Unionist	1	—	3	—	4
Independent	12	4	13	1	31*
Neutral	5	8	6	2	22††
Total	29	32	81	6	153

Note: *includes one other evening.   †includes two other mornings.
††includes one subscription evening.
Source: NPD.

Table 23: The Political Distribution of English Provincial Dailies, 1910

| | Mornings | | Evenings | | Total |
	½d	1d	½d	1d	
Liberal	5	11	34	—	51*
Independent (but Liberal)	1	1	2	—	6†
Conservative	2	7	17	—	26
Independent (but Conservative)	2	1	—	—	3
Neutral (but Conservative)	—	—	1	1	2
Unionist	—	—	4	—	4
Independent	4	2	7	—	14*
Neutral	1	8	3	2	15††
Total	15	30	68	3	121

Note: *includes one other evening.   †includes two other mornings.
††includes one subscription evening.
Source: NPD.

Table 24: Consolidated Table of the Political Distribution of English Provincial Dailies, 1868-1910

	'68	'74	'80	'85	'86	'92	'95	'00	'06	'10
Liberal	20	31	48	53	53	56	60	61	58	51
Liberal-Independent	2	2	2	2	2	1	1	1	—	—
Independent (but Liberal)	4	4	9	10	10	7	7	8	6	6
Neutral (but Liberal)	—	—	1	1	1	—	—	1	—	—
Conservative	8	12	26	35	35	34	34	33	27	26
Liberal-Conservative	1	1	—	1	—	—	—	—	—	—
Independent (but Conservative)	—	—	2	2	2	2	2	3	3	3
Neutral (but Conservative)	—	—	2	3	3	2	2	2	2	2
Unionist	—	—	—	—	—	1	1	2	4	4
Independent	1	9	17	17	19	9	13	35	31	14
Neutral	7	12	11	12	13	14	15	25	22	15
Other	—	—	2	—	—	—	—	—	—	—
Total	43	71	120	136	138	126	135	171	153	121

Note: All totals include additions noted in each of Tables 14—23.
Source: NPD.

Table 25: Concentration of English Provincial Dailies, 1868-1910

	Number of Towns Having Mornings						Number of Towns Having Evenings				
	1	2	3	4	5	6	1	2	3	4	5
1868	3	5	6	—	1	—	7	—	—	—	—
1874	10	5	5	3	—	1	13	1	1	—	—
1880	12	9	5	2	—	1	20	11	5	1	—
1885	8	6	8	1	2	—	23	14	6	1	1
1886	7	8	7	1	2	—	25	16	4	3	—
1892	14	9	4	1	1	—	28	14	4	—	1
1895	20	8	4	1	1	—	29	19	2	—	1
1900	25	11	2	3	1	—	36	21	6	—	1
1906	25	7	5	1	1	—	41	21	1	1	—
1910	14	5	4	1	1	—	32	19	—	1	—

	Number of Towns Having:			
	Mornings Only	Evenings Only	Both	At least one Daily
1868	9	1	6	16
1874	15	3	12	30
1880	10	18	19	47
1885	5	25	20	50
1886	4	26	21	51
1892	6	22	23	51
1895	9	24	25	58
1900	8	29	34	71
1906	6	31	33	70
1910	5	31	21	57

Source: NPD.

Table 26: Price Distribution of English Provincial Dailies, 1868-1910

	Halfpenny Mornings			Penny Mornings		
Year	Total	Liberal	Conser-vative	Total	Liberal	Conser-vative
1868	8	5(62)	1(12)	28	14(50)	8(28)
1874	16	9(56)	3(18)	38	21(55)	7(18)
1880	18	12(66)	6(33)	37	20(54)	8(21)
1885	19	11(58)	7(36)	36	19(52)	11(30)
1886	17	9(53)	7(41)	38	20(52)	11(29)
1892	15	9(60)	5(33)	35	17(48)	10(28)
1895	20	12(60)	5(25)	33	15(45)	10(30)
1900	30	5(16)	6(20)	36	15(41)	8(22)
1906	29	6(20)	6(20)	32	12(37)	8(26)
1910	15	6(40)	4(26)	30	12(40)	8(26)

	Halfpenny Evenings			Penny Evenings		
Year	Total	Liberal	Conser-vative	Total	Liberal	Conser-vative
1868	6	6(100)	—	1	1(100)	—
1874	12	5(41)	1(8)	2	1(100)	—
1880	59	24(40)	16(27)	1	1(100)	—
1885	71	32(45)	20(28)	5	1(20)	3(60)
1886	75	33(44)	21(28)	4	1(25)	2(50)
1892	67	34(50)	22(33)	4	1(25)	2(50)
1895	71	37(52)	22(31)	5	1(25)	2(50)
1900	92	47(51)	23(25)	7	1(14)	3(43)
1906	81	42(51)	20(24)	6	1(16)	2(33)
1910	68	36(52)	22(32)	3	—	1(33)

Note: figures in brackets are percentages of the totals.
Source: NPD.

Table 27: Morning/Evening Distribution of English Provincial Dailies, 1868-1910

Year	Mornings			Evenings		
	Total	Liberal	Conser-vative	Total	Liberal	Conser-vative
1868	36	19(52)	9(25)	7	7(100)	—
1874	55	30(54)	11(20)	16	7(43)	2(12)
1880	59	34(57)	14(25)	61	26(42)	16(36)
1885	58	32(55)	18(31)	78	34(43)	23(29)
1886	58	31(53)	18(31)	81	35(43)	23(28)
1892	53	28(52)	15(28)	73	36(49)	24(33)
1895	57	29(50)	15(26)	78	39(50)	24(30)
1900	70	22(31)	14(20)	101	49(48)	26(25)
1906	63	20(31)	14(22)	90	44(49)	22(24)
1910	47	20(42)	12(25)	71	37(52)	23(32)

Note: figures in brackets are percentages of the totals.
Source: NPD.

Table 28: Political Distribution of All English Provincial Newspapers, 1837-1887

Year	Conser-vative	Liberal	Neutral/Independent	Other	Total
1837	136	121	7	—	264
1842[i]	89	109	13	—	211
1842[ii]	90	101	14	1[a]	206
1851	85	104	45	—	234
1858	80	175	139	—	394
1860	129	266	348	—	743
1874	294	489	67	66[b]	916
1877	198	307	406	35[b]	946
1878	226	327	415	35[b]	1003
1879	228	335	417	35[b]	1015
1880	242	348	433	32[b]	1055
1881	257	356	455	30[b]	1098
1882	257	359	534	27[b]	1177
1884	268	375	557	20[b]	1220
1885	275	374	615	21[c]	1285
1886	294	396	617	24[d]	1331
1887	310	397	640	19[d]	1366

Table 29: The Political Distribution of All London Newspapers,
1837-1887

Year	Conservative	Liberal	Neutral/Independent	Other	Total
1837	19	26	11	—	56
1842[i]	25	29	41	—	95
1842[ii]	22	26	33	2[a]	83
1851	26	41	64	—	131
1858	17	39	64	—	120
1860	—	—	—	—	—
1874	25	41	332	12[b]	410
1877	23	46	381	10[b]	460
1878	25	42	410	9[b]	486
1879	26	53	417	9[b]	505
1880	27	52	426	9[b]	514
1881	30	61	451	7[b]	549
1882	38	46	463	7[b]	554
1884	33	48	514	7[b]	602
1885	30	48	572	8[d]	658
1886	34	41	586	5[c]	666
1887	30	38	607	5[c]	680

Notes: a = Chartist. b = Liberal-Conservative. c = Liberal-Conservative and
Radical. d = Liberal-Conservative Nationalist and Radical.

Sources: 1837, *Clarke and Lewis Advertising List.* 1842[i], Francis D. Lewis,
Advertising List. 1842[ii], *Hammonds Town and Country Advertising List.*
1851, *NPD.* 1858, William Dawson, *London and Country Advertising List.*
1860, Anon. *The Newspaper Press of the Present Day* (1860). 1874-1887, *May's
British and Irish Newspaper Press Guide.*

Table 30: Some Provincial Daily Circulations, 1872-1914

	'72	'80	'85	'87	'88	'89	'90	'95	'97	'00	'07	'14
*Birmingham Daily Post**						27.0[a]			27.1[a]		26.3[a]	
Northern Daily Telegraph (Blackburn)†				20.0[b]	40.0[c]							
Bradford Daily Telegraph §			22.0[d]									
*Glasgow Herald**							41.9[a]				51.2[a]	
*Liverpool Daily Post**						20.0[a]						
*Manchester Guardian**		30.0[a]								46.0[a]	35.8[a]	49.0[a]
Sheffield Daily Telegraph ‡	8.5[e]							40.0[e]				
*Sheffield Independent**	6.5[e]							16.0[e]				
Shields Gazette†					40.0[c]							
Yorkshire Post ‡	21.1[f]		46.6[f]									

Notes: all figs. are average daily circulations in '000s. *1*d morning Liberal; †½*d* morning Liberal; §½*d* morning Liberal; ‡1*d* morning Conservative.

Sources: a = A.P. Wadsworth, op. cit. b. = *Journalist*, 18 Mar. 1887. c = *Journalist*, 16 Mar. 1888. d = D.M. Jones, op. cit. e = H.J. Wilson Papers. f = M. Gibb and F. Beckwith, op. cit.

Table 31: Concentration of Ownership by Circulation in the
Metropolitan Press, 1910

Mornings

Northcliffe	controlled	39.0% of circulation[a]
Morning Leader Group	controlled	15.5% of circulation[b]
Pearson	controlled	12.4% of circulation[c]
	Total	66.9% of circulation controlled by three companies.

Evenings

Morning Leader Group	controlled	34.5% of circulation[d]
Northcliffe	controlled	31.3% of circulation[e]
Pearson	controlled	16.8% of circulation[f]
	Total	82.6% of circulation controlled by three companies.

Sundays

H.J. Dalziel	controlled	30.7% of circulation[g]
G. Riddell	controlled	22.9% of circulation[h]
F. Lloyd	controlled	15.3% of circulation[i]
Northcliffe	controlled	11.8% of circulation[j]
	Total	80.7% of circulation controlled by four companies.

Notes: These figures should be taken only as indications of a general pattern of ownership. a = *D. Mail, D. Mirror, Times;* b = *D. Express, Standard* (sold to D. Dalziel in 1910); c = *M. Leader, D. News;* d = *Star;* e = *E. News;* f = *Standard;* g = *Reynolds News;* h = *News of the World;* i = *Lloyds Weekly News;* j = *Observer, Weekly Dispatch.* Estimated total circulation, mornings = 3,625,000, evenings = 947,000, sundays = 6,525,000.

Source: T.B. Browne's Advertisers' A.B.C., 1910, with adjustments. The figures probably exaggerate the size of the morning press, and underestimate that of the evening press.

Table 32: Journalists in the House of Commons, 1880-1910

Year	Liberal	Conservative/ Unionist	Radical	Irish National- ist	Labour	Total
1880	8	—	2	1	—	11
1885	5	2	2	10	—	19
1886	4	3	3	14	—	24
1892	10	3	4	11	1	29
1895	7	5	1	15	—	28
1900	10	9	3	13	—	35
1906	27	2	—	15	5	49
1910 (Jan.)	19	3	—	18	4	43
1910 (Dec.)	18	3	—	16	4	41

Note: before 1880 'Journalists' are subsumed by Thomas under 'men of letters' and 'professional and academic'. No 'Radical' division is given after 1900. The names given in the Constitutional Year Book, 1885-96, number considerably less than the totals in Thomas.

Source: J.A. Thomas, op. cit.

Table 33: The Press in Parliament, 1892-1910

	Conservative	Liberal-Unionist	Gladstonian Liberal, Liberal, and Labour*	Nationalist	Total
Newspaper Proprietors					
1892	4	—	9	4	17
1895	5	—	4	4†	13
1900	6	—	5	2	13
1906	2	1	9	3	15
1910	3	1	8	1	13
Printers and Publishers					
1892	1	—	3	—	4
1895	3	1	2	—	6
1900	—	1	2	—	3
1906	3	—	10	2	15
1910	—	—	7	1	8
Authors and Journalists					
1892	2	—	8	10	20
1895	2	1	7	12†	22
1900	8	3	11	13	35
1906	3	1	31	15	50
1910	3	—	20	16	39

Note: *Gladstonian Liberal for 1892 and 1895; Liberal for 1900; Liberal and Labour for 1906 and 1910. †includes one Parnellite.
The 'analysis' in the Year Books, used here, exactly fits the details given for individual Members in the Books only in 1906 and 1910.

Source: Constitutional Year Books, 1893, 1896, 1901, 1906 Suppl., 1910.

Table 34: Newspaper Proprietors in the House of Commons, 1832-1900

	Whig/ Liberal	Tory/ Conservative Unionist	Radical	Irish Nationalist	Total
1832	4	—	—	—	4
1833	5	—	—	—	5
1837	4	—	—	—	4
1841	4	—	—	—	4
1847	3	—	—	—	3
1852	4	—	—	—	4
1857	4	—	⌐	—	4
1859	5	—	—	—	5
1865	4	—	—	—	4
1868	3	—	1	—	4
1874	4	—	2	—	6
1880	11	—	3	—	14
1885	10	3	3	6	22
1886	7	4	2	6	19
1892	10	5	4	11	30
1895	6	7	1	11	25
1900	8	6	1	9	24
1906	22	4	—	4	30
1910 (Jan.)	14	9	—	6	29
1910 (Dec.)	13	7	—	4	24

Note: Thomas's categories vary a little from pre- to post-1900, and I have tried to confine these figures entirely to proprietors, excluding 'men of letters', printers, publishers, stationers and paper manufacturers. No 'Radical' division is given by Thomas after 1900.

Source: J.A. Thomas, op. cit.

Table 35: United Kingdom Dailies in 1914 and 1971

	London/national		Provincial	
	mornings	evenings	mornings	evenings
1914*	14†	6	59	97
1971	9‡	2	20	79

Notes: *N. Irish papers only are included in the 1914 figures. †excludes 'class' papers, including *Financial Times.* ‡includes *Financial Times,* which had ceased to be a 'class' paper.

Source: NPD, 1914; *The Press and the People* (The Press Council, 1971).

Key to maps 2-7

▲ Liberal, Independent-Liberal and Liberal-Independent, 1d

◮   "   "   "   "   "   " , ½d

△   "   "   "   "   "   " , other price

● Conservative and Liberal-Conservative, 1d .

◖   "   "   "   " , ½d

○   "   "   "   " , other price

■ Independent, 1d

◘   "   , ½d

□   "   , other price

▬ Neutral, 1d

▭   " , ½d

▭   " , other price

◓ Unionist and Independent-Unionist, 1d

◐   "   "   "   " , ½d

○   "   "   "   " , other price

★ Labour, ½d

◢ Other, ½d

◁ Other, other price

REGIONAL DIVISIONS
used in Chapter 5.

North

East

Yorkshire

Lancashire

Midland

Eastern

Counties

Counties

The West Country

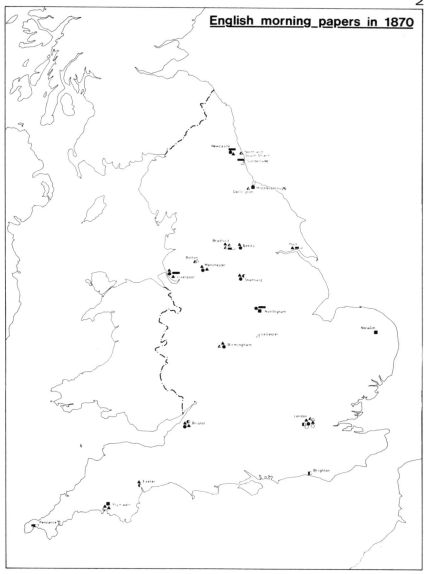

English morning papers in 1870

English evening papers in 1870

English morning papers in 1880

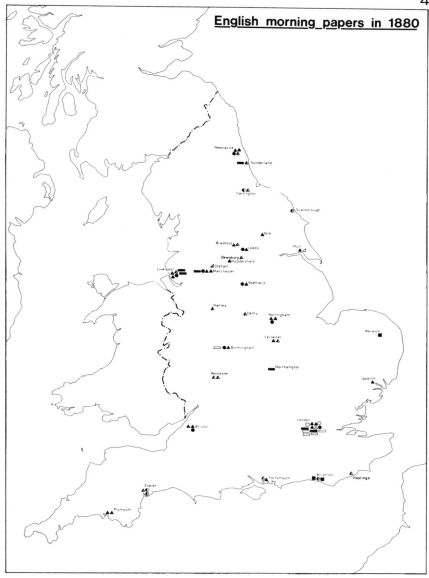

Newcastle

Sunderland

Darlington

Scarborough

York

Bradford　Leeds

Hull

Dewsbury

Huddersfield

Oldham

Liverpool　Manchester

Sheffield

Hanley

Derby

Nottingham

Leicester

Norwich

Birmingham

Worcester

Northampton

Ipswich

London

Bristol

Portsmouth

Brighton

Hastings

Exeter

Plymouth

5

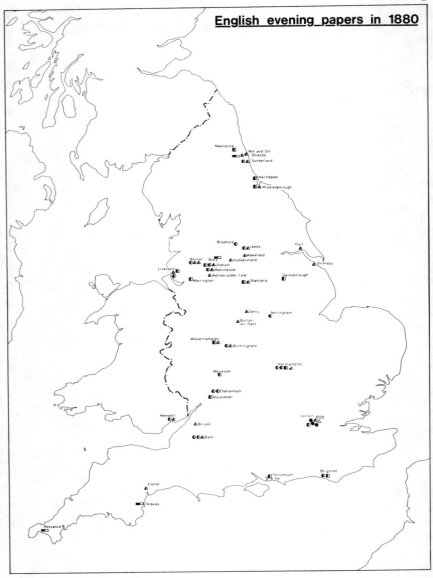

English evening papers in 1880

Newcastle
Nth and Sth Shields
Sunderland
Hartlepool
Middlesborough

Bradford
Leeds
Wakefield
Huddersfield
Bolton Bury
Oldham
Liverpool Manchester
Ashton-under-Lyne
Warrington
Sheffield

Hull
Grimsby
Gainsborough

Derby
Nottingham
Burton-on-Trent

Wolverhampton
Birmingham

Northampton

Worcester

Cheltenham
Gloucester

Newport
London

Bristol
Bath

Portsmouth
Brighton

Exeter

Torquay

Penzance

English morning papers in 1914

English evening papers in 1914

INDEX

308   *Index*

The Origins of the
Popular Press in England

1855–1914

ALAN J. LEE

CROOM HELM   LONDON

First published 1976
© Alan J. Lee 1976

Reprinted 1980

Croom Helm Ltd,
2-10 St John's Road, London SW11

ISBN 0-7099-0361-8

First published in the United States 1976
by Rowman and Littlefield, Totowa, New Jersey

Library of Congress Cataloging in Publication Data

Lee, Alan J.
   The growth of the popular press in England, 1855-1914.

   Bibliography: p. 234
   Includes index.
   1. Press - - England - - History. I. Title.
PN5117.L4 1976   072   76-17808

ISBN 0-87471-856-2

Printed in Great Britain
by Biddles Ltd, Guildford, Surrey